Critical Essays on
JOHN MILTON

CRITICAL ESSAYS
ON
BRITISH LITERATURE

Zack Bowen, General Editor
University of Miami

◆

Critical Essays on
JOHN MILTON

◆

edited by

CHRISTOPHER KENDRICK

G. K. Hall & Co.
An Imprint of Simon & Schuster Macmillan
New York
Prentice Hall International
London Mexico City New Delhi Singapore Sydney Toronto

11570675

Copyright © 1995 by Christopher Kendrick

G. K. Hall & Co.
An Imprint of Simon & Schuster Macmillan
866 Third Avenue
New York, N.Y. 10022

Library of Congress Cataloging-in-Publication Data

Critical essays on John Milton / edited by Christopher Kendrick.
        p.   cm. — (Critical essays on British literature)
    Includes bibliographical references and index.
    ISBN 0-8161-8874-2
    1. Milton, John, 1608–1674—Criticism and interpretation.
I. Kendrick, Christopher, 1953–   . II. Series.
PR3588.C69   1995
821\.4—dc20   94-36080
                                                                                        CIP

The paper used in this publication meets the minimum requirements of American National Standard for Information Sciences—Permanence of Paper for Printed Library Materials. ANSI Z3948-1984.∞™

10   9   8   7   6   5   4   3   2   1

Printed in the United States of America

Contents

◆

General Editor's Note   vii
Publisher's Note   ix
Introduction   1
    CHRISTOPHER KENDRICK

RECEPTIONS

    How to Do Things With Milton:
    A Study in the Politics of Literary Criticism   19
        CARL FREEDMAN

COMUS, PARADISE REGAINED, SAMSON AGONISTES

    Thoughts in Misbecoming Plight:
    Allegory in *Comus*   47
        VICTORIA SILVER

    Things and Actions Indifferent:
    The Temptation of Plot in *Paradise Regained*   74
        STANLEY FISH

    Paradise Regained and the Politics of Martyrdom   95
        LAURA LUNGER KNOPPERS

    "Casting Down Imaginations":
    Milton as Iconoclast   115
        DAVID LOEWENSTEIN

    Reading, Seeing, and Acting in *Samson Agonistes*   131
        WILLIAM FLESCH

PARADISE LOST

    John Milton and the Republican Mode
    of Literary Production   149
        PETER LINDENBAUM

The Genesis of Gendered Subjectivity in the Divorce
Tracts and in *Paradise Lost*   165
    MARY NYQUIST

Milton, Narcissism, Gender:
On the Genealogy of Male Self-Esteem   194
    JOHN GUILLORY

Index   235

General Editor's Note

♦

The Critical Essays on British Literature series provides a variety of approaches to both classical and contemporary writers of Britain and Ireland. The formats of the volumes in the series vary with the thematic designs of individual editors, and with the amount and nature of the existing reviews and criticism, augmented, where appropriate, by original essays by recognized authorities. It is hoped that each volume will be unique in developing a new overall perspective on its particular subject.

Christopher Kendrick's introduction seeks to get at the passion and polemics of Milton criticism—which he sees as critics' personal identification with the poet—through a history of two indicative events which occurred during the 18th Century, Richard Bently's 1732 edition of *Paradise Lost* and William Lauder's 1747 attack on Milton's honesty, both using Milton criticism to further their own ideas and/or profit. The scholarly identification with Milton—pro and con—has continued throughout Milton scholarship, culminating in the modern and contemporary critical schools which are represented in this volume. Kendrick's thesis is amplified in Carl Freedman's essay, one of four original contributions, including others by Victoria Silver, William Flesch, and John Guillory.

ZACK BOWEN
University of Miami

Publisher's Note

◆

Producing a volume that contains both newly commissioned and reprinted material presents the publisher with the challenge of balancing the desire to achieve stylistic consistency with the need to preserve the integrity of works first published elsewhere. In the Critical Essays series, essays commissioned especially for a particular volume are edited to be consistent with G. K. Hall's house style; reprinted essays appear in the style in which they were first published, with only typographical errors corrected. Consequently, shifts in style from one essay to another are the result of our efforts to be faithful to each text as it was originally published.

By way of introduction: *Bentley, Lauder, and Miltonic Identifications*

CHRISTOPHER KENDRICK

Since the early to mid-eighteenth century when one can begin speaking of a formal British literary canon, Milton has probably been, after Shakespeare, the most canonical figure in the tradition. Nonetheless Milton's works have arguably been the object of more *passionate* disagreement among subsequent readers and critics than any other writer's, and his reputation has been unusually volatile.[1] What is particularly striking is the nature of the passion involved. Beginning roughly with Dennis's and Addison's comments on *Paradise Lost*, one frequently detects an unusually personal investment in remarks and opinions about Milton, and of course especially about his classical epic.[2] Not only does the critic's reputation for learning and taste seem to be on the line; it is as if the poem as he or she constructs it were to be from that moment in some singular way the critic's own. More than the sort of sympathetic identification with the author ordinary in attentive readings, something approaching actual rivalry with Milton for his text, and not just with other critics, is put on display. This is no doubt largely to be accounted for by the fact that *Paradise Lost* was for some time a difficult poem to read as well as an intensely valued one, so that the critical struggle for meaning was comparatively free of conventional limits. Largely, but not wholly: for similar effects of unusually intense identification and rivalry have not ceased to recur, and have indeed been much in evidence within Milton studies in this century. If one attends a conference or a seminar on Milton today, one will likely on coming away hear the non-specialists in attendance expressing wonderment and irritation at the naive intentionalism of Miltonists, at the extent to which readings of Milton's poems are deemed appropriate or out-of-court depending on their accordance with "what Milton meant." And the knowledge of what Milton meant can seem simply innate to Miltonists, rather than their having to work for it anymore, to perform readings to acquire it.

Now naive identification, and a certain possessiveness in respect of one's author, are hazards of specialization in modern literature departments. Woolf and Johnson scholars, for example, manifestly exhibit a similar disposition in relation to their chosen subjects. Thus if one wants to argue that there is something about "Milton in himself," or—since one can no more abstract from Milton's cultural position and status than from that of any other writer one reads—something special to "Milton in himself as institutionalized," that encourages peculiarly intense effects of identification and rivalry, it will probably be best to do it by referring to events from the earlier history of Milton's reception, such as predate our current professional interests. Two events stand out as particularly indicative in this regard, I think, both from the middle years of the eighteenth century, both cunning attacks on Milton's reputation as *the* English classic: Richard Bentley's maverick 1732 edition of *Paradise Lost*, in which he contends that some one of Milton's friends, an irrepressible editor, had taken advantage of Milton's blindness to foist his own extravagant emendations into the received text of the poem; and William Lauder's well publicized contention, in a series of magazine articles in 1747, that Milton had translated large parts of *Paradise Lost* direct from neo-Latin texts without acknowledging his debts.[3]

These early anti-Miltonists had much in common. Both attempted to mar Milton's reputation, not by a direct assault on his ideology, form, or style, but by calling into question his poem's physical integrity, as it were, scarring it with a series of asterisks denoting spuriousness, inauthenticity, the presence of another man's hand. This strategy of dis-authentication, this indirect and qualified attempt on Milton's cultural status as symbol of literary Taste, was conspicuously (though by no means wholly) animated by that basest of all ends, the profit motive; for *Paradise Lost* was a lucrative text, and the attempt to locate the true text was bound to pay in "material" terms if successful.[4] Both attacks, meanwhile, were supported by expedient but unstably fraudulent fictions. The evidence suggests that Bentley's edition was a more or less conscious "escapade," to use William Empson's term, an ingenious, if natural, way for an editor to present critical strictures on Milton's great poem.[5] Lauder's attack was without doubt consciously fraudulent, for in order to prove that Milton had plagiarized them Lauder interpolated lines from William Hog's 1690 translation of *Paradise Lost* into the neo-Latin works he quoted. Still, no one who reads Lauder's essays can doubt that his forgeries were "honest" at least in this sense, that Lauder believed at some fairly deep level in Milton's corruptness. Like Mendel's assistant, he was forging data to prove the truth; and it perhaps lies in the nature of such an enterprise that the forger should begin to forget his own mendacity, and to believe in the appearances he has created.

Finally, and most importantly here, the attempt to undermine the integrity of Milton's text, and the honest deception it involved, attest in each case an unusually complex and thoroughgoing *identification* with the antagonist and his work. If Bentley did not believe in his editor, if his editor was at one level a parody of a scholarly editor, that finally makes his identification with Milton, though less instinctive and respectful, yet more patent and deep than had he simply offered criticisms upon the poem. The fiction of the editor provided Bentley with a way of incorporating himself into the compositional process, the authorship of the poem as it were, by replacing Milton's more copiously inclined, Renaissance editorial function with a "correct," neo-classical one (Bentley himself). The malcontented Lauder's motives were not so respectable as Bentley's, perhaps, but were caught up in a powerful identification all the same. For Lauder's general disgruntlement with literary culture, while plausibly enough fixing upon Milton and his poem as that culture's symbol, need not have turned into a conviction that the original site of Miltonic invention was a scene of crime, a swindle.[6] This conviction, coupled with Lauder's continuing (and somewhat confusing) acceptance of the poem's authentic splendor, testifies to the simple desire somehow to make himself present at the scene of composition, thus to merge with or replace Milton, to make a piece of Milton's text his own.

It might be objected at this point that, if Bentley's and Lauder's identifications are not determined by academic specialization, theirs are nonetheless very much period stories and interests. I do not want to deny this. The magnificently petty ambition and avarice, the agitated spleen and resentment which they put on display, impose themselves as immediate effects of the rapid expansion of the book market, as emanations of that emergence of Grub Street and the literary hack, without which the works of Pope and Swift, for example, would be unthinkable. The fascination with, indeed the rage for forgery so evident in both stories is also a period phenomenon, and might be read as an especially rich symptom of a certain late phase in the emergence of the concept of modern authorship. And the competition for distinction and anxiety to be marked as possessing taste can be seen as responses to the construction, the cultural consolidation, of something like a modern middle class. However one understands them, petty resentment, a reflexive fascination with forgery, and a nervous desire for distinction are present in these events, and they are all very much eighteenth-century attitudes. That ought not, however, to detract from my main aim here, which is to suggest that the tradition of Milton criticism and reception has been unusually proprietary—peculiarly subject to marked, but more or less unconscious, identification with its subject. On the contrary, since the capitalist bookmarket, modern authorship, and the modern middle class are still very much with us, we might take these examples as affording a privileged glimpse, during the long moment of Milton's institutionalization as the national poet, into the very springs of critical proprietariness.

The question remains, however, as to why Milton in particular among canonical writers should have continued to provoke such vexedly "proprietary" responses. As will already be clear, one would not expect such a phenomenon to be explicable in terms of any one or two "causes" or characteristics, whether pertaining to the poetry itself or to its institutional history. If it is to be explained at all, one must assume that it is multiply determined, and choose what seem the most important and durable from among a multitude of causes. In this introduction, I will propose four main causes for the proprietary difference in critical responses to Milton. These have respectively to do with his vocationalism, his idiosyncratic sexism, his republicanism, and his relation to British nationalism. It will be noted that the list tends to move "outward" from features of Milton's poetry considered more or less in itself, to institutional factors that have as much to do with historical developments after Milton as with the peculiarities of his verse. I would stress that the list is not intended to be exhaustive.

The explanation nearest to hand for critical fixation on and rivalry with Milton himself would seem to lie in the urgency of his presence in and to his poems, the conspicuousness of the notorious Miltonic self-esteem. Few sensitive readers, I think, have denied encountering in the poetry, and fewer would deny encountering in the prose, the author's unusually prominent sense of his own worth, which can be described accurately enough also, if a reader is in an uncharitably moralizing mood, as arrogance, as self-righteousness, or (sometimes more neutrally) as self-obsession or egotism. Probably it would be wrong to deny that what is partly at stake here are the traces of Milton's *personality*—of some utterly singular, and therefore inexplicable, way of being in the world. But from an analytical point of view it seems best, and indeed necessary, to think of this personal dimension as a structural effect, and conceive it as the residue of a determinate cultural event: namely the elaboration and enactment of a vocational poetic.[7] It has long been recognized that Milton lived his writing, his literary "career," as his "calling," in the strong Calvinist sense of that term, and that he wrote the impossible paradoxes of Protestant vocationalism into the very form and texture of his prose and poetry in an unusually thoroughgoing if not utterly unprecedented way. The biographical underpinnings of this achievement are clear enough, and have also often been noted in one way or another. Roughly speaking, they consisted in Milton's peculiar economic and political independence. On the one hand, the money his father made from the land market gave Milton the luxury of preparing himself for, and contemplating through his early years, the possibility of an autonomous literary calling/career, which is to say of one in relative freedom from the various urgencies and pressures of the patronage market.[8] On the other hand, this same relative economic freedom, combined with the anxieties attendant upon the newly abstract experience of "poetic work-in-itself," can plausibly be inferred to have enabled Milton's unusually thoroughgoing investment in the political, his powerful lay identification with the state of the nation in all its numerous emergencies. More particularly, economic position and poetic vocation respectively permitted and encouraged that dramatic series of shifts to the Left in the 1640s—the passage from fairly orthodox Presbyterianism to a rather radical form of Independency (for Milton was not just a congregationalist but a *separating* one, and became and remained a committed regicide)—which both stamped Milton as a revolutionary thinker and writer, and confirmed him in the (strong-Protestant) habit of reading his own life in allegorical relationship to the national one, so that new movements or events in the one might stand as hopeful signs of election in the other, yet leave him, in the end, relatively free of fixed party commitments.

The consequences for Milton's poetry, and more generally for his writing, go deep. They are decisively formal, rather than merely thematic ones. Vocationalism is to be seen, for example, in Milton's inveterate habit of writing his own biography into his works in an unabashed, and not unconscious, way. Thus Milton's notorious identification with Edward King in "Lycidas," with the Lady in *Comus*, with the Son in the "Nativity Ode," with Samson in *Samson Agonistes*.[9] Thus his introduction of elements of a life narrative into *Paradise Lost* through the inductions: Milton loses his sight while writing the Books of Hell, is compassed by dangers when he starts the books of Earth, and so on. So also, Milton himself is the understood hero of the divorce pamphlets: he it is, in the narrative fantasy informing those tracts, who by experiencing a bad marriage and expressing it so vigorously has attained and produced the knowledge of what marriage itself should be and is; so it is Milton who will have moved the nation to produce more signs of its own election, once it has reformed itself properly in this sphere. The typical Milton narrative is aggressively and conspicuously informed by a fantasy of identification of some kind; and accordingly it is as if Milton's narrative raw material comes pregnant with questions concerning his own fate, so that it would be impossible for the individual narrative as composed *not* to vehiculate a vocational thematics, to convey some fairly clear reflexive message as to the logic and end of his writing career.

The consequences of vocationalism are likewise to be seen in the relations between Milton's poems: in the attempt to rewrite earlier works expressly or implicitly so as to make them part of a larger unity which culminates in the last work—often enough surprisingly, so that the unity can only have been seen with this last work's appearance. The aim here is to redeem the corpus in each of its members, to make the writing life into an integral sign of election, while also preserving the sense of contingency and precariousness without which the believer's efforts in his calling will appear as mere work. The demand that each successive work of consequence "contingently reunify" the corpus determines the problem of the last, or corpus-making, work. Which is it? *Paradise Lost*, as most have had little doubt? *Paradise Regained*, whose plainer, middle style is introduced as embodying a more rigorous decorum and higher aesthetic than that represented by *Paradise Lost*, and which Milton himself reportedly would not hear to be inferior to the longer poem?[10] Or *Samson Agonistes*, his last generic and stylistic experiment, which brings so much of Milton's learning and life together, as Radzinowicz and others have shown,[11] and which it is tempting to read as revising the apparent quietism of *Paradise Regained*, or as an explanation of what that quietism really means. Partly because Milton has invested his own life narrative in them, the major poems compete with one another for the status of last or definitive work, for the honor of being the fullest sign of election. But this competition does not end there, I am suggesting. The strenuous egotism of Milton's works is also partially responsible for their being the objects of such aggressive critical appropriations.

Second, there is the peculiar salience of specifically sexual politics in Milton's lifework. In the later works this salience is not unrelated to the fact of the revolution's failure. Milton was forbidden the sustained frontal address of matters of church and state, but he remained free to represent the domestic. Thus the energy given to the representation of marital adventures in *Paradise Lost* and *Samson Agonistes*. And one can see the Son of *Paradise Regained* as a species of domestic adventurer also, if only by negation—by virtue, that is, of his refusal to leave the domestic sphere.

But even without the revolution's failure, Milton was a poet intensely interested in gender and sexuality—as his celebration of his own chastity in the 1630s, and above all his series of divorce tracts in the mid-1640s, go to prove. Appreciation of the intensity of this interest has been renewed since the 1960s, in ongoing debates about Milton's construction of gender and sexuality in the institutional and discursive movements of his time.[12] What generally seems to me to be missing in these debates—mainly I think because the assumption tends to be an automatic one that a writer so canonical should be ideologically mainstream, at least on the everyday issues of family, sex and marriage—is a steady recognition of the relative *idiosyncracy* of Milton's position within the field of sexual-political ideology. A product of a particular patriarchal society Milton certainly was; but he was far from your ordinary patriarch, as the extreme offensiveness of his argument for "divorce at will" to dominant patriarchal attitudes in his day testifies. So much—that Milton's sexism was not ordinary—is not really controversial, I think: it only tends to be *forgotten*. But not many feminists (and fewer antifeminists, for that matter) would probably agree that a good way to keep from forgetting is to invoke the somewhat crude, but still, I think, useful distinction between "paternalist" (i.e., comfortably male-supremacist) and "misogynist" attitudes, while taking to heart Linda Woodbridge's case that feminism as a matter of political principle ought to train its analysis and strategy on and against paternalism.[13] Nonetheless if a misogynist be defined, not simply as a womanhater, but as one for whom the female sex means too much as such, or has somehow become *too symbolic*, then it seems to me for reasons I can only touch on here simply a mundane diagnosis, a descriptive designation and by no means a value judgment, to say that Milton was misogynist. That is why feminist attacks on Milton as the Grand Patriarch of the poetic tradition seem misplaced, even though the readings they propose are often quite interesting; and it is why conservative defenses of Milton, while often well-informed about Milton, can seem authentically ugly, for such defenses tend not so much to misread Milton's sexual ideology as to present his misogyny, somewhat sweetened by euphemism, as normal in the period, and indeed proper for all ages.[14] My general point here is that, if Milton's construction of gender and sexuality has been partly responsible for the tendency to passionate identification and repudiation characteristic of Milton criticism, that is less because of the militancy and centrality of his sexual ideology in and to his work than it is because his oxymoronic position or identity as canonical misogynist has offered itself to critics and readers as a constant temptation to make something like a category mistake—a mistake which, once made, is likely to be a mistake with a vengeance.

One begins to understand the peculiar logic of Milton's misogyny, and it becomes yet more difficult to forget his idiosyncrasy, when one considers the extent to which his sexual ideology was bound up with his highly personal solution to the central philosophical problem of his day: his refusal of the soul-body division (i.e., his monism). To put this another way, it is less easy to forget Milton's idiosyncrasy when one sees that the imperatives determined by the monistic "solution" largely amounted to Milton's way of negotiating the problems of desire and domestic passion.[15] Technically a theological doctrine, monism seems to have corresponded, in the domain of structures of feeling, to a particular lived attitude towards the body-soul complex; one might think of it as the religious-philosophical trace of a fantasy of bodily integrity. Understood thus, the monistic fantasy helps one to grasp in its principles Milton's "extremist" rendering of Protestant domestic ideals. Some such fantasy seems to have motivated Milton's idealization of chastity in the 1630s, to which his retrospective descriptions attribute the character of a private cult aimed at the production of superior poetry. If he kept his body pure, the logic went, his soul would be too, and he would automatically write pure poetry.[16] When in the early 1640s Milton attempted and failed at more ambitious poetic designs than he had previously undertaken—when (or so I infer) this chaste poetic proved on trial to have been a lyric one, the disappointment seems to have led to the monistic fantasy's displaced reinvestment, rather than to its retirement. For the monistic attitude also helps to explain how, after his precipitate marriage's seeming failure, Milton should elaborate a theory of marriage in which the Protestant emphases on mutual support and companionship are intensified, and the normative Protestant rhetoric of spiritual wedlock is taken at face value or literalized, to the point of unconscious parody—a theory of what might be called the "consubstantial marriage," in which husband and wife are like body and soul, and thus in which the wife becomes a virtual succubus if inadequate, or the very symbol of the husband's power and salvation, if good. To insist on the peculiarity of Milton's sexual politics in this way is not, I would emphasize, to suggest that his representation of sexual-political matters was not culturally significant or central. Especially in light of the unconsciously paradigmatic status which Milton's version of the Eden and Samson stories came to occupy over the next two centuries in the novelistic tradition,[17] it seems more plausible to hold that Milton's anomalous experience and construction of gender and sexuality put him in a position, even while conspicuously pushing his own sexual ideology, to record with relative clarity, to give particularly vivid figuration to, the central moving contradictions of his time in this sphere.

The third critical determinant has been mentioned in passing, and might be seen to bridge the invisible line between the intrinsic and the extrinsic, or between features and factors. It consists in the fact that Milton was a revolutionary, both politically on the one hand and poetically or "formally" on the other—though one wants to add straightway that he was formally revolutionary in a somewhat more problematical sense than he was a formally vocational poet. In saying that Milton was a political revolutionary, what is meant is clear enough: Milton was a fairly radical species of Independent, republican in politics and disestablishmentarian in religion, and a sufficiently hardcore politico to have stuck with Cromwell, and never to have repudiated the name of the revolution, through and after the necessary violences and betrayals committed on its behalf.[18] In many respects then Milton was far "ahead" of the readers and writers who followed and emulated him. And this fact of course—that Milton's politics were relatively left-wing, and above all that he was an *unrepentant* republican and regicide—accounts for much of the overt antipathy to the man in the poetry (one thinks especially here of Dr. Johnson), and largely explains some of the attempts to dislodge him from his place in the canon (one thinks of T. S. Eliot).

Nevertheless, it cannot be denied (and indeed it is a truism) that Milton's politics are not generally on simple and condign display in the later major poems. More typically his political beliefs and desires undergo some sort of displacement or sublimation into form, as happens most clearly in the case of the Grand Style of *Paradise Lost*, whose sweeping periods Milton justifies, in a curt and aggressive note to the second issue of the poem, as a restoration of English verse to its true nature, a liberation from its diuturnal bondage by rhyme. If the sublimation into style is relatively transparent in *Paradise Lost*, it is also operative in *Paradise Regained* and *Samson Agonistes*, which likewise labor under the difficulty of being unable to speak explicitly of what they most want to be about. I would suggest that this partial repression and displacement, this necessarily imperfect formal expression of Milton's revolutionary desire, cannot but have its impact on readers, and that many have been tempted to complete Milton's struggle with the censor for him, either by replacing the poems' actual with some "true" political signified or by displacing any reference to political events utterly, by conventionalizing their form. The "romantic" reading of *Paradise Lost* (mostly associated with Blake) that makes Satan into a revolutionary without Milton's knowing it is an example of the former response. In C. S. Lewis' famous statement that, while Milton may have been an undisciplined man, he was a very disciplined poet, and in his construction of Milton's epic as a solemn game, we have an influential modern example of the latter.[19] It isn't, then, only that Milton was a notorious revolutionary that makes for an intense identification with the poet (whether this identification be for or against him); it is also, and perhaps more tellingly, the way in which the revolution inheres in his major poetry.

The final cause pertains especially, I think, to the early (pre-Victorian) reception of Milton. We have encountered it writ signally in the stories of Bentley and Lauder. Other British poets had achieved, and would achieve, much recognition. Milton, however, became *the* national poet, *Paradise Lost* *the* national poem. To put this more exactly: insofar as *Paradise Lost* became the national poem, Milton was to that extent, as its undoubted author, the national poet, in a way denied Dryden, for example, even though Dryden's opinions and works were much more representative of and authoritative within hegemonic post-Restoration culture than the zealous, republican Milton's could ever be. The reputation of Milton's epic as the single most undisputed classic of English poetry, and of Milton as the English equivalent of Homer and Virgil, was in place by the time (1712) Addison wrote his influential *Spectator* papers on the poem. Addison writes as one who can take the classic status of the poem more or less for granted, and whose task it is to teach his audience how adequately to respond to the multiform beauties (and occasional flaws) of its design and execution. He aims to show the broadening reading public how to use this now historic piece of its heritage, so recently popular yet already arriving as if handed down enshrined from a distant past—how to live up to and in the artifact which testifies indirectly to the culture's own past and current greatness.

To say that Milton's poem became the national poem is not quite to say that it became a nationalist icon. Even leaving aside the question of whether one should talk at all of Western nationalisms before the early nineteenth century, Milton's story would have presented critics desirous of wrapping themselves in it like the flag with few openings. I do not know of any eighteenth-century critics maintaining that Adam and Eve, or Milton's Son, represented peculiarly British virtues, and doubt that any did.[20] By casting Milton's poem as distinguishing itself by its sublimity, they were indeed usually allowing it to be *foreign* in a sense, foreign to their own more correct and polite moment in particular. And it was generally allowed that Milton had to struggle against the intrinsic properties of the language, to forge a somewhat un-English style, in order to achieve a truly heroic, truly classical poem. Opinions on his stylistic achievement were mixed, but it was far from generally thought that Milton's manner should stand as the precedent to be imitated, nor that he had entirely overcome the handicap of English, if by this was meant equaling the epic manner of Homer or Virgil. Yet, even if Milton could not be constructed as a nationalist poet, once the Stuarts had been removed from the throne his poem could reasonably comfortably be acknowledged as a national achievement, and be understood to speak indirectly of the resources that explained Britain's remarkable cultural consolidation and its rapid advance on the international scene in the later seventeenth and early eighteenth centuries. Thus Milton came implicitly to be appropriated, in his very foreignness, as a figure of the emergent national greatness, of its world-historical standing. Given this, it is easy to understand why *Paradise Lost* should be the natural object of peculiarly passionate reconstructions, why so many should want to make a piece of Milton their own. Though the conservative character of properly British nationalism, when it came to view in the nineteenth century, made it more difficult to read *Paradise Lost* as the national poem—one finds Matthew Arnold opining, for example, that Milton's use to the late-nineteenth-century audience lay in the stern and lofty remoteness of his style, specifically it would seem his classicism, which might serve to leaven their Anglo-Saxon vulgarity—it has probably not been completely dislodged from that status even today.[21]

It will be apparent that this sketch of reasons for the peculiar proprietariness of Milton criticism is not offered with the intention of making readers immune to the temptation to identify with or to repudiate Milton, exactly, but rather to encourage its being grasped as an objective "fact," capable of being historicized in sundry ways, and considerably more fully than the sketch has indicated. Without at all suggesting that "proprietariness" has been a special focus of recent Milton criticism (say, of the past 15 years), I would venture that the general trends in that criticism tend in the direction of such a historicization. This is to demur from a proposition commonly asserted about Milton criticism and the professional image of Milton generally, namely that the criticism has not really taken the imprint of theory and New Historicism, and that the institutional image of Milton thus has not undergone substantial alteration.[22] No doubt sixteenth-century criticism, and Shakespeare and drama studies especially, have changed more than Milton criticism (though they have not changed so radically, I think, as is often assumed). But something may be conceded to the conservative Miltonist's response to the above proposition: he will say that Milton studies has not needed to change because it has always been more philosophical and more historical-political than Shakespeare studies owing to the nature of its object. Acknowledging that such comparisons are always invidious and difficult, I still doubt that the "old historicist" counterpart in Shakespeare studies is either so rich or so finished as the line of modern Milton scholarship that begins with Masson's great biography of Milton and includes Saurat, Hanford, Woodhouse, Tillyard, and Barker.

Yet the New Historicist complaint against the older scholarship is not that it wasn't interested in a variety of historical-political contexts, but that it tended to be ethical in the guise of being historical. Thus, to take an extreme and perhaps idiosyncratic example of the old historicism, namely the type of Milton criticism dominant in the 1950s and which William

Empson, in *Milton's God*, famously dubbed neo-Christian: few such critics, perhaps, were real Christians, or if they were what was more important was that they were laboring under a kind of historicist illusion that since Milton was still living in a preliberal society in which the reigning pretense was that ethical precepts had transparent political implications, the proper thing for a historical critic to do was to respect this pretense. The result of such respect was usually to create an unconscious association between seventeenth-century religious poetry and high-minded modern political speeches. From the point of view of such a historicism, Empson's argument, in *Milton's God*, that "the poem [*Paradise Lost*] is so good because it makes God so bad" could only seem "unserious" and adolescent in its actual historical claims (of which there are several), while proving unendingly irritating for its freedom from moralistic-historicist confines. One sign that things have changed in Milton criticism is that Empson's book no longer seems either unserious or very scandalous.

This is not to say that Empson's attack on Christianity is now calmly accepted by most. From current historicist coordinates, his general argument about the poem's judgement of its God and the Christian religion seems interesting but *too* general, there having been so many Christianities; and one of the major problems with the book seems to lie precisely in the Enlightenment character of Empson's feeling for Christianity, his deep scorn and antipathy for all hierarchical monotheisms, whose very intensity tends to channel his readings too narrowly and to prevent him from attempting to articulate their theoretical underpinnings. The academic attitude toward religion may have changed in important ways since the 1950s, but this I think is not what mainly accounts for the change in attitude toward *Milton's God*. Rather, what turns out to have been scandalous about Empson's book is that it exposed the vacuousness of the older historicist assumption that Milton's was a society of real consensus, and so by implication called into question the notion that Milton could control his material and his audience in the way it tended to assume. Nothing has become more axiomatic than that writing is always "conflicted," to use the ubiquitous jargon term, or in other words that significant literature necessarily takes a position or positions in relation to the social debates and tensions of its day; and this claim is usually accompanied by an at least implicit adherence to the law of unintended consequences in the realm of authorial intention, since the reception of literary works is bound to be as conflictual as their production, in ways no one can hope to control.

If one were to mark the moment at which these assumptions become axiomatic for Milton criticism, the publication of Christopher Hill's remarkable biography of Milton would surely figure prominently.[23] Massively learned in all the genres of seventeenth-century writing, Hill's work was by no means free of non-reflective identification with its subject. Its most contentious and advertised thesis was that Milton was in active dialogue with the left-wing sects of the 1640s and 1650s (or, what is almost the same thing, that his work was partly shaped by London alehouse culture). Reviewers have not been wanting to suggest that in this thesis Hill's own populist Marxism re-members Milton in its image. But though Hill's thesis has not been generally accepted, there can be no doubt that it was largely responsible for prompting a renewed engagement with Milton's prose works in the context of sectarian writing, and encouraging new situations of the later verse narratives in relation to the various ideological tendencies of the earlier, revolutionary moment, as well as their post-Restoration refractions.[24] Moreover, Hill's focus on the sectarian moment of the revolution had the inadvertent effect, I think, of making Milton criticism that is not particularly interested in politics or in situating Milton politically more programatically aware that basic questions of social organization were at issue in the traditional political nation. Accordingly it became more difficult to maintain the pretense of religious and political consensus.[25] Meanwhile, it did not hurt the book's influence that from a strictly literary-critical point of view, it was as lacking in technique as Empson's book was (in practice) replete with it. For conservative Milton scholars could not dismiss the book by seizing on false emphases or errors in Hill's readings of poems (from a literary-critical standpoint, there were hardly any readings there); yet Hill's construction of the cultural situation, and his comments on passages and aspects of the poems, opened many doors.

The essays collected in this volume should provide a concrete sense of the change in attitude and orientation toward the figure of Milton, for they have been assembled partly for that purpose, as well as to give a reasonable sampling of the programs of critical research and the critical styles recently and currently brought to bear on Milton's works. These range from postliberal feminism (Nyquist), to something like New Historicism (Loewenstein and Knoppers) to a modified Demanianism (Flesch) to Marxism (Freedman) to Marxism-cum-psychoanalysis-and-cultural studies (Guillory)—though I would hasten to add, in case my qualifiers leave any doubt, that these categorizations are extremely rough, and that none of the following arguments has been programmed by an "-ism." It should be noted that four essays, those by Flesch, Freedman, Guillory and Silver, were written especially for this volume. This much said, the essays may be left to speak for themselves.*

Notes

1.   I assume that to be securely canonical a work or author must become the object of critical disagreement, of what comes to be seen as a tradition of debate, which sustains

*I would like to thank my research assistant, Patricia Nebrida, for much help in the preparation of this volume.

the work's (or author's) reputation. The unusual passion involved in disagreements about Milton is testified to by the frequency of more or less wholesale attempts upon his reputation. The most famous of these was T. S. Eliot's and F. R. Leavis's attack on Milton. For an informed discussion of this phase of Milton's reception, see the following essay by Carl Freedman, which can be read as a second introduction.

2.   For excerpts from John Dennis on Milton, and for Joseph Addison's *Spectator* papers complete, see John T. Shawcross, ed., *Milton: The Critical Heritage* (New York: Barnes & Noble, 1970), a useful compilation of early criticism.

3.   Shawcross, in his introduction to *Milton: The Critical Heritage, 1732–1801* (New York: Barnes & Noble, 1972) marks these off as the two major events in the history of Milton criticism in the middle part of the eighteenth century. See this volume, 135–47, 171–98, for excerpts from the Lauder affair. Lauder drew together and expanded his 1747 essays into a pamphlet in 1750, having evidently been encouraged by the articles' reception in some quarters; Dr. Johnson ghostwrote the introduction. (I should note that I have profited greatly from reading Joseph Loewenstein's paper, "Milton's Talent: The Authorial Icon in the Tonson Era," which will be published in his upcoming book on copyright and authorship.) For Bentley, see *Milton's "Paradise Lost." A New Edition* (London, 1732), which is available in a modern reprint (New York: A M S Press, Inc., 1974).

4.   Bentley received 100 pounds for his notes from the publisher Jacob Tonson, whose family had controlled publication rights to *Paradise Lost* since 1680, and who must have expected the venture to be profitable (R. J. White, *Dr. Bentley: A Study in Academic Scarlet* [London: Eyre & Spottiswoode, 1965], 209). Lauder had it in mind to publish scholarly editions of the neo-Latin works he claimed Milton had plagiarized, which he hoped would now be in demand.

5.   Joseph M. Levine, "Bentley's Milton: Philology and Criticism in Eighteenth-Century England," in *Journal of the History of Ideas*, 50:549–68. Bentley's biographers differ on how the editor is to be taken. But only Richard Jebb is sure that Bentley was utterly in earnest about him; see the chapter on Bentley's *Paradise Lost* in his *Bentley*, in John Morley, ed., *English Men of Letters*, vol. 4 (1884; reprint, New York: Harper & Brothers, 1894). The best discussion of the question is in Levine, who thinks Bentley was both ironic and ardent to render his views on Milton forcefully. It is perhaps worth noting that Dr. Johnson deemed the supposition of an editor "rash and groundless, if he thought it true; and vile and pernicious, if, as is said, he in private allowed it to be false"; see his life of Milton in *Lives of the English Poets*, ed. George Birkbeck Hill (Oxford: Oxford University Press, 1905), 181. Lauder too, who makes frequent mention of Bentley's corrections and tends to see him as an ally, claims to know that Bentley "scrupled not to acknowledge on proper occasions" his editor's chimeric status.

6.   Even with the interpolated lines, Lauder's neo-Latin passages could in fact prove no more, of course, than that Milton had imitated moderns as well as ancients. For rebuttals of the plagiarism charge and fairly calm acceptance of Milton's imitation of moderns, see Richard Richardson's and (especially) John Douglas's comments in Shawcross, 141–42 and 181–85 respectively. For Lauder's very funny story explaining how and why his plot against Milton had been conceived, see Shawcross, 192–97.

7.   Note here though Guillory's essay in this volume, which makes something like "egotism" into a period phenomenon (see especially his citation from Hegel, 214–15). For a sharp exposition of the antinomies and the historical movement of the Protestant doctrine of vocation, see his "The Father's House: *Samson Agonistes* in Its Historical Moment," in *Remembering Milton*, ed. Mary Nyquist and Margaret W. Ferguson (London: Methuen, 1987), 148–58.

8.   See, though, for arguments that Milton was not initially so free from the patronage market as all that, Lindenbaum's essay in this volume: and, with a different emphasis, Ann Baynes Coiro, "Milton and Class Identity: The Publication of *Areopagitica* and the *1645 Poems*," in *Journal of Medieval and Renaissance Studies* 22 (1992):261–89.

9. For Miltonic identification with Christ in the "Nativity Ode," see Richard Halpern, "The Great Instauration," in *Re-membering Milton*, 3–25; and for *Samson Agonistes*, see Christopher Kendrick, "Typology and the Ethics of Tragedy in *Samson Agonistes*," in *Criticism* 33 (1991):115–52.

10. For the report, see *The Early Lives of Milton*, ed. Helen Darbishire (London: Constable & Co, 1932), 75–76. Several critics have noted Milton's imitation, at the beginning of *Paradise Regained*, of the Renaissance *Aeneid*'s opening lines, and have drawn the inference that *Paradise Regained* is to *Paradise Lost* as the *Aeneid* to the *Georgics*.

11. Mary Ann Radzinowics, *Toward Samson Agonistes: The Growth of Milton's Mind* (Princeton: Princeton University Press, 1978).

12. Two of the better and more representative early feminist essays on Milton are Sandra Gilbert, "Patriarchal Poetry and Women Readers: Reflections on Milton's Bogey," *PMLA* 93 (1978):368–82, and Christine Froula, "When Eve Reads Milton: Undoing the Canonical Economy," *Critical Inquiry* 10(1983):321–47. A representative conservative response to feminist critiques is Philip J. Gallagher, *Milton, the Bible, and Misogyny* (Columbia: University of Missouri Press, 1990). A good recent collection of (mostly) feminist criticism is *Milton and the Idea of Woman*, ed. Julia M. Walker (Urbana: University of Illinois Press, 1988). Among the best feminist work done so far is Mary Nyquist's "Fallen Differences, Phallogocentric Discourses: Losing *Paradise Lost* to History," in *Post-Structuralism and the Question of History*, ed. Derek Attridge et. al. (Cambridge: Cambridge University Press, 1987), and the essay by her reprinted in this collection.

13. Linda Woodbridge, *Women in the English Renaissance: Literature and the Nature of Womankind, 1540–1620* (Urbana: University of Illinois, 1984), especially chapter 2 and page 43.

14. I take the phrase "authentically ugly" from James Turner's informative *One Flesh: Paradisal Marriage and Sexual Relations in the Age of Milton* (Oxford: Clarendon Press, 1987), who uses it to describe Milton's attitude towards marriage in the divorce tracts.

15. For Milton's monism in philosophical context, see Stephen Fallon's instructive *Milton among the Philosophers: Poetry and Materialism in Seventeenth-Century England* (Ithaca: Cornell University Press, 1991), and for the relation of monism to Milton's divorce tracts, see his "The Metaphysics of Milton's Divorce Tracts," in *Politics, Poetics, and Hermeneutics in Milton's Prose*, ed. David Loewenstein and James Grantham Turner (Cambridge: Cambridge University Press, 1990), 69–84.

16. See Milton's autobiographical excursus in the *Apology for Smectymnuus* (London, 1642), 15–18.

17. For suggestive remarks on Milton's divorce tracts and the novel, see Annabel Patterson, "No Meer Amatorious Novel?," in *John Milton*, ed. Annabel Patterson (London: Longmans, 1992), 87–101; for *Paradise Lost* and the novel, see Carrol B. Cox, "Citizen Angels: Civil Society and the Abstract Individual in Paradise Lost," *Milton Studies* 23 (1987):165–96.

18. For a good Marxist discussion of Milton's politics in the context of the Civil War, see Andrew Milner, *John Milton and the English Revolution* (London: Macmillan, 1981), 50–94.

19. C. S. Lewis, *A Preface to Paradise Lost* (London: Oxford University Press, 1942), 79, 92.

20. It is arguable that Milton's poetry had more of an effect on the everyday lives of ordinary eighteenth- and early nineteenth-century Americans than on those of Britons. This is suggested, I think, by Keith Stavely's fine *Puritan Legacies: "Paradise Lost" and the New England Tradition, 1630–1890* (Ithaca: Cornell University Press, 1989).

21. "Milton," in *The Works of Matthew Arnold in Fifteen Volumes*, vol. 5 (London: Macmillan, 1904), 42–50. This essay was composed as a speech on the occasion of a gift of a memorial window at St. Margaret's Church, in Westminster, in honor of Milton. Perhaps for this reason it is tendentious and strained even for Arnold. The "Anglo-Saxon contagion" is equated with the cult of the average man, or in other words with the democratic effects

of capitalism. From these effects, Arnold claims, *Paradise Lost* can save England; or rather, redemption is to be found, not in the religious, political, or even "perhaps" the domestic content of the poem, since these seem to be either simply outdated or somewhat contagious themselves, but in the Grand Style resounding on its own. Granted that Arnold manages to apply Milton jingoistically in his peroration ("All the Anglo-Saxon contagion, all the flood of Anglo-Saxon commonness, beats vainly against the great style but cannot shake it, and has to accept its triumph. And it triumphs in Milton, in one of our own race, tongue, faith, and morals. Milton has made the great style no longer an exotic here; he has made it an inmate amongst us, a leaven, and a power. . . . The English race overspreads the world, and at the same time the ideal of an excellence the most high and the most rare abides a possession with it forever" [98–99]); but if Milton serves imperial ends here, it is a Milton stripped of content; he cannot be made into a very full-blooded nationalist. For Arnold's better known essay on Milton, which delivers much the same judgment on Milton though in a negative key, see "A French Critic on Milton," *The Works*, vol. 10, 227–60. For British nationalism, see Tom Nairn, *The Enchanted Glass: Britain and its Monarchy* (London: Radius, 1988).

22. See, for example, for a Miltonist's rather complacent agreement with this commonplace, William Kerrigan, "Seventeenth-Century Studies," in *Redrawing the Boundaries: The Transformation of English and American Literary Studies*, ed. Stephen Greenblatt and Giles Gunn (New York: Modern Language Association of America, 1992), 73–74.

23. *Milton and the English Revolution* (New York: Viking Press, 1977).

24. For essays reflecting this interest, see Loewenstein and Turner, eds., *Politics, Poetics, Hermeneutics*; for the general interest in sectarian writing, see *Pamphlet Wars: Prose in the English Revolution*, ed. James Holstun (London: Frank Cass, 1992), and *Literature and the English Civil War*, eds. Thomas Healy and Jonathan Sawday (Cambridge: Cambridge University Press, 1990).

25. See John Peter Rumrich, "Uninventing Milton," *Modern Philology* 87 (1990):249–65, which corrects the older, neo-Christian view of Milton in light of current common sense about Milton's politics.

RECEPTIONS

◆

How To Do Things With Milton:
A Study in the Politics of Literary Criticism

CARL FREEDMAN*

If there is any single development that characterizes the varied transformation of English literary studies over the past two decades or so—the transformation often, though ambiguously, designated simply as "theory"—it is the dismantling of a certain positivism of the text, a positivism previously not only dominant but (with few exceptions) virtually unquestioned in literary criticism. For traditional humanism—and, later, in more rigorous though also, perhaps, in more limited ways, for New Criticism—the text enjoyed an unproblematic ontological and epistemological integrity that was guaranteed, at least in large part, by the living voice of the author. The text existed securely, out "there," so to speak, well away from the actual business of reading and interpreting. The task of the critic was to "approach" the text as best he (or more rarely, she) could and to unveil what the author had to offer. The critic, as distinguished from the author, was understood to be engaged in a distinctly *secondary* activity. In a representative 1963 essay, George Steiner (perhaps the last traditional literary humanist to possess distinguished intellectual credentials) chose to describe his calling in overtly self-abasing (and consistently masculine) terms: "When he looks back, the critic sees a eunuch's shadow. Who would be a critic if he could be a writer?. . . . Who would choose to be a literary critic if he could set verse to sing, or compose, out of his own mortal being, a vital fiction, a character that will endure?. . . . The critic lives at second hand. He writes *about*. The poem, the novel, or the play must be given to him; criticism exists by the grace of other men's genius."[1] The mawkish note of anguish is peculiarily Steinerian, but not the basic attitude. Indeed, on the following page Steiner adopts the most widespread and popular platitude of humanistic positivism, the notion of the critic as servant to the author or text—a metaphor meant to convey not only the empiricist dichotomy between critic and text but also the degraded, inferior, second-order status of criticism (though the figure is deconstructed into unintended complexity when we reflect that servants have usually done more and more useful work than those employing them).

*This essay was written specifically for this volume and is published here for the first time.

19

This kind of literary-critical positivism can still find proponents, but it is increasingly marginalized and on the defensive. For Marxism, for psychoanalysis, for poststructuralism and reader-response criticism—indeed, for nearly every critical method that has really achieved much positive during the past generation—there can be no question of an innocent encounter between knowing critic and known text. Literary criticism, one might say, has finally caught up with Kant's *Critique of Judgment* (1790), probably the first major intellectual statement to establish the epistemological priority of interpretation. The text is now no longer understood as a congealed effluence of the author's voice (or soul), but as a constructed artifact, a complexly structured entity that is dialectically determined in connection with the active, constructive labor of reading and criticism. The critic who poses as mere servant to the text, offering to deconceal its mysteries, affects a masochistic humility that (in just the way diagnosed by Nietzsche) masks an overweening arrogance, the arrogance of claiming a variety of certainty and intellectual mastery over the text that the very nature of intellectual activity renders impossible from the start. Every reading is inevitably an *interested* reading that does not merely respond to but participates in the construction of its object. To put the matter in the convenient Austinian terms to which my title alludes, the critical utterance is less constative than *performative*.[2] The theatrical connotations of the term (though not remarked by Austin himself) are especially pertinent in this context. Different theatre companies offering rival performances of *Macbeth* are producing unique (and interested) Shakespearian artifacts; the literally unchanging title on the several marquees advertises what can be designated the "same" play only in a very problematic and highly qualified sense. But any reading—any criticism—of *Paradise Lost* is no less a unique, interested performance. This is not, of course, to say that all performances are of equal validity or that there is not a wide variety of criteria for choosing among them. But it does mean that literary criticism does not merely respond, in second-order fashion, to the seemingly immutable attributes of the text; every act of criticism is a performative labor with its own (always overdetermined) logic.

One effect of the discrediting of positivism in literary studies has been the decline in prestige of single-author criticism as a genre, a decline related to the greatly diminished sense of literary history as a succession of individual "masters" and "masterpieces." A servant, after all, typically works for a single master and certainly feels most comfortable with such employment; and the greater the master, the more elevated the service—better to be butler of a ducal household than manservant in a bachelor flat in Wimbledon. Once criticism has managed to get beyond such naive servility, however, single-author criticism, though by no means rendered invalid, can hardly enjoy the centrality it once possessed for literary studies. The task of criticism is now not to pluck out isolated texts or authors for elevation to (or reconfirmation in) canonical status, but to understand the *general* workings of literary signification in as many varied instances as possible and in all their overdetermined complexity. Furthermore, the dialectical, as opposed to the positivistic, critic remains aware of criticism's own role in defining literature, and is thus unlikely to lie prostrate before one (or more than one) "great" name. Yet much of the major criticism of the past remains, of course, single-author criticism: and I would suggest that some of this material may provide particularly interesting and useful opportunities for the study of cultural and ideological history. For the criticism of a particular author is bound to be determined by a great many factors other than various readers' responses to the "same" text (or set of texts); and yet the fact that the text *is*, in a merely bibliographic sense, at least approximately the same imposes a certain economy convenient for the cultural historian. The history of the reputation of a frequently read author like Shakespeare or Milton may well suggest, in neatly accessible miniature, more ideological currents than could otherwise so easily be gathered into one discursive place. If we no longer write single-author criticism as much as we used to, it may be worth our while to begin studying it more than we have so far.

In this spirit, I propose to analyze some Milton criticism. I choose Milton not merely because of the volume of material available, but because I think most readers of literary criticism would agree that, as single-author criticism goes, the Milton criticism produced in English during the twentieth century is among the most provocative, subtle, and fascinating. I am especially thinking of the Milton "controversy" during roughly the first half of this century, in which perhaps more distinguished and fiercely competitive critical minds focused on the (nominally) same single author than in any other comparable instance. During a period when politics in general and revolutionary politics in particular were of considerable moment in the English literary scene, many—and variously—powerful critics chose to focus on the most active political revolutionary in the English poetic canon. But I will not, of course, attempt anything like a thorough survey. My attention will be directed to works by four uniquely important critics and controversialists: T. S. Eliot's two essays on Milton of 1936 and 1947 respectively; F. R. Leavis's chapter on Milton's verse in *Revaluation* (1936) as well as his two later essays on Milton strategically placed at the beginning of *The Common Pursuit* (1952); C. S. Lewis's *A Preface to "Paradise Lost"* (1942); and William Empson's chapter on Milton and Bentley in *Some Versions of Pastoral* (1935), as well as his much more substantial *Milton's God* (1961).[3] It is easy to think of other titles that might properly be examined, but then, the topic I have chosen could easily be the subject of a book. Not only are Eliot, Leavis, Lewis, and Empson arguably the four most influential Milton critics of their time, but they are also, of course, four *generally* important presences in modern English letters. Eliot for several decades enjoyed the rare distinction (unprecedented at least since Dryden) of being the most influential poet *and* the most influential critic writing in English. Leavis not only produced an extremely consequential body of literary criticism over his own signature; he was also the main driving force behind *Scrutiny*, easily the most important collective critical project undertaken in England during this century. Lewis—as intellectually preeminent among Oxford's English faculty as Leavis among Cambridge's—made signal contributions to the literary history of the medieval and Renaissance periods and, at the same time, achieved a much wider fame through his popular works on religion and morality, his science fiction novels, and his children's books. Empson was, like Eliot, a poet-critic, and if his poems, though highly accomplished, seem minor compared to Eliot's, it is possible that his criticism will finally be judged as the most sheerly *intelligent* of his time; in any case, of all critics of his generation, Empson's concerns resonate most strongly in literary criticism today.

The connections among these four critics are usefully close. Eliot's 1936 essay was largely, if not quite solely, responsible for launching the Milton controversy in the first place. Leavis's contributions to the anti-Milton cause were written in intensely self-conscious awareness of Eliot but also with the mixture of strongly positive and negative feelings that characterized Leavis's attitude toward Eliot in general. Lewis's book was frankly written to defend Milton against his detractors, among whom Lewis rightly perceived Eliot and Leavis to be the most consequential. Empson, also pro-Milton, offers in his book to conclude and somewhat to transcend the controversy, and he distances himself at least as much from Lewis as from Leavis or Eliot.

It is worth noting that these four critics describe a wide range of political and theological opinion, and in ways that do not simply or obviously cohere with their positions for or against *Paradise Lost*. Thus, Eliot, extreme right-wing Tory and devout Anglo-Catholic, is on the anti-Milton side with Leavis, a very conservative Liberal and, in orthodox terms, an unbeliever, though much devoted to a "religious sense" derived largely from D. H. Lawrence. On the other hand, the liberal Tory Lewis and the radical Liberal Empson both defend Milton, while remaining equally fervent and proselytizing in their orthodox Christianity and antireligious rationalism respectively. But one thing all four had in common is that they chose to write about Milton, particularly about *Paradise Lost*. Why? And how? What is the nature of the Miltonic performances under discussion here? What things, in sum, are being done with Milton?

Before trying to answer these questions, however, I had better come clean, so to speak, myself. For a discussion of this sort could with perilous ease slip (or at least appear to slip) back into just the naive positivism that I oppose. What I wish above all to avoid is the impression that, in analyzing the readings of Eliot, Leavis, Lewis, and Empson, I am implicitly contrasting them with the perfectly "true" reading of Milton that I myself possess. It is thus necessary to present very explicitly, and with overt acknowledgement of its own interestedness, the reading of Milton that will serve as my critical baseline throughout. It need not be particularly elaborate, since my own view of Milton has only a minor and indirect relevance to the main project of this paper. I will therefore simply borrow a reading of Milton offered by the critic whom I take to be the most brilliantly accomplished of living literary critics among Milton's own compatriots. But I will refer not to any of Terry Eagleton's books or articles, but to one of his drinking songs. Entitled simply the "English Literature Song," it is a wonderful survey of England's literary glories set to a tune adapted from (whom else?) Edward Elgar. Most of the song is devoted to extremely brief denunciations of various canonical figures, from Chaucer and Shakespeare—a "class traitor" and one who "hated the mob," respectively—to the "fascist" Yeats, Eliot, and Pound, the "sexist" Lawrence, and the simply "unsound" Virginia Woolf. Yet the song's attitude toward the authors whom Oxford English dons are required to discuss with their pupils is not uniformly hostile:

> There are only three names
> To be plucked from this dismal set:
> Milton, Blake, and Shelley
> Will smash the ruling class yet,
>
> Milton, Blake, and Shelley
> Will smash the ruling class yet![4]

Despite the brevity and humor, the construction of Milton suggested is, I think, tolerably clear: Milton is to be read as primarily a revolutionary and regicide, as a prophet of liberty, as one whose deepest affinities across the ages are with such later antinomian revolutionaries as Blake and Shelley as well as, implicitly, with Marx himself and the entire Marxist tradition, which of course includes Eagleton (and me). This view of Milton seems to me a good deal more congenial and, potentially, more intellectually fruitful than the views of any of the four critics I have to consider. But it is clearly a view no less interested, and its presentation in a drinking song should serve as a very plain marker that it is understood to be decidedly *partial*. Few readers, in any case, will be tempted to mistake it for the pure, simple, complete, and unproblematic truth.

Many readers, however, may be surprised to recall that the ultraconservative royalist Eliot constructs Milton in terms not wholly dissimilar to those of the revolutionary socialist Eagleton. Whatever else may be repressed in Eliot's reading, he certainly does not forget that Milton was a revolutionary. Accordingly, the 1936 essay opens by proclaiming Milton to be "antipathetic" as a man and "unsatisfactory" from various points of view, including "that of the political philosopher" (M1, 138). This is cryptic and, strictly construed, nonsensical, since not all political philosophers share one viewpoint and since Milton was, *inter alia*, a political philosopher. But as long as one remembers that for Eliot the range of permissible political thought extended roughly from Edmund Burke to Charles Maurras, then the insinuation of a specifically right-wing political case against the protoleftist Milton is not difficult to grasp. In his 1947 essay, indeed, Eliot is remarkably incisive about the political dimension of the anti-Milton position, though he takes care to enhance the respectability of his own "dispositions," as he calls them, by associating them with those of Samuel Johnson. The most relevant passage is worth quoting at length, not only for the light it throws on the formation of Eliot's reading of Milton, but for some quite acute insights about the resonance of the Great Rebellion in modern English culture:

> The fact is simply that the Civil War of the seventeenth century, in which Milton is a symbolic figure, has never been concluded. The Civil War is not ended: I question whether any serious civil war ever does end. Throughout that period English society was so convulsed and divided that the effects are still felt. Reading Johnson's essay [Life of Milton] one is always aware that Johnson was obstinately and passionately of another party. No other English poet, not Wordsworth, or Shelley, lived through or took sides in such momentous events as did Milton; of no other poet is it so difficult to consider the poetry simply as poetry, without our theological and political dispositions, conscious and unconscious, inherited or acquired, making an unlawful entry.
>
> (M1, 148)

But in exactly what sense is the Civil War "not ended"? For on the same page Eliot immediately goes on to allow that both of its main contending parties—that of the Puritans and that of the monarch whom he rather touchingly refers to as "King Charles"—are today considered unacceptable, and that the religious views of both are remote from most modern readers. How, then, do the emotions raised by the Civil War continue to move us? He does not say, except to suggest that these emotions "now take different vestures." Again, however, it is not hard to infer what these "vestures" must be. The Anglican martyr and would-be absolute monarch Charles I is an exquisitely appropriate figure for everything held dear (in the political realm) by the poet-critic whose essential Tory loyalty to the traditional English ruling elite was slightly complicated by attraction toward Continental forms of clerical fascism. On the other side, opposing both fascism and ordinary Toryism, and thus symbolically inheriting the mantle of Milton, is the chief insurgent radical movement of Eliot's lifetime, namely socialism—from the revolutionary communism that in 1936 was still an active contender in the British political arena to the Labourist social democracy of the Atlee Government that in 1947 was actually transforming, to some degree, the contours of British society.[5]

Shall we then conclude that Eliot's case against Milton is mainly a partisan hatchet job, the vilification of a great revolutionary poet as an indirect means of scoring points against the modern British left (which in

Eliot's time enjoyed a good deal of prominence in the literary world)? To a considerable extent I think that the answer is simply yes, and that no intelligent understanding of Eliot's anti-Miltonism is feasible unless the most directly and crudely political factors are given due weight. But the matter is also, of course, somewhat more complicated than that. It is certainly significant that in the organization of both essays Eliot's overtly political (and theological) objections to Milton are given priority over specifically formal matters. But it is also significant that both essays *do* go on, and at much greater length, to discuss issues of form and versification. Indeed, in the 1936 essay, Eliot describes his formal "doubts" about Milton as "more serious" (M1, 138) than Milton's general badness in the political, theological, moral, and other spheres. In the 1947 essay, Eliot explicitly announces his attempt to transcend political partisanship in order "to attend to the poetry for the poetry's sake" (M2, 149). The nature of such "attending" and its relation to overtly political questions are worth some consideration here.

It may be recalled that the 1947 essay presents itself—and has generally been accepted—as, on the formal plane, a recantation of its predecessor, a withdrawal of Eliot's condemnation of Milton's verse. There is certainly a major shift in tone. In 1936 Eliot's style is still inflected by the asperity of the outsider; to some extent, he still speaks prophetically, as the great reactionary dissident of modern English letters. By 1947 his position as the dominant force in English letters—indeed, as perhaps the most widely feared and respected literary dictator that London had witnessed since Ben Jonson—is securely consolidated, and his style is accordingly more relaxed, his tone appropriately urbane, suave, and gracious. Not by chance was Eliot's second Milton essay originally delivered as a lecture to the British Academy. But after one has made allowance for such differences in manner and presentation, the 1947 essay really concedes very little of substance (a point that Leavis was almost alone in grasping at the time, and one that he tirelessly but vainly attempted to make generally current). In the first essay, Eliot's essential objection to Milton's verse is that it lacks a certain kind of sensuous empiricism. Sharp visual images are for the most part absent, nor does the verse make any attempt to convey the pressure of actual thought or speech. Instead, the style is abstract, artificial, and hollow, a hypertrophy of sheer rhetoric whose logic, such as it is, is determined by sound, by what Eliot calls the auditory imagination. Milton, in fine, "writes English like a dead language" (M1, 141), one capable of considerable musical effect but no longer vitalized by the roughage of everyday life. Thus, for example, the descriptions of the various rustic characters in *L'Allegro* lack all human particularity: "the sensuous effect of these verses is entirely on the ear, and is joined to the concepts of ploughman, milkmaid, and shepherd." Milton, that is, "does not infuse new life into the word" (M1, 140). Or, again, when Satan delivers the famous speech to his followers in Book V of *Paradise*

Lost ("Thrones, dominations, princedoms, virtues, powers, / If these magnific titles yet remain / Not merely titular . . .", etc.), the "dark angel is not *thinking* or conversing, but making a speech carefully prepared for him" (M1, 142; Eliot's emphasis), a speech arranged on the basis of sound, not sense.[6] Eliot allows (unconvincingly) that he can enjoy the music of Milton's grandiloquence, but he insists that "this is not serious poetry, not poetry fully occupied about its business, but rather a solemn game" (M1, 144). And, because this less than serious poetry has (for reasons Eliot leaves unclear) exercised such wide influence, Milton "may still be considered as having done damage to the English language from which it has not wholly recovered" (M1, 145).

With the problematic exception of the last statement, there is nothing in this characterization of Milton's poetry that Eliot really recants in 1947. The tone is so much warmer and the absence of derogatory epithets so striking that it is easy to carry away the impression of a reversal of judgement. But Milton's verse still looks pretty much the same to Eliot. It is still rhetorical in the extreme, maintaining no vital connection to the rhythms and dictions of actual (private) speech: "there is always the maximal, never the minimal, alteration of ordinary language" (M2, 154). Indeed, it is a matter not only of remoteness from but of actual violence to the English language. Milton's style is based on "a perpetual sequence of original acts of lawlessness," so that he produces "poetry at the farthest possible remove from prose." It is also, and again, a poetry that makes little clear to the eye— as in the earlier essay, Eliot speculates at length on the stylistic importance of Milton's blindness—so that a Miltonic scene cannot really be visualized with any rigor or consistency but must simply be "accepted as a shifting phantasmagory" (M2, 156). For Milton, in sum, the "emphasis is on the sound, not the vision, upon the word, not the idea" (M2, 157). Accordingly, Eliot's original claim—that in Milton's verse magniloquent rhetorical sound reigns supreme, marginalizing both vision and meaning—still stands. Milton's verse is still understood to be lacking the sensuous empiricism so valued by Eliot and by so many others of his literary generation. Admittedly, Eliot does somewhat retract his thesis that the influence of this verse not only has in fact been bad but in the nature of the case could *only* be bad; he now sees the question as more historically variable, and even suggests that in the "now" of 1947 poets may at last be able to study Milton with profit to their own work. But Eliot's recommendation of Milton to his poetic colleagues is (as Leavis noticed) so generalized and offered with so little fervor that it is difficult to take as much more than a gesture of *politesse*. Eliot no longer presents his analysis in truculently anti-Milton terms; speaking to the British Academy, he seems to have grown more respectful of those whom the 1936 essay ridicules as persons "who regard any censure upon a 'great' poet as a breach of the peace, as an act of wanton iconoclasm, or even hoodlumism"

(M1, 139). But he has done nothing substantial to impair or disarm the anti-Milton case adumbrated by him in 1936, and thus nothing that must inhibit those of his followers who wish to continue the active fight.

F. R. Leavis is the most important of these followers, and by long odds. Indeed, in this matter as in others, even to call Leavis a "follower" of Eliot's is equivocal. It is true that in mounting a case against Milton's verse Leavis adopts the basic logic of Eliot's argument, and that Eliot's poetry as well as his criticism is an important presence in Leavis's anti-Miltonism (though Leavis's famous astringency by no means spares Eliot whenever he feels that Eliot has failed to adhere to the standards suggested by his own best work). But it is no less true that Leavis enforces his case with a combination of detail, philosophical lucidity, and close textual attention far beyond anything of which Eliot is capable. Arguably Eliot's inferior in point of originality,[7] Leavis is easily the superior critic in rigor and stamina. Since, then, the Eliotic attack on Milton's versification is given its strongest and amplest expression not by Eliot himself but by Leavis, it is necessary to examine Leavis's Milton essays before going on, as promised, to relate this strictly formal argument to the overtly political questions already discussed. First, however, it may be useful to recall a few facts about Leavis's general ideological formation.

It could hardly have been more different, in many ways, from Eliot's. While Eliot emerged from a Unitarian background in Missouri to embrace Anglo-Catholicism and High Tory monarchism, Leavis remained essentially faithful to a legacy of Whig and Liberal political views and Nonconformist religiosity. Though Leavis's Nonconformity was not expressed by adherence to any particular creed, the earnest puritanical conscience of that tradition is, as many readers have remarked, detectable on nearly every page of his work. Liberalism and Nonconformity both inclined Leavis toward autonomy of conscience and individual liberty, values that coexist in his work in often fruitful tension with the equally Nonconformist (if not particularly Liberal) ideals of community and collaboration. With such a (classically petty-bourgeois) perspective, Leavis had little sympathy for Eliot's genteel Toryism and considerable scorn for the upper-class British Establishment into which Eliot learned to fit so cozily; and he certainly had no weakness for fascism. On the other hand, an unbudging mistrust of industrial society—almost, indeed, of modernity itself—alienated Leavis from virtually all political currents on the Left. To the extent that he possessed a positive and coherent sociopolitical philosophy, it was mainly as he was able to construct one out of such works of Lawrence's as *The Rainbow*, *Women in Love*, and *Fantasia of the Unconscious*—which is to say that it is not easy to formulate a coherently Leavisite sociopolitical philosophy.[8] In the current context, one apparent conundrum may seem especially perplexing. Though the political motivation of Eliot's anti-Miltonism is easily intelligible, it is much less clear why Leavis, rooted in puritan Nonconformity and an enthusiastic critical advocate of authors similarly rooted, from Bunyan to Lawrence, should have objected so strongly to the author of *Paradise Lost*, a text generally taken to be integral to precisely the tradition that includes Leavis himself. This question must be suspended for the moment, but will be reconsidered after examining Leavis's formal indictment of Milton's verse.

Much of Leavis's analysis amounts to an amplification of Eliot's, though conducted both with closer textual attention and wider poetic erudition (of Milton himself and of other poets adduced for comparison and contrast). Like Eliot, Leavis finds Milton's style to be excessively stylized and abstract, "in the manner of a ritual" (MV, 46), and thus to display "a certain sensuous poverty" (MV, 47): the pertinent opposition is to modes of versification as diverse as those of Shakespeare, Donne, Middleton, Tourneur, Ben Jonson, the Court poets, and Marvell—all of whom, unlike Milton, display in their work "a vital relation to speech, to the living language of the time" (DM, 42). Leavis, again like Eliot, also convicts Milton of a weakness in visual imagery, though unlike Eliot he goes on to argue (partly by way of a shrewd contrasting analysis of Keats's style in *To Autumn*) that not all imagery is specifically visual, and that Milton's poverty is in *all* the senses, save perhaps the aural; and Leavis also insists that what the ear hears in Milton is something quite vague that can be described as "music" only by a clumsily specious analogy. Leavis also goes somewhat beyond Eliot (leaning heavily in this respect on A. J. A. Waldock's critique of the narrative of *Paradise Lost*) by stressing an intellectual as well as a sensuous incoherence in Milton's epic, so that, he argues, the poem repeatedly contradicts itself and makes a thorough mess of its announced aim to justify the ways of God: Milton, though of authentically heroic character, simply "hasn't the kind of energy of mind needed for sustained analytic and discursive thinking" (EM, 23). Leavis does not make it completely clear why Milton should have been so influential on English poetry for over two centuries, though, unlike Eliot, he does try to engage the question; but his construction of Milton's verse leaves little room for doubt about the good reasons (as Leavis sees them) for Milton's modern "dislodgment" (MV, 42).

If, however, Leavis displays a rigor superior to Eliot's in making the Eliotic case against Milton, he displays it above all in his articulation of the theoretical issues at stake on the level of what might be called the philosophy of poetic form. Interrogating Eliot's 1936 essay, one could simply ask (as Lewis in effect does) why remoteness from common speech and a general lack of cleanly defined images should necessarily be such damning faults in poetry. Eliot has no clear answer—which may be why in the later Milton essay he is able to suggest, if halfheartedly, that perhaps these characteristics are no longer so very bad after all. But Leavis does have an answer. Milton, he says, "exhibits a feeling *for* words rather than a capacity for feeling *through* words; we are often, in reading him, moved to comment that he is 'external' or that he 'works from the outside' " (MV, 50; Leavis's emphasis). For Leavis, then, the word itself is suspect, at least insofar as the word is considered in and of itself rather than as the means through which something else—something nonverbal—may be attained. Though the poet's business is of necessity with language, there is a danger in becoming too occupied with language for its own sake. Successful poets (Shakespeare is the supreme instance) understand and avoid this danger. But Milton does not: "We remain predominantly aware [while reading Milton] of eloquence and declamation; our sense of words as words, things for the mouth and ear, is not transcended in any vision—or (to avoid the visualist fallacy) any *realization*—they convey" (EM, 18; Leavis's emphasis). One might say that Leavis's quarrel is with writing itself, especially as writing has been understood since Barthes and Derrida, that is, writing as a self-conscious *activity* that possesses its own integrity and internal complexity, and that works to foreground itself as such. For Leavis, language is legitimate only as it functions transparently to make possible the apprehension of something beyond itself, an apprehension in which the word as such may not be wholly forgotten but in which it is organically fused with the nonverbal object. What is at issue here is not only empiricism, but also seamlessness and what Althusser might call expressive totalization. For Leavis and Eliot the original sin of literature is to be written in language, and language can be redeemed only to the degree that it dissolves itself into some virtually mystical vision of unity; it remains guilty to the degree that it remains itself, highlighting gaps and discontinuities. Leavis's preferred figure is of course *metaphor*, and he praises Wilson Knight's description of a Shakespearian play as an "extended metaphor," arguing that "the phrase suggests with great felicity [an] almost inconceivably close and delicate organic wholeness" (MV, 60–61)—the precise opposite (and Leavis is completely at one with Eliot here) of the artificial externality and detachment of the Miltonic Grand Style.

We are now in a position to appreciate the political valences of the Eliotic construction of Miltonic style. The execution of "King Charles," which Milton supported, may be seen as not only a matter of Anglican martyrdom but also—since it signalled the definitive end of the divine right of kings in England—as symbolizing the collapse of an ideology central to Eliot's reactionary Toryism: namely, the ideology of an organic hierarchical kingdom, a perfectly seamless social unity in which all the various "levels" of society are fused into one vibrant body politic, the integrity of which enjoys supernatural overtones. The Restoration could in no way undo the basic ruptures of 1642 and 1649, and by the later seventeenth century—the era of Eliot's famous "dissociation of sensibility," of course—it is clear that henceforth society is, so to speak, organized on a principle more metonymic than metaphoric. No sector of society can henceforth "express" another; rather, the various sectors grow increasingly discontinuous and relate to one another in uneasy, problematic, and sometimes violent fashion. For Eliot, Milton is responsible for this deplorable state of affairs not only because of his service in the Rebellion and the Cromwellian regime. His more subtle but in some ways more consequential guilt lies in the way that the versification of *Paradise Lost*, as Eliot (and Leavis) construe it, actually *enacts* the breakdown of organic society and thus introduces into English verse, as Milton helps to introduce into the English polity, those qualities of violence, externality, and disconnection that foreclose the reactionary Eliotic utopia. In Milton, one might say, language is allowed a certain kind of promiscuity. It is left largely to its own devices—it is not stablized by being melded with any empirical sensuous reality "beyond" itself—and in that way exhibits the "lawless" unpredictability so subversive of Eliot's Toryism. A reassuring sense of "organic wholeness" is replaced by a disturbing sense of discontinuity and fragmentation. The "dislocation" that Eliot indicts in Milton's "rhetorical style" (M1, 143) is inseparable from the sense of social dislocation that he finds so terrifying in the modern world. There is, indeed, a real parallel between the Eliotic attack on Milton and the response of reactionary twentieth-century critics to the great modernisms. The obvious irony here is that among the most important works of literary modernism are several of Eliot's own poems. Himself attacked as a "literary bolshevik" and a "drunken helot,"[9] Eliot employs numerous strategies to defuse such criticism and to erase the subversive potentialities of a work like *The Waste Land*. The antihistorical use of myth in that very poem is one such strategy. But the attack on Milton—and on his versification as well as his personality and political role—is not the least important way in which Eliot strives to repudiate the modern forces of revolution and to establish the authenticity of his own fervent but hopeless Toryism.

The case of Leavis is somewhat but not entirely different. Though he was no less wedded to social organicism than Eliot, his own lost utopia was of a rather different sort—not Eliot's Anglo-Catholic absolutist kingdom, but a commonwealth of free, proud, independent Dissenters living in a series of largely autonomous and essentially rural communities. This vision, if arguably more humane than Eliot's, remains equally allergic to the antiorganicism of Milton's poetic style, equally repelled by that refusal of wholeness which Leavis construes so incisively in the versification of *Paradise Lost*. Nonetheless, the political opposition between Leavis and Milton is not nearly so straightforward as that between Eliot and Milton; and it is noteworthy that overt political references of the sort so prominent in Eliot's Milton criticism are virtually absent in Leavis's, which confines itself almost exclusively to formal, especially stylistic, matters. But I suspect that the peculiar vehemence with which Leavis usually refers to Milton (even more intense, in tone, than Eliot's) may not be unrelated to the distant affinity between them. For if Milton is one of the founders of that Liberal and Nonconformist tradition which includes Leavis, he also illustrates—partly because of his historical moment, partly because of the particular choices he made both political *and stylistic*—how the most radical values of that tradition may at certain times tend toward social rupture rather than toward the imagined social harmony that Leavis so values in his heritage. All forms of liberalism, after all, have their origin in revolution, and revolution is necessarily the spectre that haunts every liberal tradition. Milton represents—as Bunyan and Lawrence do not—the most subversive potentialities latent within Nonconformist Liberalism and thus the possible linkages between the latter and the modern British Left that Leavis so insistently wishes to oppose. If for Eliot Milton is pretty simply the enemy, for Leavis he is the enemy within— not flatly opposing Leavisite ideology as he does Eliotic ideology, but suggesting revolutionary contradictions within Leavisite ideology that Leavis does not wish to face.

Both Eliot and Leavis, then, construct Milton as something of a *scapegoat*, a powerful figure to be rejected and stigmatized so that Eliot may maintain his right-wing Toryism (despite his experiments in modernist verse) and Leavis his *conservative* Liberalism (despite the more radical possibilities of the latter). It is in this context that we can appreciate a certain potential awkwardness in C. S. Lewis's position as he comes forward in 1942 to refute the case against Milton, at that time most consequentially voiced in Eliot's 1936 essay and the Milton chapter of *Revaluation*. Eliot and Leavis indict Milton in ways that support their distinct but congruent quarrels with the modern Left. Yet Lewis is by no means of the Left himself. He is a genially liberal Tory, antisocialist while never profascist, and with very little active or constructive interest in politics anyway. While Eliot and Leavis yearn after differently reactionary but equally impossible utopias, Lewis is genuinely dismissive of utopia and almost dismissive of politics altogether—an attitude that, in a way, is perhaps even more deeply antileftist than Eliot's ultraconservatism. Theologically, Lewis is actually Eliot's fellow Anglican—"I agree with [Eliot] about matters of such moment that all literary questions are, in comparison, trivial" (PPL, 9)—though Lewis's bluff, hearty, down-to-earth Ulster Protestantism has a cast very different from that of Eliot's genteel Anglo-Catholicism. If, then, Lewis is hardly in a position to defend Milton the revolutionary, to construct Milton as a liberating and *favorably* regarded poet of the proto-Left, one might expect him simply to deny the validity of the Eliot-Leavis reading *in toto*. But that is just what he does not do. He slyly adopts phrases from Eliot's 1936 essay in order to describe *Paradise Lost*, and at one point explicitly allows, "Dr. Leavis does not differ from me about the properties of Milton's epic verse. He describes them very accurately . . ." (PPL, 134). It is evident that, given such a perspective, Lewis must go a long way around to make a cogent defense—and that is precisely what the aptly titled *Preface to "Paradise Lost"* does.

Much of the book, indeed, has little or no *direct* concern with Milton, and it is probably safe to conjecture that these tend to be the parts that most readers have found most useful. Whatever one thinks of the way that Lewis reads the Grand Style or the character of Satan, it is hard not to be grateful for his lucid presentations of Homeric diction, of Virgil's reinvention of epic, of St. Augustine's theology of the Fall, and of the notions of angelic substance current in Renaissance Platonism. Discussions of this kind may well constitute the greatest strength of Lewis's academic writings in general, and it is perhaps tempting to describe him as essentially a glorified annotator. But the jibe is unfair, for what Lewis offers is never merely information of the sort that anyone could, with sufficient labor, ferret out of an ordinarily wellstocked university library. His chief concern is finally with the *imaginative* relevance that his far-flung scraps of erudition have to the poem under discussion. Though he devotes many pages to the exposition of "background" material, his real aim is to erase the distinction between textual and contextual criticism by showing how various historical factors are alive *within* the verse itself. Taking for granted the controlling and decisive relevance of both historical "context" and authorial intention, Lewis thus offers to present us with the textual object *wie es eigentlich gewesen*: "The first qualification for judging any piece of workmanship from a corkscrew to a cathedral is to know *what* it is—what it was intended to do and how it is meant to be used. The first thing the reader needs to know about *Paradise Lost* is what Milton meant it to be" (PPL, 1; Lewis's emphasis). In order to understand the significance of Lewis's construction of Milton, it is necessary to disentangle some of the theoretical problems here of which Lewis seems to be largely innocent.

It is not to be disputed that materials of the sort that Lewis assembles may be relevant in producing a reading of Milton. But the problem that Lewis never faces squarely (though he does not ignore it entirely) is the inevitable *selectivity* of what he deems relevant in order to know "what" *Paradise Lost* is. His omissions are astonishing. They include, indeed, nearly everything (with the exception of Renaissance—especially Cambridge—Platonism) that was actually happening during Milton's own lifetime. Contemporary politics plays an especially negligible part in the Miltonic background as Lewis sees it, so that the numerous political texts in which certain recent Milton critics have taken such an interest—whether produced (like Milton's own political writings) within the "mainstream" of the Puritan revolution or within any of the radical antinomian sects far to the Left of Cromwell—are invisible.[10] Nor does Lewis accord more than fairly minor significance to any of the heretical or esoteric religious texts, whether Christian or Jewish, that have seemed so important to numerous Milton scholars less personally devoted than Lewis to the profession and practice of strict Christian orthodoxy. Instead, Lewis emphasizes the centrality to Milton's formation of, on the one hand, the preeminent achievements of classical antiquity—especially Homeric and Virgilian epic, and Platonic and Aristotelian philosophy—and, on the other hand, the main line of orthodox Christianity, most notably as represented by the Bible and St. Augustine. Of course, Lewis is hardly the first critic to stress the fusion in Milton of

Christianity and classicism or to read *Paradise Lost* as the ultimate achievement of Christian humanism. But he delineates so compellingly and in such considerable detail how this "background" animates the sweep, the texture, and the conceptual substance of Milton's poetry that, like every other Milton critic worth reading, Lewis most certainly "produces a Milton of his own" (DM, 36), as Leavis says with misplaced (that is, positivistic) derision of E. M. W. Tillyard. Once we appreciate the *deliberateness* with which Lewis's materials are assembled, we can easily understand the many passages in which Lewis states, with what would otherwise seem incredible and breathtaking certainty, that Milton clearly meant *x* or definitely intended *y*: for who could be better qualified than Lewis (a skilled novelist, it should be remembered) to proclaim the intentions of Lewis's Milton?

It is a Milton who bears striking similarities to none other than C. S. Lewis himself. For Lewis, the author of *Paradise Lost* is a scholarly man wholly devoted to religion and to literature. He believes wholeheartedly in hierarchy and order. Despite his long political career, he seems no longer to have active political interests or even strong memories of his own partisan involvements—the contrast with the crucial importance that Eliot ascribes to Milton the politician could hardly be more clearly defined. Nor is Lewis's Milton much occupied with the theological disputes *within* Christianity, the controversies that lead the Christian Eliot to find the theology of *Paradise Lost* "in large part repellent" (M1, 144). Instead, the poem is like Lewis's own religious writings in being concerned with what is common to nearly all believing communicants, with "mere Christianity" (Richard Baxter's phrase that Lewis borrowed for the title of one of his apologetic works): "[A]s far as doctrine goes, the poem is overwhelmingly Christian. Except for a few isolated passages it is not even specifically Protestant or Puritan. It gives the great central tradition. . . . [D]ogmatically its invitation to join in this great ritual *mimesis* of the Fall is one in which all Christendom in all lands or ages can accept" (PPL, 92).

Though Milton's aim is of course to justify the ways of God to men, this is not a particularly difficult task, since the poet regards the truth and goodness of Christian orthodoxy to be so evident that virtually anyone of ordinary intelligence and unbiased mind will, with a reasonable amount of attention to the matter, easily perceive the divine justice of God—the obvious parallel is again with much in Lewis's own work (especially, perhaps, the novel *Perelandra*, whose plot is partly modelled after that of *Paradise Lost*), just as the most pertinent contrast is, as we shall see, with William Empson's reading of the poem. So far as the specifically literary context is concerned, Lewis's Milton is not particularly English. Whereas Leavis's Milton is mainly a compatriot of Donne and Jonson and, above all, Shakespeare, Lewis's Milton—as befits his centrality to the whole Western and Christian traditions—places himself in an even loftier position, alongside Homer, Virgil, and Dante.

It is by establishing this construction of Milton that Lewis is able to accept much of the descriptive formal criticism of the Eliot-Leavis case while resisting the unfavorable evaluations of the anti-Miltonists. Lewis quite agrees that the style of *Paradise Lost* is artificial and largely alien to ordinary speech: there is, he frankly allows, little "play of muscles" (PPL, 61) in Miltonic verse. If Leavis revalues Milton downwards because of the ritualistic quality in his work, Lewis unblushingly avers, "I am defending Milton's style as a ritual style." The real point, as Lewis argues at considerable length and with many ingenious variations, is that this is just what the style of the poem *ought* to be. Artificiality and remoteness from common uses of language are precisely what the high decorum of Milton's Christian epic demands; far from amounting to the poetic "lawlessness" that troubles Eliot, they are indispensable to an exquisitely majestic order. Ritual is precisely appropriate to a poem that enacts and helps us to enact the most awe-inspiringly grand and solemn truths of cosmic history—a poem whose pomp and splendor and *significance* of subject matter surpass almost everything else in the epic tradition, even the *Aeneid* itself. The case of the anti-Miltonists, then, turns on a huge misunderstanding: any hint of the ordinary speaking voice would be wholly out of place here, for "[t]he style is not pretending to be 'natural' any more than a singer is pretending to talk" (PPL, 59). If Milton's detractors persist in blaming him for achieving exactly what he meant to and what the pertinent literary and religious criteria required of him, then it is a little difficult to know how to answer them; and by the end Lewis is regarding the mighty T. S. Eliot himself rather as an exasperated schoolmaster might regard a pupil who is not innately stupid but just insists on missing the point again and again. Milton "institutes solemn games . . . in which we mourn the fall and celebrate the redemption of our species" (PPL, 134); Eliot complains that it is all "a solemn game" (M1, 144; quoted, PPL, 134). Milton's Satan makes a magnificent speech to an audience of angels; Eliot complains that it sounds as though he were making a speech. And so forth. "It reminds us," says Lewis, as he invokes one of his and his Milton's most exalted intellectual authorities, "of Aristotle's question—if water itself sticks in a man's throat, what will you give him to wash it down with?" For Lewis, clearly, the triumph over Eliot and Leavis is complete.

But Lewis's (characteristic) polemical gusto can easily obscure the important ways in which he is actually at one with his antagonists. No less, though differently, antileftist than Eliot and Leavis, Lewis performs what is probably an even more thorough job of combatting Milton the revolutionary—not by denouncing and stigmatizing him as Eliot (explicitly) and Leavis (implicitly) do, but by conjuring him out of existence, by burying him under volumes of Virgil and Augustine and others of "the great central tradition." Such a strategy of ideological containment—an academic domestication designed to make Milton acceptable in parsonage and senior common room alike—is arguably a more effective means of political warfare than

Eliot's broadside attack. Indeed, Lewis's construction of Milton as a safe and pious conservative extends even to his reading of the Grand Style itself, which as Eliot and Leavis construe it seems so unrooted, so *linguistic*, so dangerously out of control and rich with subversive possibilities; but Lewis's aesthetic turns out to be not so different from theirs as one might expect. Though he defends what they denounce—"He sees and hates the very same that I see and love" (PPL, 134), as he says of his and Leavis's views of Milton's verse[11]—he does so partly through a considered denial of that *materiality* of writing which makes Milton's verse so unacceptable to the Eliot–Leavis viewpoint. Though Lewis does not claim that the Grand Style possesses or ought to possess the Keatsian sensuousness with which Leavis so harshly contrasts it, he does maintain—in effect—that there is more than one road to that textual empiricism, that self-abnegation of language in the organicist realization of some reality beyond, which Leavis explicitly demands. Lewis's highest praise for Homeric epic diction is that it makes it "appear that we are dealing not with poetry about the things, but almost with the things themselves" (PPL, 23); and Homer's direct descendant Milton achieves much the same effect. Indeed, the high ritual quality of the verse is of special importance here, for it leads to a heightened, almost mystical state of consciousness that renders the language effectively transparent: "[W]hen we are caught up into the experience which a 'grand' style communicates, we are, in a sense, no longer conscious of the style. Incense is consumed by being used. The poem kindles admirations which leave us no leisure to admire the poem" (PPL, 61). There may be an unconscious echo of this notion in Leavis's derisive claim that the state of mind which *Paradise Lost* demands of its readers "has analogies with intoxication" (EM, 14). But he fails to notice that Lewis's defense of the Grand Style is based on an only somewhat different version of the same organicism, the same conservative empiricist aesthetic, that grounds his own revaluations.

There is, of course, another and much more overt way in which Lewis's reading of Milton is designed to serve conservative political and theological ends—namely, his construction of *Paradise Lost* as a poem of such untroubled orthodox piety and such unqualified enthusiasm for hierarchy and tradition as to rebuke all revolutionary sentiment, especially that which (most outrageously) claims the authority of Milton himself: Blake and Shelley, in other words, are Lewis's antagonists fully as much as Leavis and Eliot. Lewis's Milton is as resolute an opponent as Lewis himself of "revolutionary politics, antinomian ethics, and the worship of Man by Man" (PPL, 133). Yet because these tendencies have, in Lewis's view, largely dominated Western culture for two centuries, Milton criticism is "lost in misunderstanding" after Blake, and does not find its way again until Charles Williams and Lewis himself. Here Lewis writes most robustly as an orthodox Christian polemicist (at one point he explicitly claims that his Christianity gives him an advantage as a

Milton critic), and the skill with which he makes the case for Milton's God—even while admitting that the poet's portrayal is in places imprudently anthropomorphic—recalls the apologetic works that have gained Lewis such a large and intense following among the pious. Sometimes Lewis's reasoning appears a bit circular. Contextualizing Milton, he is almost capable of arguing that, because Milton was a Christian, and because Christians believe thus-and-such, therefore the poem *must* mean thus-and-such; while, in some of his more internal analyses of Milton's narrative logic, he can verge on dismissing the pro-Satan readings of the Blakean or Shelleyan sort by reminding us that for Christianity Satan is absolutely evil and God absolutely good *by definition*. Such points are often reinforced by brief original parables about everyday modern life designed to teach the importance of contented obedience or the wicked folly of rebellious pride. Perhaps the most remarkable moment, however, in Lewis's argument as *advocatus Dei* occurs during a mainly stylistic analysis of the poem's opening paragraph: the stress is entirely on certain atmospheric matters, and Lewis assures us that the "ostensible philosophical purpose of the poem (to justify the ways of God to Man [*sic*]) is here of quite secondary importance" (PPL, 41). It may seem an extraordinary claim to regard as "secondary" the most explicit statement that *Paradise Lost* offers of its own purpose, a statement that Milton places in the most prominent position in the entire 12 books. Yet this claim is required by the deep logic of Lewis's theological conservatism. For to take the final line of the first paragraph of Book 1 seriously tends to suggest that Milton's God—for Lewis, the Christian God—*needs* justification, and one of immense length and subtlety at that: the question would thus be raised whether Milton must be constructed as quite such an unruffled adherent of orthodoxy—as one who regards his religion quite so unproblematically—as Lewis maintains.

It is primarily in response to this question that William Empson offers to defend Milton's greatness—not only against the attackers Eliot and Leavis, but, even more, against the defender Lewis. *Milton's God* is so much more substantial and rigorous a work of criticism than any considered thus far that it is tempting to suggest that Empson renders the earlier contributions to the Milton controversy largely obsolete—though this notion will seem acceptable only to those who find Empson's general viewpoint at least somewhat congenial. But, writing in 1961, he does at any rate view the controversy in longer historical perspective, and he does have something in common with all his antagonists. Like Eliot, he writes with frank *engagement* and also with a poet's working interest in the problems of composition. Like Leavis (but much more so), he can be minutely sensitive to the nuances of particular lines. Like Lewis, he marshals considerable external evidence to help construct his own Milton, and he shares Lewis's unblushing devotion to the importance of authorial intention. Again like Lewis, Empson maintains a definite philosophical position from which his literary-critical perspective cannot be wholly disentangled: the "subject cannot be viewed in a purely aesthetic manner, as Milton himself would be the first to claim" (MG, 9). But, while Lewis's position is widely familiar, Empson's requires a brief exposition.

Empson argues that Christianity is one of the most evil belief systems ever invented and by far the most evil one to have exercised remotely comparable influence. Stalinist totalitarianism at its worst, though very bad, has never been quite so immoral; the major religions of East Asia (where Empson lived for many years) are immensely better; and a secular Benthamite liberalism is best of all. The central immorality of Christianity lies precisely in that complex of issues which engaged Milton in *Paradise Lost*. The religion teaches that, after crushing an unsuccessful rebellion against his absolute rule by a huge minority of his angels, God created Adam and Eve. He then set them a wholly arbitrary test of obedience, which they failed. As punishment for this misdemeanor, God had intended that they and all their descendants should be tortured eternally. But he does agree to a slight modification of this plan: on condition that his son agrees to be incarnated as a man on earth so that he can there be tortured to death, God agrees to spare some (probably small) fraction of mankind from unending torture. God's most important characteristic, then, is a love of torture. The religion is not only monstrously immoral but staggeringly self-contradictory. For the deity revered by Christians as the God of Love is possessed by the most evil passion imaginable: a sentient being, he somehow finds pleasing or takes satisfaction in the intense suffering of other sentient beings, including that one presumably nearest and dearest to him. In sum, the "Christian God the Father, the God of Tertullian, Augustine and Aquinas, is the wickedest thing yet invented by the black heart of man" (MG, 251).[12]

On the matter of religion, Empson may thus be seen as one of the latest and certainly not the least of that great rationalist line of morally passionate unbelievers that includes Voltaire, Tom Paine, Shelley, and Bertrand Russell. In the current context, however, what must be stressed is the somewhat unexpected mode of relevance that his anti-Christian moral philosophy has for the literary criticism of *Paradise Lost*. For Empson, though naturally unsurprised by witch burnings, Ku Kluxism and other such atrocities committed by the worshippers of a torture monster, is also genuinely impressed by the morally decent and sensitive people who, born into Christianity and unable to reject the religion, have labored mightily to make their faith into something less evil than the most authoritative statements of Christian dogma clearly reveal it to be. Among such people, Milton counts as one of the most intelligent and probably the most poetically talented. In the Milton chapter of *Some Versions of Pastoral*—written before the Milton controversy was fully launched by Eliot's original essay, and hence with little sense of a polemical context—Empson slyly uses Richard Bentley's notorious eighteenth-century emendations of *Paradise Lost* in order to highlight contradictions in the poem. In contrast to Lewis's emphasis on what he takes to be the smooth general sweep and logic of Milton's epic, Empson teases conflictive meaning out of apparently very small turns of phrase, and thereby concludes that Milton's "feelings continually cry out against his theory in favour of the Biblical implications" (MB, 181). Almost three decades later, in *Milton's God*, this somewhat unsystematic insight has grown into a fully rigorous and minutely documented theory, with which Empson offers to defend the poem against all comers by reviving "the manly and appreciative attitude of Blake and Shelley, who said that the reason why the poem is so good is that it makes God so bad" (MG, 13). Actually, though, this *mot* oversimplifies Empson's position. While Empson does read Milton's God as morally quite bad—in his cruelty, arbitrariness, deceit, paranoia, and bad temper, he bears a striking resemblance to Stalin, but also to those absolutist monarchs of the Renaissance whose claims Milton disputed—he is still measurably superior to the more normative God of Christian dogma. Milton de-emphasizes the deity's active love of pain and torture, and even supplies hints that God intends eventually to abdicate in favor of his son, thus pointing toward a heaven much happier than the one over which the father himself has ruled. The crucial critical point, however, is that the basic greatness and fascinating complexity of *Paradise Lost* result from this fundamental contradiction—whose effects are felt in the poem's smallest and largest features—between the (hideously evil) inherited Christian story and Milton's monumental attempt to embody the story in an epic of reasonable and humane character. The poet is thus continually struggling with a monstrously wicked doctrine which is deeply uncongenial to his moral character and poetic sensitivity, but to which he nonetheless remains, for the most part, intellectually committed (though Empson does see Milton's heretical Arianism as far more central to the poem than does Lewis). In other words, the most famous line of the poem must be read with total seriousness: Milton really does try to *justify* the Christian God, and (as we can know not only from *Paradise Lost* itself but from prose writings on religion by Milton and others) he understands the task to be extremely difficult. For Empson, the task is not just difficult but impossible, and the poem is, in that sense, a failure: but a "failure" of literally awesome power and beauty.

The critical method at work here has been compared to that of Macherey,[13] and the comparison is illuminating. For Macherey, a literary text does not "reflect" an ideology, but *produces* it, or, even better, *reproduces* it anew in any given act of literary composition; in so doing, literature tends to foreground ideological contradictions and gaps, evasions and antinomies, with a clarity hardly attained in any other mode of (re)presenting ideology. Empson does read *Paradise Lost* in very much this way. For him, the poem is Christian in a sense that could hardly be suspected by critics—like Eliot, Lewis, or even Leavis—who assume the truth, or at least the essential *coherence*, of Christianity. They all presume that writing an epic in justification of the Christian God must be a straightforward matter. Lewis finds that

Milton does the job splendidly, while Eliot and, even more, Leavis (especially when following Waldock) think that he botched it—taking for granted, as they do, that contradictions and absurdities produced by Milton's attempt at justification must result from his own intellectual and poetic incompetence. Empson, on the other hand, finds it a mark of Milton's greatness that his poem, in attempting to tell and justify the Christian story, is forced against its own "official" purpose to produce so rich, complex, thoroughgoing, and rigorous an interrogation of the cruel and contradictory absurdities that define the Christian religion. Whereas, however, Macherey's method of analysis consists mainly of immanent textual ideology-critique, Empson supplements such close reading by a gathering of external evidence and by an unabashed intentionalism that recall Lewis. Like Lewis, Empson is concerned to construct Milton from without as well as from within the text, but, as one might guess, he chooses his materials differently. Whereas for Lewis the relevant context is a multisecular "central tradition" both literary and theological, Empson focuses much more specifically on the seventeenth-century situation and the biographical individual John Milton. Great political realities of Rebellion, Civil War, Commonwealth, and Restoration loom large for Empson's Milton, and important details from his own life have an impact on *Paradise Lost* that Lewis can scarcely imagine. So far as the religious "background" is concerned, Empson stresses not Church Fathers like Augustine but Christian practices and theologians of Milton's own time, especially Milton himself. The general portrait that emerges is of a complex, deeply engaged, and deeply (if not purely) honest poet who attempts what is in some ways a highly personal project with full awareness of its dangers and difficulties. Empson thus produces a Milton of his own as surely as does Lewis, and one as qualified to write a fissured Machereyan text as surely as Lewis's is qualified to write a poem in (almost) total harmony with its own aims.

With the exception, therefore, of his stubborn intellectual commitment to Christianity (though in heretical Arian form), Empson's Milton bears much the same kind of resemblance to Empson that Lewis's Milton does to Lewis. For like his heroes, Voltaire and Shelley, Empson is a radical—a radical Liberal—of the old school, one whose primary political commitment is to individual liberty and the sanctity of the free conscience—"Our own consciences are therefore the final judges" (MG, 261), he says when revealing his own *credo*—and one who takes it for granted that an unflinching opposition to all forms of religion and superstition is necessary to maintain freedom of thought. As a Liberal, Empson is not without some kinship with Leavis (his fellow Cambridge man), but his Liberalism is far more militant and *purer*, lacking the admixture of conservative Lawrentian communitarianism so important for Leavis. Empson's Milton is constructed largely in Empson's own image. In sharp contrast to the delight in obedience, tradition, and hierarchy that characterizes Lewis's Milton, Empson's is the great rebel, the author of *Areopagitica* and the divorce tracts, the (early) Wordsworthian prophet of English liberty. The biographical image probably dearest to the Empsonian reading is of Milton just after the Restoration, waiting with calm courage for the death by torture which must have appeared virtually inevitable to him and continuing to compose work that could only outrage the royal authorities still further.[14]

Empson, then, sharply distinguishes himself from Lewis, Leavis, and Eliot in that (unlike Lewis) he constructs Milton as a radical but (unlike Leavis and Eliot) does so in order to vindicate rather than to dismantle the greatness of *Paradise Lost*. It is not surprising that on the much vexed question of the Miltonic style Empson also establishes a clearly contrasting position. Having no investment in any form of organicism or mystical wholeness, whether social or linguistic, Empson—the protodeconstructive theorist of ambiguity, it should be remembered—is impressed neither by the Eliot-Leavis charge that the Grand Style is too abstract and artificial to achieve oneness with its objects, nor with the Lewis defense that the style *does* achieve such organic unity, though indirectly and in a way to which the Miltonic remoteness from common speech is indispensable. More closely attentive to the poem's language than any of these three other critics, Empson finds the styles of *Paradise Lost* to be in fact quite various, and he notes a number of important passages to which the Eliotic "stock accusation of pomposity of style, too Latinized to be able to give body-feeling or a natural movement of thought" (MG, 166) is simply inapplicable even on Eliotic criteria. But perhaps the most important difference, on this score, between Empson and the three other critics is that the organicism to which Eliot, Leavis, and Lewis are all, in their different ways, committed necessarily involves a kind of *formalism* from which Empson (despite—or rather partly because of—his detailed interest in poetic form) is quite free. The organicist demand that poetic form effect a seamless and virtually mystical fusion of word with object involves a logical presupposition of form and content as cleanly *distinguishable* categories: for form, in this critical ideology, is held to determine content— or at least the precise nature of the relations between form and content— in a monocausal and historically invariable way. Thus Eliot, judging that *Paradise Lost* fails to perform the required organic fusion, claims that it is necessary to read the poem "in two different ways, first solely for the sound, and second for the sense" (M1, 143), a formulation strongly endorsed by Leavis. But equally Lewis, who *does* construe the poem as a successful organic wholeness, sees a dichotomy between form and content as logically prior to their mystical union: hence his distinct chapters on the "subject" and "style" of "secondary" epics like *Paradise Lost*. Empson, by contrast, does not understand form as a reified autonomous category in this way. He is interested not in "Miltonic style" as an abstract (and homogeneous) entity, but in the detailed ways that Milton's language moves to establish a rich delineation of theological and political contradiction (Empson thus anticipates not only

Macherey but also Derrida and, in some ways, Foucault). Concerned not only with the "official" ideology of the poem but also with the precise ways by which the latter is poetically forced into conflict with itself, Empson shows how the most complex and searching questions of "content" are inseparable from the smallest matters of poetic phrasing and rhythm. There is thus no question of "form" and "content" as distinct entities and thus no question of their being successfully or unsuccessfully combined. They are inseparable from the start, though each, one might say, is a dialectical effect of the other. Empson's freedom from formalism, in other words, enables him to perform the most frankly political and philosophical reading of *Paradise Lost* of any of these four critics, but precisely by focusing more carefully and searchingly on the poem's language than Eliot, Lewis, or even Leavis. In this protodeconstructive freedom, the Empsonian banner of radical Liberalism and classic individualism plainly waves.

It should be evident that Empson's construction of Milton is in most regards considerably closer to my own than are the readings of Eliot, Leavis, or Lewis. But there are important differences also. For Empson's radicalism is of a distinctly individualistic and thus presocialist variety. Indeed, the frequent and often apparently gratuitous anti-Communist references in *Milton's God* convey more than moral repugnance at Stalinist barbarism, and they are certainly not (what they would be in most literary critics) signs of a craven obeisance to Cold War conformism. They are, I think, to be taken as deliberately conveying the insistently middle-class character of the Empsonian Liberalism, a Liberalism for which the Kremlin may be preferable to the Vatican but only marginally so and not at any rate essentially different from it. Empson's chief ideological limitation, one might say, is that for him Christianity is not simply the enemy but almost the *only* enemy, or, more precisely, the paradigm of all evil systems: so that he is, for example, considerably more sensitive to the horrors of totalitarian thought control than to the horrors of everyday class oppression. Accordingly, Empson's Milton is a heroic champion of liberty and free thought but not really a forerunner of democracy or socialism. He is certainly a *rebel*, but not—most prominently—a *revolutionary*. Empson's careful delineation of the seventeenth-century situation is in fact notable for its lack of interest in possible connections between Milton and the far-left levelling sects of his time (though there is some perceptible shift in Empson's 1981 afterword, in which he expresses solidarity with the Marxist historian Christopher Hill and suggests that Hill's account of Milton's partial agreements with the Radical Reformers is coherent with his own reading of *Paradise Lost*). As we have seen, it is possible to make connections among Milton, the Liberal tradition, and the modern socialist Left: hence, at least in part, Eliot's antipathy to Milton and Leavis's subtextual concern to distance his own version of Liberalism from the Miltonic place of its (revolutionary) origins. But such connections do not, after all, *have* to be made, and Empson generally declines to make them. If Leavis's concerns with community and collaboration, because of their right-wing Lawrentian cast, help to alienate him from Milton the revolutionary on one side, then a similar alienation from Milton the revolutionary is effected, on the other side, so to speak, by Empson's stubborn and heroic bourgeois individualism.

It is perhaps not surprising to conclude that one big thing which all four critics have in common is that, when confronted with England's greatest revolutionary poet, they all find ways to avoid or reject the category of revolution. The radical Empson, in his vindication of Milton as a brave rebel and spokesman for the free conscience, comes closest in one sense to Milton the revolutionary, though in a different sense it is Eliot who comes closest, as the archreactionary constructs a Milton to be judged antipathetic and unsatisfactory. Eliot, Leavis, Lewis, and Empson—who may be taken as a reasonable cross section of the *best* English literary intelligence during the first half of the twentieth century—define a considerable amount of ideological space; but at its furthest left the spectrum is well to the right of revolutionary socialism, and it extends rightward to at least the fringes of full-fledged Christian fascism. Another generalization about these four has, I trust, been implicit throughout this paper. Eliot, Leavis, Lewis, and Empson were all unusually vital thinkers, who were able to write Milton criticism of fundamental importance because they were concerned with issues that extend far beyond the borders of literary criticism in the narrow academic sense. What do they know of Milton who only Milton know? Even more, the keen intelligence of these four combined with their fierce partisanships and *general* intellectual engagements to give to their Milton criticism a general interest. This criticism delineates varied ideological patterns with sufficient complexity and lucidity as to amount to a chapter of cultural history so compelling that I have thought it worthwhile to record and analyze it in some detail. Indeed, for about the two decades following the publication of *Milton's God*, the period of the Milton "controversy" could be seen in retrospect as a kind of golden age of Milton criticism. It is not that Milton criticism ceased to be written, of course. There was more of it than ever before, some of it very clever. But the characteristic Milton criticism after Eliot, Leavis, Lewis, and Empson seldom approaches the work of those four in intellectual excitement, in vital controversy, in the clash of deeply felt issues and ideologies. To borrow one of Eliot's more notorious phrases, Milton criticism after the Milton controversy tends to become less *serious*: it becomes instead a solemn game, generated more by the internal political economy of the academy than by truly wide-ranging ideological warfare. By the early 1980s, however, the situation has changed again. Owing, I think, mainly to the work of Marxist and feminist critics, Milton criticism has again become more "Miltonic," that is, more exciting, more rigorous, more partisan, and more generally engaged. I will not now attempt even the most cursory glance at this new Milton criticism. But, in concluding this survey of an episode in ideological history that is itself (at least in its own terms) concluded, I think it worth noticing that, once again now, some people are doing interesting things with Milton.

Notes

1. George Steiner, *Language and Silence* (New York: Atheneum, 1970), 3.
2. See J. L. Austin, *How To Do Things With Words* (Cambridge, Mass.: Harvard University Press, 1962).
3. T. S. Eliot, "Milton I" (hereafter cited as M1) and "Milton II" (hereafter M2) in *On Poetry and Poets* (London: Faber & Faber, 1957); F. R. Leavis, "Milton's Verse" (hereafter MV) in *Revaluation* (New York: George Stewart, 1947) and "Mr. Eliot and Milton" (hereafter EM) and "In Defence of Milton" (hereafter DM) in *The Common Pursuit* (London: Chatto & Windus, 1952); C. S. Lewis, *A Preface to "Paradise Lost"* (hereafter PPL) (Oxford: Oxford University Press, 1942); William Empson, "Milton and Bentley" (hereafter MB) in *Some Versions of Pastoral* (New York: New Directions, 1974) and *Milton's God*, Revised Edition (hereafter MG) (Cambridge: Cambridge University Press, 1981). All citations will be given parenthetically by page number.
4. Terry Eagleton, "English Literature Song," 11, 25–30. Unpublished manuscript.
5. It is worth noting that in *Little Gidding* (1942)—one of Eliot's finest poems but also highly atypical in being perhaps his *least* politically partisan major work—the legacy of the Civil War is seen quite differently, not as a matter of ongoing political controversy but rather as if *sub specie aeternitatis*. Charles I is memorialized, as "a broken king" (1. 26) and "a king at nightfall" (1. 175), but so is Milton himself—"one who died blind and quiet" (1. 179). The poem goes on to deny precisely what the passage quoted above from the 1947 Milton essay affirms:

> We cannot revive old factions
> We cannot restore old policies
> Or follow an antique drum.
> These men, and those who opposed them
> And those whom they opposed
> Accept the constitution of silence
> And are folded in a single party.
> (ll. 185–91)

The situation of his adopted country during the Second World War and especially during the German bombing (a major subtextual presence in the poem) perhaps helps to make for a unique moment in Eliot's career, one that disinclines him to dwell on the *divisions* within British society.
6. We should note the irony that the Eliotic valorization (fully shared by Leavis) of *speech* as the basis of poetic language is perfectly compatible with the denigration of *making a speech*. As my colleague Michael Dietz has suggested to me, the very political distinction is between (approved) private speech and (disapproved) public speech, the unargued assumption being that the former is necessarily superior to the latter in vitality, spontaneity, and creativity. Empson hints at the same point when he writes, "It is odd to reflect that this [Eliot's condemnation of Satan's speech-making] was written while the spellbinder Lloyd George was still a power in the country. . . . To be sure, Mr Eliot would have hated listening

to Lloyd George too, but he would not have imagined that those speeches had been cooked up by a secretary" (MG, 27).

7. Yet it should not be forgotten (though it nearly always has been) that Leavis's original treatment of Milton in *Revaluation* was written before he had access to Eliot's essay of 1936. Still, Leavis was thoroughly familiar with Eliot's earlier criticism (including scattered comments on Milton), and the logical structure of *Revaluation* (not only the Milton chapter) is pretty consistently Eliotic.

8. For a detailed attempt to situate Leavis in sociopolitical terms, see Francis Mulhern, *The Moment of "Scrutiny"* (London: Verso, 1981).

9. According to Eliot, the first of these remarkable terms was applied to himself (and to Ezra Pound) by an unnamed writer in the *Morning Post*; the second, by one Arthur Waugh. See T. S. Eliot, *The Use of Poetry and the Use of Criticism: Studies in the Relation of Criticism to Poetry in England* (London: Faber & Faber, 1964), 71.

10. At Lewis's own university I once attended a lecture on Milton given by a distinguished historian. He thought it necessary to begin—perhaps with a slyly mischievous sense of poaching on territory that the English faculty might regard as their own private preserve—by informing his audience that even great poets like Milton do spend some of their time talking with people who are alive at the same time that they are. This struck me as a neat way of making a point that could hardly be inferred from *A Preface to "Paradise Lost."*

11. It is worth noting that this sentence, with its somewhat surprising terminology of *hatred*, subtextually insinuates parallels between Lewis and Abdiel, on the one hand, and Leavis and Satan on the other: Abdiel, after all, sees and loves the very same (i.e., God) that Satan sees and hates.

12. I know this summary must seem shockingly crude, and not only to Christians; the politeness almost universally observed in academic references to Christianity influences us all. I can only refer the reader to Empson himself, who anticipates and attempts to refute accusations that his view of Christianity is woefully insensitive to all the beautiful subtleties and paradoxes inherent in such doctrines as the *felix culpa* and the Atonement.

13. See Fredric Jameson, *Fables of Aggression: Wyndham Lewis, the Modernist as Fascist* (Berkeley: University of California Press, 1979), 22; also Pierre Macherey, *A Theory of Literary Production*, trans. Geoffrey Wall (London: Routledge, 1978).

14. The first great expression of this image of Milton is, of course, offered by Milton himself in the opening lines of Book 7 of *Paradise Lost*:

> Standing on Earth, not rapt above the pole,
> More safe I sing with mortal voice, unchanged
> To hoarse or mute, though fallen on evil days,
> On evil days though fallen, and evil tongues;
> In darkness, and with dangers compassed round,
> And solitude; . . . .

(ll. 23–28)

COMUS, PARADISE REGAINED, SAMSON AGONISTES

◆

Thoughts in Misbecoming Plight:
Allegory in *Comus*

VICTORIA SILVER*

Man is a result, not an *eidos*. . . .
—Theodor Adorno

I

In *Comus*, there is a difference between what we are told by its several *dramatis personae* and what Milton's text ends up showing us; and this discrepancy has the effect of skewing the way we understand the masque. For it raises the frequent issue of how we ought to take what Milton writes—how to go about making sense of what happens in his enchanted wood and palace of illusion. For all its familiar look, duly conned from pastoral and romance, the landscape of *Comus* is yet *terra incognita* to its readers. The masque remains this way not just because John Crowe Ransom's willful poet was bound to attempt something new and idiosyncratic with his materials, but because the new things Milton does are not always perfectly evident to his readers. In fact, they only tend to make themselves known by confounding our attempts at an unequivocal reading, as when we try to make the Father or Satan the hero of *Paradise Lost*.

Such is the case here with Milton's allegory, by which I mean his personification of certain moral and religious ideas through the speeches and predicaments of his actors. Rather than compose *exempla* simple and integral in their significance, he complicates his figures' manifest roles by making them do things at odds with their allegorical character. Thus Virtue in the person of the Lady is readily entrapped by Comus, despite the Elder Brother's celebration of her clear-eyed, invincible chastity; Grace or Providence in the guise of the Attendant Spirit cannot itself save her but is obliged to seek out sublunary help; and Vice in the person of Comus gets the best lines and

*This essay was written specifically for this volume and is published here for the first time by permission of the author.

escapes unscathed. These anomalies, which any number of readers have remarked, are what I mean by a peculiar slip between the players' script for the action and the spectacle shown the audience. The bad fit could itself derive from another idiosyncrasy: namely, that *Comus* is peculiarly involved for a masque, maneuvering its few principals all over the map to what appears a foregone conclusion. Unlike most of its kind, this masque has a plot but a plot so eccentric that it seems to refute the express moral of the story.

Now the reader may refuse to acknowledge from the start that Milton's allegorical signals are so mixed, or that the world as choreographed by masques doesn't usually approach the convolutions and inconsequence of this one. Such a refusal will usually result in an argument for the Lady's transcending all manner of circumstance that might compromise her virtue or *Comus*'s ostensible meaning. And the circumstance that most disturbs an unequivocal understanding of the masque, setting in motion the Lady's transcendence, is that "marble venomed seat / Smeared with gums of glutinous heat" and redolent with connotations of sexuality, to which she becomes somehow afixed.[1] To expound a vulgar platonism foreign to all such transcendental readings of *Comus*, which include the essays of Sears Jayne and more recently, Donald Friedman, Paul Stevens, and Stanley Fish[2]: these critics prefer to regard what visibly, theatrically happens to the Lady's body, unable to move from Comus's chair, as incidental to that liberty of mind she says the enchanter cannot touch, and in which her virtue is held to consist. In other words, she is not caught or compromised by Comus; she only looks that way. Her climactic immobility thus becomes a paradox signifying exactly what the spectacle itself disputes—that she transcends the bodily or fleshly aspect of her being. That is, because she is chaste, the Lady is thought by these readers to abstain not just from the sensual or voluptuous but from all the vagaries of the phenomenal, including the mimetic in the form of *Comus*'s erratic allegory.

Her predicament thus understood resembles the martyrdom of Fides, Spes and Karitas in the medieval play of that name, who are severally flogged, mutilated, boiled and beheaded, all without feeling a pang. Or one could compare it to those Romanesque crucifixions where Christ stands at his ease on the cross, dapper and unfazed, as if he had simply come across a photo-op. In the world these images imply, suffering for truth or the good means simply to undergo without pain or passion or drama, because the phenomenal is a mere accident of the real, lacking any ultimate force. And because the Lady can be translated in this manner, rendering her virtue impervious to Comus and her own evidently incorrigible body, the same order of transcendence is extended to Milton's allegory as a whole, whose circumstantial perplexities this reading works reciprocally to evanesce. In other words, the mimetic dimension of the masque—simply put, the particular way in which it imitates an action—is not allowed to matter:

interpretation, like the Lady, elects to rise above the lapses and inexplicable exigencies of Milton's plotting. For what counts to critics of this persuasion is what we *cannot see* happening in *Comus*, not what we can: by what one might call the interpretive practice of chastity—the "willed rejection of bodily sense and desire" according to Sears Jayne[3] (which is tantamount to rejecting the conditions of mimesis), both the Lady and the reader can escape any confusion or ill consequence that might attend the position of her body, held fast in Comus's chair.

Yet there is a catch to this transcendental solution of the masque's anomalies, all of which tend to congregate around the Lady's immobile person, or rather what we are supposed to make of it. His critics—notably Balanchandra Rajan and Angus Fletcher—have long deprecated Milton's inattention to drama in *Comus*, especially in the dialogue which serves as the masque's theatrical and doctrinal centerpiece. I refer to the debate between Comus and the seated Lady, who in their speeches are held to exemplify the imperatives of Pleasure and Virtue, Indulgence and Temperance, Promiscuity and Chastity—the terms and focal conflict of the allegory. Yet their encounter amounts to little more than a staking out of ideological turf, leaving us with the impression that they not only inhabit different landscapes but speak mutually unintelligible languages, in effect denying anything like an exchange between them. The dialogue thus produces no movement of plot, much less a turn in either antagonist's understanding of the sort one gets in Bunyan, whose complex allegories are outwardly more like *Comus* than the court spectacles of Jacobean masque, which seem almost perfunctory by comparison with this one. But then, an allegory that shuns the body and the phenomenal should perhaps not succumb to mimesis in the shape of drama.

Of course *Comus* is by no means unique in this neglect. For masques convey their ideas less by the expression of character over time than by a species of imagistic or pictorial telegraphing, which tends to preclude just those circumstances conducive to moral and dramatic tension. But the dearth of drama here has to do as much with allegorical as theatrical technique: a propensity to compose tableaux both in the language and staging of masques might predict that the Lady would enter her adventure already assured of her own value, where Bunyan's Christian or Dante's pilgrim do not. For the elements of tableau must be patent to the observer and to that extent, established or conventional if the device is to have its expressive force. So in Milton's masque, we should not expect to find a dimension of pilgrimage like that Christian undergoes, where the allegory enacts not only his trial but equally his moral perplexity and need for conversion or change.

Yet Sears Jayne finds himself compelled to comment that Milton's version of a masque, as well as his own admittedly schematic reading of its action, lack even the suggestiveness or imaginative resonance he calls "emblematic" and considers typical of the form.[4] But then, emblem and tableau rely on spectacle for their effects; and this, according to Friedman, Stevens and Fish, is what Milton's platonizing allegory and his Lady together resist. For the Lady must choose, not so much between Virtue and Pleasure, as between the way things appear and how they actually mean, all of which devolve upon a figurative discrimination between the deceptions of the eye and what Friedman calls "the truth of the ear." That is, these latter-day Platonists maintain that the eye, as exemplifying a sensuous mode of understanding practiced by Comus himself, is rendered suspect while the Lady's ear, representing the inferential or abstract sense of things, is always found true. So if *Comus* seems restricted or severe in its meanings, as well as oblivious to dramatic instantiation, that is because it enacts not only some sort of Platonic doctrine but a Platonizing method of casuistry.

Since its principals must be shown performing this method of moral discrimination—for that is what *Comus* is understood to allegorize, a case of conscience—it follows that an attention to casuistical procedure, to problems of interpretation, is what makes the masque so strangely elaborate. What is more, by the Lady's own disciplined attention to "essentials" over "appearances," the reader is also taught that interpretive chastity I mentioned, which consists in ignoring what we actually *see* happening in the masque in favor of what we are told. But I would argue that the result is what long ago gave casuistry a bad name. For this dichotomy of value between eye and ear operates to ensure that we take her bondage as more ostensible than real, just one more Comean illusion that the Lady's mind and our own are able to penetrate, and therefore no index of her real condition. In consigning her bodily position to the category of things falsely imaged by the eye, every other inordinate circumstance of the allegory can then be considered similarly accidental to Milton's meaning—a point Fish frankly argues. So even in such truly circumspect accounts of the masque as these, which take great pains over the disparate particulars of Milton's allegory, the spectacle of the Lady positioned in that unctuous chair is dismissed in the triumph of Virtue over just one more specious appearance. In effect, her disdain for the person Comus becomes a proxy and an excuse for the reader to discount every difficulty encountered in *Comus* the allegory.

But if the Lady can be supposed to void her bodily plight by the way she understands it, this cannot mean that she has escaped the body's *pull* anymore than she has evaded the magician's grasp—the implication of these later readings. For we are yet obliged to ask, in the face of such claims for her transcendence, why she would even be in that position if she had not yielded in some fashion to Comus's sensuous blandishments or to her own fleshly nature. Indeed, given the sight of the Lady ambiguously immobile in Comus's seat (since we never know the precise moment she becomes stuck, only that she does), surrounded by every kind and abundance of voluptuous pleasure according to Milton's stage directions, we may be inclined like Sir

Walter Greg to doubt her much-touted chastity—or more wisely, to wonder what Milton could mean by this peculiar virtue. Because however you look at it, the Lady thus disclosed to our view is allegorically speaking the image of a change in condition and therefore of a real consequence to which we would be well advised to attend. That is, when we suppose the Lady not only undismayed by Comus but also untouched and unconstrained; when we discount the power of her beauty by exalting the claims made for her chastity; when we prefer the way some characters understand her predicament to the sight of the Lady thus ensconced; and when we preempt the anomalies of the action by choosing to view everything *sub species aeternitatis*, we just might find ourselves condoning a rape so long as it leads to a Platonic *raptio* or rapture.

Yet whatever Milton may intend by the Lady's seated position, we must also suppose that she somehow emerges morally unscathed from its embrace, and that Virtue as embodied in her person triumphs in the end. How else could she and her brothers be presented to their parents with such ceremony and acclaim in the masque's finale? So assuming we want to make the Lady's adventure suit its moral pretensions, and not just its happy ending, *Comus* presents the reader with a distinct interpretive dilemma. On the one hand, we can adopt the tack of Jayne, Fish, Friedman and Stevens, where the masque's undoubted Platonism ensures that what we see happen to the Lady, held for a long moment immovable in that muculent seat, does not describe her moral condition or complicate the masque's sense. As I said, this amounts to denying the force of representation itself, so that Milton as poet is understood to turn not only the Lady's but his own activity on its head (a point that has been variously argued for his poetry as a whole). Or we can seek some other way to read *Comus*, and to understand Milton's Platonic idiom, that without negating her predicament, might reconcile the plight of her body with the Lady's moral status. This vindication of the allegory is what I would like to pursue here.

II

Now part of the reason that the Lady's triumph raises more questions than it answers has to do with the masque's impresario of the good, the Attendant Spirit, and what he tells us about its action and his own. His account never quite squares with what we see, as when he summarizes the allegory for us at the play's end:

> Mortals that would follow me,
> Love Virtue, she alone is free,
> She can teach ye how to climb

> Higher than the sphery chime;
> Or if Virtue feeble were,
> Heaven itself would stoop to her.
>
> (1017–22)

Instead of proving Virtue's freedom and power, as Victoria Kahn has observed, the masque would seem rather to assert its irreducible ambiguity[5]; and not only by that most Miltonic optative "or," which finds its way into the Spirit's speech, but by the real uncertainty that surrounds the Lady's "weakness"—how she got in that chair, what her position means, and why it is that neither she as Virtue, the brothers, nor the Attendant Spirit as heaven's agent can get her out of it. And *Comus*'s seeming inability to comply with its stated allegory is a problem not only for the reader and the Lady, but for the masque's sundry personnel. Thus when her brothers imagine the Lady lost and solitary in yet one more mazy wood of error, they find themselves unable to agree on the very nature, never mind the consequences of her situation:

> *Sec. Bro.* But O that hapless virgin our lost sister
> Where may she wander now, whither betake her
> From the chill dew, amongst rude burs and thistles?
> . . . .
> What if in wild amazement, and affright,
> Or while we speak within the direful grasp
> Of savage hunger, or of savage heat?
> *Eld. Bro.* Peace, brother, be not over-exquisite
> To cast the fashion of uncertain evils:
> . . . .
> I do not think my sister so to seek,
> Or so unprincipled in virtue's book,
> And the sweet peace that goodness bosoms ever,
> As that the single want of light and noise
> (Not being in danger, as I trust she is not)
> Could stir the constant mood of her calm thoughts,
> And put them into misbecoming plight.
> Virtue could see to do what Virtue would
> By her own radiant light, though sun and moon
> Were in the flat sea sunk. . . .
>
> (349–74)

The brothers' disagreement over the Lady's response to her predicament—like themselves, lost and alone in the wood, but with what is seen as the peculiar vulnerability of a woman's body—prepares us for their divergent readings of the encounter between Miltonic Virtue and Vice. Now each speech says something true about what happens to the Lady: that she confronts "the direful grasp of savage heat" in the person of Comus, and that she is not "so unprincipled in virtue's book" as limply to surrender because she finds herself without her brothers' or another man's protection. But like the Spirit, it is also true that neither of the brothers quite gets it right, with the elder too complacent and the younger too sensational in imagining the Lady's circumstances. Thus while she is not without resources both personal and providential, her virtue is hardly foolproof; she is readily seduced by Comus' disguise, if not by his manners, saying as she departs the scene with him:

> Shepherd, I take thy word,
> And trust thy honest-offered courtesy
> Which oft is sooner found in lowly sheds
> With smoky rafters, than in tap'stry halls
> And courts of princes, where it first was named,
> And yet is most pretended. . . .
>
> (320–25)

And the stygian darkness of the wood does cause her anxiety—"in a place / Less warranted than this, or less secure / I cannot be" (325–27)—because she is concerned not only for herself but for her brothers. Yet they are evidently not lost in the same moral or metaphysical manner as their sister because they are men. Her sex alone makes the state of her body matter.

Just as the brothers' accounts differ in some salient respects from the preceding action in the wood, so nothing is quite as anyone says it is in *Comus*. Again, this is especially the case with the pronouncements of those who claim specially to know what is going on—the Elder Brother and the Lady's "glistering guardian" (218). Thus Fish remarks on the Spirit's odd decision to begin the masque by thoroughly deprecating the realm in which everything of moral significance takes place, calling it "this dim spot" (5), "this pinfold" (7), "this sin-worn mould" (17). Before the Lady and the brothers are even discovered to the audience, the spirit has summarized the adventure by predicting their ascent out of this earthly miasma—as Virtue's true servants who by "due steps aspire / To lay their just hands on that golden key / That opes the palace of eternity" (12–13). Suspense is hardly a concern in the composition of a masque. But such a premature abstracting of Virtue from the circumstances that express it, combined with the Spirit's conspicuous distaste for the phenomenal, naturally encourages readers to suppose that the allegory is arguing for integrity by transcendence, not just abstinence. Indeed, with this speech Milton would seem not only to preempt the action of his masque but to recant, if not revoke his own allegorizing, elemented as it is in that unwarrantable place—the bodily world of perception, desire and change.

Yet having peremptorily disposed of the mundane and mimetic together, the Spirit then launches into a republican variation on the "sceptred isle—this England" speech, celebrating an island paradise that "like to rich, and various gems inlay / The unadorned bosom of the deep," where monarchs and magistrates are as ornamental as their powers are custodial—that is, since these wonted authorities "wear their sapphire crowns / And wield their little tridents" by leave of Jove, rather than by right (26–27). On that tendentious note, he turns to "this isle / The greatest and the best of all the main":

> And all this tract that fronts the falling sun
> A noble peer of mickle trust, and power
> Has in his charge, with tempered awe to guide
> An old and haughty nation proud in arms. . . .
>
> (18–33)

In this way, the Spirit's exposition of place restores beauty to the earthly domain from which he had just unaccountably extracted it. At the same time, the actual and figurative presence of a "noble peer of mickle trust," in the person of Bridgewater himself, proves that what happens below the starry climes of Jove's court yet remains capable of moral significance and order in its own terms. But because the Spirit's metaphysical reluctance to soil himself with the sublunary as world or plot is juxtaposed with this abrupt encomium to England and the Earl, it is hard to take him at his word. For he has left us with conflicting notions of virtue—one metaphysical, the other almost topical—as well as disparate ideas of about where to locate this value: whether in the heaven we are not shown or the republican Eden we see, in the Lady's liberty of mind or in the constraint imposed upon her body. In short, the Spirit is already a dubious guide to how things mean.

In the Elder Brother's phrase, much of *Comus*'s action turns out similarly to misbecome its wonted sense. To cover a ground already well-trampled by Kahn, Fish and other more or less perplexed readers, if chastity is its own best defense, why should the Lady end up in a position that Comus's intent and Sabrina's description makes sexual? And why is it that the Spirit, whose self-proclaimed role is to relieve distressed virtue—as the Lady hopefully puts it, "To keep my life and honour unassailed" (219)—doesn't lift a finger to keep her out of Comus's hands while yet observing the whole event? And is Sabrina invoked because she was herself chaste, or because she also suffered unjustly, which emphases cast two different lights upon the Lady's predicament in that chair? Moreover, since the Spirit chooses to deceive her brothers in representing his knowledge of her plight, how are we to distinguish his kind of shepherding from the duplicity of that other supposedly unlettered hind and songster, Comus himself?

Such a conspicuous lack of coordination between script and spectacle not only jeopardizes the Lady's virtue, however conceived and embodied. It also works to undermine the credibility of the Platonism that both the Spirit and Elder Brother expound and at least try to enact (the figure of the *daimon* and the brother's emblem of the militant virgin being part and parcel of Neoplatonic idiom). For her difficulties seem rather to manifest the incompetence of the good and the inefficacy of Virtue, as well as to suggest that the "illusion" of the phenomenal is more tenacious than either Platonist will allow (not to mention Milton's platonizing readers). These apparent lapses provoke one to ask why, with so little evident intention of bearing out the argument of his house ideologists, Milton chose platonism to organize his imagery, if not his meanings.

But it is entirely possible that Milton's Platonized virtue doesn't dispense with the phenomenal or with the experience of perplexity, and that this bad fit of script with spectacle is intended to make that point. Indeed, I would argue that the vagaries of the plot methodically challenge the way we want to understand his allegory, inasmuch as they keep the reader from suiting the action to what one or other character says—unless of course we too transcend the phenomena of the text. As in *Paradise Lost*, I do not think we are supposed to approach Milton's masque in terms of single thematic ideas—that virtue is this, and vice is that—but according to the relations created among them by the action. So that if we determine to depart from the obstacles that the plot of *Comus* strews in our path, not just the Lady's, we are bound to mistake the kind of virtue for which it argues.

This is to say that meaning and value cannot be obliviously abstracted from the text of *Comus* or the spectacle it organizes, as though human and poetic facts do not count in allegories. I mean "count" in Stanley Cavell's sense of being allowed to matter, as if we could ignore our own humanity, not to mention everyone else's as the Attendant Spirit prepares to do. Until very recently, that is what has happened to the Lady in Milton studies—despite her position fixed to that sexualized seat, we choose to understand her virtue as a mode or a faculty of transcendence, ultimately redeeming her body from this tainted image, preserving her virtue from figurative compromise, and last but not least, keeping the allegory itself from inconsequence. But I don't think Milton is so facile as to suppose that what happens to the Lady's body doesn't count a great deal, especially when he makes her chastity express his virtue and subjects us to the brothers' conflicting views on her body's state—the Elder supposing it immune and intact, the Second imagining it yielding and violated. And while the Lady herself professes utter indifference to her body's viscous plight, I would suggest that her very position obliges her to do so, just as Milton's position compels him to say much the same thing in the divorce tracts. When you are told that you cannot do or be something because body is absolute, as canon law makes it in marriage or Comus in his speeches to the Lady, then you are bound to contend for the primacy of mind.

This is precisely the sort of relation in which Milton locates his own meanings, either when he is interpreting scripture or when he is composing a poem. It is also the way Jesus is described as speaking in his tracts, especially the ones on divorce, where the meaning of words and bodies are simultaneously at issue:

> [L]et us remember, as a thing not to be denied, that all places of scripture, wherein just reason of doubt arises from the letter, are to be expounded by considering upon what occasion everything is set down, and by comparing other texts. The occasion, which induced our Saviour to speak of divorce, was either to convince the extravagance of the pharisees in that point, or to give a sharp and vehement answer to a tempting question. And in such cases, that we are not to repose all upon the literal terms of so many words, many instances will teach us: wherein we may plainly discover how Christ meant not to be taken word for word, but like a wise physician, administering one excess against another to reduce us to a perfect mean. . . .[6] (596A)

In this passage and others like it, Milton is fighting the reciprocal ideas that the sexual union of bodies is identical with the marriage of persons, and that the meaning of a text consists in the simple, uncircumstanced fact of the words, rather than the way they are used. Moreover, since he is speaking of scripture, which he regards as the sole authoritative source of religious knowledge, Milton could hardly be saying that God's words and, by extension, the bodies of God's creatures don't matter. On the contrary, they matter intensely because in Milton's theology it is through words and bodies, history and nature, that we have any access to deity, and so to truth. Thus, faced with a "strange repugnant riddle" in Matthew 19 and, as he sees it, a consequent injustice in masculine affairs (618B)—between the divine motive for marriage on the one hand, which Milton understands to give in womankind a uniquely complete companionship of body and mind to the man; and on the other, an actuality where the man is bound by sex rather than his whole nature to woman—Milton does not simply void Jesus' statements against divorce. Rather, he concludes that the sense of Christ's words in this instance must be conditioned by the whole discourse of scripture— that meaning lies not in the words per se but in the complex order of relations he describes here (which, by the way, articulates the historical-grammatical method of exegesis, advocated by the Protestant reformers).

Now one can regard Milton's tack as a casuistical exercise in the pejorative sense, a denial of the manifest fact comparable to redeeming the Lady from her bondage to Comus's chair. Or one can acknowledge Milton's point in situating Christ's words, as casuistry situates moral value in occasion and practice; it is that in this world at least, there are no uncircumstanced truths either in speech or action. Hence, the role of charity as an exegetical value in Milton's theology, both in the tracts and *Christian Doctrine*.

Hence the plot in *Comus*, where the incongruity of word with action, meaning with image suggests, to take a phrase from *Il Penseroso*, that "more is meant than meets the ear" (120). This idea that an appearance can mean more and other than what is strictly or immediately evident applies to Milton's masque but not in the manner these transcendental readings assume—that is, the wholesale displacement of significance from the action we observe to the suppositional realm we can't, so that what happens on the ground and in the text of *Comus* is neatly transcended along with the Lady's body. Milton's casuistry is not of that kind. Rather, just as he does with Christ's sayings and the sense of scripture more largely, the terms of human virtue as well as his own allegory must be extenuated not to evade but instead to admit the particulars of action or image. And that precisely because appearances *do* matter in a religion and a world where deity is a hidden God, concealed even in his signs, as Luther points out. It is because God in this life can be overlooked and misunderstood that Milton is a perpetual reader of textual and historical evidence, forever alert to those moments when what we are shown does not look like what we are told to see. This is the impetus behind his exhortation to seek truth in the *Areopagitica*, rather than simply presuppose it. For "Neither is God appointed and confined, where and out of what place these his chosen shall be first heard to speak; for he sees not as man sees, chooses not as man chooses" (752B).

Thus I would argue there is ample cause to understand the Lady's chastity not so much as the single, defining term of Milton's allegory, but as one point in a relation that includes the anomalous image of her body, and which taken with other circumstances expresses Milton's idea of virtue. In this way, the contradiction between script and spectacle in *Comus* will not only assume a certain purposiveness as against inconsequence—the presumption of design that we owe any text. It should also tell us what species of Platonism and what sort of allegory Milton could write, given this virtue as his model for the convenience of human experience with the good. For it stands to reason that in retaining the Neoplatonism conventional to Renaissance masques, Milton must have found some aspects of that eclectic, amorphous ideology that were compatible with his own: specifically, arguments which do find meaning in appearance or spectacle even as a comparable discrepancy is understood to exist between the way a thing appears and how it means. Further, as a poet who writes other things besides masques, his kind of Platonism is bound to be as much iconographic as not, and the images to which he would be attracted are those we find in *Comus*—like the *Venus-Virgo* of the *Aeneid*, where desire assumes the dress and arms of chastity—which then serve to legitimate the body by reinventing how its expressions are understood.

In our chaste and transcendental preoccupations, we tend to overlook the one aspect of the Lady on which the masque insists—the beauty of her body—and which generally serves in Platonism to express the role played by appearance or phenomena in the disclosure of truth. It is a quality that gets equal time from the allegory's several expositors, who tellingly supply the Lady with all the power and effect she seems to lack in her own right. Not only do the younger brother and Comus unite to convince us of her beauty, but they each argue that this is what brings about the Lady's unbending posture in that chair. For Comus tries to make her his queen, not because he knew her chaste from the manner of her step, or holy from the sound of her song, but because he caught sight of her beauty (as the younger brother predicts).

So the image of the Lady is a composite effect not unlike the embodied God himself, especially when we join to it the ineffable force of her "sacred vehemence" (794). She is desirable and chaste, a bodily as well as a moral being, in the world but not commanded by it alone; and this compound nature is what creates the divergence in the brothers' accounts of her plight, not to mention the predicament in which they find her. For what intrigues Milton is not the fact of the composite itself, which is a philosophical topos older than both Plato and Christ, but how we experience and understand a phenomenon that exceeds its ostensible meanings. So besides its appeal to the conceptual antinomianism that Milton displays preeminently in the *Apology for Smectymnuus* and *Areopagitica*, what might interest him about these neoplatonic efforts to dignify what others decried is that they authorize a certain order of incongruity in our experience of virtue: pleasure as the end or perfecting of intellection; chastity as impassioned rapture; Venus as madonna; a noble rage similar to his claims for his own vehemence in the *Apology* (although the idea would seem for once to be original to Plato). Moreover, as Edgar Wind argues at some length, and on whose remarkable discussion I rely here,[7] the interpretive activity in Neoplatonism allowing for these surprising moral revisions also produces an asymmetry between the image and the meaning educed for it, as well as an obliqueness or complexity in the image itself. As a result, the image takes on the status of a mystery— an appearance that cannot be reduced, that remains in excess of the sense we give it, that is intelligible only up to a point and yet true.

I would like to suggest that the spectacle of the Lady fixed to Comus's chair is a revisionary image along the lines pursued by Renaissance Neoplatonism in manufacturing such iconographic allegories *cum* mysteries, where an image's incongruousness signifies that not less but more is invested in an appearance than we might suppose. So against the trend of much *Comus* criticism, the seated Lady implies a moral paradox that doesn't depend upon or evoke transcendence of her body. Rather, this focal image works to impede the very assumption that, in order to be truly good or just, one must spurn the historical in favor of the real, the body for the idea, action for inference. In other words, the Lady's predicament represents a way of dignifying human being without trying to escape it. Milton's masque, in thus disclosing to us a condition irreducibly mixed and conflicted, should provoke in his reader the recognition that appearances do not deceive us, no more than *Comus*'s inconsequence and contradiction mislead us. They both tell us something true, but not in the way we imagine.

For the real contest in Milton's masque is between how we want to approach the Lady's predicament and how the masque's curiously involved allegory demands we see her. And like the superfluity of significance that Neoplatonism elicits from its chosen icons, where the image is at once both true and equivocal, Milton presents us with a picture we cannot easily reconcile—of the Lady suffering a rape yet returning in honour to her parents. The incongruity of course has to do with "the sublime notion, and high mystery / That must be uttered to unfold the sage / And serious doctrine of virginity;" but the Lady herself never discloses what that is (784–86). Instead, she threatens Comus with something quite as profound and proleptic in its force, the idea that "the uncontrolled worth / Of this pure cause" of chastity

> would kindle my rapt spirits
> To such a flame of sacred vehemence,
> That dumb things would be moved to sympathize,
> And the brute Earth would lend her nerves, and shake
> Till all thy magic structures reared so high,
> Were shattered to heaps o'er thy false head.
>
> (792–98)

Only in a world where truth was an immanent as against a transcendent power could such a mystery and such a threat work. So, *pace* Stanley Fish in another guise, I would argue that the reader must struggle against the temptation to coherence when it involves discounting the image presented by Milton's poetry, and so confounding his enterprise of expression. Moreover, if *Comus*'s casuistry is able (as these Platonizing readers imply) to anticipate *Paradise Lost* in making the reader's interpretation a moral choice, then surely Milton must also have grasped that if our and the Lady's interpretive dilemma is to be instructive, its occasion must be equally as real and profound as its moral implications. So I would argue that Milton uses the allegory of the Lady's predicament in *Comus* to express an ineluctable order of human fact as he sees it: virtue cannot be separated from the circumstances in which it is expressed, even as it is more and other than that position; and reciprocally, that our sense of the text must incorporate what we are shown, not just told. Experience, whether mimetic or practical, counts in how we assess meaning.

III

Thus the Lady's chastity would be empty of significance without the concomitant of her beauty and the position to which it brings her, caught in the clammy embrace of Comus's chair. She speaks of her chastity precisely because the enchanter speaks only of her beauty in their debate, a circumstance already present in the brothers' exchange. The younger brother declares that no one would "rob a hermit of his weeds, / His few books, or his beads, or maple dish":

> But Beauty like the fair Hesperian tree
> Laden with blooming gold, had need the guard
> Of dragon-watch with unenchanted eye,
> To save her blossoms, and defend her fruit
> From the rash hand of bold Incontinence.
> You may as well spread out the unsunned heaps
> Of miser's treasure by an outlaw's den,
> And tell me it is safe, as bid me hope
> Danger will wink on opportunity,
> And let a single helpless maiden pass
> Uninjured in this wild surrounding waste.
> Of night or loneliness it recks me not,
> I fear the dread events that dog them both,
> Lest some ill-greeting touch attempt the person
> Of our unowned sister.
>
> (392–406)

What he describes here does indeed take place, and in the terms he supplies. For Comus does "attempt the person" of the Lady, which means that he engages in some manner of bodily assault, most likely sexual, given the brother's figures of "blossom" and "fruit" and of course that "glutinous" chair to which she finds herself fixed. In debating the proper use of nature or the world, Comus employs the younger brother's language of desire and compulsive consumption about beauty, the idea being that this quality of things was not only made to be used by others, but properly demands it. Thus he says

> Beauty is Nature's coin, must not be hoarded,
> But must be current, and the good thereof
> Consists in mutual and partaken bliss,
> Unsavoury in the enjoyment of itself.
> If you let slip time, like a neglected rose
> It withers on the stalk with languished head.
> Beauty is Nature's brag, and must be shown
> In courts, at feasts, and high solemnities
> Where most may wonder at the workmanship;
> It is for homely features to keep home,
> They had their name thence. . . .
> What need a vermeil-tinctured lip for that,
> Love-darting eyes, or tresses like the morn?

> There was another meaning in these gifts,
> Think what, and be advised, you are but young yet.
>
> (738–54)

Comus has simply extended to the Lady's beauty the economy he applied to nature or *physis* more largely, which if unused in his sense (which is to say by others) will explode from its surfeit of "odours, fruits, and flocks, / Thronging the seas with spawn inummerable . . . all to please, and sate the curious taste" (711–13). The idea of beauty as a species of exchange or currency; the erotic topos of the unplucked rose; the notion of beauty as an artifact created specially to excite admiration in the beholder: all these images imply that *the other meaning* Comus sees in the Lady is insistent attraction. In a twist on the carpe diem motif, her beauty is itself a call to pleasure. Hence, as he puts it, the *need* of "Love-darting eyes" is beauty's necessity to be used, the erotic compulsion beauty imposes on whoever perceives it. With the phrase "love-darting," Milton puts in his magician's mouth the assumptions and idiom that Satan, Adam and the speaker of *Paradise Lost* later use to describe Eve. That is, Eve's beauty is understood to *ravish* whoever sees her, rather than the other way around. One need only think of that moment when she leaves the conversation between Adam and Raphael, and the speaker says that

> With goddess-like demeanour forth she went;
> Not unattended, for on her as queen
> A pomp of winning graces waited still,
> And from about her shot darts of desire
> Into all eyes to wish her still in sight.
>
> (8.59–63)

The affinity of this description with Comus's is hardly accidental, since both suggest the image of Venus or *amor*, whose beauty is figured as erotic darts in allusion to Cupid himself, representing desire as beauty's effect upon the world.[8] So the younger brother and Comus together represent the Lady so as to emphasize the active power of her beauty to attract, to create desire in those who see her, and in that way to precipitate Comus's "attempt upon her person." That is why, when the Lady sings her song, she finds herself obliged to parley with the enchanter rather than echo, who proclaims himself seduced in every portion of his being by "such divine enchanting ravishment" (244), "Such sober certainty of waking bliss" (262).

In such loaded, ambiguously sexual language, he testifies to the Lady's erotic powers, which often tend to go unnoticed or at least unassimilated in readings of Milton's allegory. The reason for this is that, first, we have only the text in front of us, not the impersonated Lady and the theatrical spectacle which the text is supposed in some measure to explicate; second, because like Eve, it is the Lady's peculiar role in the masque to suffer interpretation, with some characters reading her one way, and some another. As a result, her significance to the allegory becomes more, not less contingent upon her appearance, since she and her predicament are approached as a species of image that not only demands action but understanding. Again, the comparison to Milton's Eve is instructive. When Adam complains to Raphael about Eve's appearance, he presents himself as "Superior and unmoved, here only weak / Against the charm of beauty's powerful glance," beauty which he considers disproportionate to her being—"on her bestowed / Too much of ornament, in outward show / Elaborate, of inward less exact" (8.532–39). Now Adam specializes in discovering just such interpretive "disproportions" because he is inclined to make appearance absolute, or in Raphael's phrase, to infer excellence from great and bright (8.27, 90–91). I would argue that Comus's own sense of burgeoning disproportion, consequent upon the disuse of nature and the Lady's beauty, is similarly the effect of his own passion, as it is Adam's. In other words, the image of woman's beauty reveals what each one brings to it; the asymmetry, not to mention Comus's hyperbole, has its origin in interpretation.

Indeed, as Fish concludes, Milton has set up *Comus* to represent an allegory of reading. Only the allegory doesn't require us to transcend the manner of the masque's expression as he suggests, but to attend to it more closely, as we should do whenever Milton decides to appropriate some well-known image or device. He always seems to turn these appropriations into self-reflexive moments, an occasion to make the reader aware of the role intepretation plays in how things are made to mean. If I may briefly draw out for *Comus* the implications of this disparity between image and meaning, like most figures of woman in Milton's writings, the Lady resembles the revealed or incarnate God in that knowing her requires that we interpret her appearances. So the *Doctrine and Discipline of Divorce* informs us that the very circumstances of intercourse between the sexes conduce to the man's mistaking what he is shown for what the woman is in herself: "for who knows not that the bashful muteness of a virgin may oftimes hide all the unliveliness and natural sloth which is really unfit for conversation? Nor is there that freedom of access granted or presumed, as may suffice to a perfect discerning till too late" (583A). In other words, mankind is perpetually faced with the problem of Eve's hair, which is that woman must be interpreted to be known and virgins especially, where it would seem—in Milton's eyes at least—that the cult of modesty has been successful in erasing all expressions of personality. Whether or not her chastity is the cause, we know the Lady in Milton's masque through the eyes of her interpreters, of which she is one, so that she stands as the icon to their allegories. As with the revelation of God in history and in the sacred text, more is meant by it than the signs in themselves, which are both the occasion and the symptom of interpretation.

So when to reassure his junior, the Elder Brother undertakes his exposition of chastity as the Lady's "hidden strength" (414), he actually renders express the image latent in Comus's account of her, as Venus armed with the power to inspire passion. Only the image is not understood in relation to the Lady's beauty, but in accordance with that new theological Virtue that the Lady claims "visibly" to see along with Faith and Hope at the masque's beginning (212–15). Consequently, the *Venus armata* is transformed into Diana and Minerva who each bear "the arms of chastity":

> She that has that, is clad in complete steel,
> And like a quivered nymph with arrows keen
> May trace huge forests, and unharboured heaths,
> Infamous hills, and sandy perilous wilds,
> Where through the sacred rays of chastity,
> No savage fierce, bandit, or moutaineer
> Will dare to soil her virgin purity.
> Yea there, where very desolation dwells
> By grots, and caverns shagged with horrid shades,
> She may pass on with unblenched majesty,
> Be it not done in pride, or in presumption.
> Some say no evil thing that walks by night
> In fog, or fire, by lake, or moorish fen,
> Blue meagre hag, or stubborn unlaid ghost,
> That breaks his magic chains at curfew time,
> No goblin or swart faery of the mine,
> Hath hurtful power o'er true virginity.
>
> (420–36)

Once again, hyperbole gives away the fact that the Elder Brother is not so much examining as projecting onto his sister's predicament; like the younger brother's allegory of beauty, his meaning is discovered to be in excess of the Lady's actuality. That is, if she cannot be brought to drink by Comus, neither does she succeed in entirely passing him by, since she is sufficiently enthralled by his spells to enter his palace and sit in his chair. So where the Second Brother gives us an image of the Lady as hapless maiden, the victim of her own desirable body and the passion it wantonly elicits, the Elder displays the Lady as virago, a virgin so militant and powerful in her chastity that she defies every danger. But as the masque's action bears out, although her predicament conforms to each of these interpretations in some part, it also resists them. John Leonard recalls in his own temperate essay on *Comus* that Sir Walter Greg had the moral obtuseness to remark that the Lady protests too much;[9] yet this is true in a sense Greg certainly did not intend, since she is passionately, articulately averse to Comus and still confined to his seat. But her predicament is owing to the allegorical fact that she is neither beauty nor chastity understood absolutely—as either a force of almost physical necessity, or the principle of transcendence that the Elder Brother describes, which casting "a beam upon the outward shape . . . turns it by degrees to the soul's essence" (459–61).

Rather, the ardent passion of Milton's Lady is a composite of both these qualities, which accordingly modify each other and convert into a new expression of her nature. And this could explain why the Lady's "sage / And serious doctrine of virginity" must remain ineffable, at least to Comus (785–86); and why her praise of temperance describes something different in character and effect from the "rigid looks of chaste austerity, / And noble grace that dashed brute violence / With sudden adoration and blank awe" which her brother likes to imagine in her case (449–51). Both elements of beauty and chastity are present in the Neoplatonic icon of Love—the *Venus-Virgo*, whose *locus classicus* is that moment in the *Aeneid* when Venus presents herself dressed as a follower of Diana (*virginis os habitumque gerens et virginis arma*).[10] As Edgar Wind observes, in transfiguring vices into virtues—like Pleasure (*voluptas*), Passion (*amor*), Madness (*furor*) or Wrath (*ira*)—the Neoplatonists invested them with something of the quality of their opposites, at once altering and dignifying them.[11] Moreover, the resulting paradox contributed to the sense of a mystery, though in the hands of Ficino and Pico it remained a mystery very much of this world—almost pagan, Wind suggests. That is because human passion itself was being ennobled, and passion describes the convergence of body with mind in the singular expression of self.

In particular, he mentions the medal of Giovanna degli Albizzi, which on one side showed the three Graces with an inscription reading *"Castitas-Pulchritudo-Amor,"* and on the other the image of "a huntress carrying bow and arrow, wearing a winged crown on her head and heavy boots on her feet, and standing on a small cloud which covers the sun, but allows its rays to be seen around it."[12] The inscription on the reverse side is the verse from Virgil describing the goddess of love dressed in the arms of chastity. Thus the image of the three Graces, understood as "the union of Chastity and Love through the mediation of Beauty is now expressed by one hybrid figure in which the two opposing goddesses, Diana and Venus, are merged into one." Wind goes on to elaborate the sense of these dual and asymmetrical images as a Neoplatonic *discordia concors*, where the arms of the *Venus-Virgo* signify the arousal of love by the exercise of restraint—Pico's definition of *pulchritudo* or beauty. For Pico argues that beauty is a composite of contrary principles, and thus distinctively a quality of human as against divine being (which as absolutely simple, cannot be called beautiful, he says).[13] Similarly, when Ficino celebrates a noble *voluptas*, it is one which unites pleasure to the good, thus producing in Wind's phrase a goodness indistinguishable from sensual bliss.[14] In either case, the point is what Wind calls the pagan impulse of their revisionary ethic: there is no such thing as a disembodied virtue to these Platonists; when Chastity herself is made the image of rapture, which she is in Wind's reading of *Primavera* by Botticelli, she is ennobled by *pulchritudo* and *voluptas*, beauty and pleasure, and Venus herself becomes the image of moderation.[15]

IV

I in no way suppose that Milton has this specific image and paradox in mind for the Lady, but rather that he imagines a comparable tension and balance between passion and restraint epitomized by the *Venus-Virgo* when he pictures her position in the debate with Comus. This fragile equilibrium may be said to characterize his concept of married love in the *Doctrine and Discipline of Divorce*, where he alludes to the *Symposium* in arguing a certain tension between what "the wanting soul needfully seeks" and "the plenteous body would joyfully give away" (584A): "When, therefore, this original and sinless penury, or loneliness of the soul, cannot lay itself down by the side of such a meet and acceptable union as God ordained in marriage, at least in some proportion, it cannot conceive and bring forth love" (584B). In other words, Milton argues that without the convenience of the soul's different passion for beauty or "proportion" with the body's impetus to pleasure, there is no love because no balance, only a growing discontinuity between what is sought and what is given. The idea of this equipoise of desires seems to be confirmed by the retrospective view of the masque's allegory that he gives us in the *Apology*, when he claims to have learned about chastity and especially love from Plato and Xenophon. "I mean that which is truly so, whose charming cup is only virtue, which she bears in her hand to those who are worthy; (the rest are cheated with a thick intoxicating potion, which a certain sorceress, the abuser of love's name, carries about); and how the first and chiefest office of love begins and ends in the soul, producing those happy twins of her divine generation, knowledge and virtue (549A–50B).

It is possible to see in this brief allegory the image of the *Venus-Virgo*, which is variously the ennobled *voluptas* or *amor* of the Neoplatonists, expressed as the distinction between a false and a true love. Now Milton may very likely be alluding to the *Eros Pandemus* or common love, as against the *Eros Uranius* or tutelary and exalting love, which Pausanius defines in the *Symposium* and which Socrates recasts as he does every previous speech on love, with his own serving to mediate between them all. For Plato intends us to understand that Pausanius mistook love when he divided it into two discrete and opposed forces, one only interested in sexual satisfaction; while the other is devoted to the virtue and well-being of the beloved. That is why, in Socrates' revisionary account of love, he embodies both orders of desire—for body and soul—in a single great *daimon* that mediates between heaven and earth. As Werner Jaeger comments, love thus becomes a mean or perpetual balance, as well as a striving for the good in all its forms.[16]

This is also the sense of the triadic conversions in which renaissance Platonism delights and which it images in the three Graces, where the dialectic of contraries may be said to create something new. And this new thing or third term is itself expressed by a *discordia concors*, an asymmetry within the otherwise harmonious grouping of Neoplatonic iconography. For usually two of the Graces are paired, while a third is averted in posture or attitude.[17]

Now what I find most intriguing about Milton's recapitulation of his own allegory is that its topic is love, not chastity, and the role of the Lady is that of lover, not abstainer, which is to say the one who seeks to generate the new thing of virtue and knowledge in the soul. And when Milton does speak about chastity here, which is almost immediately, it is in the context supplied by love and something else besides, which also pertains to *Comus*. For chastity here is a contingent or occasional topic of Milton's, because he stands accused of being unchaste. Thus his ardent pursuit of knowledge and virtue prepare the way for a testimonial to his own chaste state, against the accusations of the Modest Confuter who imagines Milton's morals to be as lax and scurrilous as his language. Not so, replies the young Milton, his opponent has misconstrued the image presented by his "vehement vein" (552B) and "tart rhetoric" (553B):

> [H]aving had the doctrine of holy scripture unfolding those chaste and high mysteries, with timeliest care infused, that "the body is for the Lord, and the Lord for the body;" thus also I argued to myself, that if unchastity in a woman, whom St. Paul terms the glory of man, be such a scandal and dishonor, then certainly in a man, who is both the image and glory of God, it must, though commonly not so thought, be much more deflouring and dishonorable; in that he sins both against his own body, which is the perfecter sex, and his own glory, which is the woman; and, that which is worst, against the image and glory of God, which is in himself.
>
> (550A)

If one reads this account of chastity from the standpoint of love, which is how I think Milton intends it, then that seemingly vacuous virtue is not about celibacy and so the negation of the body and the world. Instead, chastity is the expression of love—towards body as the self, towards the woman in marriage as other self (a phrase from the divorce tracts), and towards God whom man images as "the perfecter sex." And fornication, Milton goes on to suggest, not only denies the body this reverent love but also repudiates the expressive aspect that inspires such love—since, as Wittgenstein puts it, the human body is the best picture of the human soul. The mystery of chastity is also the mystery of incarnation for Milton, inasmuch as "the Lord is *for* the body," not just "the body for the Lord." That is, not only does Christ inhabit the body through faith, but as an act of love towards the world and humanity, assumed one of his own.

This sense of incarnation or expressiveness precisely describes the difference between Comus's approach to nature and the Lady's. To Comus, *physis* is just a generating (or excreting) mechanism that operates by necessity, without volition of its own: the pathetic desire to provide that he assigns it is only a rhetorical expedient, a personification immediately contradicted by Comus's horrendous and apocalyptic image of nature's inability to cease supplying, so that "she" "would be quite surcharged with her own weight, / And strangled with her waste fertility" (727–28). In short, nature is an object making ever more innumerable objects with no more life than itself, not excluding that beauty of the Lady's which he so palpably relishes. In the scriptural locution, Comus would have her be absolutely for her body, lacking in precisely that choice which he denies to nature. And once again, the sheer hyperbole of kinds, numbers, and degrees of things in Comus's speech is an index to allegory: it obliges us to recollect that he and the Lady are looking at the selfsame world, and like the brothers, giving that image conflicting significances.

But it should be noted that heaven is sentient in *Paradise Lost*, and that the earth groans at the fall of humanity. The Lady's speech acknowledges this and between blasts of invective at her oblivious seducer, her allegory has a different inflection: she speaks considerately of nature as having a domestic economy of its own, independent of human desires but not unresponsive to human need and moral imperative. For the well-being, the happiness, the *eudaimonia* of humankind, depends on our choosing to observe the rhythm and proportion of natural abundance, not the opposite relation of uncontrolled necessity, as Comus contends. That is why the Lady defines the virtuous as those who respect nature in this way:

> Imposter do not charge most innocent Nature,
> As if she would her children should be riotous
> With her abundance she good cateress
> Means her provision only to the good
> That live according to her sober laws,
> And holy dictate of spare temperance. . . .
>
> (761–66)

Observing the double syntax that governs the sense of "abundance" and "good," the Lady represents temperance as an understanding or reciprocity with nature, whereby the continent are the good because they live according to the good. For nature observes the deity's ordination of its goodness in the creature, which also gives creation its beauty—that "unsuperfluous even proportion" (772). So the Lady's temperance is not unlike Milton's idea of chastity in the *Apology*, insofar as they both involve a reverent attitude towards *physis*—nature being the soul of the world as well as the body that expresses God, just as the man's body expresses self and maker in the divorce

tracts, while the woman's conveys the glory of the man. Continence acknowledges and emulates this universal order of the good, as a passion held in
restraint out of reverence for beauty. Nor is Comus's imperative of pleasure
unlike Milton's fornication, a refusal to recognize that bodies convey something in addition to their appearance. All of which is to say that chastity
and fornication equally describe the practice of one's sexuality, not its avoid-
ance: since it also characterizes the married state, not to mention exceeds
the customary imposition of chastity on woman whose body only matters,
Miltonic chastity clearly means more than *virgo intacta*.

When Neoplatonic iconography argues that chastity is an expression
of love or passion mediated by beauty, it evokes no single correspondence
but a complex set of relations between matter and form, body and soul, the
person and the good, the world and God. Without beauty or appearance to
move it, passion is empty; without chastity to discipline passion, there would
be no beauty; without love or passion responding to beauty, there would be
no conversion of the person to virtue or the good. Like God, both hidden
and revealed, the good is imaged by chastity and yet distinct from it. So
Wind would have it that *Castitas*, the enraptured Grace in Botticelli's painting, turns her face towards the figure of Hermes and the possibility of
transcendence the god evokes. Milton's idea of chastity or continence observes
the same distinction even as it possesses another impetus altogether; as the
Lady's account of nature suggests, chastity is not Stoic abstinence, virtue
without passion or pleasure;[18] it is a loving and reverent inflection towards
the world and the body, the domains in which God, the soul and their
peculiar joy are made known.

That chastity is the expression of love also explains its substitution for
caritas or charity in the Lady's pantheon of theological virtues: in Luther's
idiom, it is love under a contrary appearance, which explains our propensity
to misunderstand its nature and the Lady's in *Comus*. At the same time, the
sort of love Milton intends cannot be separated from the moral action or
practice of continence, which conveys this distinctive passion to the world.
For Miltonic chastity may be said thoroughly to incarnate love by making
it a virtue one must exercise in the body and in the presence of beauty or
sexuality, without which there would be no motive for continence or passion.
Thus like the *Venus-Virgo* which is the conflicted image of love's expressions
for renaissance Platonism, the appearances of chastity are themselves composite and equivocal in Milton's world and so tend to be variously construed.

In the *Apology* itself, that conflicting appearance takes the shape of
Milton's own polemical manner, "the manner of handling that cause" whose
ugliness and virulence in the *Animadversions* brings down the charge of
incontinence upon his own head, and against which he defends himself with
language so graphic and abusive that it still embarrasses his editors (552B).
In *Comus*, the conflict appears as Greg's impression that the Lady is too
conscious to be true (so Leonard reads him). Both Milton's indecorous speech

and the Lady's indecorous position have the appearance of scandal, but they are scandalous only to those who would avoid their implications, and the same holds true of those vagaries and anomalies that readers like myself have compiled on Milton's masque. The salient implication is that truth and virtue are not obvious or transcendent, but a different, more difficult order of appearance than we suppose for them.

Indeed, Milton justifies his own and the Lady's vehemence as an excess of zeal—an ardency for truth in the face of falsehood, an impassioned if not an inspired language like that the prophets, Christ, the Lord of the covenant and Luther all employ against hypocrisy, the true enemy of God. For what hypocrisy does is to degrade appearances as the medium of deity, truth and the good; and of course this charge fits Comus. So were the Modest Confuter and Greg to point out that such vehemence does not *look* like truth, Milton would reply, as he does in the *Areopagitica*, that truth doesn't have a single look or expression anymore than does love or the unseen God, since its appearance is contingent upon the occasion of its use—that is, its embodiment. Milton's invective, like the Lady's vitriol, is how the love of goodness looks when it encounters evil, at which point chastity becomes passionate abhorrence—abhorrence not in the sense of a revulsion from the world, but in the sense of acknowledging and hating that which devalues it:

> [F]or in times of opposition, when either against new heresies arising, or old corruptions to be reformed . . . then (that I may have leave awhile as the poets use) Zeal, whose substance is ethereal, arming in complete diamond, ascends his fiery chariot, drawn with two blazing meteors, figured like beasts, but of a higher breed than any the zodiac yields, resembling two of those four which Ezekiel and St. John saw; the one visaged like a lion, to express power, high authority, and indignation; the other of countenance like a man, to cast derision and scorn upon perverse and fraudulent seducers: with these the invincible warrior, Zeal, shaking loosely the slack reins, drives over the heads of scarlet prelates, and such as are insolent to maintain traditions, bruising their stiff necks under his flaming wheels.
>
> (553A)

This explains the Lady's speech to Comus, pouring derision on her seducer even as she threatens him with a greater vehemence that will expose his illusions. Yet like the enchanter's sense that the Lady's words are "set off by some superior power" (800), there is a disparity between the allegory of Zeal's pure and ethereal substance and its image in the vulgar force of Milton's language. In another world than this, that discrepancy would compromise his claim to truth; but here vulgarity expresses the passion that comes from a close encounter with evil. So if chastity is the image of love in the *Apology* and *Comus*, a reticence that acknowledges the dignity of the creature as something more than just an object to be used up, then scorn, satire, ridicule are its reverse—the image of a just passion exercised in defense of this dignity. Just as emotion is itself an expression of the body, so this composite passion comes from being in the world, not out of it. That is, it is an expression of truth, for one can truly love or abhor only where passion counts—where the choice affects us intimately or profoundly.

So Milton famously remarks in the *Areopagitica* that it is our condition to know good by knowing evil, adding:

> [W]hat wisdom can there be to choose, what continence to forbear, without the knowledge of evil? He that can apprehend and consider vice with all her baits and seeming pleasures, and yet abstain, and yet distinguish, and yet prefer that which is truly better, he is the true warfaring Christian. I cannot praise a fugitive and cloistered virtue unexercised and unbreathed, that never sallies out and sees her adversary, but slinks out of the race, where that immortal garland is to be run for, not without dust and heat. Assuredly we bring not innocence into the world, we bring impurity rather; that which purifies us is trial, and trial is by what is contrary.
>
> (738A)

The scandal of the Lady's position is a contrary image of her virtue, like Milton's "vehement vein" and "tart rhetoric" in the *Apology*. For it is an image of injustice that, in Milton's eyes at least, teaches her the nature of the good and gives motive and force to her speech. If we take the Lady out of her predicament and her body, and treat her scorn of Comus as though it were the Attendant Spirit's disdain of this world, then she looks like a prude or a prig. But if we understand that Comus has really injured her and that she suffers by being seated in his slime, then her passion is intelligible, not trivial. The problem with our versions of the allegory is that we ourselves do not take the position of her body with the seriousness it deserves, because we are intent on transcending the spectacle that expresses it. As a consequence, our readings fail to detect the emotion that goes with the image and with Milton's idea of chastity, and what is worse, tend to be devoid of feeling themselves.

If we would but invest in the body and the world where the masque's moral action takes place, then it should not take Leah Marcus recounting the history of a Margery Evans—that is, the pertinent circumstances of an actual rape—to bring the Lady's position home to us.[19] Milton does invest, which is why the Attendant Spirit must allow her encounter with Comus and devise the brothers', so that they all gain the knowledge and choice that makes virtue not a metaphysical cipher but an ethic (Jayne makes the same point about Sabrina). And the Lady particularly honors the body, which is why Sabrina alone can rescue her—not because they are both virginal, but because they both suffer a temporal evil. That is, their chastity expresses an aversion to injustice itself, which the Spirit—not being of the body or this world—cannot know. For his virtue is but a blank compared to these two figures. This is how Milton understands tragic knowledge, where true wisdom, in the Aeschylean phrase, comes through suffering for Samson, Adam and Eve; and it is also the force he gives to Adam's cry of *felix culpa*, where guilty knowledge creates a greater joy.

The image of the Lady's predicament, seized if not caught by Comus, is a model for the manner in which we should take the masque's allegory. For her position describes something along the lines of what Luther says about believers being *simul iustus et peccator*, at once just and a sinner; or better still, the relation he expounds between spirit and flesh in his lectures on Romans, which he defines as *utrunque* or dialectical.[20] That is to say, the spiritual cannot be separated from the world, the text and the body. "We should note," Luther remarks, "that the apostle does not mean to be understood as saying that the spirit and the flesh are, so to speak, two separate entities"; for "He understands them to be one whole just as a wound and the flesh are one":

> In the light of this we can see that the metaphysical theologians deal with a silly and crazy fiction when they dispute about the question whether there can be opposite appetites in one and the same subject, and when they invent the notion that the spirit, i. e., reason, is something absolute or separate by itself and in its own kind an integral whole and that, similarly, opposite to it also sensuality, or the flesh, constitutes equally an integral whole. These stupid imaginations cause them to lose sight of the fact that the flesh is a basic weakness or wound of the whole man which grace has only begun to heal in his reason or spirit.[21]

In Milton as in Luther, "spirit" and "flesh" are conditions of the whole person, mind and body together; moreover, they do not stand for two things that can be discerned and separated out, or two discrete dimensions of being that permit us to retreat from one to the other. They describe our position towards the world, as either expressing God or denying him, even as the Lady's virtue and Comus's pleasure represent attitudes towards nature and the body taken by the whole person, imaged as continence or consumption. And when we suppose that virtue requires the Lady to void her body and appearances, and the reader to void the masque's spectacle, then we suffer from the same pathology as Luther's metaphysicians. And that lies in the desire to escape mortality by transcending the embodied condition of our humanity and all those discomfiting circumstances that go with it, like the need to interpret and choose.

It should be remembered that when Milton is through explaining his idea of virtue as a *preference*, a *felt* inclination, for the good that can only be made with knowledge of what is evil, he remarks that this is why "our sage and serious poet Spenser, (whom I dare be known to think a better teacher than Scotus or Aquinas), describing true temperance under the person of Guion, brings him in with his palmer through the cave of Mammon, and the bower of earthly bliss, that he might see and know, and yet abstain" (738B). Spenser is a better teacher not just because he knew that continence to exist must be practiced, but because unlike Scotus or Aquinas, he made that recognition real and forcible to his reader as well, through the power of allegory, or spectacle, or image.

Notes

1. John Carey and Alistair Fowler, eds. *The Poems of John Milton* (London: Longman, 1968). Subsequent references to Milton's poetry will cite this edition.

2. Jayne's "The Subject of Milton's Ludlow Mask," which represents *Comus* as a Neoplatonic symbology of the soul's rapture and return to the heavenly, appears in *Milton: Modern Essays in Criticism*, ed. Arthur Barker (Oxford: Oxford University Press, 1965), 88–111. Donald Friedman's "*Comus* and the Truth of the Ear," which addresses the predominance of neologism in Milton's masque as having an iconoclastic use, is collected in *"The Muses Common-weale": Poetry and Politics in the Seventeenth Century*, eds. Claude Summers and Ted-Larry Pebworth (Columbia: University of Missouri Press, 1988), 119–34. I have taken Stevens' argument from his essays on two kinds or functions of imagination in Milton's writings—one sensuous, one abstracting, in "Magic Structures: Comus and the Illusions of Fancy," *Milton Quarterly* 17 (1983): 84–89; and "Milton and the Icastic Imagination," *Milton Studies* 20 (1984): 43–73. Finally, Fish's account of reading according to "essentials" as against "accidents" appears in *Illustrious Evidence*, ed. Earl Miner (Berkeley: University of California Press, 1975), 115–31.

3. Jayne, "Ludlow Mask," 96.

4. Jayne, "Ludlow Mask," 104.

5. Victoria Kahn, "Virtue and *Virtu* in *Comus*," in her forthcoming book, *Machiavellian Rhetoric: From the Counter-Reformation to Milton* (Princeton: Princeton University Press, 1994).

6. Frank Allen Patterson, ed. *The Student's Milton*, rev. ed. (New York: Appleton-Century-Crofts, 1930). Subsequent references to Milton's prose cite this edition.

7. Edgar Wind, *Pagan Mysteries of the Renaissance*, rev. ed. (New York: Norton, 1968), especially, 1–151.

8. See Carey's comment to this effect, *Poems of Milton*, 816n.

9. John Leonard, "Saying 'No' to Freud: Milton's *A Mask* and Sexual Assault," *Milton Quarterly* 25 (1991): 129–40, 134. Leonard observes, quite rightly I think, that the Lady never says no to sex, or to married love; but her dangerous position demands that she concentrate on forcibly repudiating sexuality as Comus understands it. Again, we tend to misunderstand her when we fail to acknowledge the position from which she speaks.

10. Virgil, *Aeneid*, 1:315.

11. Wind, *Mysteries*, 68–69.

12. Wind, *Mysteries*, 73–78.

13. Wind, *Mysteries*, 88–89.

14. Wind, *Mysteries*, 71.

15. Wind, *Mysteries*, 117–21.

16. Werner Jaeger, *Paideia: The Ideals of Greek Culture*, tr. Gilbert Highet (New York: Oxford, 1943), 2:180–90.

17. Wind, *Mysteries*, 26–52.

18. On the development of a divine Voluptas, and pleasure or delight as the end of intellection in renaissance Platonism, see Wind, *Mysteries*, 53–71.

19. Leah Marcus, "The Milieu of Milton's *Comus*: Judicial Reform at Ludlow and the Problem of Sexual Assault," *Criticism* 25 (1983): 293–327.

20. Martin Luther, *Luther: Lectures on Romans*, ed. and tr. Wilhelm Pauck, the Library of Christian Classics (Philadelphia: Westminster, 1959), 212–13.

21. Pauck, *Luther: Romans*, 214.

Things and Actions Indifferent:
The Temptation of Plot in *Paradise Regained*

STANLEY FISH*

It has for some time been obvious to me (although perhaps not to many others) that the paradigmatic moment in Milton's poetry occurs in *Paradise Lost*, Book XII, when Adam asks Michael to specify the time and place when Christ and Satan will meet in a final battle: "Needs must the Serpent now his capital bruise / Expect with mortal paine: say where and when / Thir fight, what stroke shall bruise the Victors heel (XII, 383–85). Michael's reply is, as his replies so often are, a rebuke:

> To whom thus *Michael*. Dream not of thir fight,
> As of a Duel, or the local wounds
> Of head or heel: not therefore joynes the Son
> Manhood to God-head, with more strength to foil
> Thy enemie; nor so is overcome
> *Satan*, whose fall from Heav'n, a deadlier bruise,
> Disabl'd not to give thee thy deaths wound:
> Which hee, who comes thy Saviour, shall recure,
> Not by destroying *Satan*, but his works
> In thee and in thy Seed.
>
> (XII, 386–95)

These lines challenge the assumptions underlying Adam's question in several ways. First of all, when Michael says, "Dream not of thir fight, / as of a Duel, or the local wounds / Of head or heel," he means that Adam is wrong to think of it as a fight in which a single blow (much like the blow Michael had once thought to inflict on Satan and so end intestine war in heaven) will forever settle the issue between them. The whole point of the Incarnation and Crucifixion will have been lost if they are only to be preliminary to a battle that might have been fought without going to all that trouble: "not therefore joynes the Son / Manhood to God-head." Why then? The answer to the question alerts us to another and central aspect of Adam's error. Godhead has joined itself to manhood in order to destroy not Satan—who

---

Reprinted from *Milton Studies* 27 (1983): 163–86.

has already in the essential sense destroyed himself—but "his works / In thee." The contest, insofar as there is one, is not so much *between* the mighty antagonists as it is *for* the soul of man. Nor can the prize be won simply by claiming it as the victor's spoil; for it is only when the soul inclines to one or the other of the combatants that the victory will have occurred. Thus the fight is not only for the soul; it is in the soul, and while Adam is in some sense what the fight is about, he is also an active agent in its resolution. Resolution is of course too strong a word; for whichever way Adam inclines, that will not be the end of the matter. As Michael points out, the works of Satan must be destroyed not simply in thee, but in thy seed. Just as Adam earlier learned that death is no single stroke but a long day's dying, so must he now learn that the redemption of man will be a long day's living, in the course of which there will be innumerable reenactments of the fight—not really a fight—of which Adam here dreams. The effect of line 395—"In thee and in thy Seed"—is at once to insist on the interiority of Satan's works—they manifest themselves in tendencies of human behavior—and to emphasize the time, no less than all of time, that will be required to extirpate them.

Adam, then, is wrong on three related counts: (1) to conceive of the moral life as climaxing in a single decisive encounter; (2) to see himself in relation to that encounter as an outsider; and (3) to think of that encounter as an event in the world of circumstances rather than as a process that is continually occurring in the interior world of the spirit. He is entirely mistaken as to the nature of moral action, which he tends to identify with something that is measurable by the changes it effects in the external world. True moral action is internal and always has the form specified by Michael in the very next lines: "nor can this be, / But by fulfiling that which thou didst want, / Obedience to the Law of God" (XII, 395–97). Obedience. This is the only rule of action Michael delivers, and it is followed immediately by a perfect and exemplary illustration, the Passion. As an act, the Passion is distinguished by the immobility of the actor. It would seem from one point of view—the point of view from which Adam calls for the heroics of a duel—that Christ doesn't *do* anything, but in fact he does everything—that is, he performs the only act that merits the name; he obeys, and it is "this God-like act" that, Michael declares, "Shall bruise the head of *Satan*" (XII, 430). What is remarkable about this bruising is that it will occur without contact. Satan's wound is inflicted at long distance and is incurred not because of something that is done to him (in the crude physical sense expected by Adam) but because of something that is shown to him, a mode of being whose very presence in the world brings about his defeat. The moment of the Passion (which is here of course only anticipated) is characteristic of the "victories" enjoyed by Milton's heroes, who never clash with their great opposites but repulse them merely by declaring and holding fast to a vision of the world in which Satanic power is an illusion. This is what the

Lady in *Comus* does when she declares, "Thou canst not touch the freedom of my minde" (662), thereby denying the relevance of the (bodily) sphere over which the sorcerer has apparent power, and it is what Christ will do, again and again, in *Paradise Regained*. The declaration (whether in word or deed) is always received in the same way by the antihero, who reels as if struck by a blow, even though no blow has been landed. The pattern for this encounter (hardly an encounter at all) is set in the *Ode on the Morning of Christ's Nativity* when the fleeing of the pagan deities is attributed to the force of a recumbent babe who exerts his control without moving from his cradle and who, at the moment when his power is most felt, is in the act (if that is the word) of falling asleep (237–44).

The moral in all of these poems is the same moral Michael points to here: the true form of action is not something one does (a wound inflicted, a battle waged), but something one is. Or, to put the matter more precisely, for Milton being is an action, which therefore cannot be identified with any particular gesture or set of gestures but with an orientation or allegiance of which any gesture can be the expression.

By thus interiorizing the notion of action, Milton commits himself to a series of positions that finally have consequences for his poetry. First of all, if the form of action is interior, then any external form action happens to take is accidental and, in some sense, beside the point; and it follows that one cannot in advance make a list of actions that will always be either virtuous or evil. By the same reasoning, if all outward acts are equally the manifestation of some inner state, no one act can be said to be more important than any other; and, conversely, no act can be said to be inconsequential. Indeed, nothing is ever inconsequential. If, even in the smallest things, one is bearing witness to some kind of inner allegiance, then action is continual and admits of no respite; since obedience is not a matter of following directions but of having a direction, one has it not at particular times or in response to extraordinary circumstances, but at all times and in response to any and every circumstance. And since every circumstance presents the possibility of either keeping to or straying from the way, there is finally no meaningful distinction to be made between them. That is, one cannot speak meaningfully of moments when more is at stake than at other moments or of choices that are more or less difficult or significant than other choices; although life will present you with what appears to be a variety of situations, your obligation is to see through that variety and discern in each situation the challenge it offers to your continuing obedience; your obligation, in short, is to remember that, despite appearance to the contrary, the issues are always the same, as are the dangers. Those dangers can be enumerated simply by reversing the account of obligation. Any attempt to persuade you that one moment is more important than another, or that one action is absolutely crucial (in the sense that having performed it you can now relax), or that a change in scene means a change in what is at stake is an attempt to distract you from your commitment to obedience and substitute for that commitment the commitments that seem urged on you by empirical circumstances. One can only resist such an attempt by resisting the appeal located in words like *crisis*, *climax*, *change*, *development*, *denouement*, and *suspense*. It is in this list of things that are to be denied that one finds both the subject and the extraordinary difficulty of Milton's mature poetry. The subject is the tension between obedience, as a continuing obligation, and narrative; the difficulty, for both Milton and his reader, is the writing of poetry, and of narrative poetry, that in no way relies on crisis, climax, change, development, and suspense but instead makes them the vehicles of temptation.

I have called that temptation the temptation of plot, and it informs the strategy of Milton's villains, the most brilliant and diabolical of whom is the Satan of *Paradise Regained*. It is Satan's continual effort in *Paradise Regained* to persuade the Son of God that the Son himself is a character in a plot, in a narrative where every change of scene brings new opportunities and new risks. What defeats Satan finally is the Son's inability or unwillingness (they amount to the same thing) to recognize the fact that there is a plot at all, for as Satan discovers to his repeated frustration, the Son sees no difference at all between the various objects and actions that are offered to him and urged on him in the course of four books. The series of adverbs and adjectives that introduce the Son's replies—"unalter'd," "temperately," "patiently," "calmly," "Unmov'd," "unmov'd," "with disdain," "sagely," "In brief"—not only demonstrate the strength of his resolve but indicate that the affirmation of that resolve is made in exactly the same way—with equal ease—no matter what form the temptation takes. In no case is the son unmoved or unaltered *after* a period in which alteration or movement seems possible, nor does his firmness require more of an exertion at one point than at any other. Where Satan's rhetoric continually suggests that he is ascending a scale of progressive lures, Christ's responses have the effect of leveling that scale by refusing to recognize it. It is no wonder then that Satan exclaims in exasperation, "What dost thou in this World?", for as far as he can see the possibilities of action in response to circumstances have been exhausted by the appeals he has already made:

> Since neither wealth, nor honor, arms nor arts,
> Kingdom nor Empire pleases thee, nor aught
> By me propos'd in life contemplative,
> Or active, tended on by glory, or fame,
> What dost thou in this World?
>
> (IV, 368–72)

Or, in other words, "Since you refuse to act in the name of any one of these things, and since there are not other things in the name of which you might act, you finally are not acting at all." But in fact the Son has been acting precisely by refusing to act in the name of any of these things, for by doing so he refuses to make any one of them his God. In each of the plots Satan constructs, one or more of these things has been put forward as the highest possible value; and therefore to resist the appeal to act in its name is to resist the temptation to substitute that value for the value of obedience to God. *Paradise Regained* is sometimes characterized as a poem of rejection, but in fact the Son never rejects anything because it is evil in and of itself but because, in the circumstances as Satan has arranged them, it is presented as crucial, uniquely compelling, and, in a word, necessary.

The terms of this rejection that is not a rejection are most explicitly stated in the Son's response to the claims made by Satan for Greek philosophy:

> These rules will render thee a King compleat
> Within thy self, much more with Empire joyn'd.
>   To whom our Savior sagely thus repli'd.
> Think not but that I know these things; or think
> I know them not; not therefore am I short
> Of knowing what I aught: he who receives
> Light from above, from the fountain of light,
> No other doctrine needs, though granted true.
>   (IV, 283–90)

The Son goes on to say, "But these are false" (291), but their falsity is, as it were, an extratheoretical point and is not the reason for their being rejected. They would be rejected, as the Son is careful to point out, even if they were true, because they have been offered as indispensable to his spiritual goal ("These rules will render thee a King compleat / Within thy self") and therefore as a substitute for "light from above." The metaphor of the fountain is quite precise here: if one is fed by the fountain, one has no need for the tributaries, although in circumstances where the confusion of the two is not an issue one can drink from them or not as expedience or charity may dictate. In short, this rejection is not a judgment, and indeed the Son goes to remarkable lengths in order to avoid, and even to evade, a judgment. First of all, he refuses to identify himself either as one who knows these things or as one who is ignorant of them (although he teases Satan and the reader with these alternate possibilities), and as a result the "therefore" in "not therefore am I short" follows from either of these conditions. That is, the knowledge he *is* claiming ("knowing what I aught") depends neither on his partaking of these things nor on his abstaining from them. He therefore will neither affirm them as necessary nor condemn them as evil or forbidden, because to do either would be to make them the repository of value, whereas for the Son their value at any one moment inheres in their relationship to the obligation he has already identified as primary: "me hungering to do my father's will" (II, 259). Offered as an alternative to that obligation ("you absolutely must avail yourself to these rules") they are evil because idolatrous (one is being asked to worship them); but offered in the absence of such claims they may be embraced or not as the occasion seems to dictate. To give them a fixed value, even a negative one, would be to make them the touchstone of moral judgment; embracing them or disdaining them would in and of itself make you either a good or a bad person; and for the Son, the touchstone of moral judgment is always and unvaryingly the relationship of any alternative to his determination to serve. In short, "these things," and indeed all things, are neither good nor bad in themselves but may at different times be one or the other depending on whether their use in particular circumstances advances or subverts God's glory.

The previous sentence is a textbook definition of the doctrine of "things indifferent," or *adiaphora*, a doctrine frequently invoked by Milton and one that holds the key to the structure (if that is the word) of *Paradise Regained*. Generally speaking, the doctrine of things indifferent comes in two versions, although they are not always precisely differentiated. The first, and stronger, version originates with the Stoics, who identify virtue with the self and believe that self to be sufficient. Consequently all things external to the self are lacking in intrinsic value or disvalue and acquire value only in relation to an inner disposition or intention. Thus the entire external world for the Stoics is a mass of *adiaphora*, which, depending on the circumstances "could become either good or evil."[1] The second and more restricted version of the doctrine is theological and depends on a distinction between that which the Scripture explicitly commands or forbids and that concerning which it is silent. Francis Mason's definition is both typical and succinct: "Necessarie I call that which the eternall God hath in his word precisely and determinately commanded or forbidden, either expresly or by infallible consequence. Indifferent, which the Lord hath not so commanded nor forbidden, but is contained in the holy Scripture, rather potentially then actually, comprehended in generall directions, not precisely defined by particular determinations." Mason goes on to assert that in the absence of an explicit command or prohibition a thing indifferent falls under the jurisdiction of the civil magistrates, "the Lords viceregents upon earth, who according to the exigence of the state, may by their discretion command it to be done."[2] This is the conservative or Anglican position, which is countered by the Puritan insistence that decisions concerning things indifferent should be left to the consciences of individual believers. Otherwise, they contend, the liberty that men enjoy under the New Dispensation is unlawfully infringed: "All such humaine lawes therefore, that . . . upon any penalties, binde men to those things that are confessed indifferent, which are such things as God hath left to the free libertie of man to doe or not to . . . doe: is a deprivying of men of that libertie that God hath graunted unto them, & therefore such a lawe is neither good nor indifferent."[3] One sees immediately that the dispute over things indifferent is an aspect of the more general dispute over the authority of the ecclesiastical hierarchy in relation to the inner light of the individual. Nor is it difficult to anticipate the strategies each party pursues. The right, citing over and over again 1 Corinthians xiv, 40, "Let all things be done honestly and by order," attempts to restrict the area in which the individual has competence, and Anglican apologists point regularly to the dire consequences of allowing every man "to doe what he list." In Mason's words, "He that denieth this [i. e., Church authority over things indifferent], taketh away the Sunne out of the world, dissolveth universally the fabricke of government, overthroweth families, corporations, Churches, and king-doms, and wrappeth all things in the dismall darknesse of Anarchie and confusion."[4] To this antinomian fear the Puritan left opposes the doctrine of Christian liberty, which in its extreme form, as embraced by Milton, so expands the scope of individual conscience as to make even the commands and interdictions of the Decalogue nonbinding and things indifferent. Indeed the larger the claim made for the authority of the inner light, the larger the category of things indifferent, so that finally the left-wing definition is, like the Stoic definition, more philosophical than theological and tends toward the inclusion of everything: "There is nothing so good of it selfe, but it may be made Evill by accident, nothing so evill of it self but it may become good by accident. Nothing so good or Evil but it may become Indifferent by accident, nothing so Indifferent of it selfe but it may become Good or Evill by accident."[5]

By "accident," Bradshaw means "in a particular circumstance"; in his vision, therefore, good, evil, and indifferent are ever-present and ever-opera-tive categories, but they are not attached to any stipulated list of actions or objects. What this means is that the expansion of Christian liberty is also the expansion of Christian responsibility; for if, on the one hand, no action or object is intrinsically good or evil but, on the other hand, every action is either good or evil as it "doth either glorifie or dishonor God" in a particular circumstance, then the determination of the value of an object or action must be made again and again, and one cannot look for help to the enjoinings and forbiddings of any fixed formula, even if that formula is the Decalogue. The result is a moral life that is fraught with anxiety and danger, for in a world where every action, however small or large, is equally the potential vehicle of good or evil, no action can be taken without risk, and, indeed, "a man may by takynge up a straw or a rush commit a Moral vice. For example if he shoulde use to doe it in the time of prayer."[6] Paradoxically, then, the strong version of the doctrine of things indifferent ends by declar-ing, as does Lord Brooke in *A Discourse Opening the Nature of Episcopacy*, that nothing is indifferent.[7] The indifference of things obtains only in their existence apart from circumstances; but since our involvement with things is always circumstantial, they are never, for us at any one time, indifferent. As Milton says in a passage of the *Areopagitica*, "great care and wisdom is requir'd to the right managing of this point" (YP, II, 535). Care is required because the pitfalls are so many and so intimately related. On the one hand one must be wary lest one embrace something (an object, an action, a person) as good in and of itself and therefore as necessary, for that would be to make it one's God. This is exactly what Adam does when he decides that Eve is everything to him, and he receives a precise rebuke: "Was shee thy God, that her thou didst obey / Before his voice" (*PL* X, 145–46). On the other hand, one must be wary of declaring something (an object, an action, or a person) intrinsically evil, for that would be to shift the responsibility for evil from the intention or disposition of the agent to something external to and independent of him. This is what, in *Samson Agonistes*, Dalila does or tries to do in a number of directions as she argues in a variety of ways that the Devil made her do it. But on the third hand (that there is one is what makes the "right managing" so difficult), one must not conclude that because things (and actions and persons) are neither good nor bad in themselves, it doesn't matter very much whether one rejects them or embraces them. It always matters; it's just that the way in which it matters is not fixed once and for all in a list of intrinsically good and bad things, but must be determined, and then determined again, in the innumerable situations that make up the moral life.

Being faithful, then, to the doctrine of things indifferent (in its strong or philosophical version) requires the withstanding of three temptations: (1) the temptation of idolatry, or the temptation to label something absolutely and intrinsically good; (2) the temptation to judgment (which is at once an evasion of responsibility and an arrogation of responsibility), or the temptation to label something absolutely and intrinsically evil; and (3) the temptation to relaxation, or the temptation to think that because things are neither good nor evil in themselves they are neither good nor evil in practice. The relationship between these temptations is such that to withstand any one of them is to run the risk of courting another. In the very act of rejecting something as idolatrous, one may fall into the error of condemning it as inherently evil, and one may be so wary of the danger of either extreme that he will hazard no judgment at all and thereby abdicate his moral responsibility.

In *Paradise Regained* these are the errors that Christ is invited to make in every one of the temptations to which Satan exposes him. Thus, as we have seen, the temptation of Athens is not the temptation to accept the rules of Greek philosophy (and art and literature) but the temptation (1) to accept them as necessary, or (2) to reject them as absolutely forbidden, or (3) to say that one's relationship to them doesn't matter, for in this case, when they are being offered as necessary, it matters very much, and they must be rejected *for the time being*. The same formula (with slight variations) will do for all of the temptations. The banquet in Book II is presented to Christ as something he must eat, or alternatively as something from which he must abstain either because, (despite Satan's assertion to the contrary), the food includes "Meats by the Law unclean" (II, 328) or because the meats may have been offered first to idols. Christ's response is striking for what it does not say—for its evasiveness:

> Said'st thou not that to all things I had right?
> And who withholds my pow'r that right to use?
> Shall I receive by gift what of my own,
> When and where likes me best, I can command?
> I can at will, doubt not, as soon as thou,
> Command a Table in this Wilderness,
> And call swift flights of Angels ministrant
> Array'd in Glory on my cup to attend.
>
> (II, 379–86)

These lines have sometimes been read as an admission (or declaration) by Christ of his divinity, but they are nothing of the sort. Indeed, they admit, or declare, nothing. Rather, everything Christ says he says in the context of Satan's assertions, which he entertains as hypotheses; that is, Christ in effect argues, "Didn't you say (although I never claimed it and am not claiming it now) that everything belonged by right to me? And if what you say is true (although I am by no means affirming it), then, by your own words, there is no need for me to accept anything from you." In the second part of Christ's reply, the evasive work performed earlier by "Said'st thou not" (381) is done by "as soon as thou" (385). The boast Christ appears to make is no boast at all because the power he seems to claim—the power to command a table in the wilderness—he claims only insofar as it is also Satan's; not "I can do this," but "I can do this as well as you can." We, however, along with the two protagonists, know that Satan's power is not his own—he himself makes the point in Book I (377)—and therefore what looks like that assumption (and presumption) of Godhead is actually a refusal to claim it. The statement Christ is making is finally as complex and intricate as the doctrine (of things indifferent) he is affirming: "I don't need you, since I can do it myself just as well as you can; but since you can't in fact do it yourself, neither can I, and the only difference between us is that I know it, and glory in that knowledge." It is a remarkable linguistic performance, in which an assertion of radical dependence (on God, light from above, and so forth) is at the same time an assertion of radical independence (of Satan and his gifts). Moreover, all of this is managed, and necessarily so, without saying anything about the offered gifts (here the food) at all. The whole point of Satan's stage setting had been to get Christ to pronounce on the food one way or the other, but Christ neither embraces the food nor rejects it; instead he positions himself in such a way as to make no judgment on it at all. The strategy is available to him because the food does not correspond to a pressing need; he feels hunger but fears no harm, since he feels it

"Without this bodies wasting" (II, 256). In another situation, when the need was in fact pressing, his decision about the food—which is here to make no decision—might take another form, but here he can treat it as a thing indifferent and reject it on grounds of convenience and expediency ("as I like / The giver" [II, 321–22]).

Christ's performance here underlines a point that must be made with respect to each of the temptations: they are always more complicated than they seem at first because the terms in which they are posed are not explicitly stated. As Satan presents the issue, a temptation inheres in the embracing of a thing or action, and therefore it would seem that the proper response would be simply to reject the thing or action in question. But, as we have seen, this way of presenting the issue is as much of a trap as the proffered lure, because it makes externals rather than one's attitude towards them crucial. Christ therefore is always in the position of responding not to the overt but to the hidden terms of a temptation, and that is why his replies often seem oblique and beside the point. In fact they are reformulations of the point, in the course of which the true danger lurking in a Satanic appeal is exposed and thereby avoided. In one exchange that danger is so well hidden that only Christ and a single literary critic seem to have noticed it.[8] As Satan prepares to leave the Son at the end of the first day he makes what is apparently an almost casual request:

> Thy Father, who is holy, wise and pure,
> Suffers the Hypocrite or Atheous Priest
> To tread his Sacred Courts, and minister
> About his Altar, handling holy things,
> Praying or vowing, and vouchsaf'd his voice
> To *Balaam* Reprobate, a Prophet yet
> Inspir'd; disdain not such access to me.
>   To whom our Saviour with unalter'd brow.
> Thy coming hither, though I know thy scope,
> I bid not or forbid; do as thou find'st
> Permission from above; thou canst not more.
>   He added not.
>
>   (I, 486–97)

It would seem that the Son is here being tempted to accept the example of Balaam as an argument for permitting Satan to stay, but the real temptation is to assume that the permission is his either to grant or deny. Balaam is brought in by Satan largely as a diversionary tactic designed to draw attention away from the presumption inherent in the alternative actions the situation would seem to demand. If the Son welcomes Satan he will seem to be accepting him, if only on a social level (one of the things the Son is never guilty of in this poem is civility), and if the Son sends Satan away he will seem to claim a prerogative that belongs only to God. He of course does neither, and instead speaks in the precise and evasive language appropriate to the doctrine of things indifferent: "I bid not or forbid." It is not that he is indifferent to Satan's presence (he tells him more than once that he doesn't like him), but he knows that a power greater than his controls that presence: "do as thou find'st / Permission from above." In thus declaring the limits on Satan's freedom, the Son (characteristically) admits the limits on his own and steps out of the trap that has been set for him, a trap in which Satan himself is the bait. Later, in Book IV, Satan makes a quite different appeal, one that renders his presence far from indifferent, and Christ responds by saying what he declines to say here: "Get thee behind me" (IV, 193). The difference between this unequivocal rejection and the earlier refusal to reject is that in Book IV Satan offers himself as an idol—"On this condition, if thou wilt fall down, / And worship me as thy superior Lord" (IV, 166–67); as an idol Satan must be personally repudiated, whereas as a mere presence in the world he can be left to higher dispensation.

Again we see how nice the discriminations are that must be made and how easy it is to blur them or override them. When the narrative voice comments that the Son "added not" (497), he is paying tribute to the precision of Christ's performance; despite the opportunity to go too far in one direction or the other (by either embracing or judging Satan), the Son says just enough to establish his dependence, *and no more*. More would have almost certainly been self-assertion in some way or another, and Christ is in the business not of asserting the self but of giving it no scope—including linguistic scope—beyond that necessary to affirm his obedience. To obey or not to obey is the only issue ever at stake in *Paradise Regained*, although Satan is always trying to divert the Son's attention to other issues or, even more diabolically, to tempt him with a course of action that seems on its face to be the very manifestation of obedience. That is, the tempter urges the wrong thing but in a form that looks very much like the right one (a "false resemblance"), and in the first encounter that form is no less than charity. "But if thou be the Son of God, Command / That out of these hard stones be made thee bread; / So shalt thou save thyself and us relieve" (I, 342–44).

While it is easy to see what is wrong with working a miracle at the Devil's bidding, it is not so easy to see what is wrong with relieving the misery of others. The temptation to turn stones into bread is deliberately obvious and serves as a stalking horse for the real temptation, which is to do good works or, more precisely, to identify the doing of good works not as Milton identifies them in *Of Christian Doctrine*—as works informed by faith—but as works that answer to an empirically observable need. True works of faith may or may not redress social conditions, but when the redressing of social conditions is placed in the position of the highest obligation—as the action one *must* perform—then it becomes an action no less idolatrous than the action of falling down and worshipping a false God.

Indeed, it *is* a false God, because it has been identified as the one indispensable thing to do and therefore as necessary to salvation. All of this is comprehended in Christ's cryptic reply: "Think'st thou such force in Bread?" (I, 347). The force that Satan attributes to bread resides only with God, who of course may, if he chooses, use bread as his vehicle. As always the Son is careful not to err in either direction by making too much or too little of a thing indifferent. "Think'st thou *such* force in bread" does not deny that there is some force in bread, and "Man lives not by Bread only" (I, 349) silently insists that bread is one of the things—although not the necessary and sufficient thing—that man lives by. Again we see how great the care is that must go into the right managing of this point: if the Son had left out the word "only" he would have committed an error as fatal as the error he is explicitly tempted to commit, the error of making bread all.

The question "Think'st thou such force in ———?" identifies the danger and the way of avoiding it in every one of the scenes Satan constructs. Thinks thou such force in riches? in kingdoms? in arms? in manners? in civility? in literature? in philosophy? Satan continually offers these things as indispensable and necessary, and Christ continually rejects them *as they are offered*, while being very careful not to condemn them altogether and thus make them, rather than an interior disposition, the source of evil. My argument is not simply that the doctrine of things indifferent is to be found everywhere in *Paradise Regained*, but that *Paradise Regained* is a working out of the doctrine, and that because it is a working out of the doctrine every moment in it is necessarily the same: everything is *always* at stake. The consequences of this sameness for what one can say about the poem are far-reaching and in large part take the form of what one cannot say. One cannot say, for example, that there is any significance to the order of temptations or to the fact that more lines are devoted to some than others. I do not mean that one could not find reasons for the differences in proportion; the Athens temptation may be more elaborate than the temptation of riches because Milton felt that his readers were more likely to be literary than material idolaters. But this would not be a reason tied to the unfolding of a plot, to the gradual emergence of crisis, to a succession of choices, some of which are more important than others because they take the central figure further and further down a particular path until his destiny (for good or ill) is irreversible. In *Paradise Regained* one cannot say that this or that moment is crucial, because every moment is crucial (every moment offers an opportunity to be either faithful or idolatrous); one cannot say that *here* is where victory or defeat occurs, because the possibility of their occurrence is ever-present and ever-renewed; one cannot say that *this* decision makes all the difference, because it is a decision that will have to be made again in the very next moment; one cannot say "from this point it is all downhill," because the poem has neither steep inclines nor easy descents but is always pitched at the same level of tension that makes reading it so strenuous. Like the Son, *you* can never relax.

The fact remains, however, that these things that one cannot say about *Paradise Regained* are what critics are always saying, although they are not always saying them in the same way. To a great extent the history of *Paradise Regained* criticism is a history of attempts to establish just those kinds of distinctions (between one episode and another, between degrees of danger and risk, between the ease and difficulty of diverse temptations) that are subversive of the poem's lesson. Whether it is the triple temptation, or the three offices of Christ, or the neoplatonic tripartite soul, or the scale of ethical goods, or the responsibilities of the Church, or the recovery by the hero of his divine knowledge, the models that have been proposed as providing the structure of the poem always have the effect of dividing it up, of fore-grounding some moments at the expense of others, of identifying climaxes, resolutions, and denouements, of declaring some scenes integral and others preliminary or ceremonial—the effect, in short, of giving the poem a plot. The disagreement as to exactly what the plot is has led to differing character-izations of its shape and to a host of questions and debates. Is the gluttony temptation an extension of the bread-into-stones temptation, or does it belong to another episode? If the first temptation is the temptation of dis-trust, what do you say about the temptation of the tower? Is the answer to this question to be found in Milton's following of Luke's sequence rather than Matthew's? Since the storm scene is not found in any of the biblical accounts, is it a temptation at all, or simply a "dramatic interlude"? In fact how many temptations are there? Every number from three to nine has been given as an answer, and with each answer one or more of the temptations is divided into two, three, four, five, . . . parts. As Edward Tayler has recently observed. "The arithmetical gymnastics in this arena do not inspire confidence in our profession."[9]

There is an even severer judgment to be made: the critics who are busy debating the kinds of schematizations and formal organizations that should be kept in mind when reading *Paradise Regained* are, in effect, doing the Devil's work. It is Satan's effort in the poem to persuade Jesus to those differences and distinctions, hierarchies of values, that will obscure the sin-gleness of his obligation and get him to abandon what he knows to be the most important thing (obedience to God) for the thing (or action) that seems to be the most important in the light of some partial (that is, empirical) perspective. It is Satan's effort, in short, to divert the Son's attention from his chosen allegiance ("me hungering to do the Father's will") by urging on him the allegiances (to social reform, the arts, charitable works) that seem to be demanded by changing circumstances. That is why plot is so crucial to Satan's strategy (a strategy in which he himself believes): plot is always saying, "The situation has changed, and you must now rethink what it is that you have to do"; the Son is always saying (even when he doesn't say it), "The situation cannot have changed because there is only one situation, and what you have to do is what you have always had to do, affirm your loyalty to God." Satan builds plots (like mousetraps) by presenting inessential differences as if they were constitutive, and the Son unbuilds them by seeing through those differences to the eternal choice (between God and idols) they really present. But what the Son unbuilds, the critics build up again, multiplying distinctions, insisting on progressions, labelling beginnings, middles, and ends, and in general acting as extensions of the Satanic effort.

They are, of course, encouraged in their activities by the poem, which after all does have four books, frequent changes of scene, varying styles, temporal signatures, announced shifts of topic, shorter and longer speeches—everything, in short, that would support the assumption that different things are at stake at different times. While it is true, as I have been asserting, that the poem is everywhere the same, it is not obviously so, and it is the task of the reader to penetrate to that sameness amidst so many signs of difference. It is a task made more difficult by the performance of the Son, who sees the signs of difference *immediately* for what they are (camouflage and distractions) and therefore does not need to go through the effort of setting them aside. As a result he presents a difficult model, one who as often as not leaves out the steps that would enable someone to follow him and therefore contributes to the possibility of misunderstanding the nature of what he does.

This possibility is perhaps greatest in the tower or pinnacle scene, which has a critical literature of its own. The two points at issue are (1) whether or not this scene is a part of the temptation proper or is a "climactic epilogue" to an action already complete, and (2) whether this confrontation is decisive in a way that its predecessors were not. Those who would detach the episode from the main body of the poem take their cue partly from the narrator, who says of Satan at the conclusion of the Athens temptation, "for all his darts were spent" (IV, 366), and partly from Satan himself when he announces "Another method I must now begin" (IV, 540). To the extent that a reader takes Satan at his word (surely a questionable procedure), he will be prepared to find this scene unlike the others, but to the extent that he remains undistracted by this final stage direction (for so it is) he will be able to discern with Christ (who says at line 497, "desist, thou are discern'd") the same old trap with its attendant and familiar dangers.

That trap takes the form (as it has before) of presenting the Son with two alternative courses of actions, either of which would constitute presumption. He can "stand upright" (IV, 551) or he can cast himself down. The first would be an assertion of his divinity (an "I can command a table in the wilderness" without the saving qualification of "as soon as thou"), and the second would be to make a trial of God by commanding him to a particular performance ("See, I am putting my trust in you; now save me!"). The strategy is once again to position the Son in such a way that anything he does will be to Satan's advantage; at the very least he will finally know who his adversary is: if the Son stands upright, he is divine; if he falls, he is mere man; if he casts himself down, he will invite God to save him, and, whether God or man, he will be violating the discipline of faith and obedience. If this were all, the temptation would be subtle enough, but Satan adds another turn to its screw by offering as a *reason* for the Son's casting himself down the testimony of Scripture:

> Cast thy self down; safely if Son of God:
> For it is written, He will give command
> Concerning thee to his Angels, in thir hands
> They shall up lift thee, lest at any time
> Thou chance to dash thy foot against a stone.
> (IV, 555–59)

The brilliance of this last move inheres in its apparent fidelity to Christ's own principle of action as he has often invoked it. Man does not live by bread alone but by the Word of God, he declares at the first encounter, and in every subsequent encounter the Word of God is preferred to the various words spoken by the world. As recently as line 175, the Son has turned away a temptation with the formula "It is written," and when Satan appropriates the same formula here he seems to be inviting the Son to reaffirm an allegiance he has himself repeatedly proclaimed. This is not simply the temptation to presumption (although it is surely that), but the temptation of Scripture.

That is, in addition to the choice of standing or casting himself down Satan gives Christ the choice of either embracing the Scripture (and with it Satan's urgings) or rejecting it. He of course does neither; instead he adds it to the ever-growing and finally all-inclusive list of things indifferent. Satan presents the Scripture as if its value were independent of its use, as if it were good in and of itself, but the value of the Scripture, no less than the value of riches or learning, depends on the spirit with which it is appropriated. Like anything else the Scripture can be perverted; the Devil can quote it. What Satan offers is not the Scripture pure and simple (there is no such thing) but a reading of it which makes it an extension of the presumption he urges. The Son rejects that reading (just as earlier he rejects the signs and portents of the storm: "not sent from God, but thee" [IV, 491]), and then, in order to show that it is the interpreter and not the Scripture he rejects, he attaches himself to another verse, one that names the impiety with which a thing indifferent has been polluted: "Tempt not the Lord thy God; he said and stood" (IV, 561). It is a brilliantly compressed moment that not only illustrates in the most rigorous way the doctrine of things indifferent (by extending it to include even Scripture) but also gives definitive form to the analogous doctrine of false resemblances:

> Who therefore seeks in these
> True wisdom, finds her not, or by delusion
> Far worse, her false resemblance only meets,
> An empty cloud.
>
> (IV, 318–21)

The distinction between true and false resemblances is not a distinction between different things (one of which is superficially like the other), but between different attitudes or intentional dispositions toward the same thing, which is therefore no longer the same. Thus, in this case, the Scriptures, when they are quoted by the Devil or for diabolic purposes, are not true resemblances of themselves but are hollow forms, or, as the Son puts it, "empty clouds," just as when bread is made into an idol it does not nourish but wastes, and when poetry is detached from the praising of God, it is "As varnish on a Harlots cheek" (IV, 344). Nowhere is Milton's relentless interiorization of value more dramatically on display than it is here, when his hero looks at the Bible itself and finds it no more intrinsically valuable than the things—bread, riches, kingdom, learning—that he has earlier rejected in its name.[10]

It is by resisting the temptation to make an idol of the Scriptures that the Son can be said to stand in line 561: "Tempt not the Lord thy God; he said and stood." The correct way to read this line, and a way that will seem inevitable if one understands what the Son has done by answering Scripture with Scripture, is to read "and stood" as "and in so doing (that is, in saying that) stood firm, remained unaltered and unmoved." This reading has the advantage of deemphasizing the physical or punctual sense of "stood," which if allowed to be heard too strongly presents this as a decisive and climactic gesture: he stood up in triumph, he stood revealed as God, and so forth. But this is precisely what Satan (and some readers) want and what the Son refuses to do—that is, treat this moment as something different, as one in which *more* is at stake, in which everything is settled; as, in fact, a fight or a local duel. Instead the Son treats this moment as he has every other, not by making some definitive declaration or taking some action that would amount to the "single stroke" for which so many of Milton's heroes and villains and readers long, but by being, as he has been so many times before, creatively evasive. He does not stand up in a grand flourish of assertion, nor does he cast himself down in an impetuous hazarding of all. He does the only thing that Satan could not imagine him doing; he does nothing, or as Barbara Lewalski puts it in what remains the single best account of the moment, he calmly maintains "the impossible posture into which Satan has thrust him."[11] Just how impossible that posture is one cannot finally say; Satan is not himself sure of the matter: he only says "to stand upright / Will ask thee skill" (IV, 551–52). This comment suggests that there is a level of skill—short of miracle—that would suffice, but that Satan does not expect the Son or any other mere man to have it. That he does have it, and that it is not a skill dependent on divine intervention (whether of the Son or the Father), is evidenced by the phrase "uneasy station" (IV, 584), which suggests not a revealed God standing gloriously at front and center stage but a man who is doing the best that he can in a difficult situation to be true to the best that he knows.

The station is uneasy because it is precarious; it requires balance. It is thus a perfect visual emblem of what has been required of the Son all along, a keeping to a path so straight and narrow that the deviation of a single step to the right or left would prove disastrous. What the Son does not do here—swerve in one direction or another—is the physical equivalent of what he does not say in Book I: "he added not." In both cases the discipline of obedience is perfect, but it is a discipline, and one that must be exercised continually, rather than during a single and final moment after which all trial and struggle cease.

There is no final moment in *Paradise Regained*. In this last scene, which ends nothing, the Son does no more or less than he does before and will have to do again: he refuses to locate value in a thing indifferent, even though that thing is the Scripture, and he refuses to reduce the moral life to a single climactic action in which everything is settled once and for all. Indeed these two temptations—the temptation to either embrace or reject and the temptation to dream of a fight or a duel—are finally one and the same, for they are both invitations to externalize the moral life, either by making good and evil the property of things or by making the struggle between good and evil an event in the world of circumstances rather than a succession of events in the inner world of spiritual choice; and, by the same reasoning, they are both temptations that find their perfect expression in the dynamics of plot, which, by substituting the curve and arc of greater and lesser moments for the straight line of a moment endlessly repeated, relieves us of the obligation to be perpetually alert.

It is of course always Milton's way to present his readers with the most compelling form of the temptation he would have them resist. And in *Paradise Regained* we are certainly invited to assume that *this* is the local duel of which Adam is to dream not. For this assumption we have no less an authority than the angels of heaven, who sing "Victory and Triumph to the Son of God / Now entring his great duel" (I, 173–74). But then the qualification follows immediately: "his great duel, not of arms, / But to vanquish by wisdom hellish wiles" (I, 174–75). And when the " vanquishing" finally does occur it is like every other noncontest in Milton's poetry and prose. First of all, there is no contact; Satan falls not because he has been hit but because he has *not* been hit, because he has failed once again to draw from Christ that frontal assault, that deliberate single stroke, that would at least tell Satan where he is and with whom he is dealing ("For Son of God to me is yet in doubt" [IV, 501]). What amazes Satan is not a new revelation but the ability of his antagonist (whoever he is) to evade the demand for a revelation without resorting to easy quietism (to do something at the same time that he declines to do anything). What amazes him is the Son's perfect balance despite an "uneasy station" and, totally unbalanced himself (as he always has been), he falls.

But then he doesn't; or doesn't fall in any sense that allows us to say, "Well, that's over" or even to point to *that* fall as opposed to any other. Rather he falls and rises again and again, and for seventy-five lines. First he falls in a comparison with Anteus, who in his own career mirrors the Satanic ability to rise again ("and oft foil'd still rose, / Receiving from his mother Earth new strength, / Fresh from his fall" [IV, 565–69]); then he falls in a comparison with the Sphinx (the answer to whose riddle is like the answer to Satan's question: man [IV, 572–76]), but he falls not to the ground but into a seminar: "And to his crew, that sat consulting, brought / Joyless triumphals of his hop't success" (IV, 577–78). But this has happened before, and although we aren't told so, the diabolic consulting will no doubt produce new resolves and new plans; meanwhile Satan is not better or worse off than when Belial asked in Book II of *Paradise Lost*, "is this then worst, / Thus sitting, thus consulting?" (II, 163–64). The refrain "So Satan fell" (580) already sounds much less climactic than the first report of his "fall" (562). There are, however, other and severer falls in store for Satan, and they are rehearsed by the angelic choir beginning at line 596. They recall Satan's first fall ("and down from Heav'n cast / With all his Army" [IV, 605–06]) and speak of this new fall as if it were an act of completion ("now thou hast . . . / . . . regain'd lost Paradise" [IV, 606–08]). But then they look forward to another fall that sounds just like the first ("thou shalt fall from Heav'n trod down" [IV, 620]), and this present fall is demoted to a preliminary status:

> thou feel'st
> Thy wound, yet not thy last and deadliest wound
> By this repulse receiv'd, and hold'st in Hell
> No triumph.
>
> (IV, 621–24)

But he still holds something in Hell, and he will no doubt venture forth again, if only so that again the Son "Shall chase thee with the terror of his voice / From thy Demoniac holds" (IV, 627–28). When at line 634 the Son receives the epithet "Queller of Satan," one can only read it as referring not to an action already performed and done with but to an action that will have to be performed again and again. "Queller of Satan" is not a title you have by right after only one encounter but a title that must be earned repeatedly.

The effect of what Joan Webber has called "these remarkable lines" is to diminish the dramatic impact of any one of these falls by removing them from the story line of a plot into a timeless realm where they are eternally occurring. It is, as Webber goes on to say, a story "which is without beginning or end, and yet begins and ends at every point." I can do no better than reproduce her summary statement: "Both space and time are of infinite importance and of no importance at all. The Son is everywhere. He has warred, and has yet to war down Satan. Paradise is regained and Satan's power ended as if it had never been; Satan still rules and is yet to be cast out. His snares are broken, but Jesus has not yet begun to save mankind. The Son is everyone and the battle is within."[12] This is of course the lesson of Michael's rebuke—"Not by destroying Satan, but his works / In thee and in thy Seed"—but it is a lesson that one can never learn too often. In the closing lines of the poem Milton gives us an opportunity to learn it again as he instructs us for the last time as to how not to read his poem. The moment is, as it should be, at once small and large; its pressure barely perceptible yet as great as anything we feel in the course of four books. It is, quite characteristically, a moment *between* lines: "now thou hast aveng'd / Supplanted *Adam*, and by vanquishing / Temptation, hast regain'd lost Paradise" (IV, 606–08). There are several surprises here. First there is the slight surprise of hearing that it is Adam and not the Father who is avenged, a surprise that reminds us that this was done for our sake, and not as a matter of family honor. And then there is the complicated ambiguity of "supplanted," which means both "overthrown" or "pushed off balance," as Adam certainly was by Satan, and "superseded" or "ousted," as Adam is now by Christ, who, as George Herbert never tires of reminding us, in saving us disables us to perform in any way that he has not already made possible. But the biggest (although in presentation very small) surprise is the one that awaits us in line 608 when we discover that the object of "vanquishing" is not Satan, as the military language and the scene just past would seem to dictate, but temptation. "Temptation" is not only the word we get; it correctly names our desire for the word we didn't get. That is, it is a temptation to expect something other than (the word) *temptation*, to expect an *external* object of "vanquishing," and insofar as we succumb to it we prove again on our pulse the power and appeal of that dream to which Adam falls when he asks, "say where and when / Thir fight."[13]

Notes

1.   Bernard J. Verkamp, *The Indifferent Mean* (Detroit, 1978), p. 21.
2.   *The Authoritie of the Church in making Canons and Constitutions concerning things Indifferent* (London, 1607), p. 4. S's and u's have been modernized.
3.   William Bradshaw, *A Treatise of the Nature and Use of Things Indifferent* (London, 1605), pp. 25–26. S's and *u*'s have been modernized.
4.   *Authoritie of the Church*, pp. 9, 13–14.

5.   Bradshaw, *Treatise*, pp. 16–17.

6.   Ibid., p. 20.

7.   See Lord Brooke, *A Discourse Opening the Nature of Episcopacy* (London, 1642), p. 26.

8.   See Burton Jasper Webber, *Wedges and Wings: The Patterning of "Paradise Regained"* (Carbondale, Ill., 1975), pp. 19–20.

9.   *Milton's Poetry: Its Development in Time* (Pittsburgh, 1979), p. 254.

10.   See CD, I, xxx, where Milton makes a distinction between Scripture which is simply external, i.e., the written word, and the internal Scripture which is written on our hearts by the spirit:

> Under the gospel we possess, as it were, a two-fold Scripture; one external, which is the written word, and the other internal, which is the Holy Spirit, written in the hearts of believers according to the promise of God, and with the intent that it should by no means be neglected; as was shown above, chap. xxvii. on the gospel. Hence, although the external ground which we possess for our belief at the present day in the written word is highly important, and, in most instances at least, prior in point of reception, that which is internal, and the peculiar possession of each believer, is far superior to all, namely, the Spirit itself.
>
> (*The Student's Milton*, ed. Frank Allen Patterson [New York, 1930], p. 1041)

11.   *Milton's Brief Epic: The Genre, Meaning, and Art of "Paradise Regained"* (Providence, 1966), p. 316.

12.   See *Milton and His Epic Tradition* (Seattle, 1979), pp. 206–08.

13.   Any student of Milton criticism will know that the present interpretation builds on the work of far more predecessors than have been cited in these notes. Northrop Frye neatly articulated the doctrine of things indifferent (although he did not use that phrase) when he explained that "the moral status of the instrumental depends on the mental attitude toward; if the initial attitude is one of dependence, the instrument will become an illusory end in itself" ("The Typology of *Paradise Regained*," in *Milton: Modern Essays in Criticism*, ed. A. E. Barker [New York, 1965], p. 435). And at about the same time, A. S. P. Woodhouse *did* name the doctrine (which of course had already been extensively discussed by Barker in his brilliant and still authoritative study *Milton and the Puritan Dilemma* [Toronto, 1942]) and specify its relationship to Satan's temptations: "One must remember of course that all Satan's gifts and suggestions are offered with evil intent, to betray Christ, in one way or other, into disobedience to God. Even though what was offered were in itself a thing indifferent, like the apple in Eden, it would become evil in the circumstances as it came into competition with obedience to God" ("Theme and Pattern in *Paradise Regained*," *University of Toronto Quarterly*, XXV [1955–56], 178). Many have characterized *Paradise Regained* as static rather than as dramatic, sometimes in complaint, sometimes in praise. For the latter, see especially Jackson I. Cope, *"Paradise Regained: Inner Ritual"* (*Milton Studies*, I, ed. James D. Simmonds [Pittsburgh, 1969], pp. 51–65), and Tayler, *Milton's Poetry*, passim. Ralph Condee has commented well on the extent to which Milton in this poem "rejects the normal devices of suspense in a plot," allowing a moment of suspense occasionally only in order to "dismiss it" (*Structure in Milton's Poetry* [University Park, 1974], pp. 167, 168). This rejection of course also entails the rejection of those psychological readings in which the point of the poem is the hero's development or growing self-awareness. Here I stand with Irene Samuel when she writes that "to read [*Paradise Regained*] as a 'Who Am I?' poem is to limit it to a mimesis of the particular, a matter for the historian-chronicler-biographer-theologian; to read it as a 'How am I to live?' poem is to see its availability as the mimesis of a universal action, a program for every man" ("The Regaining of Paradise," in *The Prison and the Pinnacle* [Toronto, 1973], p. 126). It seems to me (as it does to Samuel) equally limiting to read the

poem as an attempt by Satan to discover the identity of his adversary, at least if one assumes in such a reading that discovery is possible. Given Milton's radical identification of perception with moral status, it would be impossible for Satan to know who the Son is unless he himself were "a composition and patterne" of the same "best and honourablest things" (YP, I, 890). Sameness, in short, is a condition of recognition, so that for Satan to recognize the Son, he would first have to be like him, and then he would no longer be Satan. Finally, for a reading that appeared after this one was already in press, but which is supporting and confirming, see Alan Fisher, "Why is *Paradise Regained* So Cold?" (*Milton Studies*, XIV, ed. James D. Simmonds [Pittsburgh, 1980], pp. 195–217). Fisher's essay is preceded in that same volume by two pieces—Mary Wilson Carpenter, "Milton's Secret Garden," and William B. Hunter, Jr., "The Double Set of Temptations in *Paradise Regained*"—which demonstrate that the impulse to understand the poem by distinguishing and arranging its episodes into some structure or plot is still very much alive.

Paradise Regained and the Politics of Martyrdom

Laura Lunger Knoppers*

At the later end of the year 1648 I had leave given mee to goe to london to see my Father & during my stay there at that time at Whitehal it was that I saw the Beheading of King Charles the first; He went by our door on Foot each day that hee was carry'd by water to Westminster, for hee took Barge at Garden-stayres where wee liv'd, & once hee spake to my Father & sayd Art thou alive yet! On the day of his execution, which was Tuesday, Jan. 30, I stood amongst the crowd in the street before Whitehal gate, where the scaffold was erected, and saw what was done, but was not so near as to hear any thing. The Blow I saw given, & can truly say with a sad heart; at the instant whereof, I remember wel, there was such a Grone by the Thousands then present, as I never heard before & desire I may never hear again.

—Philip Henry diary[1]

The execution of Charles I followed nearly a decade of fighting in print and with arms over the nature and limits of kingship.[2] The revolutionary Independents had, with the support of the army, purged parliament and set up the Court of High Commission, which tried, condemned, and sentenced Charles. Both the trial and execution were public displays, designed to persuade the people that Charles was being justly punished for capital offenses against them. But the groan of the crowd as the king's head was severed from his body might have warned the revolutionaries of an audience not quite so tractable or convinced as they had hoped. In its response the audience demonstrated that the effects of punishment cannot be fully controlled by the mechanisms of exemplary power. The public display of punishment, dependent upon its audience, was immediately challenged and subverted by the discourse of martyrdom. The execution was followed shortly by the publication of *Eikon Basilike*, the "King's Book," which interpreted Charles's refusal to submit to the court not as obstinacy but as constancy, and his death not as just punishment for treason but as martyrdom. The cult of royal martyrdom which the *Eikon Basilike* initiated would meet with a deter-

* From *Modern Philology* 90 (November 1992): 200–19, Reprinted by permission of The University of Chicago Press.

mined and defiant opponent in John Milton. But, paradoxically, the royal
martyr would not die.

I

Despite their victory over Charles in the field, the revolutionaries struggled
in the trial and execution to win the ideological battle. On January 6, 1649,
the Commons accused Charles of tyranny, treason, and murder, charging
that he had "a wicked designe totally to subvert the antient and fundamentall
lawes and liberties of this nation. And in theire place to introduce an arbitrary
and tiranicall government . . . and hath prosecuted it with fire and sword,
levied and maintayned a cruell warre in the land against the Parliament and
kingdome."[3] The public trial of Charles I shows a transitional stage of
power between what Michel Foucault has delineated as the arbitrary torture
perpetrated by the ancien régime in France—a means of inducing horror
and terror in the viewer—and more condign punishment which links the
ideas of crime and penalty in the minds of the viewers.[4] The trial and
execution were part of the dramaturgy of state, designed to convince its
audience that the text of Charles's life must be read as treason, his death as
"exemplary and condigne punishment." The high court appealed to the
rhetoric of justice and divine providence to supplement or, more accurately,
occlude the force underlying the trial. John Cook, lawyer for the prosecution,
described the proceedings as "the most Comprehensive, Impartial and Glorious piece of Justice that ever was acted and Executed upon the Theatre of
England."[5] The Court of High Commission had not only a juridical but
also a moral and theological function. Shifting among various Old Testament
models by which their actions could be interpreted and justified, the court
fastened on the notion of bloodguilt. According to Cook, they acted for a
higher court in trying and judging Charles, "whom God in his wrath gave
to be a King to this nation, and will, I trust, in great love, for his notorious
Prevarications and Blood guiltiness take him away from us." In a drama
that is allegorical and didactic, Charles "stands now to give an account of
his stewardship and to receive the good of justice, for all the evil of his
injustice and cruelty.[6]

By staging the trial as a public display, the regicides strove to justify
but also exposed to open challenge the legitimacy of their cause. And Charles
refused to play his given role. The king acted out the part not of a penitent
sinner, which would have confirmed their case, but of a constant sufferer
for liberty and truth. Refusing to recognize the authority of the court, he
continually exposed the force which the display of justice attempted to cover:
"it is not my case alone, it is the Freedom and the Liberty of the people of
England; and do you pretend what you will, I stand more for their Liberties.

For if power without law may make lawes, may alter the fundamental laws of the kingdom, I do not know what subject he is in England, that can be sure of his life or any thing that he calls his own."[7] Charles rewrites the script, recasting the regicides' justice as a power which unlawfully threatens king and subject alike. As a king betrayed and tried by his own subjects, not allowed to speak in a court claiming justice, Charles soon found a more effective paradigm by which he could sustain and explain his case—that of martyrdom and, in particular, the royal martyrdom of Christ.

The scaffold as a theater for punishment, twinned with the public trial, shows the force of law and justice inscribed in the very body of the condemned. Yet the display of the punished traitor does not produce a single meaning. As Foucault explains, there is "an ambiguity in this suffering that may signify equally well the truth of the crime or the error of the judges, the goodness or evil of the criminal, the coincidence or the divergence between the judgement of men and that of God."[8] Ironically, the Independents themselves make Charles a martyr by trying and executing him publicly. Charles's speech and demeanor during his trial and execution, fully reported and put into circulation, have unexpected consequences. On the scaffold, as during the trial, Charles refuses to play his assigned role. No scaffold confession, acknowledging his own guilt and the justice of the state which punishes him, is forthcoming. On the contrary, Charles asserts his innocence and models himself on the royal martyr, Christ. Like Christ, he forgives his enemies: "I have forgiven all the world, and even those in particular that have been the chief causes of my death . . . I pray God forgive them." Claiming to die as "the Martyr of the people," Charles looks to a crown of martyrdom: "I go from a corruptible to an incorruptible crown, where no disturbance can be, no disturbance in the world." He bravely meets the execution which follows: "After a little pause, the King stretching forth his hands, the Executioner at one blow severed his head from his body, and held it up and shewed it to the people, saying, 'Behold the head of a Traitor.' "[9] But already the theater of punishment was crumbling.

In ceremonies of public execution the main character was the crowd, whose presence and belief was required for the performance. But the audience at Charles's execution was unreliable. Philip Henry reports that the soldiers, apparently fearing a negative reaction, immediately dispersed the crowd: "There was according to Order one Troop immediately marching from-wards charing-cross to Westm[inster] & another from-wards Westm[inster] to charing cross purposely to masker the people, & to disperse & scatter them, so that I had much adoe amongst the rest to escape home without hurt."[10] The audience did not cooperate in the official spectacle but sought another meaning, another kind of tragedy. A Royalist newspaper, *Mercurius Elencticus* (Tuesday, January 30), reports that the people rushed to buy relics of the dead king. For the people Charles was a martyr; for the soldiers he was a means of making money: "When they had murdered him, such as desired to dip their handkerchiefes or other things in his blood, were admitted for moneys. Others bought peeces of board which were dy'd with his blood, for which the soldiers took of some a shilling, of others half a crowne, more or lesse according to the quality of the persons that sought it. But none without ready money." The soldiers continued to profit: "And after his body was coffin'd, as many as desired to see it were permitted at a certaine rate, by which meanes the soldiers got store of moneys, insomuch that one was heard to say 'I would we had two or three more such Majesties to behead, if we could but make such use of them.' "[11] The soldier's wish would be granted, although not in the form he might have imagined. Charles would indeed reappear in the ensuing cult of royal martyrdom which left the regicides and Cromwellian government with many Charleses to confront, many new majesties to behead.

II

The publication of *Eikon Basilike* immediately after Charles's execution marked a new stage in the struggle between the monarch and his foes. "Prayers and tears" would ultimately be more effective than the weapons of warfare which had failed to make good the king's cause, the discourse of martyrdom more effective than the spectacle of treason. After the Restoration, the probable coauthor (or true author) of *Eikon Basilike*, John Gauden, exulted in martial metaphor over its publication: "When it came out, just upon the King's death; Good God! What shame, rage and despite filled hys Murtherers! What comfort hys friends! How many enemyes did it convert! How many hearts did it mollify, and melt! . . . What preparations it made in all men's minds for this happy restauration . . . In a word, it was an army, and did vanquish more than any sword could."[12] Although much of the *Eikon Basilike* gives a detailed defense of Charles's political actions and decisions, most compelling are its rhetoric of piety and claim to a Christlike martyrdom for Charles that skillfully adapts the precedent of John Foxe's "Book of Martyrs."[13] *Eikon Basilike* impresses Charles's story with the distinctive contours of Foxe's martyrology as the king endures affliction, remains true to his conscience, and suffers the rage and malice of his enemies. But the "King's Book" also conflates Charles's sufferings with Christ's, merging the Foxean portrait of the martyr with the rich and resonant biblical and literary tradition of royal martyrdom. In so doing, *Eikon Basilike* develops a powerful discourse for idealizing Charles and stigmatizing his enemies.

Like the "Book of Martyrs," *Eikon Basilike* is self-consciously concerned with defining and portraying true martyrdom. Charles explicitly claims this status: "They knew my chiefest arms left me were those only which the ancient Christians were wont to use against their persecutors—prayers and tears. These may serve a good man's turn, if not to conquer as a soldier, yet to suffer as a martyr" (p. 47). And he denies martyrdom to his political opponents: "Some parasitic preachers have dared to call those 'martyrs' who died fighting against me, the laws, their oaths, and the religion established. But sober Christians know that glorious title can with truth be applied only to those who sincerely preferred God's truth and their duty in all these particulars before their lives and all that was dear to them in this world" (pp. 118–19). Charles claims the martyrs' constancy, commenting: "Here I am sure to be conqueror if God will give me such a measure of constancy as to fear him more than man and to love the inward peace of my conscience before any outward tranquility" (p. 38), for, "what they [my enemies] call obstinacy, I know God accounts honest constancy" (p. 138). Charles also prays: *"Give me that measure of patience and constancy which my condition now requires"* (p. 139). Such frequent references to conscience, patience, and constancy create a compelling portrait of Charles, the martyr-king.

While the "King's Book" portrays Charles as suffering and dying for the church as well as for the more strictly political cause of monarchy, the issues are inseparable because this martyr's truth is bound even more to an internal political power struggle than are those in Foxe's massive tome. While it would be naive to deny the political implications in Foxe's virulently anti-Catholic accounts of martyrdom, his Marian martyrs at least debate theological issues, albeit ones with political import—transubstantiation, purgatory and the penitential system (confession, indulgences, meritorious works), marriage of the clergy, and papal supremacy. *Eikon Basilike* appropriates and further politicizes the discourse of martyrdom, employing its rhetoric to interpret such specific events and points of dispute in the English civil war as "His Majesty's Calling This Last Parliament," "The Listing and Raising Armies against the King," "Their Seizing the King's Magazines, Forts, Navy, and Militia," and "The Various Events of the War: Victories and Defeats" (pp. vii–viii). But despite the increased attention to details of contemporary political events, Gauden (with Charles) is able to draw much more fully than Foxe had on the tradition of Christ as royal martyr. Foxe's own relationship to monarchy is complex if not problematic.[14] Foxe writes to support Elizabeth and the established church, to advise the queen in her destined role as true sovereign; yet the martyrdoms he most vividly and elaborately recounts are those of middle- and lower-class subjects under conformity proceedings mandated by another monarch—bloody Queen Mary. Although Foxe briefly recounts Christ's passion and crucifixion, he makes no real use of the resonant biblical and literary tradition of Christ as royal martyr. *Eikon Basilike* thus draws on and dramatically revises the Foxean tradition in its compelling portrait of the martyr-king.

Associations with Christ's sufferings, passion, and death resonate throughout the "King's Book," elevating Charles's cause and stigmatizing his political enemies as traitors. "His Majesty's Retirement from Westminster" and his refusal to comply with parliamentary demands are presented as a choice of kingly martyrdom: "I will rather choose to wear a crown of thorns with my Saviour than to exchange that of gold, which is due to me, for one of lead" (p. 28). Foregrounding his divine type, Charles implicitly compares "Raising Armies against the King" with the crucifixion of a forgiving Christ: *"when Thy wrath is appeased by my death, O remember Thy great mercies toward them and forgive them, O my Father, for they know not what they do"* (p. 46). The "Troubles in Ireland" (in which the king stood accused of fomenting a Catholic uprising) are depicted in terms of Christ's suffering on the cross: "Therefore with exquisite malice they have mixed the gall and vinegar of falsity and contempt with the cup of my affliction" (p. 63). Similarly, the "Scots Delivering the King to the English" is compared to Judas's selling of Christ: "If I am sold by them, I am only sorry they should do it and that my price should be so much above my Saviour's" (p. 137).

Finally, in the "Meditations upon Death" which conclude *Eikon Basilike*, Charles moves from justifying specific actions to constructing more fully the myth of the royal martyr by which his life and death may be interpreted. Charles refers to "those greater formalities whereby my enemies, (being more solemnly cruel) will, it may be, seek to add (as those who crucified Christ) the mockery of justice to the cruelty of malice" (p. 174). Echoing Christ's words in the garden of Gethsemane, Charles professes willingness to accept the bitter cup: *"Thou givest me leave as a man to pray that this cup may pass from me; but Thou hast taught me as a Christian by the example of Christ to add, not my will, but Thine be done"* (p. 181). He claims conformity with Christ's martyrdom: "If I must suffer a violent death with my Saviour, it is but mortality crowned with martyrdom" (p. 179). And Charles is explicit in acknowledging that his martyrdom will be a paradoxical victory: "My next comfort is that He gives me not only the honor to imitate His example in suffering for righteousness' sake, (though obscured by the foulest charges of tyranny and injustice), but also that charity which is the noblest revenge upon and victory over, my destroyers" (p. 176). Like Foxe's martyrs whose constancy in burning at the stake astonished and amazed onlookers, and like Christ on the cross, to whom the Roman centurion pays tribute, Charles will experience death but no defeat. The regicides' apparent failure to understand the power of martyrdom is a crucial and ultimately irreparable mistake.

III

The "King's Book" brilliantly subverted the exemplary power of the state, recasting the public trial and execution of Charles as a drama of suffering and martyrdom. Gauden's colleagues responded in kind. The book initiated an outpouring of elegies and hyperbolic laments on Charles the royal martyr.[15] Focusing on his final days and his death, the martyrologies greatly elaborate the parallels with Christ's passion and crucifixion, paying little attention to details of the political struggle. Diverging from Foxe and elaborating on the *Eikon Basilike*, the martyrologies construct a full picture of Charles as a uniquely royal martyr. For the first time, Charles is given a sympathetic—even weeping—audience. The author of *An Elegie Upon the Death of Our Dread Soveraign Lord King CHARLS the MARTYR* is typical:

> Com, com, let's Mourn; all eies, that see this *Daie*,
> Melt into Showrs, and Weep your selvs awaie:
> O that each Private head could yield a Flood
> Of Tears, whil'st *Britain's Head* stream's out His Blood.[16]

Flouting state censorship, the martyrologies poignantly link Charles with Christ in his passion and death, blackening the regicides with the powerfully resonant myth of the crucifixion.

The martyrologies recast the alleged justice of Charles's public trial and execution as a false, theatrical reenactment of Christ's trial and crucifixion. In a sermon which he would preach again eleven years later before Charles II, the bishop of Downe turns from the passion and death of Christ "to present unto you another sad tragedy, so like unto the former, that it may seem but *vetus fabula per novos histriones*, the stage onely changed, and new actors entred upon it."[17] *A Deep Groane Fetch'd At the Funerall of that Incomparable and Glorious Monarch, Charles the First* elaborates more fully on the tragic play:

> Such was their Bedlame Rabble, and the Cry
> Of Justice now, 'mongst them was *Crucifie*:
> *Pilates* Consent is *Bradshawes* Sentence here;
> The *Judgement hall's* remov'd to *Westminster*.
> Hayle to the Reeden Scepture the Head, and knee
> Act o're againe that Cursed Pageantrie.[18]

In this mock trial, Charles bears a unique resemblance to Christ. The Independents become the "Bedlame Rabble," Bradshaw takes the role of Pilate, and the trial at Westminster reenacts the "Cursed Pageantrie."

Focusing thus on the final days and hours of the king's life, elegies and sermons multiply links between the sufferings of Charles and Christ, much to the detriment of the king's accusers. *A Hand-Kirchife for Loyall Mourners* asserts,

It is a heavy thing to think on, that he should suffer by his own Judasses. But a joyfull and glorious thing it is to think on, that he suffered so like his own Jesus, so like him in the manner, and circumstances of his sufferings being betrayed by his owne servants, arraigned before Jewes and *Pilate*, at the best, reviled, reproached, and they say spit upon by an unworthy varlet, scorned and contemned & condemned unto death: so like him in the temper of his sufferings, with so much meeknesse and fortitude, undauntedness of spirit, and submission to the will of God.[19]

A number of tracts and sermons insist that the parallels between Charles and Christ are both striking and singular. *The Scotch Souldiers Lamentation Upon the Death of the most Glorious and Illustrious Martyr, King Charles* concludes, "There have beene many Martyrs, but no Martyr-Kings that I know of but my blessed Saviour Christ Jesus, and my late gracious Soveraigne Lord King Charles."[20]

In 1660, the martyrology tracts again proliferated with the restoration of the king's son, Charles II. Royalists republished and embellished *lachrymae ecclesiasticae* whose pathos and hyperbole were much the same as those in elegies, sermons, and memorials published just after the execution eleven years earlier. But now the tragedy turns to tragicomedy, even to comedy; the king's murderers are banished from the stage and the new king installed in the leading role. Anthonie Sadler's *The Loyall Mourner, Shewing the Murdering of King Charles the First: Fore-shewing the Restoring of King Charles the Second* traces the developments of the past decade:

> The King's Beheaded: and the Royall Crown's
> Script of *Monarchall* Rule: the Nobles down:
> The Souldier sways the Judge: the Sword, the Law:
> A Lawless Sword doth all the Kingdom awe.

Suddenly now the play has changed:

> the Theater's new Hung,
> A Proclamation made, the Bells are Rung,
> The King's Receiv'd, Loyalties Return'd;
> All in a night, and welcome Formes Reform'd,
> Peace Crowns the Kingdome, *all* in each degree,
> Act *pleasant* parts, and play a Comedy.[21]

The triumphal return of Charles II and the punishment of those who had supported the regicide seemed to confirm the martyrdom of Charles I; the true church, afflicted under the republic, was now restored.

The publishing and republishing of the martyrologies and the *Eikon Basilike* thus had important political ramifications in Restoration England. Like Foxe's "Book of Martyrs" dedicated to Elizabeth, the martyrologies implicitly or explicitly pointed to Charles II as the true monarch about to restore the church. And also like Foxe, the martyrologies instructed and guided Charles in the manner of establishing that church. The cult of the royal martyr exonerated the Anglican clergy, blackened the Independents, and provided a text by which to interpret the display of the new, even more theatrical Restoration monarchy. Even in their political victory, the Royalists seemed to retain firm control of the powerful discourse of martyrdom.

IV

In publishing the text of Charles's trial and execution and allowing the *Eikon* and the martyrologies to escape censorship, the Independents had seriously miscalculated the effects of the public execution. Too late, the new government commissioned John Milton to answer the "King's Book." Milton's *Eikonoklastes* (1649), although primarily a point-by-point rebuttal of the *Eikon Basilike*, also recognizes the cult of royal martyrdom which the "King's Book" had fostered. Milton rebukes the preachers who "howle in thir Pulpits" after the dead Charles and he tries (futilely, in the event) to repel the rhetoric of martyrdom with a combination of scorn and reason.[22] Milton attacks the *Eikon Basilike*, first of all, by reversing the charges of stagecraft: Charles's alleged martyrdom is false theatricality dependent on a deluded and idolatrous audience.[23] The frontispiece of the *Eikon Basilike*, which depicts a kneeling Charles about to exchange his golden crown for a crown of thorns, aims, according to Milton, to "Martyr him and Saint him to befool the people" (p. 343). The "conceited portraiture" of Charles is sleight-of-hand stage work, "drawn out to the full measure of a Masking Scene, and sett there to catch fools and silly gazers" (p. 342). Such "quaint Emblems and devices begg'd from the Old Pageantry of some Twelf-nights entertainment at *Whitehall* will doe but ill to make a Saint or Martyr" (p. 343). The "King's Book" is to be rejected as false and theatrical: "Stage-work will not doe it; much less *the justness of thir Cause*" (p. 530).

And yet the people are easy prey. Milton heaps scorn not only on the royal actor but on his gullible, doting, idolatrous audience: "The People, exorbitant and excessive in all thir motions, are prone ofttimes not to a religious onely, but to a civil kinde of Idolatry in idolizing thir Kings" (p. 343). The "King's Book" shows "what a miserable, credulous, deluded thing that creature is, which is call'd the Vulgar" (p. 426). Charles will never "stirr the constancie and solid firmness of any wise Man" but will only "catch the worthles approbation of an inconstant, irrational, and Image-doting rabble" (p. 601). The people, like a "credulous and hapless herd, begott'n to servility, and inchanted with these popular institutes of Tyranny" are themselves witness to "thir own voluntary and beloved baseness" (p. 601).

Charles's claim to martyrdom, then, is false and theatrical; the people's responses to such a claim are idolatrous and deluded. Milton scornfully dismisses Charles's claim to a Christlike crown of thorns since Charles, unlike Christ, suffers for his own faults: "Many would be all one with our Saviour, whom our Saviour will not know. They who govern ill those Kingdoms which they had a right to, have to our Saviours Crown of Thornes no right at all. Thornes they may find anow, of thir own gathering, and thir own twisting . . . but to weare them as our Saviour wore them is not giv'n to them that suffer by thir own demerits" (pp. 417–18). According to Milton, Charles's self-promotion undermines his own cause since "Martyrs bear witness to the truth, not to themselves": "If I beare witness of my self, saith *Christ*, my witness is not true. He who writes himself *Martyr* by his own inscription, is like an ill Painter, who, by writing on the shapeless Picture which he hath drawn, is fain to tell passengers what shape it is; which els no man could imagin" (p. 575). Suffering or dying with constancy, Milton objects, does not make a martyr: "Lastly, if to die for *the testimony of his own conscience*, be anough to make him Martyr, what Heretic dying for direct blasphemie, as som have don constantly, may not boast a Martyrdom?" (p. 576).

In discounting Charles's suffering and emphasizing the truth for which genuine martyrs suffer, Milton implicitly revives the etymology of martyrdom—"witnessing." If Milton primarily focuses in *Eikonoklastes* on denying Charles the name of martyr, he also constructs his own text as a counterexample, a true martyr or witness to the truth before God and man. *Eikonoklastes* comes to counter the king's false claims to the truth, impelled by the king's "making new appeale to Truth and the World" and leaving "this Book," *Eikon Basilike*, "as the best advocat and interpreter of his own actions" so that "his Friends by publishing, dispersing, commending, and almost adoring it, seem to place therein the chiefe strength and nerves of thir cause" (p. 340). Milton will oppose the *Eikon Basilike* by "remembring them the truth of what they themselves know to be heer misaffirm'd" (p. 338). Milton insists that this truth needs no reinforcement but is simply sent out "in the native confidence of her single self, to earn, how she can, her entertainment in the world, and to finde out her own readers; few perhaps, but those few, such of value and substantial worth, as truth and wisdom, not respecting numbers and bigg names, have bin ever wont in all ages to be contented with" (pp. 339–40).

Yet Milton's truth, like the king's, is embedded in and shaped by seventeenth-century politics. As an object of political debate and ideological struggle, such truth is not, in Foucault's words, "outside power, or lacking in power."[24] When, as confuter of Charles, Milton claims to be part of the "sole remainder" or remnant selected by God "to stand upright and stedfast in his cause; dignify'd with the defence of truth and public libertie" (p. 348), he politicizes not only martyrdom but also the truth to which martyrs bear witness. Later in the work, he more radically conflates truth with justice and claims both were operative in executing the king: "either Truth and

Justice are all one, for Truth is but Justice in our knowledge, and Justice is but Truth in our practice . . . or els, if there be any odds, that Justice though not stronger then truth, yet by her office is to put forth and exhibit more strength in the affaires of mankind" (pp. 583–84). Writing thus, Milton hopes to "set free the minds of English men from longing to returne poorly under the Captivity of Kings, from which the strength and supreme Sword of Justice hath deliverd them" (p. 585). Like the Royalists, Milton strives to appropriate and deploy justice and truth for his political cause: once again, it is clear that such truth is a thing of this world, produced and defined in ideological struggle.

Central to *Eikonoklastes*, then, is Milton's rebuttal of Charles's claim to cap the Foxean tradition of martyrdom. To Charles's false, theatrical martyrdom, Milton opposes his own witness to the truth, a revised and reconstituted kind of martyrdom. Ironically, after the Restoration, *Eikonoklastes* itself suffered the traditional fate of a martyr—public burning by the common hangman. But Milton was left alive to contemplate and develop new modes of witness, of standing upright for the truth.

V

After 1660, although Milton's "left hand" no longer produced polemical prose, he continued his fight against kingship in the more allusive medium of poetry. *Paradise Regained*, seemingly so remote from contemporary political issues, is centrally concerned with depicting a Christ who cannot be associated with the Stuart monarchy. Milton's Son of God recalls the *Eikon Basilike* and the martyrologies of Charles I precisely to critique the claims of one who suffers for the preservation of an earthly monarchy.[25] If in *Eikonoklastes* Milton primarily sought to rewrite the figure of Charles so as to deny him martyrdom with Christ, in *Paradise Regained* he strives, even more radically, to rewrite the meaning of martyrdom. Milton constructs a Son of God who embodies many of the characteristics of Foxe's martyrs—constancy in affliction, plain speaking of the truth, self-composure. Yet the Son is no martyr in the traditional sense employed by Foxe and elaborated by Gauden and the martyrologies; he is a victor who does not die to achieve his conquest. Rejecting the theatrical suffering and lachrymose exaltation of the recent English royal martyr, Milton reinvents in *Paradise Regained* the root sense of martyrdom as witnessing to the truth. *Paradise Regained* counters the Royalist appropriation of the discourse of martyrdom by radically rewriting both recent English political history and the centuries-old literary and cultural tradition of the royal martyr.

The long-standing problems of the poem are significant with regard to this revisionary project. The Son of God in *Paradise Regained* has been termed a "celibate detective," "heartless, prissy, or downright cold," a "peevish obscurantist," and an "inhuman snob."[26] The Son refuses to act or even to show any emotion. Faced with its spare style, austere setting, and paucity of action, readers have found the poem, as well as its hero, baffling and cold.[27] Even the most basic questions remain unsettled. Why this subject? Why not the crucifixion? Is there development? Does the Son learn anything? Is there a miracle atop the temple tower? Why does Satan fall astonished? Such cruxes are not resolved by classifying the poem as brief epic. Indeed, Milton's use of that genre is equally puzzling. Why no heroic action, figurative richness, poetic allusiveness, divine intervention?[28]

Viewing *Paradise Regained* as participating in the political discourse of martyrdom clarifies a number of these issues. Here epic action, narrative, and plot are circumscribed by the single action of the martyr who must speak the truth—repeatedly, constantly. The hero's actions consist precisely in his witness to the truth—speaking out, enduring fraud and force, standing upright to the end. Divine intervention comes by way of the inward consolations which fortify martyrs. Epic allusiveness and figurative richness become Satanic snares, pitfalls to the plain and simple truth. While the Royalist tracts focus on the passion and crucifixion of Christ with only scant attention to the wilderness temptation as preparation for Christ's martyrdom, for Milton the temptation not only prepares for but essentially replaces the passion and crucifixion. Paradise is regained not by theatrical suffering but by an intellectual debate in the wilderness; the genre is not tragedy but brief epic, the protagonist not the crucified, kingly Christ but the constant, unmoved Son of God.

Unlike the Royalist martyrologies, *Paradise Regained* offers no physical suffering and death, no pathos, no public spectacle, no weeping audience. The poem is deliberately antitheatrical, or, rather, it links theatricality with Satan, who has a full complement of props, costumes, scenery, and dramatic ploys. While Satan seems to do all the acting, he also continually presses the Son to say or do something dramatically interesting.[29] The character of the Son—private, terse, unemotional—is the opposite of that of the king, who acts out a well-calculated pageant before a gullible audience. The Royalists may have the theater, but Milton has the truth.

The contemporary political discourse which linked Charles Stuart with Christ thus clarifies both Milton's choice and treatment of his subject in *Paradise Regained*. There is, to begin with, the simple, essential, but continually overlooked point that the hero of *Paradise Regained* is never called Christ. He is the "Son of God" (thirty-six times), the "Son" (fifteen times), "our Saviour" (eighteen times), "Jesus" (five times), "Messiah" (seven times), but never Christ, the one in whom the kingly line of David had been fulfilled.[30] Critics, however, invariably call this character Christ, thus coloring the character and poem with the sacramental associations of earthly kingship which Milton consciously avoided. The Christ of the Gospels is dramatically attractive as he suffers for others, forgives and prays for his enemies. The passion of Christ is central in the Gospels, and it was the language of the passion narratives which Charles so powerfully appropriated. Christ's passion takes place in the capital, Jerusalem; his agony in the garden, trial, condemnation, and carrying of the cross are all publicly accessible events. The Christ of the Gospels does not eschew the notion of kingship, although he also states, paradoxically, that "My kingdom is not of this world" (John 18:36, King James Version). Charged before Pilate with claiming to be the king of the Jews, Christ simply replies, "Thou sayest it" (Matt. 27:11; Mark 15:2; Luke 23:3).[31] The passion of the gospel Christ is compelling because of the pathos he evokes as a figure tragically misunderstood and unjustly put to death. What Milton leaves out of a poem on paradise regained is, from this perspective, astonishing. In rejecting the passion narratives as models for telling how Christ regains paradise, Milton represses the main emphases of the Gospels—Christ misunderstood, suffering for others, redeeming humanity through his death and resurrection. The witness of Milton's Son of God counters and challenges the pathos and dramatic appeal not only of the martyred Charles but also of the Christ whom Charles imitates.

Suffering and death, the traditional marks of martyrdom, are invoked in *Paradise Regained*, but then only to be pushed beyond the margins of the narrative. God the Father explains the Son's future mission:

> To conquer Sin and Death the two grand foes,
> By Humiliation and strong Sufferance:
> His weakness shall o'ercome Satanic strength
> And all the world, and mass of sinful flesh.
>
> (1.159–62)

The Son knows from the beginning that his claim to his promised kingdom will ultimately consist in a traditional martyr's witness: "my way must lie / Through many a hard assay even to the death, / Ere I the promis'd Kingdom can attain" (1.263–65). Satan, too, forecasts the Son's future suffering and death: "Sorrows, and labors, opposition, hate, / Attends thee, scorns, reproaches, injuries, / Violence and stripes, and lastly cruel death" (4.386–88). Rejecting an earthly kingship, the Son envisages his God-appointed mission thus:

> What if he hath decreed that I shall first
> Be tried in humble state, and things adverse,
> By tribulations, injuries, insults,
> Contempts, and scorns, and snares, and violence,
> Suffering, abstaining, quietly expecting
> Without distrust or doubt, that he may know

> What I can suffer, how obey? who best
> Can suffer, best can do; best reign, who first
> Well hath obey'd.
>
> (3.188–96)

While the Son's rejoinder to Satan here seems to refer to future martyrdom, his speech (which significantly omits any mention of the crucifixion) also strikingly describes the action of *Paradise Regained* itself. In a very material sense, the wilderness temptation—during which the Son is tried by "injuries, insults, / Contempts, and scorns, and snares, and violence" and responds by "Suffering, abstaining, quietly expecting / Without distrust or doubt"—substitutes for traditional martyrdom in Milton's poem. The Son's suffering here consists of endurance as he abstains from earthly political power. Martyrdom thus delineated can encompass all the faithful republicans in Restoration England (including those who do not bear the ultimate witness of death). In Milton's hands, the martyrdom of the Son of God becomes an inclusive condition, no longer unique and no longer linked with his kingship—or with that of Charles I.

Although the Son does not suffer death in *Paradise Regained*, he nonetheless shows throughout his temptations the constancy which centrally defines Foxean martyrs. This, however, has been perhaps his most frustrating and puzzling trait for readers. In response to Satanic temptations, the Son replies "sternly" (1.406), "with unalter'd brow" (1.493), "temperately" (2.378), "patiently" (2.432), "calmly" (3.43), "fervently" (3.121), "unmov'd" (3.386, 4.109), "with disdain" (4.170), and "sagely" (4.285). During the Satanic storm he is "patient" (4.420), "Unshaken" (4.421), and "unappall'd" (4.425). Satan names the trait that constitutes the Son's central defense when he rejects Belial's suggestion of a temptation involving women: "with manlier objects we must try / His constancy" (2.225–26). The simile which opens book 4 of *Paradise Regained* recalls the frontispiece to *Eikon Basilike* as well as Charles's claims (repeated by the martyrologies) of his constancy in faith through storms of popular rage:

> [As] surging waves against a solid rock,
> Though all to shivers dash't, th'assault renew,
> Vain batt'ry, and in froth or bubbles end;
> So Satan"
>
> (4.18-21).[32]

Likewise, Satan later complains that he has found the Son "Proof against all temptation as a rock / Of Adamant, and as a Center, firm" (4.533–34). This constancy reaches its apex (literally and dramatically) in *Paradise Regained* in the temptation of the Tower, when the Son stuns Satan by the untheatrical action of standing still: "To whom thus Jesus. Also it is written, / Tempt not the Lord thy God; he said and stood / But Satan smitten with amazement fell" (4.560–62).

And yet, as Milton himself had argued in *Eikonoklastes*, such constancy is in itself insufficient. Milton wants to show that the Son of God, unlike Charles, is constant in his witness to the truth. The Son declares early in *Paradise Regained* that even as a child he felt himself "born to promote all truth, / All righteous things" (1.205–6). Military might allures him to subdue tyrannic power to these specific ends: "Till truth were freed, and equity restor'd" (1.220). By contrast, Satan is repeatedly defined in terms of falsehood. The Son reproaches Satan as "compos'd of lies / From the beginning, and in lies wilt end" (1.407–8). Later, he charges Satan: "For lying is thy sustenance, thy food. / Yet thou pretend'st to truth" (1.429–30). Even Satan praises (though guilefully) the Son's truthfulness:

> Hard are the ways of truth, and rough to walk,
> Smooth on the tongue discourst, pleasing to th' ear,
> And tunable as Silvan Pipe or Song;
> What wonder then if I delight to hear
> Her dictates from thy mouth?
>
> (1.478–82)

This praise is blandishment offered as a response to the Son's characterization of himself in terms of truth:

> God hath now sent his living Oracle
> Into the World to teach his final will,
> And sends his Spirit of Truth henceforth to dwell
> In pious Hearts, an inward Oracle
> To all truth requisite for men to know.
>
> (1.460–64)

Truth, as embodied in the Son, becomes inward, not visible, not subject to display. Such a definition is politically charged, formed in a nexus of political struggle. Thus *Paradise Regained* dissociates truth from kingship, as the Son confirms his unlikeness to Charles by rejecting an earthly throne and redefining kingship:

> But to guide Nations in the way of truth
> By saving Doctrine, and from error lead
> To know, and knowing worship God aright,
> Is yet more Kingly.
>
> (2.473–76)

Once the Son has definitively denied any association with earthly political power, the narrator concludes: "So spake *Israel's* true King, and to the Fiend / Made answer meet, that made void all his wiles. / So fares it when with truth falsehood contends" (3.441–43).

Finally, as opposed to Charles's false kingly witness, the Son's true witness is private. While Charles courts publicity as a martyr, publishing his meditations and seeking through theatrics to rouse the people, Milton's Son of God is alone in the wilderness. Milton moves his hero's public role—not only his suffering and death, but his entire ministry—beyond the poem's purview. Although it opens with the public baptism of the Son, the action then relocates to a private sphere. Unlike Charles, Milton's Son of God is found "tracing the Desert wild, / Sole, but with holiest Meditations fed" (2.109–10). Satan mocks the Son's circumstances—

> Thou art unknown, unfriended, low of birth,
> A Carpenter thy Father known, thyself
> Bred up in poverty and straits at home;
> Lost in a Desert here and hunger-bit
>
> (2.413–16)

—and tempts him to seek fame: "These Godlike Virtues wherefore dost thou hide? / Affecting private life, or more obscure / In savage Wilderness" (3.21–23). But the Son harshly rejects public acclaim, the "people's praise," in language which strikingly recalls Milton's earlier polemic against the "herd" in *Eikonoklastes:* "And what the people but a herd confus'd, / A miscellaneous rabble, who extol / Things vulgar, and well weigh'd, scarce worth the praise?" (3.49–51). The link with Milton's *Eikonoklastes* clarifies the otherwise puzzling severity of these lines. Milton's Son of God, unlike Charles, rejects popular fame because he witnesses not to himself but to God: "Shall I seek glory then, as vain men seek / Oft not deserv'd? I seek not mine, but his / Who sent me, and thereby witness whence I am" (3.105–7).

The human bystanders in *Paradise Regained* neither see nor hear about the Son's temptation in the wilderness. Andrew and Simon are disappointed and baffled by the Son's disappearance; nonetheless they summon up their faith:

> But let us wait; thus far he hath perform'd,
> Sent his Anointed, and to us reveal'd him,
> By his great Prophet, pointed at and shown,
> In public.
>
> (2.49–52)

Mary is not present at the baptism but hears by report that her son, "Private, unactive, calm, contemplative" (2.81), has now been "acknowledg'd . . . / By *John* the Baptist, and in public shown, / Son own'd from Heaven by his Father's voice" (2.83–85). Apprehensive about her son—"But where delays he now? Some great intent / Conceals him" (2.95–96)—Mary too keeps faith: "But I to wait with patience am inur'd" (2.102). The poem hence provides a model for the faithful few in Milton's Restoration audience, as the poet conceived them and his hero alike. The Son's true witness never finds a human audience in the poem. After withstanding Satanic temptation, the Son simply goes home: "hee unobserv'd / Home to his Mother's house private return'd" (4.638–39).

Yet the Son is not wholly unobserved for he has, in the first place, a divine audience. God the Father explains that he is sending the Son

> That all the Angels and Ethereal Powers,
> They now, and men hereafter, may discern
> From what consummate virtue I have chose
> This perfect Man, by merit call'd my Son,
> To earn Salvation for the Sons of men.
>
> (1.163–67)

Satan too, of course, closely tracks the Son's witness and is ultimately stunned and defeated by it. Finally, the Son is not unobserved because Milton himself publishes as he textualizes the Son's "private" witness in the wilderness. The narrator will

> tell of deeds
> Above Heroic, though in secret done,
> And unrecorded left through many an Age,
> Worthy have not remain'd so long unsung.
>
> (1.14–17)

In order to lodge his insistence that the true Son of God has no real earthly audience, Milton must speak to some earthly audience. This audience might be those few of "value and substantial worth" with whom, in *Eikonoklastes*, Truth is contented. For Milton, the very inaccessibility of *Paradise Regained* throughout its reception history, its lack of drama and popular appeal, would paradoxically confirm the truth of his discourse.

Paradise Regained thus inscribes a specifically Miltonic witness to the truth in the context of popular reaction to the crisis of Stuart monarchy. Charles's assimilation of himself to the Christ of the Gospels—suffering for the people and unjustly put to death—was so brilliantly successful that Milton could no longer use this discourse. In a number of ways *Paradise Regained* shares the mission of *Eikonoklastes*, but, instead of deconstructing the martyr King Charles, the poem deconstructs the Christ of the Gospels. *Paradise Regained* is not an orthodox work, no matter how much critics downplay its manifold difficulties. Milton's highly politicized redaction of the temptation of Christ in the wilderness, fully implicated in the contemporary politics of martyrdom, might be better named the (new) gospel according to John.

Notes

1. Matthew Henry Lee, ed., *Diaries and Letters of Philip Henry* (London, 1882), p. 12.

2. For general accounts of Charles's life and death, see C. V. Wedgwood, *A Coffin for King Charles* (New York, 1964); and John Bowle, *Charles I: A Biography* (London, 1975). On the civil war controversies, see Merritt Y. Hughes, intro. to *The Complete Prose Works of John Milton*, ed. Don Wolfe et al., 8 vols. (New Haven, Conn., 1953–82), 3:1–189.

3. "An Act of the Commons of England assembled in Parliament for erecting of a High Court of Justice for the Trying and Judging of Charles Steward King of England" (London, January 6, 1649), reprinted in *The Trial of King Charles the First*, ed. J. G. Muddiman (London, 1929), app. A, p. 193.

4. Michel Foucault, *Discipline and Punish: The Birth of the Prison*, trans. Alan Sheridan (New York, 1979). Clearly, Foucault's argument regarding the display of punishment is also altered when the king himself is the subject of punishment.

5. "King Charls, His Case, or an Appeal to all Rational men Concerning his Tryal at the High Court of Justice Being for the most part that which was intended to have been delivered at the Bar, if the King had pleaded to the Charge and put himself upon a fair Tryal," (London, 1649), reprinted in Muddiman, ed., app. C, p. 234.

6. Ibid.

7. *A perfect Narrative of the whole Proceedings of the High Court of Justice, in the Trial of the King . . . Published by Authority, to prevent false and impertinent Relations* (London, January 20–27, 1649), in Thomas Bayly Howell, *A Complete Collection of State Trials*, 33 vols. (London, 1816–26), 4:998.

8. Foucault, *Discipline and Punish*, p. 46.

9. Howell, 4:1138–41. A number of contemporary newspapers reported extensively on Charles's trial and execution, most following *A perfect Narrative* almost verbatim. These newspapers, dated in the Thomason tracts from January–February 1649, include *The Perfect Weekly Account*, *The Moderate Intelligencer*, *The Kingdomes Faithful Scout*, *The Kingdomes Weekly Intelligencer*, and *The Moderate*. Bruce Boehrer points astutely to the theatrical nature of Charles's execution in "Elementary Structures of Kingship: Milton, Regicide, and the Family," *Milton Studies* 23 (1987):97–98.

10. Lee (n. 1 above), p. 12.

11. *Mercurius Elencticus* (London, 1649), reprinted in *A History of English Journalism to the Foundation of the Gazette*, ed. J. B. Williams (London, 1908), app. A, p. 205.

12. Quoted in introd., *Eikon Basilike*, ed. Philip Knachel (Ithaca, N.Y., 1966), p. xxxii. Knachel discusses the vexed question of the authorship of the "King's Book" in this introduction. All quotations from *Eikon Basilike* are from this edition and are noted parenthetically in my text.

13. Foxe's *Acts and Monuments of these latter and perilous days, touching matters of the church . . . from the year of Our Lord a thousand to the time now present*, popularly known as the "Book of Martyrs," was first published in English in 1563 and frequently reprinted; after 1570 a copy was placed with the Bible in every English church. On the enormous influence of Foxe, see William Haller, *Foxe's Book of Martyrs and the Elect Nation* (London, 1963). The influence of Foxe on the *Eikon Basilike* is discussed by Florence Sandler, "Icon and Iconoclast," in *Achievements of the Left Hand: Essays on the Prose of John Milton*, ed. Michael Lieb and John T. Shawcross (Amherst, Mass., 1974), pp. 160–62; and John Knott, Jr., " 'Suffering for Truths Sake': Milton and Martyrdom," in *Politics, Poetics, and Hermeneutics in Milton's Prose*, ed. David Loewenstein and James G. Turner (Cambridge, 1990), pp. 159–62.

14. For Foxe and the imperial tradition, see Janel Mueller, "Embodying Glory: The Apocalyptic Strain in Milton's *Of Reformation*," in Loewenstein and Turner, eds., pp. 15–16.

15. See Helen Randall, "The Rise and Fall of a Martyrology: Sermons on Charles I," *Huntington Library Quarterly* 10 (1947):135–67.

16. *An Elegie Upon the Death of Our Dread Soveraign Lord King* CHARLS *the* MARTYR (London, 1649), n. p. The martyrologies which I am citing are found in *Pamphlets, Books, Newspapers, and Manuscripts relating to the Civil War, the Commonwealth, and Restoration, Collected by George Thomason*, 1640–1661 (British Library).

17. The Bishop of Downe, *The Martyrdom of King Charls I: Or his Conformity with Christ in his Sufferings: In a Sermon preached at Bredah, Before his Sacred Majesty King Charls the Second* (The Hague, 1649; reprint, London, 1660), p. 16.

18. *A Deepe Groane Fetch'd At the Funerall of that Incomparable and Glorious Monarch, Charles the First, King of Great Britaine, France and Ireland, & c. On Whose Sacred Person was acted that execrable, horrid & prodigious Murther* (London, 1649), p. 3.

19. *A Hand-Kirchife for Loyall Mourners or a Cordiall for Drooping Spirits, Groaning for the bloody murther, and heavy losse of our Gracious King, Martyred by his owne Trayterous and Rebellious Subjects* (London, 1649), pp. 5–6.

20. *The Scotch Souldiers Lamentation Upon the Death of the most Glorious and Illustrious Martyr, King Charles* (London, 1649), p. 18.

21. Anthonie Sadler, *The Loyall Mourner, Shewing the Murdering of King Charles the First: Fore-shewing the Restoring of King Charles the Second* (London, 1660), pp. 2–3.

22. *Eikonoklastes*, in Wolfe et al., eds. (n. 2 above), 3:365. Further references are included parenthetically in my text.

23. For a fuller discussion of Milton's attack on theatricality in *Eikonoklastes*, see Lana Cable, "Milton's Iconoclastic Truth," in Loewenstein and Turner, eds. (n. 13, above), pp. 143–45; and David Loewenstein, *Milton and the Drama of History: Historical Vision, Iconoclasm, and the Literary Imagination* (Cambridge, 1990), chap. 3.

24. "Truth and Power," in *Power / Knowledge: Selected Interviews & Other Writings by Michel Foucault*, ed. Colin Gordon, trans. Colin Gordon et al. (New York, 1980), p. 131.

25. Recent critics have variously explored the political significance of *Paradise Regained*. Christopher Hill sees Christ as rejecting those things which led the revolutionaries astray; see his *Milton and the English Revolution* (New York, 1977), pp. 413–27. Andrew Milner argues that Christ's rejection of Satan's political offers reflects Milton's own quietism in face of the collapse of the Commonwealth (*John Milton and the English Revolution* [Totowa, N. J., 1981], pp. 167–79). Michael Wilding also finds quietism in the poem (*Dragon's Teeth: Literature in the English Revolution* [Oxford, 1987], pp. 249–53). David Quint argues that the poem challenges the Davidic claims of Charles I and II ("David's Census: The Politics of *Paradise Regained*," in *Re-membering Milton: Essays on the Texts and Traditions*, ed. Mary Nyquist and Margaret Ferguson [New York and London, 1987], pp. 128–47). My own essay, which implicitly counters the claims of quietism, is indebted to John Knott's brief but compelling discussion of *Paradise Regained* (n. 13 above), pp. 166–68.

26. See John Carey, *Milton* (London, 1969), p. 137; Alan Fisher, "Why Is *Paradise Regained* So Cold?" *Milton Studies* 14 (1980): 206; and Northrop Frye, "The Typology of *Paradise Regained*," in *Milton: Modern Essays in Criticism*, ed. Arthur E. Barker (London, 1965), p. 439.

27. See, e. g., Fisher. For a challenge to this view, see Wayne Anderson, "*Is Paradise Regained* Really Cold?" *Christianity and Literature* 34, no. 4 (Summer 1983): 15–23.

28. For a full account of the history and nature of brief epic, see Barbara Lewalski, *Milton's Brief Epic* (Providence, R. I., 1966).

29. From a different perspective, and without exploring the political implications, Stanley Fish has examined the antitheatrical nature of *Paradise Regained* in "The Temptation of Plot in *Paradise Regained*," *Milton Studies* 17 (1983): 163–85 [reprinted in this volume], and "Inaction and Silence: The Reader in *Paradise Regained*," in *Calm of Mind: Tercentenary*

Essays on "Paradise Regained" and "Samson Agonistes" in Honor of John S. Diekhoff, ed. Joseph Anthony Wittreich, Jr. (Cleveland, 1971), pp. 25–47.

30. *John Milton: Complete Poems and Major Prose,* ed. Merritt Y. Hughes (Indianapolis 1957). Further references are included parenthetically in my text.

31. Christ's reply to Pilate in the Gospel of John is strikingly different: "Thou sayest that I am a king. To this end was I born, and for this cause came I into the world, that I should bear witness unto the truth. Every one that is of the truth heareth my voice" (John 18:37). Interestingly enough, while Milton's Son of God seems closest to this Christ, the Gospel of John has no temptation account. Milton seems to meld the Christ of the Gospel of John with the temptation episode found in the other Gospels.

32. On the connection with *Eikon Basilike*, see Knott, p. 167.

"Casting Down Imaginations": Milton as Iconoclast

DAVID LOEWENSTEIN*

"The weapons of our warfare are . . . mightie through God to the pulling down of strong holds; casting down imaginations and everie high thing that exalts it self against the knowledge of God . . . having in a readiness to aveng all disobedience." This passage from Paul's second epistle to the Corinthians (10:4–6) had special significance for Milton's controversial writings: he cited it three times in his polemics—once in his antiprelatical tracts of the early 1640s, once during the period of his regicide polemics, and once in his late pre-Restoration works.[1] While it involved the breaking of images and the pulling down of strongholds, iconoclasm for Milton, the major literary iconoclast of his revolutionary age, was a renovating activity with both crucial artistic and social implications. Here I will explore the creative and historical dimensions of Milton's iconoclasm in *Eikonoklastes* and *Samson Agonistes*, two texts which are closer in social vision than commentators have usually recognized.[2]

Eikonoklastes is Milton's longest and most sustained revolutionary polemic: with immense passion and skill it demolishes the fiction, spectacle, and arguments of *Eikon Basilike*, a work of royalist propaganda displaying Charles I as the greatest martyr of his age. Iconoclasm emerges in Milton's controversial tract, which appeared in early October 1649 (and which was written in response to an order from Parliament), as an essential expression of the poet-polemicist's dynamic and creative response to the historical process. In *Eikonoklastes* Milton attempts to free history from the tyranny of the king's image—a powerful icon of Charles projected and fashioned with considerable visual and rhetorical art in the frontispiece and text of the king's book. Recognizing the extraordinarily alluring power of the king's theatrical image and text, Milton seeks to deconstruct point by point the arguments of *Eikon Basilike*, thereby relentlessly breaking to pieces, with his verbal iconoclasm, the royal ideology and its symbolic icon. Iconoclasm for Milton consequently emerges as a profoundly radical and creative response that

*Reprinted from " 'Casting Down Imaginations': Milton as Iconoclast" in *Criticism* 31 (Summer 1989): 253–70, by David Loewenstein by permission of the Wayne State University Press.

cannot be divorced from his dramatic sense of social transformation: it represents his attempt to undermine an entrenched ideological and historical perspective, so as to bring about a new mode of social vision.

The vehement iconoclasm of Milton's regicide polemic develops out of his antiprelatical tracts of 1641–1642 in which Milton had repeatedly cast down the icons of episcopacy. But in *Eikonoklastes* Milton's iconoclasm gains a newer complexity. For here—in a tract explicitly concerned with the ideological and theatrical nature of an image—Milton proves more anxious and even divided about the powers of the human imagination. His polemic provides a devastating critique of the king's image in *Eikon Basilike*, while uneasily acknowledging the power of that representation as spectacle; he fiercely dismantles the fiction and symbolic icon of the royal text and then, drawing upon his own powers of historical interpretation and literary invention, recasts that icon.[3] This complex relationship to the dynamics of iconoclasm accounts for the imaginative and literary achievements of Milton's radical polemic. His sense that iconoclasm is itself a creative means of affecting the historical process, moreover, sustains his perception of history as a process which may be actively altered by vehement polemic: by demolishing and refashioning the theatrical image of the king as martyr, the revolutionary iconoclast asserts his power to disrupt and reshape the drama of history. A specifically literary activity—both here and in *Samson*—Milton's iconoclasm represents a crucial dimension of his imaginative response to the historical process.[4]

Iconoclasm had of course achieved renewed fervor during the English Reformation of the sixteenth century when religious rites, icons, and relics were often seen by Protestant reformers as competing with the unmediated power of the Word.[5] Indeed, as the work of Ernest Gilman and Michael O'Connell has recently stressed, it was because Protestant reformers were sensitive to and anxious about the power of images and visual representations that they needed to cast them down so vehemently.[6] Iconoclasm acquired renewed fervor again during the period of the English Revolution when Puritans wielded the hammer to break images (which they associated with the Laudian church) as they asserted the primacy of the Word. In his antiprelatical tracts Milton had already placed himself in a line of iconoclasts beginning with Leo the Iconoclast, the Byzantine emperor who had begun the first wave of iconoclasm in Christian history in 725, when he issued an edict resulting in the destruction of all icons and relics in churches;[7] Milton again invokes the name of that original iconoclast near the beginning of his regicide polemic: Leo the Iconoclast, who "took courage, and broke all superstitious Images to peeces" (3:343), is the prototype for this Puritan iconoclast who, however, realizes his vocation not with the hammer but with the pen.

Nevertheless, iconoclasm for Milton proves problematic and somewhat paradoxical: as a poet he is *unusually* sensitive to the power of the image and yet as a revolutionary iconoclast he feels compelled to cast it down virulently.

On one level, as we shall see, Milton's iconoclasm is an antitheatrical gesture; on another, it proves to be deeply theatrical. When it culminates in *Samson Agonistes* with Samson's destruction of the temple and theater of Dagon, it is paradoxically a highly theatrical gesture: the messenger describes Samson's extraordinary act as nothing less than a "horrid spectacle" (1542).[8] Milton was fascinated by the theatricality of power and the power of theatricality—even more so than other Puritan writers (one could hardly imagine Bunyan, for example, attending the theater).[9] Indeed for Milton iconoclasm could be deeply theatrical, poetic, and historically renovating.

There are two points I wish to make in a brief way about Milton's revolutionary polemic before turning to a detailed discussion of iconoclasm in *Samson Agonistes*. First, *Eikonoklastes* offers a powerful critique of what the new historicism has described as Renaissance self-fashioning, though its relation to self-fashioning is complex and somewhat ambivalent since Milton himself goes about refashioning the image of Charles.[10] And second, I believe that Milton envisioned his violent polemic as a shaping and creative force in the turbulent process of history: he saw his iconoclastic text as actively taking part in the eschatological drama. The cultural practices and displays of power, which the new historical criticism has made one of its central subjects, aroused Milton's deepest suspicion and incited his iconoclastic rage; nevertheless, the new historicist concern with the text as deeply implicated in historical and social processes—not set off or detached from them—is valuable for understanding Milton's sense of his revolutionary text actively effecting historical transformation, and for assessing the relation between his iconoclasm and his literary imagination.[11]

Eikon Basilike dramatized the king as a martyr on the stage of history: this book aimed to catch the conscience of the people, and that it did beginning with its first appearance on the very day of Charles's execution, going through no less than thirty-five English editions printed in England before the end of the year.[12] Composed by the divine John Gauden from Charles's own notes, the work offers a series of reflections and meditations on the king's career from the beginning of his troubles to his imprisonment in Carisbrooke Castle in 1647. It represents Charles as a martyr who has suffered terrible afflictions in the hands of violent and mutable enemies—Parliament and its supporters characterized impersonally as "they" throughout the text. Numerous biblical comparisons—especially to David, Job, Samson, and Solomon—help to reinforce this portrait of a wise and penitential king more sinned against than sinning. Moreover, the book's famous emblematic frontispiece showing the king praying in a basilica with his earthly crown at his feet, while his eyes are focused on the illuminated heavenly crown, suggests his Christ-like innocence. He appears not as a figure of power, but as a martyr of God who has suffered under arbitrary political and ideological forces. Depicting a large unmoved rock in the midst of raging waters, the frontispiece is, among other things, emblematic of the king's saintlike constancy and patience in the face of historical mutability, turbulence, and one might add, iconoclasm. Attempting to counteract the iconoclasm of Puritan radicals, who envision the millennium overturning his authority and "perturbing the civil state," the king asserts that "Christ's kingdom may be set up without pulling down mine."[13]

There are almost no theatrical references at all in *Eikon Basilike* and yet it is precisely in terms of theatricality that Milton interprets the text and image of the king. The king has made a spectacle of himself and transformed "Tyranny into an Art" (3:344), his text and icon becoming a "great shew of piety" (3:536). Full of theatrical tropes, *Eikonoklastes* attests to both the lure and dangers of the theatrical representation of power which so effectively exploits pathos and sentiment. For Milton Charles's self-fashioned martyrdom is a piece of "Stage-work" (3:530) and Milton will cast it down as passionately and as vehemently as Samson casts down the theater of Dagon. Milton suggests, moreover, that Charles's theatrical gestures render symbols and images themselves highly equivocal: when Charles compares that powerful autocrat, the Earl of Strafford, to the sun, the royal emblem, Milton is disturbed by the manipulative use of "figurative" language to praise "a Subject" (3:372): the disjunction of image and reality, signifier and signified leads Milton to conclude that the stagework of *Eikon Basilike* is full of what he calls "equivocal interpretations" (3:495). Indeed the numerous theatrical tropes in *Eikonoklastes*—there are references to interludes, revels, comedies, Sunday theater, and so on—suggest that the king's court and his activities have all been skillfully stage-managed. The king's "conceited portraiture" is "drawn out to the full measure of a Masking Scene," though "quaint Emblems and devices begg'd from the old Pageantry of some Twelf-nights entertainment at *Whitehall*, will doe but ill to make a Saint or Martyr" (3:342–43). The revolutionary polemicist saw through the cult of Renaissance self-fashioning and the equivocal spectacle of power, analyzing a self in a text that was pure theatrics—"a meer artificiall *Adam*, such an *Adam* as he is in the motions," to quote from *Areopagitica* (2:527), where Milton imagines a hollow Adam as a puppet figure.

While Milton's literary sense is considerably more sophisticated than that of other Puritan contemporaries (such as William Prynne), he nevertheless shares something of the Puritan uneasiness with spectacular invention, the counterfeiting of the self, and outward exhibitionism.[14] But the controversial polemicist is distinctly more radical in his response than other Protestant reformers: a sixteenth-century reformer such as John Jewel might well abhor what Milton calls the "Image-doting rabble" (3:601) and the theatrics employed in religious ceremonies and rituals so that "men's eyes [are] fed . . . with mad gazings and foolish gauds"; yet Jewel, aware that his reformist views might well lead to ideological radicalism, would check himself by noting that "neither do we disorder realms, neither do we set up or pull

down kings, nor translate governments."[15] And that is precisely what the
iconoclasm of Milton's revolutionary polemic does attempt to do.

The sense of unparalleled, even terrifying upheaval emphasized by the
iconoclastic radicals of mid-seventeenth-century England is absorbed into
the literary iconoclasm of Milton's virulent polemic. John Owen, Cromwell's
chaplain, observed that the Kingdom of Christ would be preceded by "great
Warres, desolations, alterations," at which time many nations "shall be
shaken, broken, translated, and turned off their old foundations, and constitutions."[16] For Milton iconoclastic polemic could itself operate as a powerful
and violent force—an expression of what another contemporary called the
age's "many new, unusual emergencies, such as our forefathers have not
known"[17]—in a renovating social process that promised to be profoundly
unsettling. Iconoclasm was nothing less than a revolutionary act—"a direct
act of violence against the accepted social myth."[18] Or to use the formulation
of Perez Zagorin, it was a gesture of "symbolic violence"—an act of verbal
aggression "in deliberate transgression and reversal of prevailing social norms
. . . intended to destroy the sanctity or prestige of ruling persons and
institutions."[19] Milton's magisterial tract concludes with a series of apocalyptic and prophetic passages which virulently break to pieces the text and
symbolic icon of the king's book, just as Milton believed that the Word of
God would ultimately "break to peeces and dissolve" the "great power and
Dominion" of Charles (3:509). Milton Iconoclastes emerges as a mighty
activist in the turbulent eschatological drama of his age; and as he wields
the power of *his* word and *the* Word in order to break to pieces the king's
text and equivocal signs, his verbal iconoclasm expands to what Roland
Barthes has called an active "semioclasm."[20]

Milton's iconoclastic response to the King's book, however, is further
complicated by the fact that Milton does not simply cast down the image;
he radically refashions it as well.[21] His new image of the king is itself a
fashioned representation of considerable skill. This is the iconoclasm of a
writer, then, who understands very well the ideological, fictive, and emotive
power of images, and who must somehow confirm the value of his own
imaginative art, even as he proceeds virulently to cast down imaginations.
Milton completely mutes the king's tragic potential and transforms him into
a paradigmatic despot; there is not a tinge of sympathy for the king and his
martyrdom, no attempt on Milton's part to achieve some sense of poise and
detachment in his portrait of Charles, as Marvell would so skillfully do in
his Horatian Ode. Rather Milton draws upon numerous despots from history
and aligns them with the king: Nero, Caligula, Domitian, Rehoboam, Ahab,
Herod, Nebachudnezzar, Nimrod, Pharaoh, William the Conqueror, to
mention only some of the tyrants Milton selects for comparison.[22] Milton
draws as well on mythological analogy, highlighting the parallel between
Charles and Circe: the king's rhetoric and theatrics resemble the Circean arts

(as well as the arts of Comus, her son) which completely enchant the people—that "Cup of deception, spic'd and temperd to thir bane" so that "they should deliver up themselves to these glozing words and illusions of him" (3:582; cf. 3:488). The grotesque image of man bestialized and made subhuman through illusion and enchantment (men in Milton's text become "slaves, and arrant beasts" and "clamouring & fighting brutes" [3:581]) recalls Comus followed by his *"rout of Monsters, headed like sundry sorts of wild Beasts."*[23]

By transforming Charles into a Circe-Comus figure, Milton creates a wholly fictional and imagined representation of the king and his powers, as Milton goes about recasting and reinventing, quite drastically, the royal image. Iconoclasm proves to be as much of an art for Milton as tyranny is for the king. The polemicist employs mythopoetic invention to discredit the authority of the king's icon and text, even as he suspects that the king wears "a garb somewhat more Poetical then for a Statist" and that his "whole Book might perhaps be intended a peece of Poetrie" since "The words are good, the fiction smooth and cleanly; there wanted only Rime" (3:406).[24] Consequently, his regicide polemic, its rhetoric often astonishingly violent and unsettling, emerges as both a destructive and creative response to the events and texts of his age—a response that tested his polemical skills in new and impressive ways.

Both *Eikonoklastes* and *Samson Agonistes* present literary renderings of iconoclasm: in *Samson* Milton does not radically refashion an image; but he does theatricalize iconoclasm. From the beginning of the drama Milton associates the Philistines and their treatment of Samson with theater. Himself a source of mockery and spectacle, Samson is "the scorn and gaze" (34) of his enemies and visitors; he has fallen prey to the Circean Dalila's "wonted arts" (748), which include feigning and her ability to put on a good show—as her colorful entrance amply demonstrates (710–24). Samson bitterly resents playing the part of "fool or jester" (1338), especially after having been, in the past, "assign'd" by heaven a much more central "part" (1217) in the drama of history and having been, in effect, the "gaze" of God's "special eye" (636). The officer who comes to collect Samson increases the sense of theatrical performance, when he expresses concern about the way Samson will "appear" at the "solemn Feast," "Triumph, Pomp, and Games" in honor of Dagon (1310–18). Samson finds nothing more demeaning than the thought of having his calamities transformed into "sport" and "game" (1328, 1331) as he "play[s] before" Dagon (1340) in the Philistine theater:

> A *Nazarite* in place abominable
> Vaunting my strength in honor to thir *Dagon*?
> Besides, how vile, contemptible, ridiculous,
> What act more execrably unclean, profane?
> (1359–62)

Consequently, Samson's reference to "some great act" at that crucial turning point when he feels inwardly "Some rousing motions" and consents to perform in the Philistine festival, expresses considerable ambiguity and indeterminacy: it refers simultaneously to his great performance in the spectacle of Dagon and to his "remarkable" performance in the iconoclastic spectacle of history (1381–89). Its powerful vagueness manages to embrace *both* theatrical occasions.

This complex sense of theatricality intensifies as the play moves towards its iconoclastic dénouement. The messenger's description of Samson's impending performance at the Philistine festival is particularly rich in theatrical references. Samson's "spectacle," he notes, was held in

> a spacious Theater
> Half round on two main Pillars vaulted high,
> With seats where all the Lords and each degree
> Of sort, might sit in order to behold,
> The other side was op'n, where the throng
> On banks and scaffolds under Sky might stand.
> (1604–10)

Milton has transformed the "house" in Judges 16:26–27 into a sumptuous classical amphitheater, thereby heightening the sense of dramatic occasion. Among the analogues for Milton's play, only Vondel's *Samson* approaches Milton's self-conscious theatricalism: expected to perform in a masque at Dagon's temple, Samson transforms, with a sense of irony, the theatrical occasion into "A holy drama that the Philistines / Will carry in remembrance evermore."[25] Both Milton and Vondel exploit the ironies inherent in the competition between the dramas of Dagon and God, though Milton explores the relation between the two spectacles more deeply and resists the overtly typological interpretation of Samson's terrifying act.

That "great act" will set spectacle against spectacle, as Samson's iconoclasm paradoxically turns out to be a highly theatrical performance displaying his radical activism in the historical process. Heavily ironic, Samson's final words contrast the spectacle he has just performed in with the spectacle he is about to enact:

> Hitherto, Lords, what your commands impos'd
> I have perform'd, as reason was, obeying,
> Not without wonder or delight beheld.
> Now of my own accord such other trial
> I mean to show you of my strength, yet greater;
> As with amaze shall strike all who behold.
> (1640–45)

Performing of his "own accord," Samson becomes an "actor" in both senses of that word—as doer and stage player.[26] Employing the language of theater, Samson thus underscores *his* activism in the eschatological drama of history. No mere "sport and play" (1679), his "great act," evoking a theatrical response of wonder and amazement, turns out to be a "horrid spectacle" (1542) of iconoclasm—a dramatic gesture that vividly recalls the radicalism of Milton's major polemic, *Eikonoklastes*, and which, in one terrifying moment, brings to a climax the iconoclasm of Milton's career.

II

In his controversial prose writings of the 1640s and 1650s, Milton often represented historical transformation in violent, turbulent, and iconoclastic terms. He seemed to believe that great iconoclastic disturbances, though deeply violent and unsettling, could also have healthful and purgative effects on the nation: since reformation is rarely perfected "at the first push" (1:536), he concluded in *Areopagitica* that God must sometimes shake a kingdom "with strong and healthful commotions to a generall reforming" (2:566). In *An Apology for Smectymnuus* Milton singled out for praise Parliament's execution of the Earl of Strafford in 1641: one violent act might well alter, with extraordinary decisiveness, the whole course of history—thus with "one stroke" they won "againe our lost liberties and Charters" (1:924).[27] And with equal swiftness and decisiveness, Samson's own iconoclastic act in Milton's play brings about a sudden, dramatic change: "All in a moment," the messenger tells Manoa and the Chorus, the sons of Gaza were "overwhelm'd and fall'n" (1559). The violence and passion of Milton's revolutionary rhetoric in his polemics reminds us that he was not at all afraid of "sudden extreams" (1:601), as he puts it in *Of Reformation*, or "the sudden assault of [God's] reforming Spirit" (1:704), as he states in *Animadversions*.[28] The day of the Lord itself, Milton noted in the *Christian Doctrine*, "will be sudden" and characterized by unexpected destruction (6:615). Milton is particularly fascinated, then, by the dramatic potential of iconoclasm, with all its turbulence, immediacy, and implications for social change.

Thus while much of *Samson* is a profoundly dark work, it is also a work of fierce rage against outward authority—a work in which Milton's radicalism expresses itself in a passionate gesture of iconoclasm. In that sense the play as a whole highlights rather than harmonizes divided responses to history— its disturbing pessimism offset by its violent yet liberating act of iconoclasm.[29] Samson's destruction of the temple of Dagon (both theater and place of idolatrous worship) recapitulates the spirit of Milton's revolutionary iconoclasm—his violent attacks in his controversial polemics on the images of prelatical and royal power. Envisioning history as a profoundly iconoclastic process, Milton warns the prelatical Remonstrant of *Animadversions* that "wee shall not doubt to batter, and throw down your *Nebuchadnezzars* Image and crumble it like the chaffe of the Summer threshing floores" (1:700). Samson displays the irony and scorn of those martyrs who, as Milton writes in *The Reason of Church-Government*, "*rip up the wounds* of Idolatry and Superstition *with a laughing countenance*" (1:903). Furthermore, his inwardness—as he stands between the pillars of the temple "With inward eyes illuminated" (1689)—resembles the "inward power" of a late polemic like *A Treatise of Civil Power* (1659), in which the act of iconoclasm grows out of the "inward perswasive motions" of God's spirit (7:261): here, for the last time in his radical prose career, Milton recalled the biblical text about "casting down imaginations" (7:257). Indeed we find ample evidence of his iconoclastic vision even in those works which seem to stress withdrawal from activism in the public sphere.

Thus we should note that *Paradise Regained*, for all its emphasis on Christ's inwardness, his withdrawal from the world, and his rejection of brute military power, does portray the saviour as a kind of iconoclast who, when his time comes to assume David's throne, will "to pieces dash / All Monarchies besides throughout the world" (4.149–50). Like *Samson*, Milton's brief epic is a work about waiting for "due time" (3.182) to act in history: Satan, after all, takes Christ up a hill of history in Book 3 and tempts him to play the part of the epic activist by assuming the Parthian throne as a means to regain David's seat. And in Book 4 Satan again tempts Christ with the spectacle of history—the "majestic show" (4.110) of a magnificent yet decadent Rome under the reign of Tiberius, a vision of luxury and power which simultaneously evokes a decadent post-Restoration milieu. But Satan misconstrues the kind of activism and historical role for which Christ stands and waits. When his due time does come, Christ will not, as he tells his adversary, be "slack" (3.398) like the "carelessly diffus'd" (118) Samson at the beginning of Milton's drama; rather he will emerge an iconoclastic activist in the eschatological scheme of history—a radical stance already suggested by his vehement and scornful responses to Satan's temptations in Book 4 (ll. 170–94).

The iconoclasm, rage, and violence of *Samson Agonistes*, however, resembles most closely the vehement polemics of *Eikonoklastes*, where Milton demolishes, with such unrelenting rancor and fury, the image and spectacle of royalty projected in *Eikon Basilike*. I have already suggested that Milton aligned this impassioned attack on the royal text and icon—and especially the "Stage-work" of its emblematic frontispiece—with the unfolding of God's dramatic judgments in history. But *Eikonoklastes* was a text also fervently expressing Milton's sense of his own decisive activism and power in the iconoclastic historical process. Milton considered his revolutionary text a dynamic, iconoclastic weapon—an expression of the power and imagination of the polemicist to alter the very shape of history itself. With great polemical force, he dashes to pieces the icon of Charles I, that idol which catches "the worthles approbation of an inconstant, irrational, and Image-doting rabble" (3:601). And with an equally disturbing power, his fiercely iconoclastic play dramatizes the sudden pulling down of strongholds and spectacles, along with the terrible "desolation" (1561) awaiting those who worship "in Temples at Idolatrous Rites" (1378).

Milton presents the drama of Samson's iconoclasm in terrifying detail. His destruction of the theater and temple of Dagon conveys the sheer ferocity and awesomeness of apocalyptic history fulfilling itself. This is the militant Samson who resembles, to use Dalila's words, an "Eternal tempest never to be calm'd" (964). Before the Last Judgment, Milton observes in the *Christian Doctrine*, quoting from Luke (21:25–26), there will be "on the earth panic among the nations, not knowing which way to turn, with the sea and the waves roaring: and men will faint with fear" (6:619). So Manoa and the Chorus hear not only a "hideous noise" that is "Horribly loud," but a "universal groan / As if the whole inhabitation perish'd," causing "Blood, death and deathful deeds"—"destruction at the utmost point" (1509–14). According to George Hakewill's *Apologie or Declaration of the Power and Providence of God*, God's power at the Apocalypse will be profoundly iconoclastic, striking with the fury of a tempest unleashed: then He will come "breaking and throwing downe whatsoever standeth in his way, as a rage of many waters that flow and rush together." He will appear flanked "on every side of him [with] a violent tempest" and "the mountaines shall meet and fly away at his presence."[30] The messenger's account in Milton's drama highlights the iconoclastic energy and violence Samson unleashes from *within himself* as he performs his great act:

> straining all his nerves he bow'd;
> As with the force of winds and waters pent
> When Mountains tremble, those two massy Pillars
> With horrible convulsion to and fro
> He tugg'd, he shook, till down they came, and drew
> The whole roof after them with burst of thunder
> Upon the heads of all who sat beneath.
> (1646–52)

Like the Cromwell of Marvell's Horatian Ode, Samson destroys "Pallaces and Temples" with a natural force of extraordinary dimensions—though Samson's iconoclasm is apocalyptic, whereas Cromwell's, at least in that poem, is not.[31] Such, then, is the cataclysmic force of God's power in history—that unappeasable fury of "wrath divine" (1683) which brings swift and resistless destruction to God's enemies.[32]

The terrifying drama of iconoclasm in *Samson Agonistes*, moreover, expresses something of a deep wish fulfillment on Milton's part—the impulse not only to remake and overturn history, but, in the process, to devastate one's enemies by means of a spectacular act. Rather than muting the cataclysmic devastation in his biblical source, Milton has highlighted it. Samson demolishes his enemies not in any indiscriminate fashion, but in a calculated act that decimates their "choice nobility and flower," including "Lords, Ladies, Captains, Counsellors, [and] Priests" (1653–54)—a detail that Milton has expanded from the less descriptive biblical phrases, "all the lords of the Philistines" and "all the people that were therein" (Judges 16:27, 30). We need only remind ourselves here how astonishingly often Milton the revolutionary polemicist relishes the thought of his enemies suffering some devastating destruction or punishment: recall "the divine vengeance" and "punishing force" he implores Parliament to "rain down" upon its "godlesse" enemies at the very end of *The Reason of Church-Government* (1:861); or "the invincible warriour Zeale" he envisions in *An Apology* driving "over the heads of Scarlet Prelates . . . brusing their stiffe necks under his flaming wheels" (1:900); or Milton's obvious admiration in his *First Defense* for the younger Pliny's description of the bloody death of the emperor Domitian: " 'no one so checked his delight as to feel that the sight of his torn and bleeding joints and limbs, his grim and terrible statutes cast down and thrown into the flames, was anything but vengeance overdue' " (4:446). *Samson Agonistes* thus expresses yet again this aggressive, violent impulse we so often encounter in Milton's polemical tracts. Even in his *Christian Doctrine* Milton marshals the support of numerous biblical texts to justify the act or wish of vengeance against God's enemies, and he stresses that some kinds of hatred may be nothing less than a religious duty, such "as when we hate the enemies of God or of the church,"[33] or when (to recall another Miltonic work) the disappointed husband hates the wife he wants to divorce. Nevertheless, in stressing Samson's process of regeneration, commentators have too often tended to soften the "inexpiable hate" dramatized in Samson's spectacular act of iconoclasm.[34]

This discomfort with the violence and passion of Milton's iconoclasm suggests that critics have yet to come to terms with its disturbing implications. Still it is important to emphasize that iconoclasm and vehemence could have a distinctly literary or poetic dimension for Milton, and that he understood iconoclasm as much more than simply a gesture of violence. In *Tetrachordon*, to cite a particularly suggestive example from the prose, Milton describes that highly dramatic moment when Christ confronts and casts down the Pharisees on the controversial issue of the law of Moses: "So Christ being demanded maliciously why *Moses* made the law of divorce, answers them in a vehement *scheme*" (2:664). Milton gives vehemence itself a literary or poetic quality: "scheme" here is a "*trope* of indignation," a literary-critical term that serves to valorize the poetics of Christ's vehemence—his "art of powerful reclaiming," as Milton describes it a few pages later (2:668). The iconoclastic exegete aims "to dazle" and "amaze" the literal-minded Pharisees with his hermeneutic performance (to use Milton's words in *The Doctrine and Discipline of Divorce*, 2:308), just as the less intellectual Old Testament iconoclast aims to dazzle and amaze the Philistines as he kills them. In his final act, Samson is both hero and stage manager, as he forces his enemies to be both audience and victims.

In this way we can see Milton valorizing Samson's iconoclasm: Milton gives Samson's greatest expression of vehemence a literary dimension by presenting it in terms of an iconoclastic spectacle which competes with and outdazzles the spectacle of Dagon. Just as Christ meets vehemence with vehemence, so Samson meets hate with hate: but in both cases Milton has drawn our attention to the highly literary nature of these aggressive and iconoclastic responses. For all its attendant violence, then, Milton's iconoclasm is simultaneously poetic, theatrical, and liberating. Both an act of power and a kind of poetics, his iconoclasm cannot be divorced from his sense of drama or literary creativity. Consequently, we must understand the iconoclasm in *Samson Agonistes* as a radical gesture that is deeply renovating for Milton in both social and artistic ways.[35]

The fulfillment of God's iconoclastic judgment in history evokes a complex response—a mixture of terror, wonder, and mystery all at once—which stretches the human imagination itself. As the Chorus observe, God has performed some "incredible" (1532) deed through Samson, a fact immediately confirmed by the messenger who arrives in a frenzy pursued by "dire imagination" (1544). And similarly God's enemies "who behold" the spectacle of His power are struck "with amaze" (1645), as they experience the sense of wonder appropriate to all who witness the awesome drama of iconoclasm. "At once delight and horror on us seize," as Marvell perceptively remarked about Milton's daring and inspired efforts in *Paradise Lost*. (Marvell, we recall, wonders at first whether the poet resembles Samson groping "the Temple's Posts in spite" as though "The World o'er whelming to revenge his sight.")[36] Indeed such a response might well be applied to the iconoclastic spectacle at the end of Milton's play, a gesture that expresses on one level a deep and primitive impulse of hatred and revenge—that "inexpiable hate" raised in Samson but never wholly assuaged. A sense of horror, dread, and amazement balances the Chorus' celebration of Samson's victory over his enemies—"dearly bought revenge, yet glorious!" (1660). Samson has quit himself like Samson, but it has been a terrifying fulfillment preceded by extraordinary anguish, doubt, and pain, and culminating in a spectacular act of destruction and desolation. No simple, one-sided response can adequately convey the power and horror of Samson's great act. The historical process remains a mystery and God's iconoclastic power a source of wonder.

But if the power of God is a force of immense iconoclasm, as Milton's radical polemics and *Samson* amply demonstrate, it may also achieve an inverse effect that is no less dramatic: "in one instant," the Word of God, as Milton declares elsewhere, "hushes outrageous tempests into a sudden stilnesse and peacefull calm" (*The Doctrine and Discipline of Divorce*, 2:333), a passage that conveys something of the effect at the very end of *Samson Agonistes*—"calm of mind, all passion spent" (1758). Nevertheless, the play refuses to let us settle into a comfortable view of the historical process and the meaning of Samson's iconoclastic performance. The Israelites' apparent certainty about the clarity of the providential scheme stands in striking contrast to Samson's solitary, painful, humiliating attempt to comprehend the "mystery of God" (378); their assertion that all is "well and fair" (1723) stands in contrast to Samson's cataclysmic act of iconoclasm.

As an expression of inexpiable rage and iconoclasm, *Samson Agonistes* will continue to challenge those commentators who wish to see Milton as a more temperate thinker and writer in his great poems. Can we really conclude that the outcome of Samson's struggles confirms Milton's views of reason and grace or the value of turbulent passions tempered and purified? The vehement iconoclasm of *Samson Agonistes*, I have argued, dramatizes a turbulent side of Milton that was deep in his writings from at least the early revolutionary tracts. This iconoclasm, which found its greatest polemical expression in *Eikonoklastes*, possessed a poetic and theatrical attraction for Milton; it was a dramatically liberating gesture that was profoundly violent yet also regenerative. Consequently, we need to be more alert, as we approach the great poems, to the various and contradictory dimensions of Milton's imaginative responses to the drama of history in his age: the pulling down of strongholds and the casting down of imaginations, for this writer, was to prove as vital and as radical a response to the historical process as seeking in the paradise within quiet refuge from the tribulations of history. Rather than ignoring, apologizing for, or softening the extraordinary vehemence of Milton's iconoclasm, we need to confront its unsettling and dramatic power, and to acknowledge the ways in which it generated some of his greatest imaginative and literary achievements—both in the controversial prose and major poems.

Notes

I wish to thank Gerald MacLean and Robin Grey for their comments on an earlier draft of this paper.

1. See the *Complete Prose Works of John Milton*, ed. Don M. Wolfe *et al*, 8 vols. (New Haven: Yale Univ. Press, 1953–82), 1:848; 3:310; 7:257 (the version cited); cf. 5:446. References to Milton's prose are from this edition and cited parenthetically within my text

2. Milton's iconoclasm has nonetheless begun to receive more critical attention. Florence Sandler's "Icon and Iconoclast," in *Achievements of the Left Hand: Essays on the Prose of John Milton*, ed. Michael Lieb and John T. Shawcross (Amherst: Univ. of Massachusetts Press, 1974), pp. 160–84, studies Milton's regicide tract in its intellectual context; my own

essay attends more to the interconnection between Milton's revolutionary iconoclasm and his imaginative strategies. Ernest B. Gilman, *Iconoclasm and Poetry in the English Reformation*: *Down went Dagon* (Chicago: Univ. of Chicago Press, 1986), chap. 6, examines Milton's poetry in its Reformation context. Richard Helgerson has recently considered Milton's regicide tract in relation to print culture: see "Milton Reads the King's Book: Print, Performance, and the Making of a Bourgeois Idol," *Criticism*, 29 (1987), 1–25. On Milton's polemic as a response to the idolatry of words, see Lana Cable, "Milton's Iconoclastic Truth," in *Politics, Poetics, and Hermeneutics in Milton's Prose*, ed. David Loewenstein and James G. Turner (Cambridge: Cambridge Univ. Pres, 1990).

3. Cf. Joan S. Bennett, "God, Satan, and King Charles: Milton's Royal Portraits," *PMLA*, 92 (1977), 441; I place greater emphasis on Milton's iconoclasm in relation to his refashioning of the king's image.

4. I explore more fully Milton's imaginative responses to history in *Milton and the Drama of History: Historical Vision, Iconoclasm, and the Literary Imagination* (Cambridge: Cambridge Univ. Press, 1990); see chapters 3 and 6 for extensive treatments of *Eikonoklastes* and *Samson*.

5. On iconoclasm in England, see John Phillips, *The Reformation of Images: Destruction of Art in England, 1535–1660* (Berkeley: Univ. of California Press, 1973). See also Carlos M. N. Eire, *War Against the Idols: The Reformation of Worship from Erasmus to Calvin* (Cambridge: Cambridge Univ. Press, 1986), for a valuable study of Reformation iconoclasm.

6. Gilman, *Iconoclasm and Poetry in the English Reformation*, chap. 2; Michael O'Connell, "The Idolatrous Eye: Iconoclasm, Anti-Theatricalism, and the Image of the Elizabethan Theater," *ELH*, 52 (1985), 285–99.

7. See *Of Reformation* (1:577–78) and *Of Prelatical Episcopacy* (1:648–49). Cf. *The Tenure of Kings and Magistrates* (3:218) where Milton suggests that Charles is a counterfeit king by quoting from Leo the Iconoclast's legal compendium, the *Eclogue*.

8. References to Milton's poetry are from *John Milton: Complete Poems and Major Prose*, ed. Merritt Y. Hughes (Indianapolis: Odyssey, 1957).

9. Puritans, of course, were by no means consistently antagonistic to the stage: see Martin Butler, *Theatre and Crisis, 1632–1642* (Cambridge: Cambridge Univ. Press, 1984), chap. 5.

10. On this cultural phenomenon in the English Renaissance, see Stephen Greenblatt, *Renaissance Self-Fashioning: From More to Shakespeare* (Chicago: Univ. of Chicago Press, 1980).

11. On the relation between texts and history in the new historical criticism, see Louis Montrose, "Renaissance Literary Studies and the Subject of History," *English Literary Renaissance*, 16 (1986), 5–12.

12. The number of English editions that year reached forty, if one counts those printed on the continent. Francis F. Madan examines *Eikon Basilike's* many editions, as well as the question of its authorship in *A New Bibliography of the Eikon Basilike of King Charles the First* (Oxford: Oxford Univ. Press, 1950).

13. *Eikon Basilike: The Portraiture of His Sacred Majesty in His Solitudes and Sufferings*, ed. Philip A. Knachel (Ithaca: Cornell Univ. Press, 1966), p. 127.

14. On Puritan antitheatricalism, see Jonas Barish, *The Antitheatrical Prejudice* (Berkeley: Univ. of California Press, 1981), chapters 4 and 6.

15. For the citations from Jewel, see *An Apology of the Church of England*, ed. J. F. Booty (Ithaca: Cornell Univ. Press, 1963), pp. 35–36, 63.

16. *A Sermon . . . Concerning the Kingdom of Christ and the Power of the Civile Magistrate* (Oxford, 1652), pp. 19, 15. See also *The Advantage of the Kingdome of Christ in the Shaking of the Kingdoms of the World* (Oxford, 1651), pp. 7–9, 11–12, 26–28, 31, 33.

17. John Wilkins, *A Discourse Concerning the Beauty of Providence* (London, 1649), cited in Keith Thomas, *Religion and the Decline of Magic* (London: Weidenfeld and Nicholson, 1971), p. 431.

18. Eire, *War Against the Idols*, p. 151; see pp. 151–65 and chap. 8 for his full discussion of the revolutionary dimensions of iconoclasm.
19. *Rebels and Rulers, 1500–1660*, 2 vols. (Cambridge: Cambridge Univ. Press, 1982), 1:18.
20. See Barthes's discussion of *"sémioclastie"* in his preface to *Mythologies* (1957; rpt. Paris: Seuil, 1970), p. 8.
21. Cf. Greenblatt, *Renaissance Self-Fashioning*, p. 188, who notes, in discussing Spenser's Bower of Bliss, how iconoclasm may be related to "the act of fashioning."
22. I examine the implications of these historical analogies in greater detail in *Milton and the Drama of History*, chap. 3.
23. See the stage direction following line 92.
24. Helgerson, "Milton Reads the King's Book," pp. 15–20, stresses the conflict between iconoclast and poet in Milton's writings, though he recognizes that Milton's language may be "theatrical and iconic" (p. 20); I would place greater emphasis on the interconnection of iconoclasm, poetics, and performance in both the prose and poetry.
25. Joost Van Den Vondel, *Samson, of Heilige Wraeck, Treurspel* (1660), in *That Invincible Samson: The Theme of "Samson Agonistes" in World Literature*, trans. Watson Kirkconnell (Toronto: Univ. of Toronto Press, 1964), p. 115; see also pp. 102–03, 108–09, 136–37, 139. Cf. Francis Quarles's poetic version of the story, *The Historie of Samson* (London, 1631): there the "Revengefull *Samson*" is likewise an *"Actor"* (pp. 86, 88), but Quarles, by contrast, makes no attempt at all to heighten the theatricality of Samson's performance.
26. See e. g. the definition of "actor" in Edward Phillips, *The New World of English Words* (London, 1658).
27. See also Parliament's letter of 2 April 1649, Latinized by Milton, to the Senate of Hamburg: "we have thought that it is better to strike the yoke of slavery from our necks at once [*servitutis jugum semel . . . a cervicibus nostris dejicere*] than to risk endless struggles for this cause and to face so often the repeated hazard of war against ever new men intent upon mastery" (5:479–80). For the Latin, see *The Works of John Milton*, ed. Frank Allen Patterson, 18 vols. (New York: Columbia Univ. Press, 1931–38), 13:468. The verb *"dejicere"* has the violent implication of casting or throwing down. Cf. Milton's description of "the Axe of Gods reformation hewing at the old and hollow trunk of Papacie" (*Of Reformation*, 1:582).
28. Cf. his defense of "Speedy and vehement" reformation: 1:602.
29. For the view that the play is "intensely, almost unbearably pessimistic" and "Milton's darkest piece of writing," see William Riley Parker, *Milton: A Biography* (Oxford: Clarendon Press, 1968), 2:937.
30. 2nd ed. (London, 1630), p. 508.
31. "An Horatian Ode upon Cromwel's Return from Ireland," 1.21, in *The Poems and Letters of Andrew Marvell*, ed. H. M. Margoliouth, rev. Pierre Legouis and E. E. Duncan-Jones, 3rd. ed., 2 vols. (Oxford: Clarendon Press, 1972). Marvell associates Cromwell more explicitly with apocalyptic themes in *The First Anniversary*.
32. The drama of iconoclasm in *Samson* demonstrates, to quote Stephen Marshall's Civil War sermon, *Reformation and Desolation* (London, 1642), that "Gods wrath may be so far kindled, that he will accept of no attonement, but will inexorably proceed to desolation" (p. 26); cf. p. 28: "no mortall man can possibly determine when the *precise time* of this or that Nations utter ruine is certainly come." See also John Benbrigge, *Gods Fury, Englands Fire* (London, 1646), pp. 13–14.
33. On Milton's justification for hatred and revenge, see 6:743, 755, where he mentions such scriptural authorities as Ps. 18:38–43, Ps. 139:21–22, Ps. 41:10–11, Jer. 11:10 and 15:15, Rev. 6:10, among others. Cf. the emphasis on God's vengeance in the scenario for "Sodom" in the Trinity College manuscript: see 8:558–59, and James Holly Hanford's remarks on p. 593. Michael Lieb has recently discussed the *odium Dei* as a central theological

concept in *Paradise Lost*: " 'Hate in Heav'n': Milton and the *Odium Dei*," *ELH*, 53 (1986), 519–39.

34.   See e. g. William O. Harris, "Despair and 'Patience as the Truest Fortitude' in *Samson Agonistes*," *ELH*, 30 (1963), 107–20; Sherman Hawkins, "Samson's Catharsis," *Milton Studies*, 2 (1970): "Yet even as we watch, [Samson's] passions—so powerfully raised—are purified, reduced, and tempered" (p. 224). In the most impressive study of the poem, *Toward "Samson Agonistes": The Growth of Milton's Mind* (Princeton: Princeton Univ. Press, 1978), Mary Ann Radzinowicz offers a reading that likewise stresses the tempering and composing of turbulent passions: see pp. 7, 351, 354.

35.   Here I find myself dissenting from Joseph Wittreich's recent conclusion that the code of vengeance in the drama makes "it necessary that we entertain Samson's final action as a negative, as a foolhardy embracing of self-destruction, while he is engaged in the slaying of others" (*Interpreting "Samson Agonistes"* [Princeton: Princeton Univ. Press, 1986], p. 231). While I sympathize with his effort to cast down the Dagon of Milton critical orthodoxy, especially with its tendency to treat Milton's Samson as simply a saint or hero of faith, I believe that he presses too hard the argument that Samson, though "no villain," "*is* deeply flawed and thus ambiguous in his heroism" (p. 306). Wittreich assumes throughout his study that we are to consider Samson's violence only in negative terms.

36.   "On Mr. Milton's *Paradise Lost*," 11. 35, 9–10, in Margoliouth, 1:138.

Reading, Seeing, and Acting in *Samson Agonistes*

WILLIAM FLESCH*

At the end of *Samson Agonistes* the chorus praises God, or at least "the unsearchable dispose / Of highest wisdom" (1746–47), for—well, for the end of the drama, that is, for ending it appropriately: its witnesses, God's servants, made "calm of mind all passion spent." "Dispose" used as a noun here and as the subject of the sentence is an odd word[1]: probably its nearness to being a verb means to underline God's agency in the *final* disposition or state of affairs, just because that agency is (or has been) unsearchable and so unrepresentable, and God has taken no part in the events of the drama. The question of agency is a difficult one, as the chorus's attempt at an explanation of what God has caused to happen to the Philistines may show:

> While their hearts were jocund and sublime,
> Drunk with idolatry, drunk with wine
> And fat regorged of bulls and goats,
> Chanting their idol, and preferring
> Before our living dread who dwells
> In Silo his bright sanctuary:
> Among them he a spirit of frenzy sent,
> Who hurt their minds,
> And urged them on with mad desire
> To call in haste for their destroyer;
> They only bent on sport and play
> Unweetingly importuned
> Their own destruction to come speedy upon them.
> So fond are mortal men
> Fallen into wrath divine,
> As their own ruin on themselves to invite,
> Insensate left, or to sense reprobate,
> And with blindness internal struck.
>
> (1669–86)

* This essay was written specifically for this volume and is published here for the first time by permission of the author.

The chorus is hedging the question of agency here, and the ambiguities are worth noting. God causes the Philistines to call for their own destruction, yet it is their own blameworthy fondness that makes them invite their ruin. This fondness may be the manifestation of divine wrath, or on the other hand it may be that God's wrath at their fond preference for Dagon is the reason that he does not rescue them from the destruction it will inevitably cause. They are only bent on sport and play, which means that they had no intention of importuning their own destruction, but also that their intention, their bent on dissipation was a frenzied desire for what would destroy them. They're either insensate, which is not their fault, or reprobate to sense, which is.[2]

The apparent contradiction here is one Luther tried to explain in his account of God's hardening of Pharoah's heart in Exodus: the origin of the will comes from God, but the will itself, regardless of its origin, is intent on evil and for this it is deservedly punished. If God creates an evil thing, then it certainly is evil, and so worthy of destruction. This doctrine of compatabilism is not quite Milton's, however, and the chorus seems to be finessing the question how much credit God should get for the operations of a certain dramatic fatality. If he receives credit at all it is for the intimate impulses that drive the Philistines to wish for what they would wish for anyhow—the spectacle of Samson's humiliation; this is the pendant to the intimate impulse, the "rousing motions . . . which *dispose* / To something extraordinary [Samson's] thoughts" (1383–84; my emphasis), which cause Samson once more to see whether going along to Dagon's feast will give him the opportunity he seeks to confound his enemies. What God actually does is stage-manage a confrontation that its principles might not have arrived at on their own, but the confrontation itself occurs without any interference on his part. His agency effectively consists in his making their agency possible, not in actively interceding.

It is in this sense that God's agency in the drama takes the form of his "dispose." The word echoes the prefatory epistle to the poem. There Milton defines tragic plot as "nothing indeed but such economy, or *disposition* of the fable as may stand best with verisimilitude and decorum" (my emphasis). To some degree this reverses Aristotle, for whom plot is primary and preliminary, and not simply a distribution of events "standing" well with decorum. Milton may thus be felt to be downgrading the activeness of the tragic action, which Aristotle says constitutes the plot (*Poetics*, 6), and to promote a kind of economy or disposition of its elements over a direct causal sequence under the full control of any agent. For the dramatist, disposition of the fable is a decision as to how to present a series of given events, which is of course what Milton is doing in retelling a biblical story (in the two epics as well). The issue of presentation of incident is important enough to Milton that the Argument alerts us to the fact that he dramatizes it: "an Hebrew comes in haste confusedly at first; and afterwards more distinctly relating the catastrophe. . . ." Disposition consists in the *timing* of the presentation of events. True, for God (in *Samson* as in *Paradise Lost*) what would need timing would be opportunities for his creatures' agency, for their capacity to cause events, rather than the presentation of the events themselves. But in a way this could be seen as God's dispose of foreseeable events; the difference is a temporal and modal one, God allowing confrontations between free agents to occur which will result in a certain disposition of incident.[3] Thus in his dispose God would have so arranged the economy of the fable, so distributed the timing of his creatures' own causally independent desires, that the Philistines would call upon themselves their own greatest destruction just through their victorious celebration. Rather than interceding ex machina (even Samson's intimate impulse is merely the discovery of the potential disposition of the plot), God's dispose underscores the tragic irony of the Philistines' destruction. The irony, to be irony, lies in the Philistines' agency in their own demise, not in God's. But the question of Samson's agency is more difficult.

The "mere [] management . . . of the events,"[4] or "ordering of the incidents,"[5] makes it unclear who is responsible for the sense of heroism and triumph that the Chorus and the poem feel in the close. Is it God or is it Samson? When at the end of the poem, the chorus says that God "to his faithful champion hath in place / Bore witness gloriously" (1751–52) there's something strangely passive about what God has done—he's done what we've done, he's been a witness, and it's not quite clear what there is in the act of bearing witness that differs from witnessing here, nor what there is in witnessing that can be done gloriously.[6] No doubt the chorus means that God has testified to his own support of Samson; rhetorically such testimony would be performative and self-validating. But in Samson's case it can only mean that he allowed the witnessed event to occur and thus to be witnessed, by God, by the messenger, and through him by the chorus and by us. Bearing witness is precisely a question of the presentation and disposition of incident, "in place," which must mean both at the proper place in the story but also so coincidentally to Samson's witnessed deed as to be indistinguishable from it. The emphasis is on witness, rather than intervention. The glory of agency in *Samson Agonistes* is so attenuated as to seem nearly empty, as though the difference between agency and the better fortitude of patience has come undone.[7]

As I've already suggested, the question of who or what is responsible for the triumph at the end of *Samson Agonistes* has to do partly with the vexed questions of free will and agency that come up in any discussion of Milton's Arminianism. Using Max Weber's conceptual vocabulary, John Guillory has recently reframed these questions in terms of the ambiguity of the notions of vocation, work, and election in the history of Protestantism.

I want to take from Guillory the sense that *Samson Agonistes* inevitably raises questions of agency—or causal initiation—that may finally be psychologically insoluble.[8] For Guillory, the way Samson puts an end to this problem is through a labor of destruction—a spectacular display of agency which results in the abolition of the problem, through its self-destruction. But Samson's solution and Milton's own stance in post-Restoration England do not coincide, and if Samson engages in an act of triumphant violence this makes vivid the contrast between his action and the almost notorious restraint of the poem, its very nearly complete economy as to any action at all, as though its only action were in its series of dispositions of the fable.

It is on this restraint that I want to concentrate. *Samson Agonsites* is a poem in which almost nothing happens. What the reader (and writer) share with Samson is a sense of waiting for the "event" of the poem, but that event has very little to do with the events in the poem itself.

This is what Dr. Johnson insisted. I want to use Johnson in order to try to characterize the stillness of *Samson Agonistes*, a stillness that is Samson's entire state of being within the poem, as he waits for something to happen, whether intimate impulse or death (or both). The reader similarly waits for something to happen, and I think finally the poem is about the experience of *that* contentless event—not the "true experience [of the] great event" (1756) that takes place offstage, but the phantasmatic event of waiting.

Johnson famously complained that "the poem . . . has a beginning and an end which Aristotle himself could not have disapproved; but it must be allowed to want a middle, since nothing passes between the first act and the last, that either hastens or delays the death of Samson." The notion of middle here seems to mean what resists the collapse of a story into its result; even if that resistance hastens the arrival of the story's end, it fills out the account of how that end arrives. Thus Johnson goes on to say, "The whole drama, if its superfluities were cut off, would scarcely fill a single act; yet this is the tragedy which ignorance has admired, and bigotry applauded" (*Rambler* 139). Johnson's metaphors here oddly recapitulate the beginning and end of the poem, or at least of the story in *Judges*. Because Samson's hair—an apparent superfluity—is cut off, he begins the play in captivity; his performance in the Temple of Dagon earns the admiration of ignorance and the applause of bigotry. "Hitherto, Lords, what your commands impos'd / I have perform'd, as reason was, obeying, / Not without wonder or delight beheld" (1640–42).

Such recapitulatory language is present also, I think, in Johnson's praise of the account of the destruction of the Temple: "this is undoubtedly a just and regular catastrophe, and the poem, therefore, has . . . an end. . . ." The catastrophe (literally, *overturning*) is just and regular, both as an account and as an event—just and regular as poetry, and just and conformable to divine law in its destruction of the Philistines. And in the next *Rambler*,

Johnson continues employing the terms of the poem he criticizes when he writes that "The everlasting verdure of Milton's laurels has nothing to fear from the blasts of malignity; nor can my attempt produce any other effect, than to strengthen their shoots by lopping their luxuriance." This partially identifies Johnson with Dalila again, even as it echoes Manoa's plan to bring Samson home, where he will "build him / A Monument, and plant it round with shade / Of Laurel ever green. . ." (1733–35).

I suspect that the echoes in Johnson's language arise out of a fundamental anxiety at the heart of the closet drama—an anxiety about the act of reading itself. The privacy and intimacy of reading—the fact that this drama does take place only in the study—do not sort well with the separation of actor and spectator, of speaker and hearer, that is the very constitution of the public, of all public life, including public theatre. Samson can justify his public appearance at Dagon's festival because of the private presages that allow him to continue a Nazarite (1386–87), and so "separate to God" (31).[9] But no clear separation between public and private characterizes the act of reading the poem, where the reader's engagement is at once less intense and less distanced than a spectator's would be: less intense because there is nothing to *see*; less distanced because there is nothing to turn from or to turn to. The action only occurs as I read it, and cannot be said ever to go on without me.

There is therefore, I think, exemplary value in the fact that the language of *Samson Agonistes* should contaminate the language that would describe it and pronounce strictures upon it. This contamination occurs both because the commentator cannot clearly distinguish commentary from reading (witnessing from bearing witness), and because the commentator is partly attempting to dramatize, to publicize, an act of confrontation, with all that this implies of duality and separation, that it is his complaint that the play lacks. (Johnson adumbrates the ambiguity in the modern critical notion of reading, which can range from passive perception to active commentary.) Indeed, Johnson has begun this second *Rambler* with an observation that sounds like a continuation of his criticism, that the drama wants a middle, which has ended the last *Rambler*: "It is common, says Bacon, to desire the end without enduring the means." But this is actually about his own "attempts to show, however modestly, the failure of a celebrated writer." Thus Johnson's critical reading of *Samson* constitutes the middle that the poem itself lacks, and itself provides the means—the medium and middle absent from drama— to the end of appreciating its just and regular catastrophe and of strengthening the shoots of its author's laurels.

Johnson's reading, in other words, seeks to render more substantial the play's wispy evanescence. For to say that the play wants a middle is another way of saying that in some sense it is all middle, all interstices. The play, through most of its length, is a kind of marking of time. Aristotle's definition of the middle, in chapter 7 of the *Poetics*, permits both senses, resistance and suspension. It is "that which follows something else, although something else exists or comes about after it" (p. 41). Johnson's sense of middle as what hastens or delays the catastrophe is something like Hume's idea of causation as a kind of ghostly connection between cause and effect; indeed in his *Life* of Milton Johnson will bring in the concept of cause in repeating his strictures against *Samson*: "the intermediate parts have neither cause nor consequence, neither hasten nor retard the catastrophe." Hume's skepticism about causation might be regarded as another element of his antipodal relation to Johnson, for Hume did not see how such a mediating moment between cause and effect could occur. This skepticism arises from the consideration that causation itself would have to be immediately related to the cause and to the effect (otherwise the problem would simply be displaced: how does causation cause what it causes—through a second-order causation? and so on). To prevent simultaneity of cause and effect (so that every chain of causes would reduce to a single instant, all dominos falling at once) you have to reify causation itself as a state, a kind of syncope or suspension of action falling between every cause and its effect. Causation thus would be the moment when nothing happens. Every mediation between cause and effect would be a period of suspension of action.

I've argued elsewhere that Hume's philosophical claim stems in some ways out of Shakespeare, and that Kant's argument against Hume is a recapitulation of Aristotle's *Poetics*.[10] Here I follow this detour only in order to characterize what it is that is so unsettling about *Samson*: that sense of suspension. And, as I say, I think that that suspension is most aptly character-ized as a kind of experience of reading. Paul de Man has famously described the resistance to reading, but perhaps more important is the phantasmal resistance *of* reading.[11] This resistance is oddly bound up with its opposite. The phenomenology of literacy is such that nothing is less resistant than reading, than the eye gliding over words on a page; and yet somehow we want, or are compelled, to invest this extraordinary physical ease with difficulties of a high order. In a sense—and this is what I think Johnson is finally objecting to—the difficulty of *Samson* lies in its ease, in the fact that nothing except sheer reading separates its beginning and its end. There is no causal structure to resist a kind of always imminent immediacy, no event connecting and separating the beginning from the end it would hasten or delay, or better, both hasten *and* delay. Johnson's airily summarizing ventriloquization of the central reversal—"during the absence of the messen-ger, having a while defended the propriety of his conduct [in refusing to go along to the feast for Dagon, Samson] at last declares himself moved by a secret impulse to comply, and utters some dark presages of a great event to be brought to pass by his agency, under the direction of Providence"— points up the absence of any sort of causation in the play: nothing need come before this middle, and what comes after could have come at any time. Despite the heroic attempts of many critics with very different allegiances, from Arthur Barker to Christopher Hill, to make of *Samson* a powerful and inexorable mental drama (attempts which are almost always a display of the profound and dramatic mental life of the critic), a kind of blank, a vacancy of *any* event, physical or mental, is central to the work's effect. Johnson, at least, does not deny this, although he does lament it.

Is this effect accidental? Milton's own early relation to drama, well before the Puritan revolution and the closing of the theatres, was one of reading. His 1630 poem "On *Shakespear*" already describes reading as the exchange of stances between work and audience:

> Thou in our wonder and astonishment
> Hast built thy self a live-long Monument.
> For whilst to th'shame of slow-endeavouring art,
> Thy easy numbers flow, and that each heart
> Hath from the leaves of thy unvalu'd Book,
> Those Delphick lines with deep impression took,
> Then thou our fancy of it self bereaving
> Dost make us Marble with too much conceaving;
> And so Sepulcher'd in such pomp dost lie,
> That Kings for such a Tomb would wish to die.
>
> (7–16)

In the wonder and astonishment produced by *reading* Shakespeare, by taking the impression of his lines from the leaves of his book onto our hearts, we are turned to marble, even as his numbers keep flowing. This, in a sense, is the opposite of Johnson's complaint, which will be that nothing of any significance happens in *Samson*; for Milton it is the reader who becomes unable to act. But although vectored differently, the connection between reader and text is the same.

The difference between Shakespeare and *Samson* may feel like the difference between middles and their absence. A middle, as Johnson conceives it, might be described as the action that takes place on stage, at least in Milton's classical sources; beginnings and endings are the offstage, already known events connected by the causation provided by the middle. To say that *Samson* wants a middle, or to say that it is all middle, is to say that nothing happens onstage. *Samson Agonistes* is of course the English play most notorious for what happens offstage, as compared with the very little that we might see. Like Samson's our relation to the action of the drama is one of blindness. We don't see it, but only hear about it. Indeed, as readers we can only be aware of what some person in the drama reports to us: nothing can happen for us apart from its description. Our eyes neither represent nor misrepresent any event. Their only function is the relationship, alien at once to proximity and to distance, of reading. In this lies the curiously affectless safety of our relationship to the theatrical events, an affectless safety entirely opposed to the experience of sitting in a theatre. It is safe because we cannot be involved, and affectless because there is nothing that we could be said to have escaped. It is of course no accident that the building Samson destroys is a theatre, as the messenger who escapes to report Samson's death emphasizes:

> all abroad was rumoured that this day
> Samson should be brought forth to show the people
> Proof of his mighty strength in feats and games;
> I sorrowed at his captive state, but minded
> Not to be absent at that spectacle.
> The building was a spacious theatre. . . .
>
> (1600–5)

To see Samson perform means to risk death; to hear about his performance means to be absent from the theatre, whether as Manoa and the chorus are absent, or as the reader reading the "work" is absent.[12] This sounds like an experience of purgation without its enabling condition of pity or terror, and the question is what content such an experience might have.

Here it is worth returning to Milton's curious version of Aristotle. Milton sets as mottoes to the prefatory epistle a truncated quotation of Aristotle's Greek (tragedy is the imitation of a serious action, etc.), followed by his somewhat less truncated Latin rendering (tragedy is the imitation of a serious action, etc., with pity and terror causing the purgation of such affects); part of what he elides is Aristotle's insistence that tragedy occurs "in the form of action, not narration" (p. 39). Milton then translates into English and improves: "Tragedy, as it was antiently compos'd, hath been ever held the gravest, moralest, and most profitable of all other Poems: therefore said by *Aristotle* to be of power by raising pity and fear, or terror, to purge the mind of those and such like passions, that is to temper and reduce them to just measure with a kind of delight, stirr'd up by reading or seeing those passions well imitated."

That is, in Milton's rendering, tragedy purges the mind of those passions that it comes to experience in reading or seeing the imitation of such passions. Pity and terror are emotions that arise from reading or seeing pity and terror well imitated; the imitation is prior to what it imitates. A deconstructive-style vicious circle can be discovered here. The real passions of the audience come before their imitation on stage, and yet those passions are produced through the imitation.[13] This can be saved, of course, by stressing the importance of the idea that the passions are "stirr'd up"—an ambiguous phrase possibly suggesting that they exist more or less latently in human beings and can be raised in a variety of ways, including their imitation on stage. Perhaps there's no surprise there. But it's still worth dwelling on the idea that Milton's definition of tragedy goes something like this: an imitation of the emotional experience of attending to a tragedy. This is clear also in the idea that the audience's passions are produced in response to the imitation of fear and pity, not as in Aristotle in response to the action.[14] It is the chorus who experience fear and pity, and so the audience responds to the chorus, to the fear and pity imitated by an onstage audience, and not to what happens to the protagonist.

This suggests—though again I don't want to place too much emphasis on this—something resembling a Bloomian paradigm. *Samson Agonistes* is a tragedy in some ways imitative of Milton's own experience of tragedy. Naturally, Greek tragedy is what he has primarily in mind, but the idea that tragedy will reduce the passions to "just measure with a kind of delight" probably also glances at *Antony and Cleopatra*:

> Nay, but this dotage of our general's
> O'erflows the measure.
>
> > (1.1.1–2)
>
> * * *
>
> > His delights
> Were dolphin-like, they show'd his back above
> The element they liv'd in.
>
> > (5.2.88–90)

I may seem to be finding a lot of allusiveness in two words, but the play alludes almost obsessively to *Antony and Cleopatra*,[15] and it seems reasonable to take those allusions as a context even for the prefatory matter. This is especially true given the complexity of the word "delight" in *Samson*: thus Samson refers to the "various objects of delight" which belong to light itself (71) as well as the "wonder or delight" of his Philistine audience. This latter phrase returns us to the "wonder and astonishment" of "On *Shakespear*." There too the formulation is slightly odd: "Thou in our wonder and astonishment / Hast built thy self a live-long monument," as though our affect, our wonder and astonishment, preceded the poet who makes use of it to build his monument by causing it.

Milton's description of the experience of tragedy as "reading or seeing those passions well imitated" allows respectively for both Miltonic and Shakespearean tragedy. But reading and seeing are hardly commensurate activities. To see a passion well imitated is to see an actor doing the imitation. To read a passion well imitated is to attend to the language and not the performance of the language. Aristotle doesn't talk about the experience of reading tragedy, but of seeing it: "Now since the representation is carried out by men performing the actions, it follows, in the first place, that spectacle is an essential part of tragedy."[16] The difference between the two modes to which Milton refers corresponds to the difference between two kinds of imitation, performance and writing, and I think that Milton is consciously attempting a theory of reading in *Samson*, partly as an evasion or alternative to Shakespeare, both in the preface and in the poem as a whole.[17]

It is certainly the experience of reading that the opening of *Samson* aims at: "SAMSON: A little onward lend thy guiding hand / To these dark steps, a little further on; / For yonder bank hath choice of sun or shade . . ." (1–3). The list of persons in the drama does not mention Samson's guide, who has a curiously elusive life in the play. Of course he has no lines; but he enters with Samson at the opening of the play, and may, according to the messenger's account, be killed by Samson in the general slaughter:

> At length for intermission sake they led him
> Between the pillars; he his guide requested
> (For so from such as nearer stood we heard)
> As over-tired to let him lean a while
> With both his arms on those two massy pillars
> That to the arched roof gave main support.
> He unsuspicious led him. . . .
>
> (1629–35)

The request for intermission (the suspended middle which turns out to be the climax) and the chance for rest and relief echo the opening of the poem, and there's a sense in which Samson's feat recapitulates the poem in miniature. It may be that Samson, at his exit from the poem, is led by the guide (or it could be that he's led by the Philistine officer); at any rate the chorus imagines another guide for him: "Go, and the Holy One / Of Israel be thy guide . . ." (1427–28).

At the start of the poem, though, the guide represents a silent addressee, and it is very hard to say where Samson moves from addressing the guide to soliloquy. Certainly he's still talking to the guide at line 11 ("leave me to respire") and certainly we can forget about the guide by line 23 ("O wherefore was my birth from heaven foretold . . . ?"). The point is, first of all, that the guide has to be a ghostly presence, available when needed, but completely effaced, as a visible character on stage would not be, when we are caught up in the reading.[18]

But the guide is of course the reader as well, leading the reading on. The dark steps of Samson are also the dark steps of Milton, and of Milton's poetic measure.[19] Thus at the end of his speech, Samson will announce the entrance of the chorus (which otherwise we would not know about): "But who are these? for with joint pace I hear / The tread of many feet steering this way" (110–11). The joint pace of many feet is prosodical as well, indicating that the chorus is in monostrophe, as the dedicatory epistle has already declared.[20] To lend a hand to Samson's steps is to move a hand under the lines that you are reading; complementarily this also describes a kind of writing, Samson's steps guided onwards by Milton's composition. The choice of sun or shade thematically alludes to light and blindness, but also to ink on the page.

The play eschews all notion of mutual physical presence—of the bodies that make theatre. Samson clasps the hand only of his ghostly guide; he refuses to touch Dalila, and Harapha refuses to touch him.[21] This, I think, is another way of thematizing the nonpresence of reading; certainly its effects, like the effect of the ghostly guide, depend upon reading rather than seeing. Thus, Samson's first indication of the bench couldn't work on stage, since he's blind and any attempt to point it out would look either incongruous or ludicrous (unless awfully dignified). Only in reading can language reasonably point to an unseeable object. And, as already noted, Samson's apostrophes in his first speech can slide imperceptibly from an address to the guide to a general lamentation, and thence to an apostrophe to the loss of sight (67). And thus also it can be unclear for a while when exactly the chorus actually addresses him. The chorus enters resolved to leave him alone: "This, this is he; softly a while, / Let us not break in upon him; / O change beyond report, thought, or belief!" (115–17). This apostrophe to change gives rise to the passionate rhetorical questions: "Or do my eyes misrepresent? Can this be he, / That heroic, that renowned, / Irresistible Samson?" (124–26). The evidence of seeing undoes the evidence of renown. The story takes place on a different plane from the spectacle, and Samson present is for the chorus Samson absent. The chorus continues its account of Samson's past glories, and then begins another apostrophe:

> Which shall I first bewail,
> Thy bondage or lost sight,
> Prison within prison
> Inseparably dark?
> Thou art become (O worst imprisonment!)
> The dungeon of thyself. . . .
> The rarer thy example stands,
> By how much from the top of wondrous glory,
> Strongest of mortal men,
> To lowest pitch of abject fortune thou art fallen.
> (151–69)

But it turns out that none of this is an address to Samson, that the chorus's apostrophe, while overheard by the reader is neither heard nor meant to be heard by its addressee. "I hear the sound of words, their sense the air / Dissolves unjointed ere it reach my ear" (176–77), Samson says, and makes of the joint pace of the chorus an unjointed sound. Also unjointed and dissolved are the eye-rhymes here: "their sense the air" / "ere . . . reach the ear," a play of language visible but probably not audible, like the rhyme *desire* / *destroyer* (1677–78), or the repeated slant rhymes on *life* and *light*, or the rimes riches on *light*. Only then does the chorus actually address

Samson: "He speaks, let us draw nigh. Matchless in might, / The glory late of Israel, now the grief; / We come thy friends and neighbors. . . ." (178–80).

There's an almost cinematic quality to the closet drama's ability to obscure the totality of interaction.[22] The speeches serve as close-ups, but we can never be sure who's present on stage; we don't know who is talking to whom at any given time, and who is overhearing what speech. All this tends to place the focus very heavily on language as a sort of ritual soliloquy, and I think that the only deep (Shakespearean) dialogue is between Samson and Dalila. All the more remarkable, then, is Samson's odd and bitter charity to her, "At distance I forgive thee, go with that" (954), which emphasizes again the ways in which Samson is about a world reduced to a purely linguistic space of distances where theatrical presence is impossible.

I think that this is thematized most clearly in the report of Samson's last act. The guide unsuspiciously leads Samson to the pillars for support,

> which when Samson
> Felt in his arms, with head a while inclined,
> And eyes fast fixed he stood, as one who prayed,
> Or some great matter in his mind revolved.
> At last with head erect thus cried aloud,
> Hitherto, lords, what your commands imposed
> I have performed, as reason was, obeying,
> Not without wonder or delight beheld.
> Now of my own accord such other trial
> I mean to show you of my strength, yet greater;
> As with amaze shall strike all who behold.
> (1635–45)

The theatre is the place for the display of power, but not tragedy, since at this theatre delight precedes greater—even measureless—terror. But the mental theatre of report in which *Samson* is played out eschews display. (As with the bench, this makes it possible to imagine Samson's "eyes fast fixed" as though intentionally oblivious to the visible as he revolves his thoughts; as though the visible *could* be visible to him.) Those who see Samson's show of strength are those who die watching it—all except the Jobean witness who has escaped to tell what he has seen. All that remains of Samson's feat is the story reported of him; like the phoenix, he comes back to another sort of life: "And though her body die, her fame survives, / A secular bird, ages of lives" (1706–7). Samson's fame is the issue for the remainder of the poem (1717, 1736–39); indeed, it is the fact that his story ends as it does that shows how God "to his faithful champion hath in place / Bore witness gloriously."

It is part of Milton's iconoclasm that God's presence can only be part of the report, rather than ever witnessed directly.[23] The hidden God of the

Israelites corresponds to the antirepresentational character of the poem, a poem in which, as Johnson complained, nothing happens. Everything mentioned in the poem is in some odd aspectual (in the grammatical sense) relation to the actual interaction between characters; and this strange incommensurability of aspect seems always at work. Samson and Dalila speak not as lovers but as people disappointed with each other. Samson's own past seems put into question by the present state to which he has degenerated. The promises of the past all seem blasted through his defeat by the Philistines. And his final glory takes place offstage. In *Samson*, even destruction lacks material status; where Shakespeare has built a live-long monument in our wonder and astonishment, all those struck with amaze (1644) by Samson's feat die. Manoa, indeed, intends to build him a material monument (1734), but his eternizing wishes for its everlasting laurels are in some sense empty, since no such monument survives; by the seventeenth century, Samson's tomb has disappeared. Opposed to any monument, to any idol—even that of a name like Shakespeare's—is the empty process of reading. What else is the "new acquist / Of true experience" that leaves the servants of God "calm of mind, all passion spent" (1755–58)? The acquisition of experience is the expenditure of the passion experienced in acquiring it, and what finally remains is the end of the act of reading, the suspended middle of the poem merging with the suspension of the poem itself in its ending. I think that this is the version of divinity that Milton finally read in the text of the history he participated in: God indistinguishable from his absence; both presence and absence reduced to just measure with a kind of delight indistinguishable from loss of hope. If *Antony and Cleopatra* theatricalizes the beginning of Christian history, and if for Milton Shakespeare stands for the beginning of English drama, *Samson Agonistes* marks their empty interminability, their issue in a perpetually suspended intermission, the suspension of all causation, of all divinity in history, with the end of the Good Old Cause.

The notorious difficulty of dating the work is appropriate (and for me is evidence of its lateness), because in a certain sense *Samson Agonistes* is posthumous from the start, the residue of defeated agency, of a vanished middle which would lead to some appropriate end. *Samson* records the fact that it records nothing but the experience of its reading. Samson's own history means nothing to his death, is unrelated to it, which is why Milton casts off the biblical thematic of revenge in Samson's final act. *Samson* is not a revenge drama, the drama of causation par excellence. It is about the purgation of history as cause or as caused. What remains is a belatedness as to all incident, even the apocalyptic defeat of the Philistines, or of Charles I. Events turn into history, into historical narrative, and narrative is read until it comes to an end not very different from the act of reading itself, whose passions are stirred up and spent in the same perpetual belatedness.

Notes

1. It's also used as a noun twice in *Paradise Regained*, to mean "disposal;" thus Satan tells Jesus: "It shall be my task / To render thee the Parthian at dispose" (3.368–69). Neither time is it the subject of a sentence.

2. Earlier Samson too has straddled the question of God's disposition. Manoa complains that Samson's indignities are fouler than he deserves, to which his son answers:

> Appoint not heavenly disposition, father,
> Nothing of all these evils hath befall'n me
> But justly; I myself have brought them on,
> Sole author I, sole cause. . . .
>
> (373–76)

Manoa ought not complain about heavenly disposition, either because it has nothing to do with what has happened to Samson, or because its decrees are perfectly just.

3. Thus God's Arminian position in *Paradise Lost* still preserves the sense that the future is disposed by him, although not through absolute decree or foreknowledge:

> They therefore as to right belonged,
> So were created, not can justly accuse
> Their maker, or their making, or their fate,
> As if predestination overruled
> Their will, disposed by absolute decree
> Or high foreknowledge; they themselves decreed
> Their own revolt, not I: if I foreknew,
> Foreknowledge had no influence on their fault,
> Which had proved no less certain unforeknown.
>
> (3.111–19)

This is an answer to Satan's earlier equation of disposing with decreeing: "he / Who now is sovereign can dispose and bid / What shall be right" (1.245–47). God does foreknow, and through this foreknowledge makes sure to confound Satan and save the elect. But his disposition is not decree—it is not causal but demonstrative or expository, allowing evil opportunity to confound itself through its own operations.

4. John Carey, in his note to the prefatory epistle to *Samson Agonistes*, in *The Poems of John Milton*, ed. Carey and Alastair Fowler (New York: Norton, 1972), 345.

5. Aristotle, *Poetics*, in *Classical Literary Criticism*, trans. T. S. Dorsch (London: Penguin, 1965), 39.

6. "Bore witness gloriously" has the same interestingly incongruous feel as the chorus's reference to God's "uncontrollable intent" (1754). The strength of the modifier seems out of proportion to what it modifies, which I think is verbally and conceptually homologous to the problematization of agency here. "Intent" also resonates with the idea of reading rather than acting, since "this work never was intended" to the stage.

7. Samson too is an arranger, and his own death is part of his final disposition, occuring both "by accident" (i.e. incidentally) and "inevitably," since he is "tangled in the fold / of desire necessity, whose law" he cannot abrogate.

8. John Guillory, "The Father's House: *Samson Agonistes* in its historical moment," in *Re-membering Milton: New Essays on the Texts and Traditions*, ed. Mary Nyquist and Margaret W. Ferguson (New York: Methuen, 1988), 148–76.

9. For an extraordinary account of the adventures of election and vocation in *Samson*

Agonistes, and their relation to issues of the public and private, see Guillory's "The Father's House."

10. In "Proximity and Power: Shakespearean and Cinematic Space," *Theatre Journal* 39 (October 1987), 277–93.

11. Here I am thinking of the account of reading given by de Man's great precursor, Maurice Blanchot, in *L'Espace littéraire* (Paris: Gallimard, 1955).

12. A paranthesis in the last sentence of the first paragraph in the prefatory epistle calls *Samson* "this work," alluding, as Gary Taylor observes, to the seventeenth-century debate begun by Ben Jonson as to whether or not plays were properly called "works."

13. The most careful reading of this passage and its relation to Aristotle is John M. Steadman's " 'Passions Well Imitated': Rhetoric and Poetics in the Preface to *Samson Agonistes*," in *Calm of Mind*, ed. Joseph Anthony Wittreich, Jr. (Cleveland: Case Western Reserve University Press, 1971), 175–207. Although alert to many possibilities of ambiguity in both Aristotle and in Milton, Steadman is typical in taking "stirr'd up" to modify "delight," rather than "those and such-like passions." On this reading delight is stirred up through the purgation of the passions, and there may be something to that notion. But I maintain that it's odd to think of delight as stirred up, which has an overtone of anxiety about it; also that "stirr'd *up*" looks back to "*raising* pity and fear, or terror;" and finally that there's something over-casual about the idea that Milton would simply say that the purgation of pity and fear would also bring in its wake the purgation of "such like passions." "Such like passions" needs qualification: "those and such like passions . . . stirr'd up by reading or seeing those passions well imitated."

14. Aristotle, on the other hand, wrote "In tragedy it is the action that is imitated" (39).

15. John Guillory notes some of this allusion in "Dalila's House: *Samson Agonistes* and the Sexual Division of Labor," in *Rewriting the Renaissance: The Discourses of Sexual Differences in Early Modern Europe*, ed. Margaret W. Ferguson and Nancy J. Vickers (Chicago: University of Chicago Press, 1986), 106–22, but on the whole I think that no one has noticed how frequent those allusions are. I observe almost at random 165, 173–77, 710–724, 878, 1208, 1557, 1562–70; and these are only the more obvious allusions. After *Antony and Cleopatra*, but much less often alluded to, one can detect *King Lear*, *Othello*, and *The Merchant of Venice*. In a longer version of this essay I attempt to argue in some detail that Milton's sense of belatedness with respect to Shakespeare took the form of placing a premium on reading as the relation to theatre most adequate to what Shakespeare was attempting, but (for Milton) failing to achieve, on stage. Thus the very fact of his belatedness, the fact that he *reads* Shakespeare (rather than *seeing* his work performed), could already begin representing for Milton, made older than Shakespeare's age through eyesight lost (cf. 1489), a literary stance unavailable to Shakespeare.

16. Aristotle, *Poetics*, 6,4 (39). But see also 6, 19: "Spectacle, or stage-effect, is an attraction, of course, but it has the least to do with the playwright's craft or with the art of poetry. For the power of tragedy is independent both of performance and of actors" (41).

17. Hence his oft-quoted approval of the idea of *Revelations* as having the form of a tragedy.

18. I don't deny that a decent production of *Samson* could make the guide as uncanny as he is in the reading; his presence could actually disappear on stage, as Bunraku puppeteers disappear although always present; but if this were the case the stage presentation would have some of the force of reading.

19. Measure, throughout *Samson*, as also (I argue) in *Antony and Cleopatra*, combines the meanings of poetic meter and emotional restraint. This is a very old conceptual pun.

20. There may be a pun on the idea of the prosodical foot in *Paradise Lost* as well:

> and now at foot
> Of Heav'ns ascent they lift their feet, when loe

> A violent cross wind from either Coast
> Blows them transverse ten thousand Leagues awry
> Into the devious Air.
>
> (3.485–89)

The last foot of line 486 crosses up the fools' attempts to make their feet coincide with the steps ascending heaven at its foot. At any rate, the pun is found passim in *Samson*. Manoa, for example, enters "with careful step" after the chorus because their feet are younger, and his feet come "lagging after" (327–37); later when he thinks he can ransom Samson he returns "With youthful steps" (1442); similarly Dalila arrives "With doubtful feet and wavering resolution" (732). All of this emphasizes how much it is precisely walking on foot that manifests itself to the reader only in reading the chorus's poetry.

21.   Although Samson suggests the pairing of touch and sight which I argue stands for the distanced immediacy of reading—"thou seest it in thy hand" (1105)—Harapha's hand is not like the reader's or writer's guiding hand. This phrase—"thou seest it in thy hand"—probably means something like, you can see this immediate possibility at hand. But it does go with other moments in the poem of a kind of synesthesia which I would equate with the difference between reading and seeing; reading literally depends on seeing, but it also depends on not seeing, or on understanding something different from what you are literally seeing. Thus, for example, the chorus's grotesquely metonymic announcement of the arrival of Harapha, after Dalila's departure: "Look now for no inchanting voice, nor fear / The bait of honied words; a rougher tongue / Draws hitherward, I know him by his stride" (1065–67), where Samson might *look* for a voice, where words might be *honied*, but especially where *tongues* stride, as though on metrical feet. Shortly after this Harapha himself talks of striding or walking sound: he has "come to see of whom such noise / Hath walk'd about, and each limb to survey, / If thy appearance answer loud report." And Samson replies: "The way to know were not to see but taste" (1088–91); later he warns Harapha to "take good heed my hand survey not thee" (1230). Samson earlier has threatened Dalila to "tear thee joint by joint" after she desires to "approach at least, and touch thy hand" (951–53)—this after Samson has declared that his *feet* will never enter her doors, so that again actual physical contact in the poem is being opposed to poetry and to the relation to poetry that reading names.

22.   I mean this in a way roughly consonant with my article on Shakespearean and cinematic space.

23.   David Loewenstein, in *Milton and the Drama of History: Historical Vision, Iconoclasm, and the Literary Imagination* (Cambridge: Cambridge University Press, 1990), 126–51, reads *Samson* as a complex negotiation whereby Milton's radical iconoclasm can nevertheless manifest itself in an extraordinarily theatrical spectacle. In some ways this reading resonates with Guillory's in "The Father's House." Guillory sees Samson's act of destruction fulfilling the contradictory vocational demands of Manoa and of God; it does so when the difference between work and destruction becomes undone.

PARADISE LOST

◆

John Milton and the Republican Mode of Literary Production

PETER LINDENBAUM*

"It is a shame," lamented Boswell in 1773, acting yet once more as straight man to Dr Johnson, "that authors are not now better patronized." To which the unabashed free marketeer of learning responded: "No sir. If learning cannot support a man, if he must sit with his hands across till somebody feeds him, it is as to him a bad thing, and it is better as it is. With patronage, what flattery! what falsehood! While a man is in equilibrio, he throws truth among the multitude, and lets them take it as they please: in patronage, he must say what pleases his patron, and it is an equal chance whether that be truth or falsehood."[1] Boswell was no doubt merely drawing his friend out, since Johnson had, a moment before, exultantly proclaimed "We have done with patronage." Literary critics have tended to disagree over what exactly might have constituted the death knell of the aristocratic patronage system, whose passing Johnson celebrated on several different occasions. A past generation looked most often perhaps to Johnson's own famous 1755 letter to the Earl of Chesterfield, berating that lord for gratuitous commendation after having ignored Johnson seven years earlier when he needed real help, of a monetary kind. Maynard Mack has recently resubmitted an alternative event, Pope's 1714 contract with the publisher Lintot for the subscription and publication of the poet's *Iliad*.[2] As a result of the eight to nine thousand pounds Pope took home from *The Iliad* and *The Odyssey*, he became the first poet to achieve financial independence by means of his poetry alone, without having to rely upon the munificence of some single great figure. I should like to drive the event farther back yet, to Milton's act of publishing *Paradise Lost* on the open market, for what amounted to the meagre sum of ten pounds.

Actually, it is not the publication of *Paradise Lost* alone that might be said to mark the watershed, but the whole shape or progress of Milton's career up to and including the publication of his epic in 1667. For Milton

* *Milton and the Republican Mode of Literary Production* by Peter Lindenbaum. The *Yearbook of English Studies*, Vol. 21, 1991. Copyright © Modern Humanities Research Association, 1991. All rights reserved. Reprinted by permission of the Editor and the Modern Humanities Research Association.

provides us with an example of someone who began his career within the aristocratic patronage system and worked his way free of it. His first major published work was the masque we call *Comus*, the masque itself of course an aristocratic form and written to honour the Earl of Bridgewater's family on the occasion of the Earl's installation, in 1634, as Lord President of Wales. *Comus* is by no means an ordinary celebratory piece; it constitutes, as several critics now have well shown, an effort to educate its aristocratic audience and is, if anything, critical of the cavalier, courtly taste and attitudes that one normally associates with masques.[3] It in no way fawns. But there is ample evidence that the young Milton was enormously pleased not simply with the work itself but also with the aristocratic connexions it implied. He participated in the preparation of the 1637 printing of the masque, restoring some passages from the pre-performance manuscript, adding significant new passages that make its moral point clearer and more substantial; yet he seemed willing to let the work appear anonymously in 1637, as if the property of those for whom it was performed. When he did finally put his name to the masque in print, in the 1645 edition of his *Poems*, he gave *Comus* pride of place, perhaps as the volume's most substantial work, taking it out of chronological order and putting it last among his English poems, after "Lycidas" of 1637. And he assigned the masque a separate title page in the volume and prefaced it with Henry Lawes's Dedicatory Letter to the Earl of Bridgewater's son, taken from the 1637 edition, and with a letter of commendation to the author from Sir Henry Wotton, provost of Eton College and former ambassador to Venice. In the 1645 volume Milton and his publisher Humphrey Moseley are in part trying to make Milton's name on the coat-tails of others. The title page of the whole volume informs us that "The SONGS were set in Musick by Mr. HENRY LAWES Gentleman of the KINGS Chappel, and one of his MAJESTIES Private Musick."

By 1645 Milton had already embarked on his public career as a prose writer, and his twentieth-century biographer, William Riley Parker, has suggested that Milton published the 1645 volume in order to establish a name for himself as something other than a Puritan pamphleteer and a "divorcer."[4] But the 1645 volume went virtually unnoticed and it was in prose and public service that Milton's public career remained for the period 1641 to 1660, as he wrote polemical works first on behalf of his religious party, then the government, and then a republic of his own devising. When he did get back to writing and publishing poetry as his main concern, his own religious and political causes were so out of favour that there may well have been no patron willing to be viewed as his supporter. And, of course, to a certain extent Milton did have a patron for *Paradise Lost* after all; please that one reader, God, and no others matter. But the decision to publish *Paradise Lost* on the open market and without benefit of protection or support of some great man represents not simply a religious decision but a political one. In his desire to educate a whole nation through *Paradise Lost*, Milton was making an essentially republican gesture, one that can be said to be an outgrowth of his own increasing republicanism in the period 1640 to 1660.

To see the full significance of Milton's manner of publishing *Paradise Lost*, we need to consider the various publishing and writing models he had before him, and to do that we can best look back to the Italy Milton visited in 1638–39. For it was there that one could see postulated side by side, and in relatively distinct and pure form, two very different modes of producing literature, what I shall be calling the ducal (or aristocratic) and republican modes respectively. I do not claim that the Italian trip was in any way responsible for Milton's move from the first to the second. Milton's whole Italian trip in fact presents many difficulties and the account Milton provides of it in his *Second Defence of the English People* is fraught with inconsistencies and contradictions. He makes virtually no comment at all on what we have reason to expect ought to have been, for an emergent republican Milton, the culminating point of his whole tour, the stay in Venice. The account, though written in 1654 when Milton was in the midst of his career of public service and leading a life very different from his more private existence of the 1630s, betrays much the same kind of thinking that the 1645 volume of poems does. Milton is eager to tell us about the learned friends he made and to gain his readers' respect by that means. Sir Henry Wotton again makes an appearance and is thanked for that same letter which prefaces *Comus*. And, wishing to portray himself as a Protestant patriot, Milton mentions that sad tidings of civil war in England, which he received when in Naples, forced him to abandon his plans to visit Sicily and Greece, and yet the account he provides reveals that it took him six more months to meander home (and when he got there he did not immediately throw himself into the fray, but rather devoted himself to setting up a school for boys and to two more years of reading). If the trip to Italy does not appear, then, to have been the turning point in Milton's artistic career or his thinking generally that his biographers, following Milton's own lead, like to suggest, the trip does remain of major interest.[5] For, as I have suggested, the Italy Milton saw provides us with fully articulated paradigms of two rather different approaches to literature and the men who create it, paradigms which postulate very different roles for writers in their respective societies.

If Venice did not seem to interest Milton much in 1639, what excited him on his trip, and excited him a great deal, was the welcome he received in Florence and Naples. In Florence, where he remained four months in all, he was evidently taken quickly under the wing of a group of men "eminent in rank and learning," members of two different private literary academies, the *Apatisti* and the *Svogliati*, the meetings of both of which Milton attended and from which he emerged with great praise both for his poetic skill and his learning.[6] In Naples he was given the signal honour of particular attention from Giovanni Battista Manso, Marquis of Villa, a nobleman of distinguished rank and former patron to Italy's last great epic poet, Torquato Tasso, and to whom that poet had dedicated his *Dialogue of Friendship*. Manso was a figure of considerable influence, a great patron of the arts and founder and long-time leader of a literary academy, the *Oziosi*, whose meetings were held at his villa. Manso himself seems to have guided Milton around Naples, taken him to the palace of the viceroy, and even visited Milton at his own lodgings. Milton's reception at both these cities, then, plainly appealed to the twenty-nine year old Englishman aspiring to be, and to be recognized as, an up-and-coming poet and scholar. But the account of those two triumphs points to something besides an admiration for John Milton that those two cities had in common, and that is a shared mode of literary production, one very different from that promoted in Venice and that which Milton might be said to have participated in himself in his own later literary career.

The account of the stay in Naples presents us with an arrangement that is familiar enough: it is the traditional patronage system in which the artist strives to gain the attention of a rich patron who in turn provides the material means to enable the artist to continue to ply his artistic or literary trade. The system in Florence implied in the account is a bit more complex, although ultimately the same. Those two literary academies whose meetings Milton attended were both offshoots of the larger, public *Accademia Fiorentina* and that parent academy began its career in the 1540s by being quickly appropriated by Cosimo I, then Duke of Florence and later to be first Grand Duke of Tuscany. Cosimo had provided the members of the academy with a place to meet (initially the Palazzo Medici), with stipends for lectures, and made their elected head a salaried magistrate within his own government, responsible for public instruction and for supervising the book trade within the city. Cosimo secured, as well, the adoption of provisions prohibiting the performance of speeches without permission of his *auditore*.[7] What such measures did of course was to render the literati of Florence politically harmless, those intellectuals, many of whom had been stirred in the period 1527 to 1530 by Florence's final attempt to banish the Medici and re-establish a republican form of government.

The founders of the *Accademia Fiorentina* in 1540 had included members of the merchant class as well as professional scholars and one of the reasons for gathering was a desire to bridge the cultural gap between artisans and intellectuals. By the time of Milton's trip to Italy such aims seem to have been long since abandoned and the various private academies founded by members of the Florentine Academy existed primarily for the amusement of their upper-class members.[8] A favourite form of entertainment at meetings of the *Apatisti* from 1649 on was a game in which members were called upon to provide learned expositions, studded with quotations from classical and modern sources, of immediate, unthinking, no doubt often meaningless, responses to questions put either to a young member of the academy or to a youth brought in from the street for the occasion.[9] Despite the implications we might draw from that game, the academies were serious enough undertakings, promoting piety, the study and practice of literature, philosophy, philology, in some cases even science. But they were distinctly *not* the place the Medici rulers would go for political advice or for discourses in political theory. The very names of the two academies whose members befriended Milton in Florence—the *Apatisti*, meaning passionless or dispassionate, and the *Svogliati*, will-less or disgusted—express all too conveniently the institutions' detachment from political and social issues of their time. Such names are gestures in self-deprecation, but they point up nicely that these academies, like Manso's *Oziosi* in Naples, were in effect pastoral ventures: as the names suggest, such groups seek detachment from everyday political and social life; they are élitist enclaves, whose members seek separation from more humble sorts, from trade, from *negotium*, in order to devote themselves to art, poetry, the life of the mind. Whether they explicitly state it or not—in the way that Ficino's Platonic Academy, founded for him in 1462 by Cosimo "Il Vecchio," did state it—such institutions endorse the contemplative life over the active. And much the same stand is implicit in Manso's kind of patronage system. The intellectuals, those *Oziosi*, whom Manso with all the good will in the world led and supported were expected to go about their literary and artistic business at some distance from those holding direct political power. It was expressly written into the statutes of that academy that its members were forbidden to discuss theological questions, Scripture, or issues dealing with public government, which last were to be left to the care of the princes who ruled over them.[10] The reason why Manso did not see even more of Milton than he did, Manso told the Englishman on his departure and Milton duly reports in the *Second Defence*, was that Milton had been so outspoken on matters of religion. Manso's attention and patronage were at bottom, then, incompatible with forthright, uncensored statements of controversial religious or political positions.

Venice, too, had its aristocratic patrons and its literary academies, the latter complete with self-deprecatory names. And there is much evidence that Venice's academies did not differ greatly from their counterparts in Florence and Naples. The published work of the leading Venetian literary academy at the time of Milton's visit, the *Accademia degli Incogniti*, suggests that the same kinds of topics were discussed there as in academies in other city-states, questions ranging from the light-hearted or silly (defences of the colour grey, or diatribes against cheese) to those dealing with love (whether absence does in fact make the heart grow fonder) to potentially more serious issues (the dangers of eloquence, or whether that prince is wiser who encourages learning among his subjects or he who seeks to extirpate it). A published collection of biographies of the *Incogniti* reveals that perhaps only a tenth of its members were actually Venetian; the *Incogniti* in their meetings could thus hardly be said to be expressing a particularly Venetian sensibility on behalf of the Venetian populace as a whole.[11] But Venice in the late Renaissance had something besides literary academies and which made for quite a different model of intellectual activity within its bounds: it had the only remaining independent and significant republican form of government among the city-states of Italy. And it had an ideology to match, one which was perceived as a direct extension of that republican form of government. This ideology, a version of that strand of Renaissance humanism that Hans Baron, particularly, has labelled for us as "civic humanism," favoured the active life and promoted the ideal of direct participation in the concerns of government on the part of all citizens in society, among which, naturally enough, would be its intellectuals.[12] Venice thereby endorsed a literary system quite at odds with one that sets intellectuals apart from the rest of society, cloistered in élitist enclaves.

In talking about Venice in the Renaissance, though, we have quickly to acknowledge that we are talking about two different Venices—overlapping entities to be sure, but still different—the actual city with its basically aristocratic mode of governing and what historians call "the myth of Venice."[13] The myth in its fullest form claimed that Venice's government had survived unchanged for over a thousand years and had done so primarily because it possessed from its very beginning the ideal combination of balance of the three forms of rule Plato and Polybius had argued was necessary for enduring governmental stability: monarchy, aristocracy, and democracy. The doge represented the monarchic element, the Senate the aristocratic, and the Grand Council the democratic. The resulting stability had in turn given rise to a high degree of personal and civil liberty, as was often noted by writers on and travellers to the city. As critics of the myth like Jean Bodin pointed out though, Venice's government was not really so mixed after all. The power of the doge, despite the fact that he was elected for life, was severely limited: he could not act on his own without four of his six elected councillors present, while any four of those councillors could act with him absent; and his actions were subject to review by the Grand Council at his death and his heirs fined if he were found guilty of impropriety. More importantly, the "many" that the Grand Council, the main electoral body, was purported to represent never at any point in the period from 1500 to 1645 numbered significantly more than one and a half per cent of the total population of Venice: to be a member of the Grand Council and eligible for high elected office, one had to be an adult male descendant of one of the families recorded in the *Libro d'Oro* of 1381. This meant that in 1581, for instance, there were 1,843 members in the Grand Council out of a total population of some 134,890.[14] Venice was in actuality then what we would call today simply a closed aristocracy or an oligarchy, not a mixed polity.

Had there been a legitimately democratic element in the Venetian governmental system, the connexion between the actual Venice and civic humanist dedication to the active life and service to the state (for all citizens) would have been logically firmer and more complete.[15] And it must be admitted as well that the patricians who had complete governmental control of the city-state by no means consistently acted in the high-minded, self-sacrificing, patriotic, and decorous way that their own myth suggested they ought to.[16] In any case and despite this, several generations of writers from and on Venice devoted themselves to promoting a view of the Venetian state as a republican Sparta or Rome and in fact better than those earlier mixed polities because dedicated to peace and civil ends rather than war. And for contemporary Europeans of the mid-seventeenth century, Venice provided a more forceful example of republican dedication to the active life and service to the state than did the Florence where the ideals of civic humanism seem first to have taken root in the Renaissance. This was because Venice's republic continued to live on in the present whereas the period of Florence's vibrant republicanism—in the first half of the fifteenth century and revived briefly from 1494 to 1512 and even more briefly again from 1527 to 1530—was by now well in the past. And for someone like John Milton in the 1640s and 1650s, Venice's republicanism lived on in a particularly important and relevant way, in the recent examples it provided of scholars and writers like himself who had dedicated themselves to state service.

Foremost among these was Gasparo Contarini, perhaps the single figure most responsible for the dissemination of the myth of Venice throughout Europe, as a result of his having written the *De Magistratibus et Republica Venetorum*, a work which proceeded through some twenty different editions from 1543 to 1650 and in four different languages.[17] By no means a mere governmental propagandist, Contarini was a theologian and a philosopher, a member of the patriciate whose family had provided several doges and who himself served in a number of high governmental positions (ambassador, senator, procurator of St. Mark) before being in effect seized by the church and made a cardinal in 1534. In the next generation Paolo Paruta, though of a lesser noble family, served in a similar series of governmental positions and as official historian of the city. It was his dialogue *Della perfettione della vita politica* of 1579 which gave fullest expression to the Venetian civic humanist preference for and dedication to the active life. Set in the last session of the Council of Trent in 1563, the *Vita politica* pitted Venetian ambassadors and representatives to the Council against prelates who presented Counter-Reformation arguments against commitment to anything in this debased world; they thereby favoured contemplative withdrawal from such a world. What the figures Paruta plainly sympathized with expressed in opposition to such a view was not simply a preference for the active life in this world but an active life dedicated to service to the specifically Venetian state, the mixed or balanced polity of which the then dead Contarini (by the device of remembered conversation from the past) is brought in to praise in the work's final pages.

By far the most important and direct Venetian model for Milton, though, was Paolo Sarpi: Servite friar, philosopher, theologian, historian, religious reformer, friend of Galileo, and acquaintance of Sir Henry Wotton, that writer of recommendations for John Milton. Sarpi was a many-sided scholar who in his mid-fifties was appointed official theologian to the Venetian Republic and called upon to defend Venice at the time of one of its greatest crises, during the Papal Interdict of 1606–07. Unlike Contarini and Paruta, Sarpi was not a member of the patriciate, but he plainly lived out the republican civic humanist ideal of service to the state. He is, as well, one Venetian with whose life and work we know Milton to have been very familiar, and increasingly so as Milton himself embarked on his own public career. In his *Of Reformation* (1641), Milton reveals an awareness of Sarpi, albeit a distant one, as "the great Venetian antagonist of the Pope" (*CPW*, 1, 581). Then, evidently in 1643–44, he proceeded to read Sarpi's *History of the Council of Trent* with care and interest, recording some thirteen entries from it in his Commonplace Book under disparate headings ranging from Marriage to Civil War.[18] He then proceeded to make use of this material and other passages as well in his various proposals for the improvement of conditions in England, in the second edition of *Doctrine and Discipline of Divorce, Areopagitica, Tetrachordon, Eikonoklastes*, and *Likeliest Means to Remove Hirelings*, revealing an awareness of Sarpi's work in both its Italian and English versions. He found no occasion to refer to Sarpi's work in his own flurry of pamphlets arguing for a republic in 1659–60, but it is clear that Venice was on his mind as a possible model—if only in his decision to call his commonwealth's main governing body a Grand Council and to urge that its members sit for life. His true debt to Venice and to independent figures like Sarpi that Venice seemed to foster, though, is not to be seen so much in specific proposals at that time of political desperation as in his phrasing which in itself recalls civic humanist idealism, when for instance in *The Readie and Easie Way* he compares "the perpetual bowings and cringings of an abject people" under a monarchy to conditions in a free commonwealth (or republic) "wherein they who are greatest, are perpetual servants and drudges to the public at thir own cost and charges . . . yet are not elevated above thir brethren . . . [but] walk the streets as other men, [and] may be spoken to freely, familiarly, friendly, without adoration" (*CPW*, VII, 426, 425).

Plainly these Venetian examples do not in themselves account for the increasing political involvement of John Milton. But what I think we can say is that in the course of his public career Milton made the ideals of republican civic humanism his own and secondly, as he did so, he moved from the Neapolitan-Florentine mode of literary production to the Venetian one. It was not a move he made quickly, in the manner of a conversion. Indeed, in many ways Milton can be said to have lived his life in slow motion. Just as he was slow to return to England after having decided to do so in Naples, he was slow to get the 1645 *Poems* into print (publishing in that volume works almost all of which were written before 1637), and he was slow to deliver on his long-standing promise, made implicitly in

"Lycidas" and explicitly in *Reason of Church Government* of 1642, to write something that after times would not willingly let die. And his movement or progress was by no means steady. The 1645 *Poems* probably *was* an attempt to gain respectability, but in the terms I am outlining here, it was a step backward from the type of public, political stance assumed in the anti-prelatical tracts and *Areopagitica* which posit as their ideal subject and audience active, engaged figures who think for themselves and do not seek the protection of established institutions. With its poems in four different languages, its masque and other forms of aristocratic entertainment, its letters of commendation and recommendation, the volume appeals to a coterie audience, insists upon its connexions with the court, and reflects a literary system in which gentlemen-poets do not wish to seem eager to appear in print (it is Humphrey Moseley's claim in the Preface to the volume that he sought out John Milton rather than vice versa).

But if we look at Milton's writing career as a whole, the differences between early and late practices are considerable. One reflection of the change is in the differing presentation of *Comus* within the two editions of Milton's minor poems to appear in his lifetime. In the 1673 edition of *Poems, &c, on Several Occasions*, the privileging of *Comus* has been eliminated. It is still placed after "Lycidas" but it is no longer last among the English poems, being followed this time by the translations of the Psalms. It no longer has a separate title page and its prefatory material (Lawes's Dedicatory Letter to Viscount Brackley and Wotton's Letter to Milton) has been cut. John Creaser has suggested that the reason for this last change is Milton's dislike of the increasing and increasingly evident royalist politics of the Bridgewater family.[19] This is certainly possible, but it does not explain why Wotton's Letter has disappeared along with that of Lawes and the announcement of who played the masque's various parts. It seems more likely that Milton merely wished to be rid of all the extra paraphernalia that set *Comus* apart in the volume and associated it so strongly with its original setting of aristocratic privilege. The 1673 edition as a whole obviously has much the same flavour and effect as the 1645 *Poems of Mr John Milton* since the later volume reproduces all of the 1645 poems along with some fifteen additions. The Latin part of the volume is particularly close to the 1645 form and continues to include the poems and letters of flamboyant praise from Milton's Italian friends. But the volume as a whole ends with the prose tract *Of Education* and this, along with the changes in the presentation of *Comus*, reveals a movement, perhaps slight, away from aristocratic privilege and reminders of high-level connexions, in the direction of meritocratic independence, that is, the goal for which one educates young men to begin with; in effect, in a more republican direction.

If we wish, though, to see Milton-as-poet in a fully republican guise and adopting a republican mode of literary production, it is to *Paradise Lost* that we should turn. And to see first of all to what extent Milton had become a follower of Paruta and Sarpi, how attached he had become to the values of civic humanism, we might best look to his whole handling of the active and contemplative lives in his epic.

The old debate between the active and contemplative lives comes up most explicitly in *Paradise Lost* in the council in Hell, in the paired speeches of Moloch and Belial. Both fallen angels present debased versions of the respective stands. Moloch, for instance, favours constant, unthinking action in a suicidal argument that is all too easy for Belial to demolish. Belial, on his part, *sounds* better as he defends the life of the mind and asks, "who would lose, / Though full of pain, this intellectual being, / Those thoughts that wander through Eternity" (II. 146–48).[20] But as the narrator points out, these are words only "cloth'd in reason's garb" (II 226): the lascivious Belial, as his name might well tell us, is not really interested in the life of the mind at all. What is odd and particularly interesting about Milton's handling of the debate is that he is willing to let Moloch's speech go by without comment, whereas he felt impelled to have his narrator place warnings around Belial's speech, evidently so as to put his reader on guard against its false appeal. The appeal to the contemplative life that Belial's speech embodies was, it would appear, perceived by Milton to be particularly and insidiously dangerous.

Milton, in fact, betrays an edginess or uneasiness over the contemplative life and appeals that might be made to it at numerous points in his poem. He grants full contemplation only to the fallen angels in Hell, where a group of lesser devils while away the time until the more active Satan, working on behalf of the whole nation of fallen angels, returns from his scouting expedition. These minor angels "apart sat on a Hill retir'd" and "reason'd high / Of Providence, Foreknowledge, Will, and Fate" (II. 557–59), the reward for their intellectual efforts being to find themselves "in wand'ring mazes lost" (II.561). They have, in effect, set up an academy of the Italian sort and, given the fact that "Passion and Apathy" is one of the topics of their discourse, we might (a bit unfairly) call it an infernal branch of the *Apatisti*. And hermits, who might be presumed to practice the contemplative life, are placed among those who sought to reach heaven by vain or too sudden means, a class of beings that seems to have troubled or annoyed Milton to the extent that he departed from his usual adherence to Mortalism in order to give their souls immediate, appropriate punishment after death. The souls of hermits are thus to be found in the Paradise of Fools, along with the builders of the Tower of Babel, Empedocles, Cleombrotus, and embryos, idiots, and friars (III. 444–75). Paolo Paruta passed judgement upon contemplatives in similar terms, likening them to Semele who sought immediate and full apprehension of Jove, only to be struck down by that god for desiring to rise above her proper nature.[21]

But nowhere is Milton's favouring of the active life over the contemplative more remarkable than in his portrayal of Adam and Eve's life in Paradise before the Fall. Paradise is, as we might expect, a place of both action and contemplation in their ideal forms. But there was a theological tradition, and one we can see Milton arguing with, which suggested that Paradise was above all a place particularly suited for the practice of contemplation. It is a tradition reflected in Francis Bacon's statement that though "it is set down unto us that man was placed in the garden to work therein," that work "so appointed to him could be no other than work of contemplation."[22] St John Damascene, to take just one earlier voice from that tradition, thought that "the one work" man was to perform in Paradise was "to sing as do the angels . . . the praises of the Creator, and to delight in contemplation of Him."[23] Milton's particular achievement or distinction was to construct the most uncontemplative Paradise in the whole hexameral tradition. His treatment of Paradise was marked by two relatively original emphases. First, whereas other writers may have insisted that there was some labour to be done in Eden (though of a thoroughly delightful sort),[24] Milton provided Adam and Eve with a particularly exuberant garden that made keeping it in check more difficult than was true of any previous paradisal garden. Much more so than any previous Adam and Eve, Milton's pair had very legitimate work to do.[25] And secondly, Milton took the highly unusual stand of presenting our first parents with the gift of sexual love before the fall.[26] Contemplation tends to be de-emphasized in Milton's Paradise, then, simply because there proves to be so much else for Adam and Eve to do. He has endowed his Paradise with distinctive features which weight the balance on the side of the active life, and thereby provides a pastoral analogue to the type of stand a civic humanist like Paolo Paruta advocates in his political realm.

Twenty years ago Barbara Lewalski published an article on Adam and Eve's life in Eden, showing how as part of their particularly active prelapsarian existence our first parents undergo an education through trial and error;[27] this education is part of the process whereby Adam and Eve are to be "improv'd by tract of time" and by steps ascend to God (V. 498, 512). Recently Mary Ann Radzinowicz followed up that study with an article showing how this education continues in the poem after the fall and takes on a particularly political form. Abdiel, Adam, and the reader are expected to correct the false linguistic and political usages and practices of a Satan and a Nimrod and thereby discover for themselves the true bases of freedom, order, and degree. The poem everywhere insists upon freedom of choice, both before and after the fall, and is concerned to promote the discipline and industry that produce an educated meritocracy.[28] While *Paradise Lost* does not, as Radzinowicz observes, endorse any particular political programme or course of action, there is a distinctly republican cast to the whole epic with its insistence upon responsibility for one's own decisions, upon earning one's own freedom and knowledge through a constant process of self-correction. One must be actively engaged at all times in establishing what is politically correct and morally true, just as, in *Areopagitica*, a man may become a heretic in the truth if he accepts that truth merely on the advice of his pastor or the Assembly.

It is in *Paradise Lost*'s thoroughgoing endorsement of constant activity, its portrayal of human life as process, its rejection of stasis as an ideal, that we can see its author's adherence not simply to the tenets of radical Protestantism but to the ideals of civic humanism as well, and to the republicanism closely associated with those ideals. And what is true inside the poem is of course true outside it as well, in the manner of its publication. Milton may ultimately be most interested in finding a "fit audience . . . though few" for his epic, just as he favoured resting power in the hands of the few in *The Readie and Easie Way* (in an aristocracy of virtue or merit, not blood); but he did not, in publishing his poem on the open market, without patronage, and without introductory commendations, affect to identify that audience in advance. He is letting that fit audience identify itself by its active reading of the poem and is certainly not suggesting that the fit audience is to be found within a certain class of inherited wealth or taste. It can well be argued that *Comus* insists upon the same independence, activity, and personal responsibility that *Paradise Lost* does; but the masque appears in a context that calls up other kinds of associations as well, those of privilege and connexion, a social world in which one advances by virtue of the Henry Wottons one knows rather than by one's own active moral virtue.

Humphrey Moseley, the publisher of the 1645 *Poems*, was given in his prefaces to claiming that the works he was issuing were coming naked into the world, even as he pointedly mentioned that various learned "Academicks" had applauded the poems that follow or indulged in praise of his own high-mindedness for publishing such works for the benefit of his intelligent, clear-sighted, and gentle readers.[29] Although Milton was certainly a known figure after the Restoration, *Paradise Lost* really did come close to entering the world naked in 1667. And this, I would suggest, was as important for later writers seeking independence as the subscription method of publishing which was establishing itself in the course of Milton's lifetime. It is of some significance that it should have been the incipient republican and Puritan prophet, George Wither, who *almost* invented the subscription method of publishing in 1615. In between one work dedicated "To Himself" (*Abuses Stript and Whipt* (1613)) and another dedicated "To Anybody" (*Wither's Motto* (1621)), fresh out of Marshalsea Prison and in desperate need of funds, Wither "put . . . out for an adventure amongst [his] acquaintance, upon a certaine consideration" his *Fidelia*, and then at the last minute thought better of the idea, returned all monies, and distributed all copies of the 1615 edition free.[30] But subscription publishing was, initially at least, a commercial venture more than a political one and did not in itself necessarily spell the end of the aristocratic patronage system and lead to political and moral independence for authors, as the fourth edition of *Paradise Lost*, published by subscription by Jacob Tonson in 1688, might well remind us. As was customary in such a mode of publication, the names of the subscribers are provided within the volume itself. For this particular venture, the names are divided according to each letter of the alphabet, but within each letter they are listed in order of aristocratic and social rank, a practice that would presumably make John Milton turn in his grave.

Samuel Johnson both misrepresented and detested Milton's "acrimonious and surly" republicanism, which he viewed as "founded in an envious hatred of greatness, and a sullen desire of independence."[31] But in discussing the originality of Milton's invention at the end of the "Life of Milton," Johnson had recourse to phrasing that suggests he admired Milton the man and his republican independence more than he let on: "From his contemporaries he neither courted nor received support; there is in his writings nothing by which the pride of other authors might be gratified, or favour gained; no exchange of praise, nor solicitation of support" (p. 194). Johnson is ostensibly talking here about literary rather than monetary indebtedness; but the references to courting, soliciting, and receiving support, gaining favour and exchanging praise, all call up the spectre of the patronage system which Johnson, at some level of his consciousness, saw Milton as helping to lay to rest. There was plainly a great deal more in common between the two writers than Johnson was always willing to acknowledge.

Notes

1. *Boswell's Life of Johnson*, edited by George Birkbeck Hill, revised by L. F. Powell, second edition, 6 vols (Oxford, 1964), v, 59.

2. *Alexander Pope: A Biography* (New York, 1985), p. 863.

3. See Cedric C. Brown, *John Milton's Aristocratic Entertainments* (Cambridge, 1985), and John Creaser, "The present aid of this occasion: The Setting of *Comus*," in *The Court Masque*, edited by David Lindley (Manchester, 1984), pp. 111–34.

4. *Milton: A Biography*, 2 vols (Oxford, 1968), 1, 288; see too the related argument of Thomas N. Corns "Milton's Quest for Respectability," MLR, 77 (1977), 770–79.

5. For the view of the trip as a turning point in Milton's artistic career, see Parker, I, 179–82. In noting the various contradictions in the *Second Defence* account of the journey, I am indebted to a number of papers delivered at the Third International Milton symposium, held in Vallombrosa and Florence, 12–18 June 1988, most particularly that of Dustin Griffin, "Milton in Italy: The Making of a Man of Letters."

Milton's detailed account of his journey, in *The Second Defence of the English People*, is to be found in the *Complete Prose Works*, edited by Don M. Wolfe and others, 8 vols (1953–82), IV, 614–20. Subsequent references to Milton's prose will be from this edition and marked *CPW*.

6. Milton's attendance at meetings of the *Svogliati* on 17, 24, 31 March 1639 has long been known (it is recorded in the second edition of Volume 1 of David Masson's *Life of John Milton* [1875]); that he attended meetings of the *Apatisti* too has been assumed but only recently confirmed, by Alessandro Lazzen's transcription of an eighteenth-century manuscript in Florence's Biblioteca Marucelliana (MS A. 36). The manuscript provides a

record of the early history of the academy by a later member, Antonio Gori, and on page 53ʳ, in the midst of a list of members for 1638, appears the name of "Giovanni Milton inglesi," see Lazzeri, *Intelletuali e consenso nella Toscana del Seicento: L'Accademia degli Apatisti* (Milano, 1983), p. 74.

7. For my knowledge of the *Accademia Fiorentina* and the private academies deriving from it, I am indebted to the first chapter of Eric Cochrane's *Tradition and Enlightenment in the Tuscan Academies*, 1690–1800 (Chicago, 1961) and his *Florence in the Forgotten Centuries*, 1527–1800 (Chicago, 1973); Claudia di Filippe Bareggi, "In nota alla politica culturale di Cosimo I: L'Accademia Fiorentina," *Quaderni Storici*, 8, no. 23 (1973), 527–73; Armand L. De Gaetano *Giambattista Gelli and the Florentine Academy*: The Rebellion Against Latin (Firenze, 1976), esp. pp. 100–30; Lazzeri (see Note 6 above); the various entries in Michale Maylender's *Storia delle accademie d'Italia*, 5 vols (Bologna, 1926–30).

8. Cochrane, *Florence in the Forgotten Centuries*, pp. 204–05; Lazzeri, pp. 8–10.

9. On the *Sibillone*, see Cochrane, *Tuscan Academies*,p.4, and Lazzeri, pp. 26–27.

10. Maylender, IV, 184; for a more detailed study of the procedures and activities of this academy, see Vittor Ivo Comparato. "Società civile e società letteraria nel primo Seicento: L'Accademia degli Oziosi," *Quaderni Storici*, 8, no. 23 (1973), 359–88.

11. Of the 106 biographies included in *Le Glorie degli Incogniti* (Venezia, 1647), only eleven of the members described (not the total membership) are Venetian. The most authoritative studies of Venetian academies of the late Renaissance are those of Gino Benzoni, "Aspetti della cultura urbana nella società veneta del '5–'600: Le Accademie," *Archivio Veneto*, 108 (1977), 87–159, and *Gli affanni della cultura Intelletuali e potere nell' Italia della Controriformo e barocca* (Milano, 1978), pp. 144–200, and of Paolo Ulvioni "Accademie e cultura in Italia dalla controriformo all' Arcadia: Il caso veneziano," *Libri e Documenti* (Archivio Storico Civico e Biblioteca Trivulziana), 5, no. 2 (1979), 21–75. Both Benzoni and Ulvioni paint a relatively bleak picture of intellectual life in the academies covered, noting their increasing homogenization and marginalization as the seventeenth century and the Counter-Reformation wore on, as the academicians talked more and more merely to each other and less to the outside world. In defence of this particular academy, the *Incogniti*, we might note however that, in existence from 1630 to 1660, it came relatively early in the period of Venice's artistic and intellectual decline in the seventeenth and eighteenth centuries and that there is evidence of some unusual intellectual activity among its members, if not always in the performances within the academy's meetings themselves.

12. See, among many works by Baron, "Cicero and the Roman Civic Spirit in the Middle Ages and the Early Renaissance," *Bulletin of the John Rylands Library*, 22 (1938), 72–97, and *The Crisis of the Early Italian Renaissance*, revised edition (Princeton, 1966). Eugenio Garin, though concerned more with philosophical than political attitudes, describes much the same phenomenon on his *Italian Humanism: Philosophy and Civic Life in the Renaissance*, translated by Peter Munz (Oxford, 1965 (originally *Der italiensche Humanismus* [Bern, 1947]), I follow William J. Bouwsma (in *Venice and the Defense of Republican Liberty: Renaissance Values in the Age of the Counter Reformation* [Berkeley, 1968]) in viewing Baron's conception of civic humanism as applicable to Venice.

13. The amount of material on the myth of Venice and its effect on the rest of Europe is now vast. For studies in English alone, see: Zera S. Fink, *The Classical Republicans: An Essay in the Recovery of a Pattern of Thought in Seventeenth-Century England*, second edition (Evanston, 1962), esp. pp. 28–51; Brian Pullan, "Service to the Venetian State: Aspects of Myth and Reality in the Early Seventeenth Century," *Studi Secenteschi*, 5 (1964), 95–148 (pp. 95–108); William J. Bouwsma, *Venice and the Defense of Republican Liberty* and his "Venice and the Political Education of Europe," in *Renaissance Venice*, edited by J. R. Hale (London, 1973), pp. 445–66; Felix Gilbert, "The Venetian Constitution in Florentine Political Thought," in *Florentine Studies: Politics and Society in Renaissance Florence*, edited by Nicolai

Rubinstein (Evanston, 1968), pp. 463–500; Eco O. G. Huitsma Mulier, *The Myth of Venice and Dutch Republican Thought in the Seventeenth Century*, translated by Gerard T. Moron (Assen, 1980), pp. 1–54; and Edward Muir, *Civic Ritual in Renaissance Venice* (Princeton, 1981), pp. 13–61.

14.   These figures are taken from Fink, *The Classical Republicans*, p. 30, who is indebted for them, by way of John Addington Symonds, to Charles Emile Yriarte, *La Vie d'un patricien de Venise au seizième siècle* (Paris, 1874), p. 96. Yriarte's figures are in basic agreement with more modern studies on Venice's population, for instance, that of James Cushman Davis, *The Decline of the Venetian Nobility As a Ruling Class* (Baltimore, 1962), pp. 62–68.

15.   Defenders of the Venetian political system tended to get around this difficulty either by following the lead of Gasparo Contarini (in *De Magistratibus et Republica Venetorum*, translated by Lewes Lewkenor as *The Commonwealth and Government of Venice* (London, 1599), p. 16) in arguing that the middle classes and lower were mercenary people who work for a living and hence are public servants, not rightly, then, considered citizens; or, alternatively, by talking of the means by which Venetians below the patrician class might participate in the communal life of the city and thereby have reason to feel the government their own, thus instilling in them a sense of loyalty to the state (or at least rendering them quiet). These means included service in governmental offices reserved for professional bureaucrats, participation in the Scuole Grandi (in which long-standing members of the merchant class might serve as officers and work alongside patricians in dedicating themselves to acts of charity parallel to those of the state's procurators), and even popular election of parish priests when vacancies appeared. Contarini touches on this latter approach late in his work (Lewkenor translation, pp. 142–46) and it was developed further by Giovanni Botero in his *Relatione della republica venetiana* (Venice, 1605), fols 42–43, 97–98, and 107–08. It was by such means that the republican civic humanist ideal of active involvement in the affairs of the state might become the ideology not simply of the Venetian patriciate alone but of a fairly large proportion of the Venetian populace. See Brian Pullan, "Service to the Venetian State," pp. 100–05, and *Rich and Poor in Renaissance Venice* (Oxford, 1971), pp. 99–108.

16.   See Robert Finlay, *Politics in Renaissance Venice* (New Brunswick, New Jersey, 1980), and Donald E. Queller, *The Venetian Patriciate: Reality versus Myth* (Urbana and Chicago, 1986).

17.   A check of the *National Union Catalogue* and those of the *British Museum* and *Bibliothèque Nationale* reveals: Latin editions in 1543 (Paris), 1544 and 1547 (Basel), 1551, 1557, 1589, and 1592 (all Venice), 1599 (Lübeck), 1626 and 1628 (Leiden), 1636 (Amsterdam); editions of Domenichi's Italian translation in 1544, 1545, 1548, 1551, 1564, 1591, 1630, and 1650 (all Venice); two editions of Charrier's French translation, in 1544 (Paris) and 1557 (Lyon); and Lewkenor's English translation of 1599 (London).

18.   The assumption that Milton read Sarpi's *History* in 1643 and made those entries in his Commonplace Book at that time is based on the fact that the first reference in Milton's prose showing direct awareness of Sarpi's writing comes in a passage added for the second edition of *The Doctrine and Discipline of Divorce* (published probably very early in 1644) and not included in the first edition (published before 1 August 1643); see James Holly Hanford, "The Chronology of Milton's Private Studies," *PMLA*, 36 (1921), 251–314 (pp. 268–69), and Ruth Mohl's Notes to Milton's Commonplace Book in *CPW*. 1, 396 ff. And after *DDD* comes the extensive reliance upon Sarpi in *Areopagitica*, written later in 1644. It is of course possible that Milton started reading Sarpi earlier.

19.   "The present aid of this occasion," p. 117.

20.   Quotations from *Paradise Lost* are from the text of John Milton, *Complete Poems and Major Prose*, edited by Merritt Y. Hughes (New York, 1977).

21.   *Della perfezione della vita politica*, in Paruta's *Opere politche*, edited by C. Monzani, 2 vols (Firenze, 1832), 1,123.

22. *The Advancement of Learning*, in Bacon's *Works*, edited by James Spedding, Robert Leslie Ellis, and Douglas Denon Heath, 15 vols (Boston, 1860–64), VI, 137–38.

23. John of Damascus, *De Fide Orthodoxa*, translated by S.D.F. Salmond, in *A Select Library of Nicene and Post-Nicene Fathers of the Christian Church*, edited by Philip Schaff and Henry Wace, Second Series (Grand Rapids, 1955), IX, 29 (Book II, Chapter II).

24. See for instance, among many: John Calvin, *Commentaries on the First Book of Moses Called Genesis*, translated by John King, 2 vols (Edinburgh, 1847), 1, 125; Gervase Babington, *Certaine Plaine, Briefe, and Comfortable Notes upon Everie Chapter of Genesis* (London, 1592), fol. 10^r; and Thomas Adams, *Meditations upon Some Part of the Creed*, in *Workes* (London, 1629), p. 1130.

25. See J. M. Evans, *Paradise Lost and the Genesis Tradition* (Oxford, 1968), pp. 242–71.

26. See my *Changing Landscapes: Anti-Pastoral Sentiment in the English Renaissance* (Athens, Georgia, 1986), pp. 158–77, a reworking of my earlier 'Lovemaking in Milton's Paradise', *Milton Studies*, 6 (1974), 277–306.

27. "Innocence and Experience in Milton's Eden," in *New Essays on Paradise Lost*, edited by Thomas Kranidas (Berkeley, 1969), pp. 86–117.

28. "The Politics of *Paradise Lost*," in *Politics of Discourse: The Literature and History of Seventeenth-Century England*, edited by Kevin Sharpe and Steven N. Zwicker (Berkeley, 1987), pp. 204–29.

29. For Moseley's characteristic praise of himself, see his prefatory epistles to Milton's *Poems* (1645), Launcelot Andrewes's *Private Devotions* (1647), and John Suckling's *Last Remains* (1659); and for variations on his publications going forth into the world naked or in unsophisticated manner, see the prefaces to Waller's *Poems* (1645), Cowley's *The Mistress* (1647), and Raleigh's *Judicious and Select Essays* (1650). Moseley's prefaces are conveniently gathered in John Curtis Reed's 'Humphrey Moseley, Publisher', *Oxford Bibliographical Society Proceedings and Papers*, II, Part 2 (1928), 57–142 (pp. 73–103).

30. The quoted phrase is from the prefatory matter to the 1615 edition of *Fidelia*, sig. A5^r; publisher George Norton provides further information in his Preface to the 1617 edition. The prize for having introduced subscription publishing must go instead to John Minsheu for his *Ductor in Linguos* of 1617.

31. *Lives of the English Poets*, edited by George Birkbeck Hill, 3 vols (Oxford, 1905), 1, 157.

The Genesis of Gendered Subjectivity in the Divorce Tracts and in *Paradise Lost*

MARY NYQUIST*

It appears that one can now speak of "third-wave feminism" as well as "post-feminist feminism." Like other labels generated by the historical moment to which they refer, these await a lengthy period of interrogation. But if they should stick, their significance will be associated with the variety of attacks mounted against Western bourgeois or liberal feminism over the past decade and a half. Now, as never before, what has to be contended with—precisely because it has been exposed in the process of contestation and critique—is the historically determinate and class-inflected nature of the discourse of "equal rights." The questions, equal with whom, and to what end? have been raised in ways that have begun to expose how, ever since the early modern period, bourgeois man has proved the measure. They have also shown how the formal or legal status of this elusive "equality" tends by its very nature to protect the status quo.

Because much academic criticism on *Paradise Lost*, especially that produced in North America, has been written within a liberal-humanist tradition that wants Milton to be, among other things, the patron saint of the companionate marriage, it has frequently made use of a notion of equality that is both mystified and mystifying. The undeniable emphasis on mutuality to be found in *Paradise Lost*—the mutual dependency of Eve and Adam on one another, their shared responsibility for the Fall—is for this reason often treated as if it somehow entailed a significant form of equality. Differences that in *Paradise Lost* are ordered hierarchically and ideologically tend to be neutralized by a critical discourse interested in formal balance and harmonious pairing. To take just one, not especially contentious, example, Milton is said to go out of his way to offset the superiority associated with Adam in his naming of the animals by inventing an equivalent task for Eve: her naming of the flowers. In this reading, Milton, a kind of proto-feminist, generously gives the power of naming to both woman and man.[1] The rhetorical effectiveness of this point obviously depends in important ways upon the

---

*Reprinted from *Re-membering Milton: Essays on the Texts and Traditions*, ed. Mary Nyquist and Margaret W. Ferguson (New York: Methuen, 1987), 99–127.

suppression of features suggestive of asymmetry. Left unquestioned must be the differences between Adam's authoritative naming of the creatures—an activity associated with the rational superiority and dominion of "Man" when it is presented by Adam, who in Book VIII relates to Raphael this episode of the creation story in the second chapter of Genesis—and Eve's naming of the flowers, which is revealed only incidentally in her response to the penalty of exile delivered in Book XI. In a speech that has the form of a lament for the garden she has just been told they are to leave, Eve's naming in Book XI appears in such a way that it seems never to have had the precise status of an event. It is, instead, inseparably a feature of her apostrophic address to the flowers themselves: "O flow'rs / . . . which I bred up with tender hand / From the first op'ning bud, and gave ye Names" (XI.273–7).[2] Here Eve's "naming" becomes associated not with rational insight and dominion but rather with the act of lyrical utterance, and therefore with the affective responsibilities of the domestic sphere into which her subjectivity has always already fallen.

In recent years, a remarkably similar critical current, intent on neutralizing oppositions, has been at work in feminist biblical commentaries on Genesis. Within the Judeo-Christian tradition, claims for the spiritual equality of the sexes have very often had recourse to Genesis 1.27, "So God created man [hā'ādām, ostensibly a generic term] in his own image, in the image of God created he him; male and female created he them."[3] This verse, which is part of what is now considered the Priestly or "P" creation account (Genesis 1–2.4a), has always co-existed somewhat uneasily with the more primitive and more obviously masculinist Yahwist or "J" creation account in chapter 2, where the creator makes man from the dust of the ground (thereby making hā'ādām punningly relate to hā'ādāmâ, the word for ground or earth) and woman from this man's rib. Within a specifically Christian context, the relationship between the two accounts has been—at least potentially—problematical, since I Timothy 2:11–14 uses the Yahwist account to bolster the prohibition against women taking positions of authority within the Church: "Let the woman learn in silence with all subjection. But I suffer not a woman to teach, nor to usurp authority over the man, but to be in silence. For Adam was first formed, then Eve. And Adam was not deceived, but the woman being deceived was in the transgression." Recently, in an effort to reconcile feminism and Christianity, Phyllis Trible has tried to harmonize the differences between the Priestly and the Yahwist creation accounts. Trible holds that the exegetical tradition alone is responsible for the sexist meanings usually attributed to the Yahwist creation story, which she renarrates using methods that are basically formalist.

More specifically, Trible argues that the second chapter of Genesis tells the story not of the creation of a patriarchal Adam, from whom a secondary Eve is derived, but the story of the creation of a generic and androgynous earth creature or "man" to whom the sexually distinct woman and man are related as full equals. Throughout, Trible's retelling is strongly motivated by the desire to neutralize the discrepancy between the "P" and the "J" accounts by assimilating "J" to "P," which is assumed to recognize the equality of the sexes and therefore to provide the meaning of the two creation accounts taken together as one. Because "P" suggests the possibility of a symmetrical, non-hierarchical relationship between male and female, "J" is said by Trible to tell the story of the creation of a sexually undifferentiated creature who becomes "sexed" only with the creation of woman. The simultaneous emergence of woman and man as equals is signalled, she argues, when Yahweh brings the newly fashioned partner to the previously undifferentiated *hā'ādām* or "man," who responds with the lyrically erotic utterance: "This is now bone of my bones, and flesh of my flesh: she shall be called Woman, because she was taken out of Man" (Genesis 2:23) (in Trible's reading "taken out of" means "differentiated from").[4]

Trible's revisionary and profoundly ahistorical reading is significant in large part because it has been so widely influential. Among feminist theologians it would seem to have established a new orthodoxy. And it has recently been ingeniously elaborated for a secular readership by Mieke Bal, who assumes with Trible that the commentator can, by an effort of will, position herself outside the traditions of masculinist interpretation; and that Genesis bears no lasting traces of the patriarchal society which produced it.[5] Yet it is far too easy to adopt the opposing or rather complementary view that Genesis is a text inaugurating a transhistorically homogeneous patriarchal culture. This is, unfortunately, a view that is frequently expressed in connection with *Paradise Lost*. For in spite of the existence of scholarly studies of Genesis in its various exegetical traditions, the view that the relationship of *Paradise Lost* to Genesis is basically direct or at least unproblematically mediated continues to flourish. And so, as a result, does an entire network of misogynistic or idealizing commonplaces and free-floating sexual stereotypes, relating, indifferently, to Genesis and to this institutionally privileged text by Milton, English literature's paradigmatic patriarch.

The notion of a timeless and ideologically uninflected "patriarchy" is of course vulnerable on many counts, not least of which is its capacity to neutralize the experience of oppression. I would therefore like to attempt to situate historically Milton's own appropriation of the Genesis creation accounts. In the process, I hope also to draw a preliminary sketch, in outline, of the genealogy of that seductive but odd couple, mutuality and equality. It is certainly not difficult to recognize the reading given Genesis by Trible and Bal as a product of its time. Especially in North America, the notion of an originary androgyny has had tremendous appeal to mainstream or liberal feminism. Taken to represent an ideal yet attainable equality of the sexes, androgyny is often associated metaphorically with an ideal and egalitarian form of marriage. A passionate interest in this very institution makes itself felt throughout Milton's divorce tracts, in which his interpretation of the two creation accounts first appears. Milton's exegesis, too, is the product of an ideologically overdetermined desire to unify the two different creation accounts in Genesis. Not surprisingly, at the same time it is representative of the kind of masculinist "mis"-reading that Trible and Bal seek to overturn. By emphasizing its historical specificity, however, I hope to show that it is so for reasons that cannot be universalized.

II

Milton appropriates these two texts, first in the divorce tracts and then in *Paradise Lost*, by adopting the radically uni-levelled or this-worldly Reformed method of reconciling them. For leading commentators such as Calvin and Pareus, the two accounts do not correspond to two stages in the creation of humankind, the intelligible and the sensible, as they do in an earlier, Greco-Christian tradition. Indeed there are not in their view two accounts in this sense at all but instead one story told in two different ways, once, in the first chapter of Genesis, in epitome, and then, in the second chapter, in a more elaborated form. Simplifying matters considerably, and using terms introduced into the analysis of narrative by Gérard Genette, one could say that in the view articulated especially cogently by Calvin and then elaborated, aggressively, by Milton, the *story* consists of the creation in the image of God of a single being supposed to be representative of humankind, Adam, and then the creation of Eve; the *narrative discourse* distributes this story by presenting it first in a kind of abstract and then in a more detailed or amplified narrative fashion. More specifically, the first two statements of Genesis 1:27, "So God created man in his own image, in the image of God created he him," are thought to refer to the creation of the representative Adam, told in a more leisurely and graphic fashion as a creation involving the use of the dust of the ground in the second chapter; while the concluding "male and female created he them" is taken to refer to the creation from this Adam of his meet help, Eve.

Echoing similar statements by Pareus, Milton writes of the second chapter's narrative of Eve's creation for Adam: "This second chapter is granted to be a commentary on the first, and these verses granted to be an exposition of that former verse, 'Male and female created he them.' "[6] Yet the second chapter can have the status of a commentary in part because of the gaps, ambiguities, or troublesome suggestions to be found in the first. Commenting on the blessing of fertility in Genesis 1:28, for example, Calvin says that it is actually given to the human couple after they have been joined in "wedlocke," even though this event is not narrated until the following chapter.[7] As this indicates, for Protestant commentators, in so far as the rhetorically amplified second version is capable of interpreting and completing the account that comes before it in this way, it is the last creation account that tends to take precedence over the first.

If the Protestant exegetes Milton cites in his divorce tracts find the meaning of "male and female created he them" in the narrative of the creation of a help meet for Adam, they do so by reading that narrative ideologically, as proving that marriage, far from being what in their view the Roman Church would have it, a remedy prescribed for the spiritually weak, is divinely instituted, indeed recommended. That woman was created solely or even primarily for the purposes of procreation is the low-minded or "crabbed" (Milton's adjective) opinion the Protestant doctrine of marriage sees itself called to overturn.[8] Emphasizing, eloquently, the psychological needs sanctioned by the deity's words instituting marriage ("It is not good that the man should be alone," Genesis 2:18), the Reformers enable an emerging bourgeois culture to produce what has the appearance at least of an egalitarian view of the marital relation. The very phrase "meet for him" is said by Calvin to suggest in the Hebrew *kĕneged*, the quality of being "like or answerable unto" (*quia illi respondeat*) the man and to indicate vividly that psychological rather than physical likeness founds marriage as an institution.[9] Milton endorses this view when he takes the untranslatably expressive Hebrew "originall" to signify "*another self, a second self, a very self itself*" (*T* 600), and also when he has the divine interlocutor promise Adam, "Thy likeness, thy fit help, thy other self, / Thy wish, exactly to thy heart's desire" (*PL* VIII.450–1).

As has often been pointed out, in the divorce tracts Milton raises to unprecedented and undreamt of heights this early modern tendency to idealize the marriage bond. The extent to which he relies upon an implicit privileging of "J" over "P" (indeed, over the other texts he treats, as well) in order to do so has, however, not been commented upon. Milton's advocacy of a more liberalized interpretation of the grounds for divorce proceeds by countering the mean-spirited misinterpretations of scripture promulgated by scholastics and canonists.[10] On its more constructive front, it seeks to harmonize different and radically conflicting scriptural texts. The most taxing exegetical feat Milton has to perform is the reconciliation of Matthew 19:3–11, which suggests that remarriage after divorce is forbidden on grounds other than "fornication," and Deuteronomy 24:1–2, which Milton reads as sanctioning divorce for reasons of what we would now call incompatibility. *Tetrachordon*, the tract in which Milton's skills as exegete are most on display, announces in its very title his determination to establish unity and sameness in the place of seeming difference and contradiction. Meaning "four-stringed," and thus referring to the four-toned Greek scale, *Tetrachordon* attempts to harmonize what on the title page are referred to as the "foure chief places in Scripture, which treat of Mariage, or nullities in Mariage." The first text given on the title page is "Gen. 1.27.28 compar'd and *explain'd by* Gen. 2.18.23.24" (*T* 577; my emphasis).[11]

The explaining of Genesis 1 *by* Genesis 2 is of multi-fronted strategic importance to Milton's polemical attack on existing English divorce laws, which don't properly recognize the spiritual nature of marriage. First and foremost, it permits Milton to exploit rhetorically the sexual connotations of "male and female," essential to the divorce tracts' central, most tirelessly worded argument, which is that neither sexual union in and of itself nor procreation is the primary end of marriage as originally constituted. Commenting directly on "Male and female created he them" in *Tetrachordon*, Milton states it has reference to "the right, and lawfulness of the mariage bed." When relating this text to its immediate context, he claims that sexual union is an "inferior" end to that implied by the earlier "So God created man in his own image, in the image of God created he him" (Milton's detailed exegesis of which I'll be coming back to later on) (*T* 592). As this suggests, a bi-polar and hierarchical ordering of the spiritual and physical dimensions of experience structures many of the exegetical moves in these tracts. The following commentary on "male and female" is fairly representative, and illustrates, in addition, the important role played by "J:"

> He that said *Male and female created he them*, immediately before that said also in the same verse, *In the Image of God created he him*, and redoubl'd it, that our thoughts might not be so full of dregs as to urge this poor consideration of *male and female*, without remembering the noblenes of that former repetition; lest when God sends a wise eye to examin our triviall glosses, they be found extremly to creep upon the ground: especially since they confesse that what here concerns mariage is but a brief touch, only preparative to the institution which follows more expressly in the next Chapter. . . .
>
> (*T* 592)

The divorce tracts seek to persuade the mind that doesn't want to creep upon the ground that it should be duly impressed with the fact that in Genesis 2:18 God himself speaks, revealing in no uncertain terms what the end of marriage is: "And the Lord God said, It is not good that the man should be alone; I will make him an help meet for him." Expounding the true meaning of the earlier verse, "Male and female created he them," this verse declares "by the explicite words of God himselfe" that male and female is none other "than a fit help, and meet society" (*T* 594). Milton is willing to put this even more strongly. It's not just that we have here the words of God himself, expounding the meaning of an earlier text. God here actually explains *himself*: "For God does not heer precisely say, I make a female to this male, as he did briefly before, but expounding himselfe heer on purpos, he saith, because it is not good for man to be alone, I make him therefore a meet help" (*T* 595).

In Milton's exegetical practice, then, "J" 's narrative makes possible a spiritualized interpretation of the more lowly and bodily "male and female."

Indeed, "J" 's narrative, understood as instituting a relationship primarily psychological, provides the very basis for the passages emphasizing mutuality to be found throughout the divorce tracts. The above citations don't begin to convey the eloquence with which Milton can celebrate the pleasures of a heterosexual union that is ideally—that is, on the spiritual plane intended by its divine institution—fitting or meet. And there are numerous other moments in these works where without rhetorical flourish mutuality is clearly asserted or implied. The woman and man of the marriage relation can, for example, be referred to as "helps meete for each other."[12] On a more practical level, and of direct relevance to the legal reforms he is proposing, is the statement Milton offers of his position when opening the first chapter of *The Doctrine and Discipline of Divorce*: "*That indisposition, unfitnes, or contrariety of mind, arising from a cause in nature unchangable, hindring and ever likely to hinder the main benefits of conjugall society, which are solace and peace, is a greater reason of divorce then naturall frigidity, especially if there be no children, and that there be mutuall consent*" (*DDD* 242). The explicit reference to "mutuall consent" here is matched or perhaps even deliberately introduced by the opening words of the subtitle appearing in both the first and second editions of this work: "Restor'd to the Good of Both Sexes, From the bondage of Canon Law, and other mistakes. . . ."

Yet much as the dominant discourse of the academy might like to celebrate this praiseworthy attention to mutuality, there are very few passages of any length in the divorce tracts that can be dressed up for the occasion. For over and over again, this laudable mutuality loses its balance, teetering precariously on the brink of pure abstraction. And the reason it does so is that it stands on the ground (to recall the play on *hā'ādāmâ*) of a lonely Adam who is not in any sense either ungendered or generic. It becomes clear, finally, that the concluding phrase of Milton's position-statement— "and that there be mutuall consent"—is not expected to stand up in a court of law. In the penultimate chapter of the second edition of *The Doctrine and Discipline of Divorce*, Milton states his view "that the absolute and final hindring of divorce cannot belong to any civil or earthly power, against the will and consent of both parties, *or of the husband alone*" (*DDD* 344; my emphasis). Even if this could, improbably, be attributed to a moment's forgetfulness on the part of an author busy revising and enlarging his original, it still wouldn't be able to pass itself off as an instance of simple self-contradiction. For as I hope to show, this particular assertion is also the self-consistent outcome of the deeply masculinist assumptions at work in Milton's articulation of a radically bourgeois view of marriage.

Time and again, the language of the tracts passes through the use of plural forms potentially inclusive of both sexes only to come to rest with a nongenerically masculine "he." As the discussion up to this point has indicated, in so far as the story of Eve's creation from Adam's rib is thought to articulate the Protestant doctrine of marriage, it is not her creation *after*

Adam *per se* that is so significant but her creation *for* him, to remedy his loneliness. The egalitarian sentiments expressed, sporadically, throughout the divorce tracts therefore cannot finally obscure Eve's secondary status as a "gift" from one patriarch to another. Created for Adam, Eve is, as Adam puts it in *Paradise Lost*, "Heav'n's last best gift" (V.19). Yet Eve is also, of course, created *from* Adam, as well as *for* him. And in Milton's view, as Adam's "likeness" Eve does not even have the status—to use Satan's description of "man" in *Paradise Lost*—of the Father's "latest," meaning most recent, "image" (IV.567). For by unifying the two creation stories in the way Reformed principles permit him to, Milton's exegesis makes possible the production of two ideologically charged and historically specific readings, contradictorily related: on the one hand an interpretation of "male and female" that psychologizes heterosexual union and dignifies marriage, and on the other an explication of "created man in his image" that tends to restrict the meaning of "man" to an individual Adam, from whom and for whom the female is then made.

It is important to put this exactly, for of course biblical commentators always claim that woman is also in some sense made in the image of God. Calvin, like Milton, however, locates the generic sense of "man" directly in the first and gendered man's representative status. Commenting on Genesis 2:18, "I will make him an help meet for him," Calvin responds to the question, why isn't the plural form "Let us make" used here, as it was in the creation of "man"?:

> Some think, that by this speach, the difference which is betweene both sexes is noted, and that so it is shewed, how much more excellent the man is, then the woman. But I like better of another interpretation, which differeth somewhat, though it be not altogether contrarie: namely, that when in the person of man, mankinde was created, the common worthinesse of the whole nature, was with one title generally adorned, where it is said, *Let us make man*: and that it was not needful to be repeated in the creating of the woman, which was nothing else but the addition and furniture of the man [quae nihil aliud est quam viri accessio]. It cannot be denied, but the woman also was created after the image of God, though in the seconde degree. Whereupon it followeth, that the same which was spoken in the creation of the man, perteineth to womankind.[13]

Milton's stridently masculinist, "Hee for God only, shee for God in him" in *Paradise Lost* obviously goes much further than Calvin in drawing out the masculinist implications of this hermeneutical practice, which forges an identity between the generic and the gendered "man." In *Tetrachordon*, too, Milton pursues the logic of this exegesis with a maddening and motivated precision. In his commentary on "in the image of God created he him," the intermediate statement of Genesis 1:27, he states that "the woman is not primarily and immediately the image of God, but in reference to the man," on the grounds that though the "Image of God" is common to them both, "had the Image of God been equally common to them both, it had no doubt bin said, In the image of God created he them" (*T* 589).

So it continues to matter that Adam was formed first, then Eve. As a further means of taking the measure of Milton's interest in this priority, I would now like to discuss three seventeenth-century texts more favourably disposed towards an egalitarian interpretation of Genesis. Although research in this area is still underway, it is safe to say that Milton could not but have known that questions of priority figure prominently in the Renaissance debate over "woman" we now know as the "Querelle des Femmes." In *A Mouzell for Melastomus, the cynicall bayter of, and foule mouthed barker against Evahs sex*, for example, one of the feminist responses to Joseph Swetnam's *The Araignment of lewd, idle, forward and unconstant women*, Rachel Speght appeals several times to the privilege assumed to be a property of firstness. Speght mentions that although it is true that woman was the first to sin, it is also woman who receives the "first promise" that God makes in Paradise; she argues that the dignity of marriage is proved by Jesus honouring a wedding ceremony with "the first miracle that he wrought;" and that the spiritual equality of the sexes is shown when after his Resurrection Christ "appeared unto a woman first of all other."[14]

In the restricted intellectual economy of the "Querelle," orthodox views of male superiority are frequently countered by paradoxical assertions of female superiority. Lastness is therefore placed in the service of overturning firstness, as in Joan Sharpe's poetic defense of women against Swetnam's *Araignment*, where it is claimed: "Women were the last worke, and therefore the best, / For what was the end, excelleth the rest."[15] Speght, however, deliberately avoids the use of this kind of paradox. Like other Renaissance and Reformed commentators, preachers and courtesy-book writers, Speght places a strong emphasis on marriage as involving the "mutuall participation of each others burden." And this emphasis is sustained rhetorically throughout the tract. For example, while accepting the conventional view that woman is "the weaker vessel," Speght supplies a subtly polemical reference to man as "the stronger vessel."[16] In deploying a linguistic stress on balance and mutuality to neutralize hierarchical oppositions, this young, early seventeenth-century Protestant may very well be the most important unsung foremother of modern liberal feminist commentators on Genesis and on *Paradise Lost*.

Speght does not offer any programmatic statements on the relation of "P" to "J," nor does she attempt systematically to assimilate one to the other. But like all feminist participants in the "Querelle des Femmes," she assumes that Genesis 1:26 and 27 provide a clear statement of the spiritual equality of the sexes. The passage in which she briefly explicates Genesis 1:27 is distinctive, however, in its provisional but decidedly revisionary reconciliation of the two creation accounts: "in the Image of God were they both created; yea and to be brief, all the parts of their bodies, both externall and internall, were correspondent and meete each for other."[17] By referring to both woman and man, and in relation to one another, the terms "correspondent and meete" ("correspondent" being, as modern commentators point out, a good translation of the Hebrew *kĕneged*) deftly unite the "male and female created he them" of the "P" account with the account in "J" of Eve's creation for Adam, which here, momentarily, loses its narrative identity. Speght's brief exegesis carefully preserves an emphasis on bodily fitness, while pointedly ignoring questions of chronology that might threaten the egalitarian statement.

At one point Speght refers to marriage as "a merri-age, and this worlds Paradise, where there is mutuall love."[18] The same celebratory word-play ("the very name whereof should portend unto thee merry-age") appears in a work published just two years before Swetnam's provocative tract, Alexander Niccholes' *A Discourse, of Marriage and Wiving*. Interesting for, among other things, its citation of lines from the Player Queen's speech in *Hamlet*, Niccholes' *Discourse* eulogizes the special pleasures of marital friendship in one of the very phrases used in *Tetrachordon*: the wife is "such a friend, which is to us a second selfe."[19] Niccholes' brief commentary on the two creation accounts differs significantly from Milton's, however. Appearing in the first chapter, "Of the First Institution and Author of Marriage," Niccholes' exegetical remarks follow the citation of Genesis 2:18 ("It is not good for the man to bee alone"):

> so the creation of the woman was to be a helper to the man, not a hinderer, a companion for his comfort, not a vexation to his sorrow, for *consortium est solatium*, Company is comfortable though never so small, and Adam tooke no little joy in this his single companion, being thereby freed from that solitude and silence which his lonenesse would else have bene subject unto, had there beene no other end nor use in her more, then this her bare presence and society alone: But besides all this, the earth is large and must be peopled, and therefore they are now the Crowne of his Workemanship, the last and best and perfectest peece of his handiworke divided into Genders, as the rest of His creatures are, Male and Female, fit and enabled *Procreare sibi similem* to bring forth their like, to accomplish his will, who thus blessed their fruitfulnesse in the Bud: Increase and multiply, and replenish the earth.[20]

In this passage, as in the divorce tracts, the two different creation accounts, presented in their "real" order of occurrence, are discussed as if each revealed a different end or benefit of the first institution. And "J"'s narrative of the creation of a meet help for Adam, given a strictly psychological and social interpretation, is given priority over "P"'s. But Niccholes significantly omits any discussion of the creation of "man" in God's image. This absence permits the plural "they" easily to take over, so that it is the (now happily united) first man and woman alike who are "the last and best and perfectest peece of his handiworke." Although Niccholes mentions that woman was made both "for" and "out of" man, he maintains his emphasis on mutuality by erasing any explicit or evaluative commentary on her having been made *after* man, as well.

The commentary I would like to examine next is one produced during the same period as the divorce tracts, that is, at the very time when egalitarian issues of all kinds were being hotly contested, and when women in the sectaries not only laid claim to their spiritual equality with men on the basis of Genesis 1:27 and other texts, but publicly proclaimed the extra-textual significance of this equality by preaching and prophesying.[21] Unlike Speght's and Niccholes', the text I turn to now belongs, officially, to the commentary genre. Issued in association with the Westminster Assembly and published in 1645, the annotations on Genesis in *Annotations Upon All the Books of the Old and New Testaments* have not, to my knowledge, ever been studied.[22] Yet they shed an extraordinarily clear, not to say glaringly bright, light on the distinctive and motivated features of Milton's exegesis.

An annotation on 1:26 takes up directly the question of the meaning of the signifier "man" or "Adam." With reference to the phrase "let them" (in "And let them have dominion over the fish of the sea," etc.), the annotation states: "The word *man*, or the Hebrew, *Adam*, taken not personally or individually for one single person, but collectively in this verse, comprehendeth both male and female of mankind: and so it may well be said, not *let him*, but *let them* have dominion." Here the generic sense of *hā'ādām* is made completely to override the gender-specific sense. To this end, the use of the plural pronoun in the latter section of Genesis 1:26 is privileged over the singular pronoun, used with reference to the image ("in the image of God created he him"). This annotation alone therefore reveals a process of interpretation diametrically opposed to that at work in *Tetrachordon*, where, as we have seen, Milton seizes upon the difference between singular and plural forms in Genesis 1:26 and 27 to argue that only the gender-specific Adam is made immediately in the image of God.

What makes comparison of the *Annotations* with *Tetrachordon* possible and of crucial importance is that both accept the Reformed view of the relationship between the two creation accounts. Adam and Eve are said to be formed on the same, that is, the sixth, day, but their creations are presented first in chapter I, where "their creation in the generall was noted with other creatures," and then again in chapter 2, where "in regard of the excellencie of mankind above them all, God is pleased to make a more particular relation of the manner of their making, first of the man, vers. 7. and here [vers. 22] of the woman." Yet as these words suggest, the *story* assumed by the *Annotations* is slightly different from Milton's, which starts unabashedly with a "man" taken personally or individually. The difference is fine, but extremely significant. Like Milton and other Protestant commentators, the *Annotations* rejects the view that male and female were created

simultaneously, together with the view that both sexes were originally embodied, hermaphrodite-like, in a single being. "J"'s narrative ordering is
respected, which means that woman was indeed created after man. But this
is how the gloss on verse 27's "male and female" puts it:

> Not at once, or in one person, but severally; that is, though he united them
> in participation of his image, he distinguished them into two sexes, male and
> female, for the increase of their kinde: their conformitie in participation of
> Gods Image is clearly manifest by many particulars, for in most of the
> respects fore-mentioned, Annotation in ver. 26, the image of God is equally
> communicated to them both, and Eve was so like to Adam (except the
> difference of sexe which is no part of the divine image) in the particulars fore-
> mentioned, that in them, as she was made after the image of Adam, she was
> also made after the image of God: as if one measure be made according to
> the standard, an hundred made according to that, agree with the standard as
> well as it.

By associating differences between the sexes solely with reproduction, this
comment seems to hearken back to a Platonically inflected division between
the spiritual and the physical. The concluding analogy, however, shows
this truly remarkable text grappling with hierarchically ordered notions of
secondariness. Working with reference to the production of things in the
form of commodities, the analogy attempts to take on the difficulties resulting from the view that man and woman were made "severally." And it
tries to effect, on its own, an egalitarian synthesis of "P" and "J." That man
was first made in the image of God is implicitly conceded. But that woman
was made "after" man becomes a statement referring not so much to an
order of temporality as to an order of materiality. Woman is made "after"
the image of Adam in the sense of being made "according to the standard"
of the image of Adam. The analogy argues, by ellipsis, that since Adam
was himself really created "after" the image of God, which is the original
"standard," being created "after" Adam's image, Eve is equally created
"after" the image of God. Thanks to this highly ingenious and polemically
motivated analogy, Eve's being created "after" Adam loses its usual sense
of secondariness.

Read in the context of other learned Protestant biblical commentaries,
this analogy has a jarring effect since, in exceeding by ninety-nine the
requirements of logic, it seems to testify to the contemporary phenomenon
of the growth of mercantile capital. For the sake of an egalitarian synthesis
between "P" and "J," this workmanly analogy tries to undermine not only
a hierarchically inflected logic of temporality but also the generally Platonic
logic whereby original is privileged over copy. It is true that man is still,
quite literally, the "measure." And to give the analogy its force, woman is
placed in the position of being not the first commodity made "after" this
measure but rather the "hundred" that can be produced on its basis. The

logic deployed by the analogy from production insists, however, that it is not really possible to measure any residual differences between the image of God, man, and woman. Of the great variety of attempts made in the Renaissance and seventeenth century to come to Eve's defense, this must be the least chivalrous in content, the most lacking in conventional grace or charm. But it definitely does the job. And it certainly establishes, dramatically, the possibilities open to Milton, which he rejected.

In rejecting a position like that of the *Annotations*, Milton implicitly takes what would seem, from another perspective, though, to be a "progressive" stance, namely that the difference between woman and man is not a simple matter of biology; that it is not a difference of sex *per se*. In both *Tetrachordon* and *Colasterion* Milton rejects the view that Adam would have been given a male not a female partner had companionship been the end of marriage. The following passage from *Tetrachordon*, which comments on the all-important "*It is not good for man to be alone*," suggests why Milton would not want to imagine Eve's being created according to the same "standard" as Adam: "And heer *alone* is meant alone without woman, otherwise *Adam* had the company of God himself, and Angels to convers with; all creatures to delight him seriously, or to make him sport. God could have created him out of the same mould a thousand friends and brother *Adams* to have bin his consorts, yet for all this till *Eve* was giv'n him, God reckn'd him to be alone" (*T* 595). By specifying a desire that only "woman" can satisfy, and by associating that desire with a transcendence of sexual difference as vulgarly understood, the divorce tracts seem almost to open up a space for the category of "gender." Yet that this space is in no sense neutral can be seen in the language with which friendship between men gets differentiated from the marital relation. In *Colasterion* Milton opposes "one society of grave friendship" to "another amiable and attractive society of conjugal love."[23] Elsewhere Milton can associate the marriage relationship with the need man has for "sometime slackning the cords of intense thought and labour" (*T* 596); or he can refer to the seeking of "solace in that free and lightsome conversation which God & man intends in mariage" (*DDD* 273). It should go without saying that man can have this need for companionship remedied, can intend to enjoy "lightsome conversation" as opposed to "grave friendship," only if woman is constituted as less grave, more attractive, more lightsome and more amiable than her male counterpart; and if both she and marriage itself are associated with a world apart.

III

As has already been suggested, the priority bestowed upon Adam in Milton's divorce tracts is not associated directly with the order of creation. It tends, instead, to be inscribed in the divine words instituting marriage, "It is not good that the man should be alone; I will make him an help meet for him" (Gen. 2:18). These words, which Milton frequently refers to simply as "the institution," are in turn often taken to gesture towards a prior loneliness or "rational burning" experienced by the first man, Adam. I have already argued that the priority Milton gives "J" over "P" is inscribed indelibly in every one of his major rhetorical and logical moves. In concluding this discussion of the divorce tracts, I would like to show how consistently or systematically this priority is associated with the deity's instituting words and thus, by implication, with Adam's needs.

It has not yet been mentioned that Matthew 5:31, 32 and Matthew 19:3–11, which together constitute one of the four texts treated in *Tetrachordon*, and which appear unequivocally to forbid divorce except for fornication, are susceptible to Milton's polemical appropriation of them precisely because in chapter 19 Jesus is represented as quoting from Genesis. The relevant verses, cited by Milton, are the following, verses 3–6: "The Pharisees also came unto [Jesus], tempting him, and saying unto him, Is it lawful for a man to put away his wife for every cause? And he answered and said unto them, Have ye not read, that he which made them at the beginning made them male and female, And said, For this cause shall a man leave father and mother, and shall cleave to his wife: and they twain shall be one flesh? Wherefore they are no more twain, but one flesh. What therefore God hath joined together, let not man put asunder." The two texts cited here are the now-familiar "male and female created he them" in Genesis 1:27 and "Therefore shall a man leave his father and his mother, and shall cleave unto his wife: and they shall be one flesh" (Gen. 2:24). Milton's strategy in commenting on the verses from Matthew is to subvert their literal and accepted meaning by referring the citations back to the divine words of institution, which, he points out, are *not*, significantly, quoted. Although the tempting Pharisees, his immediate interlocutors, aren't worthy of receiving this instruction, Jesus's intention, Milton argues, is to refer us back to the uncited words of institution in chapter 2, "which all Divines confesse is a commentary to what [Jesus] cites out of the first, the *making of them Male and Female*" (*T* 649). The instituting words are thus made to govern the manner in which those cited by Jesus from chapter 1 are to be interpreted.

Also cited is Genesis 2:24, which Milton regards as spoken by Adam. Yet Milton's exegesis has already determined that Adam's speech too has meaning only with reference to the words of divine institution. In the first part of Adam's speech ("This is now bone of my bones, and flesh of my flesh: she shall be called Woman, because she was taken out of Man," Gen. 2:23), Milton finds Adam referring to and expounding his maker's instituting words, regarded as constituting a promise now fulfilled (*T* 602). By establishing a dialogic relation between Adam's words and those of his maker, Milton can argue that anyone who thinks Adam is in these words formulating the doctrine of the indissolubility of marriage "in the meer flesh" is not only sadly mistaken but guilty of using "the mouth of our generall parent, the first time it opens, to an arrogant opposition, and correcting of Gods wiser ordinance" (*T* 603). It is the next part of Adam's speech, however, verse 24, which is commonly thought to be "the great knot tier," as Milton correctly points out: "Therefore shall a man leave his father and his mother, and shall cleave unto his wife: and they shall be one flesh." In Milton's view, *by* opening with "therefore," this verse clearly indicates that Adam confines the implications of his utterance only to "what God spake concerning the inward essence of Mariage in his institution" (*T* 603). With reference to both parts of Adam's speech, Milton's position thus is that the deity's words are the "soul" of Adam's and must be taken into Adam's utterance if it is properly to be understood.

This is not, interestingly, the reading given these verses by Calvin, who assigns verse 23 to Adam, but draws attention to the interpretative choices open with regard to 2:24, for which three different speakers are eligible: Adam, God, and Moses. After a brief discussion Calvin opts for Moses, suggesting that, having reported what had historically been done, Moses in this passage sets forth the end of God's ordinance, which is the permanence or virtual indissolvability of the marriage bond.[24] For reasons that are obvious, Milton would want to reject this reading. By making Adam the speaker of this passage, Milton weakens its authority as a text enjoining the indissolubility of marriage. Since this is the very text cited by Jesus in Matthew, such an assault on its status as injunction is a decisive defensive move. But it is also more than that. For by assuming Adam to be its speaker, Milton also strengthens the contractual view of the first institution his exegetical practice implicitly but unmistakably develops.

That Milton's understanding of the first institution is implicitly both contractual and masculinist can perhaps be seen if his exegetical practice is compared with that of Rachel Speght. Towards the beginning of *A Mouzell for Melastomus*, Speght argues that Eve's goodness is proved by the manner of her creation:

> Thus the resplendent love of God toward man appeared, in taking care to provide him an helper before hee saw his owne want, and in providing him such an helper as should bee meete for him. Soveraignety had hee over all creatures, and they were all serviceable unto him; but yet afore woman was formed, there was not a meete helpe found for *Adam*. Mans worthinesse not meriting this great favour at Gods hands, but his mercie onely moving him thereunto: . . . that for mans sake, that hee might not be an unit, when all other creatures were for procreation duall, hee created woman to bee a solace unto him, to participate of his sorrowes, partake of his pleasures, and as a good yokefellow beare part of his burthen. Of the excellencies of this Structure, I meane of Women, whose foundation and original of creation, was Gods love, do I intend to dilate.[25]

Were Milton to have read Speght's tract, I suspect that midway through the first sentence here he would have discovered himself a resisting reader. The notion that God acted on Adam's behalf "before hee saw his own want" would have seemed highly provocative, if not downright offensive. Speght draws strategically on orthodox Protestantism's doctrinal emphasis on divine grace as radically transcendent, as an active principle utterly unconnected with human deserts. In the process, Adam becomes a passive recipient of a gift, meetness abounding, while Eve is subtly positioned in relation with her true "original," divine love.

By contrast, in the divorce tracts and, as we shall see, in *Paradise Lost* as well, Milton foregrounds an Adam whose innocent or legitimate desires pre-exist the creation of the object that will satisfy them. But this is to put it too abstractly. In Milton's exegesis, the significance of the gift—woman— passed from maker to man is determined by two speeches, first the maker's and then Adam's, precisely because these speeches are construed as a verbal exchange that is basically contractual. In Genesis 2:18 Adam's maker prom- ises him that he will assuage his loneliness and provide him with a meet help; in 2:23 and 24, Adam accepts this gift by acknowledging it is exactly what was promised him, and then promises to honour it on these very grounds. Eve's status as a divinely bestowed gift is exploited polemically by both Speght and Milton. But unlike Speght's transcendent lord of love, Milton's veiled but systematic insistence on the contractual form of the first institution is produced by a Protestantism pressed into the service of an historically specific form of individualism, an individualism paradigmatically masculine, autonomous, articulate, and preternaturally awake to the implica- tions of entering into relations with others.[26]

IV

One of the questions concerning *Paradise Lost* that this discussion of the divorce tracts has, I hope, made it possible to address is: why does Milton's Eve tell the story of her earliest experiences first, in Book IV? Why, if Adam was formed first, then Eve, does Adam tell *his* story to Raphael *last*, in Book VIII? An adequate response to this question would require a full-scale analysis of the ways in which *Paradise Lost* articulates a putative sequential order of events or story with the narrative discourse that distributes this story. As a genre, epic is of course expected to develop complicated relations between a presumed chronological and a narrative ordering of events. But *Paradise Lost* would seem to use both retrospective and prospective narratives in a more systematic and motivated manner than does any of its predecessors, in part because it is so highly conscious of the problematical process of its consumption. I would like to argue here that *Paradise Lost*'s narrative distribution of Adam and Eve's first experiences is not just complexly but ideologically motivated, and that the import of this motivation can best be grasped by an analysis aware of the historically specific features of Milton's exegetical practice in the divorce tracts.

This practice is crucially important to *Paradise Lost*'s own use of the Genesis creation texts. In the case of the passage it most obviously informs, Raphael's account of the creation of "man" on the sixth day of creation in Book VII, certain features are intelligible only in the light of this historically specific context. If commenting on this passage at all, critics have tended to suggest that Raphael gives something like a heavenly, as compared with Adam's later more earthly, account of creation.[27] This doesn't, however, even begin to do justice to the intricately plotted relations of the "P" and "J" accounts in the following:

> Let us make now Man in our image, Man
> In our similitude, and let them rule
> Over the Fish and Fowl of Sea and Air,
> Beast of the Field, and over all the Earth,
> And every creeping thing that creeps the ground.
> This said, he form'd thee, *Adam*, thee O Man
> Dust of the ground, and in thy nostrils breath'd
> The breath of Life; in his own Image hee
> Created thee, in the Image of God
> Express, and thou becam'st a living Soul.
> Male he created thee, but thy consort
> Female for Race; then bless'd Mankind, and said,
> Be fruitful, multiply, and fill the Earth,
> Subdue it, and throughout Dominion hold
> Over fish of the Sea, and Fowl of the Air,
> And every living thing that moves on the Earth.
> Wherever thus created, for no place
> Is yet distinct by name, thence, as thou know'st
> He brought thee into this delicious Grove,
> This Garden, planted with the Trees of God,
> Delectable both to behold and taste;
> And freely all thir pleasant fruit for food
> Gave thee, all sorts are here that all th' Earth yields,
> Variety without end; but of the Tree
> Which tasted works knowledge of Good and Evil,
> Thou may'st not; in the day thou eat'st, thou di'st;
> Death is the penalty impos'd, beware,
> And govern well thy appetite, lest sin
> Surprise thee, and her black attendant Death.
> Here finish'd hee.

(VII.519–48)

Genesis 1:26–8 is here given in what is virtually its entirety. But the principal acts of Genesis 2:7–17 are also related: Yahweh's making of "Man" from the dust of the ground (2:7), his taking of this man into the garden of Eden (2:15), and his giving of the prohibition (2:16,17). One could argue that even Milton's "artistry" here hasn't received its proper due, since this splicing economically makes from two heterogeneous accounts a single one that is both intellectually and aesthetically coherent.

Yet it does more, far more, than this. For Raphael's account removes any trace of ambiguity—the residual generic dust, as it were—from the Priestly account of the creation of *hā'ādāmâ* or "man" in the image of God. This it does by a set of speech-acts unambiguously identifying this "man" with Raphael's interlocutor, Adam. The direct address in "he form'd thee, *Adam*, thee O Man / Dust of the ground" has what amounts to a deictic function, joining the representative "Man" to Raphael's gendered and embodied listener, who is specifically and repeatedly addressed here, while Eve (though still an auditor) very pointedly is not. It is clearly significant that these very lines effect the joining of the Priestly and Yahwistic accounts. By placing "thee O Man / Dust of the ground" in apposition to the named "Adam," it is suggested that this individualized "Adam" actually is *hā'ādām* or representative man and the punning *hā'ādāmâ* "ground," an identity that only the joining of the two accounts reveals.

The impression this joining creates is that the two accounts have always already been one in narrating the creation of Adam. The same cannot be said of Raphael's account of the creation of Eve, however. For in contrast (I would like to say something like "in striking contrast," yet it has not really been noticed) to the ingenious joining that takes place for the sake of Adam, Raphael refers to Eve's creation only in the statement immediately following, which is again, significantly, addressed to Adam: "Male he created thee, but thy consort / Female for Race" (529–30).[28] Outside of this meagre "but thy consort / Female for Race," Raphael's account does not otherwise even allude to the creation of Eve, although, as we have seen, other details of the narrative in the second chapter are included in it. Indeed, if we examine the matter more closely, it appears that the Yahwist account is made use of only up to and including Genesis 2:17 (the giving of the prohibition) precisely because Genesis 2:18 inaugurates the story of the creation of a help meet for Adam.

But of course the story of Eve's creation is not excised from *Paradise Lost* altogether, which is, presumably, why readers have not protested its absence here. It is told later, by another narrator, Adam. One of the effects of this narrative distribution is that in Milton's epic Adam's story comes to have exactly the same relation to Raphael's as in the divorce tracts and in Protestant commentaries the second chapter of Genesis has to the first: it is an exposition or commentary upon it, revealing its true import.[29] Yet the second telling can have this status only because it is Adam's. As my discussion indicates, Milton's argument in the divorce tracts rests on a radical privileging of "J" over "P" in the specific form of a privileging of the words of divine institution in Genesis 2:18. Had Milton interpolated the story of Eve's creation into Raphael's creation account, he would have had to record these words in the form of indirect speech (as he does the words of prohibition in lines 542–7) or else to have reproduced both the creator's speech and Adam's. In either case, the instituting words would have been displaced from their centres of authority. By transferring the entire narrative to Adam and by interpolating a dramatic colloquy into this narrative, *Paradise Lost* ensures the coincidence of narrator and auditor of the instituting words, of narrator and of the first man's instituting response. By dramatizing this commentary, this necessary supplement to Raphael's account, in the form of a colloquy narrated by Adam, *Paradise Lost* makes sure that the doctrine of marriage is both produced and understood by the person for whom it is ordained, just as in the divorce tracts it is the privileged male voice, Milton's, which expounds the true doctrine of divorce.

As the divorce tracts never tire of insisting, the true doctrine of marriage relates only to the satisfaction of that which the wanting soul needfully seeks. In *Paradise Lost* this doctrine is co-authored by Adam and the "Presence Divine," who work it out together. It is also communicated, formally, by the extraordinary emphasis placed on Adam's subjectivity, on his actual experience of desire. As Milton has masterminded the exchange, the divine instituting words come *after* Adam has been got to express his longing for a fitting companion (VIII.444–51), so that this longing has the kind of priority that befits the first man. Yet the longing is also clearly a rational burning. With its strong filiations to the disputation, the very form of the colloquy establishes that this desire is rational, and that merely reproductive ends are certainly not what Adam has in mind. Although procreation is referred to, it is presented as a kind of necessary consequence of the conjunction of male and female, but for that very reason as a subordinate end. Adam's language cleverly associates it with a prior lack, a prior and psychological defect inherent in his being the first and only man (VIII.415–25). The way Milton's Adam responds to the deity's formal presentation to him of his bride, Eve, is just as motivated. The Genesis 2:23–4 speech is cited, but only after it has been introduced in a way that joins it explicitly to the causes implicit in the deity's instituting words:

> This turn hath made amends; thou hast fulfill'd
> Thy words, Creator bounteous and benign,
> Giver of all things fair, but fairest this
> Of all thy gifts, nor enviest. I now see
> Bone of my Bone, Flesh of my Flesh, my Self

> Before me; Woman is her Name, of Man
> Extracted; for this cause he shall forgo
> Father and Mother, and to his Wife adhere;
> And they shall be one Flesh, one Heart, one Soul.
> (VIII.491–9)

This speech is presented as a species of spontaneous lyrical utterance ("I overjoy'd could not forbear aloud" [490]) and according to Adam is "heard" by Eve. Yet it is obviously addressed *not* to her but to her maker, who is thanked for the gift itself, but not until he has been praised for having kept his word. Before letting Adam commit himself to the project of becoming one flesh with Eve, Milton has to make it clear that Adam does so believing that the "Heav'nly Maker" has done what he has promised, that is, created a truly fit help.

Not only the placement of Adam's narrative after Raphael's but also its most salient formal features can thus be seen to be motivated ideologically, and to illustrate the causes joining the divorce tracts and *Paradise Lost*. Before turning to Eve, I would like to summarize the discussion so far by emphasizing that these causes are joined, and to man's advantage, both when "P" and "J" are united and when they aren't. By joining "P" and "J" as it does, Raphael's account specifies the gendered Adam of *Paradise Lost* as the "man" who is made in the divine image. By disjoining them, Raphael's account lets Adam himself tell the story of the creature made to satisfy his desire for an other self.

We can now, more directly, take up the question, why does heaven's last best gift tell her story first? One way of approach might be to suggest that had Eve's narrative of her earliest experiences appeared where "naturally," in the order of creation, it should have, that is *after* Adam's, *Paradise Lost* might have risked allowing her to appear as the necessary and hence in a certain sense superior creature suggested by what Jacques Derrida has called the logic of the supplement, undeniably set in motion by Adam's self-confessed "single imperfection." *Paradise Lost*'s narrative discourse would seem to want to subvert this logic by presenting Eve's narrative first. And it seems to want to subvert it further by placing immediately *after* Adam's narrative a confession in which Eve's completeness and superiority is made to seem an illusion to which Adam is, unaccountably, susceptible. In this part of Adam's dialogue with Raphael, the language of supplementarity as artificial exteriority seems curiously insistent: Eve has been given "Too much of Ornament" (VIII.538); she is "Made so adorn for thy delight the more" (VIII.576) and so on.

Yet a displaced form of the logic of supplementarity may nevertheless be at work in the place of priority given Eve's narrative. For if Eve is created to satisfy the psychological needs of a lonely Adam, then it is necessary that *Paradise Lost*'s readers experience her from the first as expressing an intimately subjective sense of self. From the start she must be associated in a distinctive manner with the very interiority that Adam's need for an other self articulates. Or to put this another way, Eve's subjectivity must be made available to the reader so that it can ground, as it were, the lonely Adam's articulated desire for another self. Appearing as it does in Book IV, Eve's narrative lacks any immediately discernible connection with the Genesis creation accounts on which the narratives of both Raphael and Adam draw. Its distance from Scripture as publicly acknowledged authority is matched by Eve the narrator's use of markedly lyrical, as opposed to disputational, forms. Set in juxtaposition to the rather barrenly disputational speech of Adam's which immediately precedes it in Book IV, Eve's narrative creates a space that is strongly if only implicitly gendered, a space that is dilatory, erotic, and significantly, almost quintessentially, "private."

In a recent essay, Christine Froula reads Eve's first speech thematically and semi-allegorically, as telling the story of Eve's (or woman's) submission of her own personal experience and autonomy to the voices (the deity's, then Adam's) of patriarchal authority. As the very title of her essay— "When Eve Reads Milton"—indicates, Froula wants to find in Milton's Eve if not a proto-feminist then a potential ally in contemporary academic feminism's struggle to interrogate the academic canon together with the cultural and political authority it represents. Milton's Eve can play the part of such an ally, however, only because for Froula the privacy of Eve's earliest experiences and the autonomy she thereby initially seems to possess are equivalent to a potentially empowering freedom from patriarchal rule.[30] Given the liberal assumptions of the feminism it espouses, Froula's argument obviously does not want to submit the category of personal experience to ideological analysis.

In attempting to give it such an analysis, I would like to suggest that Eve's speech plays a pivotal role, historically and culturally, in the construction of the kind of female subjectivity required by a new economy's progressive sentimentalization of the private sphere.[31] It is possible to suggest this in part because the subjective experiences Eve relates are represented as having taken place before any knowledge of or commitment to Adam. That is, they are represented as taking place in a sphere that has the defining features of the "private" in an emerging capitalist economy: a sphere that appears to be autonomous and self-sustaining even though not "productive" and in so appearing is the very home of the subject. In Book VIII Adam recalls having virtually thought his creator into existence and having come up with the idea of Eve in a dialogue with his fellow patriarch. By contrast, Eve recalls inhabiting a space she believed to be uninhabited, autonomous, hers—but for the "Shape within the wat'ry gleam." It is, however, precisely because this belief is evidently *false* that it is possible to see this space as analogous to the "private" sphere, which is of course constituted by and interconnected with the "public" world outside it. Illusory as this autonomy

is, inhabiting a world appearing to be her own would nevertheless seem to
be the condition of the subjectivity Eve here reveals.

It has long been a commonplace of commentaries on *Paradise Lost* that
a network of contrasts is articulated between Eve's narration of her earliest
experiences and Adam's, the contrasts all illustrating the hierarchically ordered nature of their differences. Yet it has not been recognized clearly
enough that while shadowing forth these bi-polar oppositions, Eve's narrative
is supposed to rationalize the mutuality or intersubjective basis of their love.
For by means of the Narcissus myth, *Paradise Lost* is able to represent her
experiencing a desire equivalent or complementary to the lonely Adam's
desire for an "other self." It is not hard to see that Adam's own desire for
an other self has a strong "narcissistic" component. Yet Adam's retrospective
narrative shows this narcissism being sparked, sanctioned and then satisfied
by his creator. By contrast, though in Book IV Eve recalls experiencing a
desire for an other self, this desire is clearly and unambiguously constituted
by illusion, both in the sense of specular illusion and in the sense of error.
Neo-Platonic readings of the Narcissus myth find in it a reflection of the
"fall" of spirit into matter. Milton transforms this tragic tale into one with
a comic resolution by instructing Eve in the superiority of spirit or, more
exactly, in the superiority of "manly grace and wisdom" over her "beauty."
But because this happily ending little *Bildungsroman* also involves a movement
from illusion to reality, Eve is made to come to prefer not only "manly grace
and wisdom" as attributes of Adam but also, and much more importantly,
Adam as embodiment of the reality principle itself: he whose image she
really is, as opposed to the specular image in which her desire originated.

To become available for the mutuality the doctrine of wedded love
requires, Eve's desire therefore must in effect lose its identity, while yet
somehow offering itself up for correction and reorientation. As has often
been noted, Eve's fate diverges from that of Narcissus at the moment when
the divine voice intervenes to call her away from her delightful play with
her reflection in the "waters." We have seen that in Book VIII Adam's desire
for an other self is sanctioned by the divine presence's rendering of "It is
not good that the man should be alone; I will make him an help meet for
him." When the divine voice speaks to Eve, it is to ask that she redirect
the desire she too experiences for an other self:

> What thou seest,
> What there thou seest fair Creature is thyself,
> With thee it came and goes: but follow me,
> And I will bring thee where no shadow stays
> Thy coming, and thy soft imbraces, hee
> Whose image thou art, him thou shalt enjoy
> Inseparably thine.
>
> (IV.467–73)

Unlike the instituting words spoken to Adam in Book VIII, these have no basis in the Yahwist creation account. Yet they are clearly invented to accompany the only part of that account which Milton has to work with here, the brief "and brought her unto the man" (Gen. 2:22), which in Genesis immediately precedes Adam's words of recognition. Marked inescapably by literary invention and uttered by a presence that is invisible to Eve, the voice's words have a curiously secondary or derivative status, at least compared with those spoken to Adam. They seem indeed, fittingly, to be a kind of echo of the divine voice.

In so far as it effects a separation of Eve from her physical image, this word in a way echoes what Milton calls the creator's originary "divorcing command" by which "the world first rose out of Chaos" (*DDD* 273). But the separation of Eve from her image is not the only divorce effected here. Before this intervention the "Smooth Lake" into which Eve peers seems to her "another Sky," as if the waters on the face of the earth and the heavens were for her indistinguishable or continuous. The divine voice could therefore much more precisely be said to recapitulate or echo the paternal Word's original division of the waters from the waters in Genesis 1:6–7. Before describing her watery mirror and her other self, Eve mentions "a murmuring sound / Of waters issu'd from a Cave"—murmurs, waters and cave all being associated symbolically with maternality, as critics have pointed out. When the paternal Word intervenes, Eve's specular autoeroticism seems to become, paradoxically, even more her own, in part because it no longer simply reflects that of Ovid's Narcissus. And when Eve responds to the verbal intervention by rejecting not only his advice but also Adam, "hee / Whose image" she is, preferring the "smooth wat'ry image," an analogical relationship gets established between female autoeroticism and the mother-daughter dyad. But—and the difference is of crucial importance—this implicit and mere analogy is based on specular reflection and error alone. Grounded in illusion, Eve's desire for an other self is therefore throughout appropriated by a patriarchal order, with the result that in *Paradise Lost*'s recasting of Ovid's tale of Narcissus, Eve's illusion is not only permitted but destined to pass away. In its very choice of subject, Milton's epic seems to testify to the progressive privatization and sentimentalization of the domestic sphere. That this privatization and sentimentalization make possible the construction of a novel female subjectivity is nowhere clearer than in Eve's first speech, in which the divine voice echoes the words originally dividing the waters from the waters, words which in their derived context separate Eve from the self which is only falsely, illusorily either mother or other.

This takes us to the very last feature of Eve's story-telling to be considered here. As has been suggested, Protestant exegetes consider Adam's declaration in Genesis 2:24, "This is now bone of my bones, and flesh of my flesh," to be part of the first wedding ceremony. A version of this ceremonial utterance appears in Adam's narrative and (highly abridged) in Eve's. In Genesis, this declaration follows "and brought her unto the man," a verse which is translated into action in both of *Paradise Lost*'s accounts. Calvin, when commenting on this phrase, views the action from Adam's point of view, as involving the exchange of a gift: "For seeing Adam tooke not a wife to him selfe at his owne will: but tooke her whome the Lord offered and appointed unto him: hereof the holinesse of matrimonie doeth the better appeare, because we know that God is the author thereof."[32] Yet Milton is not alone in seeing this moment from Eve's point of view as well as from Adam's, for Diodati, commenting on "And brought her unto him," says: "As a mediator, to cause her voluntarily to espouse her self to Adam and to confirm and sanctify that conjunction."[33] In *Paradise Lost*, the story Eve tells stresses with remarkable persistence both the difficulty and the importance of Eve's "voluntarily" espousing herself to Adam. Many years ago Cleanth Brooks mentioned that Eve's speech in Book IV seemed to anticipate Freud's observations on the comparative difficulty the female has in the transition to adult heterosexuality.[34] But if it does so, it is in a context that constitutes female desire so as to situate the process of transition within competing representational media, within what is almost a kind of hall of voices and mirrors.

This entire discussion of the relation between *Paradise Lost*'s retrospective creation narratives and the divorce tracts can therefore be put in the following, summary terms. If in Book VIII's recollected colloquy Adam is revealed articulating the doctrine of marriage, in Book IV's recollected self-mirroring Eve is portrayed enacting its discipline. Or to formulate this somewhat differently, by associating Eve with the vicissitudes of courtship and marriage, and by emphasizing her voluntary submission both to the paternal voice and to her "author" and bridegroom, Adam, *Paradise Lost* can *first* present the practice for which Adam *then*, at the epic's leisure, supplies the theory. In doing so, *Paradise Lost* manages to establish a paradigm for the heroines of the genre Milton's epic is said to usher in. In the Yahwist's creation account, Adam may have been formed first, then Eve. But Milton's Eve tells her story first because the domestic sphere with which her subjectivity associates itself will soon be in need of novels whose heroines are represented learning, in struggles whose conclusions are almost always implicit in the way they begin, the value of submitting desire to the paternal law.

Of course the female authors and readers associated with the rise of the novel are not always willing to submit to this discipline. And in what is perhaps the most strongly argued critique of the institution of marriage to be written by a feminist before this century, "Milton" is prominently associated with the very ideological contradictions that get exposed. In *Reflections upon Marriage*, Mary Astell submits the notion of "subjection" to an analysis that is devastatingly sharp and in certain ways deconstructive, since she wants to undo the notion that subjection is synonymous with "natural" inferiority. Arguing, even if with heavy irony, by means of the very rationalist and individualist principles that came to prevail during the Civil War period, Astell urges women who are considering marriage to become fully conscious of the liberties they will have to surrender if they are to enter into this state of institutionalized domestic subjection. Her wry reference to Milton is fairly well-known: "For whatever may be said against Passive-Obedience in another case, I suppose there's no Man but likes it very well in this; how much soever Arbitrary Power may be dislik'd on a Throne, not *Milton* himself wou'd cry up Liberty to poor *Female Slaves*, or plead for the Lawfulness of Resisting a Private Tyranny."[35]

As I have suggested, the appearance, at least, of Active-Obedience is far more important to *Paradise Lost* and to Milton's rationalism than this remark would suggest. Might an awareness of this be registered in Astell's reflections on Genesis in the supplementary "Preface"? Like other feminists writing from within the Christian tradition, Astell finds 1 Timothy 2:11–14, with its unambiguous assertion of the Genesis Adam's priority over Eve, exceedingly troublesome: she offers a rather laboured allegorical interpretation, and then adds the caveat that if the "Learned" don't accept it, it will be because "Learning is what Men have engros'd to themselves."[36] Though less defensive, her remarks on Genesis itself are no less acerbic. After mentioning, approvingly though tentatively, the opinion that "in the Original State of things the Woman was the Superior," Astell proceeds to this brilliantly savage rebuttal of the notion of woman's "inferior" secondariness:

> However this be, 'tis certainly no Arrogance in a Woman to conclude, that she was made for the Service of GOD, and that this is her End. Because GOD made all things for Himself, and a Rational Mind is too noble a Being to be Made for the Sake and Service of any Creature. The Service she at any time becomes oblig'd to pay to a Man, is only a Business by the Bye. Just as it may be any Man's Business and Duty to keep Hogs; he was not made for this, but if he hire himself out to such an Employment, he ought conscientiously to perform it.[37]

Like other feminist commentators, from participants in the "Querelle des Femmes" to Phyllis Trible and Mieke Bal, Astell here implicitly privileges "P" over "J." In overturning the view that woman was created "for" man, Astell, however, applies to the domestic sphere the historically determinate notion of contractual relations that Milton helps to articulate in his divorce tracts, political treatises and in *Paradise Lost*. With dazzling, Circe-like powers, Astell's analogy works to disabuse bourgeois "Man" of his delusions of grandeur. But in exploiting, however archly, a contractual notion of "Service," it also illustrates some of the hazards involved in the project— ongoing—of trying to call a spade a spade.

Notes

1. For this, see Barbara K. Lewalski, "Milton and women—yet once more" (*Milton Studies*, 6, 1974, 8). Other defenses have been written by Virginia R. Mollenkott, "Milton and women's liberation: a note on teaching method" (*Milton Quarterly*, 7, 1973, 99–102); Joan M. Webber, "The politics of poetry: feminism and *Paradise Lost*" (*Milton Studies*, 14, 1980, 3–24) and Diane K. McColley, *Milton's Eve* (Urbana, University of Illinois Press, 1983). Generally speaking, an apologetic tendency is a feature of much North American academic literature on Milton.

2. Quotations from Milton's poetry are from *John Milton: Complete Poems and Major Prose*, ed. Merritt Y. Hughes (New York, Odyssey, 1957).

3. Biblical quotations are from the King James version.

4. Phyllis Trible, *God and the Rhetoric of Sexuality* (Philadelphia, Fortress, 1978), 100–1. The discussion in chs 1 and 4 of this work revises and extends the influential "Depatriarchalizing in biblical interpretation" (*Journal of the American Academy of Religion*, 16, 1973, 30–48). For a fuller discussion of some of the exegetical issues touched upon here, see an earlier version of this essay, "Genesis, genesis, exegesis, and the formation of Milton's Eve," in *Cannibals, Witches and Divorce: Estranging the Renaissance*, ed. Marjorie Garber (Baltimore, Johns Hopkins Press, 1987), 147–208. The present essay is part of a full-length study on Genesis, gender, discourse and Milton to be published by Cornell University Press and by Methuen.

5. Mieke Bal, "Sexuality, sin, and sorrow: the emergence of the female character (a reading of Genesis 1–3)" (*Poetics Today*, 6, 1985, 21–42).

6. *Tetrachordon*, ed. Arnold Williams, in vol. II of *The Complete Prose Works of John Milton*, ed. Ernest Sirluck (New Haven, Yale University Press, 1959), 594. Subsequent references to this edition of *Tetrachordon* will appear parenthetically introduced by "T." See David Paraeus, *In Genesin Mosis Commentarius* (Frankfurt, 1609), 267, 293.

7. John Calvin, *A Commentarie of John Calvine, upon the first booke of Moses called Genesis*, tr. Thomas Tymme (London, 1578), 47.

8. Margo Todd argues persuasively for the importance of relating Protestant to humanist views in "Humanists, Puritans and the spiritualized household" (*Church History*, 49, 1980, 18–34). For a discussion of the distinctively Puritan development of this ideology see William and Malleville Haller, "The Puritan art of love" (*Huntingdon Library Quarterly*, 5, 1942, 235–72); William Haller, "Hail Wedded Love" (*English Literary History*, 13, 1946, 79–97); see also John Halkett, *Milton and the Idea of Matrimony: A Study of the Divorce Tracts and "Paradise Lost"* (New Haven, Yale University Press, 1970), and James T. Johnson, *A Society Ordained by God: English Puritan Marriage Doctrine in the First Half of the Seventeenth Century* (Nashville, Abingdon, 1970). For a negative evaluation of the impact on women of the development of bourgeois marriage doctrine, see Linda T. Fitz, " 'What says the married woman?:' marriage theory and feminism in the English Renaissance" (*Mosaic* 13, Winter) 1980, 1–22. For a wide-ranging, comparatist discussion of these socioeconomic and ideological changes as they affect the relations of the sexes, see the introduction to *Rewriting the Renaissance*, ed. Margaret W. Ferguson, Maureen Quilligan and Nancy J. Vickers (Chicago: University of Chicago Press, 1986), xv–xxxi.

9. Calvin, op. cit., 74. Latin cited from *Mosis Libri V, cum Johannis Calvini Commentariis* (Geneva, 1563), 19.

10. The political, legal and social contexts for Milton's tracts are discussed by Chilton L. Powell in *English Domestic Relations, 1487–1653* (New York, Columbia University Press, 1917), 61–100, and by Ernest Sirluck (ed.), vol. II of *Complete Prose Works*, 137–58. Milton's rhetorical strategies are examined by Keith W. Stavely, *The Politics of Milton's Prose Style* (New Haven, Yale University Press, 1975), 54–72, and by John M. Perlette, "Milton, Ascham, and the rhetoric of the divorce controversy" (*Milton Studies*, 10 1977, 195–215).

A relevant and illuminating study of the "crossing" of rhetorical, judicial and other discursive codes can be found in Pat Parker's "Shakespeare and rhetoric: 'dilation' and 'delation,' " in *Othello, Shakespeare and the Question of Theory*, ed. Patricia Parker and Geoffrey Hartman (London, Methuen, 1985), 54–74.

11.   For a discussion of the title, see the preface by Arnold Williams, *Tetrachordon*, 571.

12.   *The Doctrine and Discipline of Divorce*, ed. Lowell W. Coolidge, vol. II of *Complete Prose Works*, 240. Further references will be introduced by *"DDD."*

13.   Calvin, op. cit., 72; *Mosis Libri* V, 18.

14.   Rachel Speght, *A Mouzell for Melastomus, the cynicall bayter of, and foule mouthed barker against Evahs sex* (London, 1617), 6, 14, 16. Joseph Swetnam, *The Araignment of lewd, idle, forward, and unconstant women* (London, 1615). For further discussion of this controversy, see Coryl Crandall, *Swetnam the Woman-Hater: The Controversy and the Play* (Lafayette, Purdue University Studies, 1969), and Linda Woodbridge, *Women and the English Renaissance: Literature and the Nature of Womankind, 1540–1620* (Chicago, University of Illinois Press, 1984). The "Querelle des Femmes" has recently been studied by Joan Kelley, *Women, History and Theory* (Chicago, University of Chicago Press, 1984), 65–109. See also Ian Maclean, *The Renaissance Notion of Woman* (Cambridge, Cambridge University Press, 1980), as well as the discussion of "feminist polemic" in *First Feminists: British Women Writers, 1578–1799*, ed. Moira Ferguson (Bloomington, Indiana University Press, 1985), 27–32.

15.   Joan Sharpe, chapter VIII of *Ester Hath Hang'd Haman : A Defense of Women, Against The Author of the Arraignment of Women* by Ester Sowernam, reprinted in *First Feminists*, 81.

16.   Speght, op. cit., 4, 5.

17.   ibid., 11.

18.   ibid., 14.

19.   Alexander Niccholes, *A Discourse, of Marriage and Wiving: and of the greatest Mystery therein Contained: How to Choose a good Wife from a bad* . . . (London, 1615), 5.

20.   ibid., 2.

21.   See the influential discussion by Keith Thomas, "Women and the Civil War sects" (*Past and Present*, 13, 1958, 42–62). Phyllis Mack examines some female prophets and the ways in which their activities were "limited by traditional beliefs about woman's passivity, her low social position, and her basic irrationality," in "Women as prophets during the English Civil War" (*Feminist Studies*, 8, 1, 1982, 25). For a discussion of more overtly political interventions, see Patricia Higgins, "The reactions of women, with special reference to women petitioners," in *Politics, Religion and the English Civil War*, ed. Brian Stuart Manning (London, Edward Arnold, 1973), 177–222.

22.   *Annotations Upon All the Books of the Old and New Testaments . . . By the Joynt-Labour of Certain Divines* . . . (London, 1645). For its insistence on the generic sense of Genesis "Man," the *Annotations* would seem to be indebted to the text ordered by the Synod of Dort and published in 1637, later translated as *The Dutch Annotations Upon the Whole Bible* . . ., tr. Theodore Haak (London, 1657).

23.   *Colasterion*, ed. Lowell W. Coolidge, vol. 2 of *Complete Prose Works of John Milton*, 739–40.

24.   Calvin, op. cit., 77–8.

25.   Speght, op. cit., 2, 3.

26.   Catherine Belsey examines the development and representation of liberal-humanist "Man" in *The Subject of Tragedy: Identity and Difference in Renaissance Drama* (London, Methuen, 1985). Francis Barker suggestively locates in the seventeenth century the emergence of a distinctively bourgeois subjectivity; see *The Tremulous Private Body: Essays in Subjection* (London, Methuen, 1984). Jean Bethke Elshtain critiques the rise of liberal ideology in *Public Man, Private Woman* (Princeton, Princeton University Press, 1981), 100–46. For a discussion of

the divorce tracts that sees them expressing an alienated bourgeois individualism, see David Aers and Bob Hodge in their very important " 'Rational burning:' Milton on sex and marriage" (*Milton Studies*, 12, 1979, 3–33).

27. J. M. Evans, *"Paradise Lost" and the Genesis Tradition* (London, Oxford University Press, 1968), 256.

28. If commented upon at all, the emphasis on procreation here is naturalized so that it becomes an expression of Raphael's character or situation. Aers annotates these lines by suggesting that Raphael is revealing a typically "distorted view of sexuality," *John Milton, "Paradise Lost:" Book VII–VIII*, ed. David Aers and Mary Ann Radzinowicz, *Cambridge Milton for Schools and Colleges*, ed. J. B. Broadbent (Cambridge, Cambridge University Press, 1974), 99. Halkett (op. cit., iii) points out that Raphael later (VIII.229–46) reveals that he was not present the day of Eve's creation. But since both are supposed to take place on the same "Day," Raphael's absence obviously cannot explain the different treatment given Adam's creation and Eve's in his account. I would argue that such character- and situation-related effects are part and parcel of the ideologically motivated narrative distributions examined here.

29. In emphasizing the lines of continuity between the divorce tracts and *Paradise Lost*, I am questioning the position developed by Aers and Hodge, who see *Paradise Lost* gesturing towards "a more adequate view of sexuality and the relationship between women and men" (op. cit., 4). Like other readers, Aers and Hodge stress the importance of the following speech, suggesting that in it "Adam makes the equation Milton did not make in his prose works, the crucial equation between mutuality, equality, and delight" (23):

> Among unequals what society
> Can sort, what harmony or true delight?
> Which must be mutual, in proportion due
> Giv'n and receiv'd.
>
> (VIII. 383–6)

In my view, however, this produces a mystifying view of "equality," since what Adam is here rejecting is the society of creatures belonging to a different species; Eve is "equal" only in the restricted sense of being a member of the human species. Although I do not here explore the various tensions and contradictions of Milton's views on gender relations in *Paradise Lost*, I make an attempt to do so in "Fallen differences, phallogocentric discourses: losing *Paradise Lost* to history," in *Post-Structuralism and the Question of History*, ed. Derek Attridge, Geoff Bennington, and Robert Young (Cambridge, Cambridge University Press, 1987).

30. Christine Froula, "When Eve reads Milton: undoing the canonical economy" (*Critical Inquiry*, 10, 1983, 321–47). That Derrida's *Supplement* can productively expose motivated contradictions in the not unrelated field of Renaissance rhetorical theory is demonstrated by Derek Attridge in "Puttenham's perplexity: nature, art and the supplément in Renaissance poetic theory," in *Literary Theory / Renaissance Texts*, ed. Patricia Parker and David Quint (Baltimore, Johns Hopkins University Press, 1986), 257–79.

31. For a sharp analysis of the ways in which, among the upper classes, the development of an affective domestic sphere served to reinforce masculinist modes of thought, see Susan Moller Okin, "Women and the making of the sentimental family" (*Philosophy and Public Affairs*, 11, 1981, 65–88).

32. Calvin, op. cit., 76–7.

33. Annotation on Genesis 2:22 in John Diodati, *Pious and Learned Annotations upon the Holy Bible*, tr. (R. G.), 3rd edn (London, 1651).

34. Cleanth Brooks, "Eve's awakening," in *Essays in Honor of Walter Clyde Curry* (Nashville, Vanderbilt University Press, 1954), 283–5. Brooks says that to the student of

Freud, Eve's psychology may seem "preternaturally" convincing; he also remarks that Eve is "charmingly feminine withal"!

35.   Mary Astell, *Reflections upon Marriage, The Third Edition, To Which is Added A Preface, in Answer to some Objections* (London, 1706), 27. Ruth Perry examines this work's political discourse in her recent biography, *The Celebrated Mary Astell: An Early English Feminist* (Chicago, University of Chicago Press, 1986), 157–70. See also Joan K. Kinnaird, "Mary Astell and the conservative contribution to English feminism" (*Journal of British Studies*, 19, 1979, 53–75); and see the discussion by Hilda Smith, *Reason's Disciples: Seventeenth-Century English Feminists* (Chicago, University of Illinois Press, 1982), 131–9.

36.   Astell, op. cit., Preface, a2, a3.

37.   ibid., A2.

Milton, Narcissism, Gender:
On the Genealogy of Male Self-Esteem

JOHN GUILLORY*

THE WAY WE ALWAYS WERE

For reasons that have as much to do with the dissemination of psychoanalytic terms in our culture as with the intention to use these terms consistently or rigorously, it has become almost impossible to consider Milton's representation of Eve in *Paradise Lost* without invoking the concept of "narcissism." Further reflection upon this fact compels one to the perhaps surprising conclusion that the casual invocation of narcissism is less likely to raise the charge of anachronistic reading than the attempt to produce a fully psychoanalytic interpretation of Milton's poem. The latter project is sure to run afoul of the scrupulously historicist methodologies prevalent today, which have deprived a good many "theoretical" approaches of their critical good conscience—or rather, their naïveté. In this essay I would like to reconsider the question of narcissism in the reading of Milton's poem. I propose to demonstrate that the association of narcissism with female subjectivity is accompanied by the simultaneous occultation of the male body-image and assertion of a specifically male "self-esteem."

If the category of male self-esteem solicits identification with male narcissism, it should be recalled that the status of the latter in psychoanalysis is very uncertain. While it is possible for Freud to undertake a general account of narcissism in infantile life without reference to gender, narcissism inevitably returns in his analysis of femininity on behalf of epitomizing the difference of the feminine. Such a theoretical agenda either makes male narcissism disappear, or reduces it to a version of female narcissism in the male. The question I would like to pose in this essay is addressed initially to the feminization of narcissism in both Milton and Freud, but beyond that, to the problem of accounting historically for the recurrence of a constitutive link between femininity and narcissism in two discourses so widely separated as a seventeenth-century epic poem and the Freudian metapsychology.

*This essay was written specifically for this volume and is published here for the first time by permission of the author.

The problem raised here is not resolved by the hypothetical enclosure of both Milton and Freud within the domain of "modernity" (though the problem itself may very well be a mark of that epoch). For the concept of narcissism continually escapes from that enclosure in order to sustain the most transhistorical claims of psychoanalysis. Thus Lacan asserts with customary assurance in his famous essay on the "Mirror Stage" that the "predestination" of the subject to this stage is "sufficiently indicated by the use, in analytic theory, of the ancient term, *imago*."[1] Lacan's appropriation of this word from a text of imperial Rome—the "imago" with which Ovid's Narcissus falls in love—argues for the recurrence of certain fundamental psychic structures in human beings over the *durée* at least of Western history. Yet the relative decline of psychoanalytic interpretation in recent years as an approach to older literatures would seem to suggest either that such enduring psychic structures as Lacan remarks no longer seem convincing, or that current historicist paradigms have no way of apprehending such structures as *historical*. I shall argue ultimately for the latter of these alternatives, while acknowledging that interpretive exercises which take the form of "A Freudian (or Lacanian) reading of X" have indeed become increasingly suspect, and for entirely good reasons.

Let us say that what historicism seems to have a right to demand is a certain caution in the use of twentieth-century theory to explain cultural works of an earlier era. Such caution has been advocated with characteristic thoughtfulness by Stephen Greenblatt in a brief essay entitled "Psychoanalysis and Renaissance Culture," in which he directly confronts the fact that "the universalist claims of psychoanalysis are unruffled by the indifference of the past to its categories."[2] Interrogating these claims more closely, Greenblatt is forced to conclude that "psychoanalysis seems to follow upon rather than explain Renaissance texts" (221). Nevertheless, the relation of psychoanalysis to Renaissance culture cannot be reduced to one of simple irrelevance. Greenblatt remarks on our sense of an "obscure link" between Renaissance culture and the "way we are," on the basis of which one can argue that psychoanalysis must be "causally linked" to that culture at the same time that it is "causally belated." The belatedness might be said to legitimize the project of historicist criticism, as the thought of cultural difference; but the positing of a "link" or continuity seems to demand another sort of explanation. If we are then to follow Greenblatt's final dialectical turn, and understand Renaissance culture as in some sense the *origin* of psychoanalysis (leaving aside for the present the question of what "origin" might mean here), historicizing psychoanalysis in this way would still seem to imply that psychoanalytic terminology must remain suspect as a means of illuminating Renaissance texts. While Greenblatt himself does not recommend abandoning entirely the attempt at "psychologically deep readings of Renaissance texts," it is less than apparent what part of psychoanalysis would survive the project of "historiciz[ing] its own procedures" (221) sufficiently intact to serve as an apparatus of interpretation for Renaissance texts.

The dubious utility of psychoanalysis in the interpretation of older cultures is more than evident in the case study offered in Greenblatt's essay, the celebrated story of Martin Guerre. If the latter's displacement by the imposter Arnauld du Tilh raises the question of how individual identity is determined in the Renaissance, this is not a question, Greenblatt reminds us, which could be adjudicated by appealing to the authority of a psychological discourse. The identity of Guerre was determined in a court of law by testimony concerning his body as a unique collection of physical traits ("scars, features, clothing, shoe size") rather than his mind as a unique constellation of psychic traits. This body was the only legitimate basis for a claim to Guerre's "name and property," and its identification bypassed altogether the question of "subjectivity," that is, of identification as an interior or psychological process (203). The manifest exteriority of identity concepts in the Renaissance is further confirmed for Greenblatt by the age's ubiquitous reliance upon theatrical models of self-representation, with their implicit conflation of identity with the public performance of a social role. Given the fact that "proprietary rights to a name and a place in an increasingly mobile social world" are always at stake in such performances, Greenblatt's argument moves toward the conclusion that the body-property relation was of greater social consequence than the body-psyche relation for the formation of identity during this period, and thus that the precursor of the psyche (in our sense) is the concept of property.

Yet here one might pose a question that by no means invalidates Greenblatt's genealogical conjecture, but rather enhances its capacity to surprise us: Is there no "link," obscure or otherwise, between psychoanalysis and Renaissance *psychology*? It would be very odd indeed if a genealogy of psychoanalysis found no precedents in earlier psychological discourses. The puzzle of this genealogy is only deepened when we consider that the determination of legal identity in our own time, just as much as in the Renaissance, would exclude psychological evidence. If the trial of Arnauld were held today, the testimony of psychoanalysis would hardly be probative. And yet the very incommensurability of psychoanalytic and legal constructions of identity may well have an origin in the early modern period, specifically in the "mind-body" problem consequent upon the decline of scholasticism and the emergence of a "mechanical philosophy." These metaphysical debates give us the Cartesian *cogito*, with its predication of an immaterial mind, as a favorite site of inception of modernity. But what relation does this site have to Renaissance psychology, with its tripartite division of the soul into vegetative, animal, and rational spirits, its taxonomy of "faculties," its circulation of "humors," its dynamics of body-heat?

What emerges from Greenblatt's essay is the perception of a certain marginality in the Renaissance of psychology itself, its subordination in a social system in which identity is typically exteriorized, in which inner states, apart from the moral question of the state of one's soul, have only a tenuous cultural reality. This condition might be expressed more accurately by the proposition that psychology does not then exist as a *discourse*. In a study of conceptions of "self-interest" from Descartes to La Bruyère, A. J. Krailsheimer has well remarked that what we call psychology in the early modern period looks upon closer inspection like a "mixture of physiology, theology, and ethics."[3] While the long-standing scholastic synthesis of Aristotelian, Galenic, and Christian conceptions of body-soul relations seeks to reconcile an ethical / theological system of virtues and vices with a physiology of faculties and humors, one need not credit this reconciliation with having achieved the synthesis which is its nominal end. The manifest incoherence of the syncretic mode renders Renaissance psychology entirely inadequate as a conceptual framework for addressing those questions of interiority in which we might presently have an interest. If psychology defines a domain which *for us* can be reduced neither to physiology nor to ethics, it would be rather difficult to find a distinct set of concepts governing this domain at all in the Renaissance. This deficiency is without doubt the occasion for the recourse to psychoanalysis in the interpretation of Renaissance texts, with its attendant risk of anachronism.

It is also by reason of this deficiency that one should resist the temptation to translate the concept of "narcissism" into an ethico-theological equivalent such as "pride" or "vainglory." I propose to take up instead a hint afforded by Ian Maclean in his compendious study, *The Renaissance Notion of Woman*, regarding the consequences of the ongoing attack on the scholastic synthesis in the sixteenth and seventeenth centuries, particularly as this attack affected the status of women in Renaissance discourses.[4] Despite the fact that the cumulative effect of these discourses was to confirm the inferiority of women on many different and often inconsistent grounds, the weakening of the scholastic system tended to bring inconsistencies to the fore, producing what Maclean calls "dislocations of thought especially in the area of psychology" (89). These dislocations opened certain limited spaces within discourse for new kinds of profeminist as well as antifeminist positions; but just as consequentially, the attack on the scholastic synthesis provided new opportunities for reflection on the axis of relation between the body and the psyche. We cannot enumerate all the sites of such reflection; but they are to be found explicitly in critiques of Aristotelian or Galenic physiology, in the obsession of the period with theories of melancholy which oscillate between humoral and affective etiologies,[5] and perhaps most consequentially, in the great philosophical debates around the ontological distinction of matter and spirit, which eventuate by the end of the century in a triumphant dualism of mind and body. I will argue finally that in addressing the question of "narcissism" to Milton's text, we are really raising a question about the relation in his work between the body and the psyche, and thus implicitly about the relation between gendered bodies and gendered psyches. We shall see that the same "dislocation of thought" in the early modern period which occasions Milton's allusion to Ovid's Narcissus provokes Milton's critics to a citation (however casual) of Freud.

ON THE BODY-IMAGE IN PSYCHOANALYSIS

In order to recover a sense of that dislocation, however, it will first be necessary to "work through" the concept of narcissism itself, and in this way to inoculate our methodology against the anachronism of psychoanalytic interpretation. This inoculation must proceed first by bringing to the fore the question that motivates the invocation of narcissism both for Freud and for readers of *Paradise Lost*. That question, we can say immediately, is the same one that troubles Greenblatt's meditation: the question of identity. Nothing is more obvious—and yet, in a certain way, harder to grasp— about Freud's allusion to Narcissus than the fact that narcissism locates the process of self-identification in a particular relation between the body and the psyche. What is at issue in both Freud's essay of 1914, "On Narcissism: An Introduction," as later in Lacan's theory of specular identification in the mirror stage, is the very formation of the human subject, the first appearance of the "I" or the "ego" as a psychical agency.[6] In either version of this theory narcissism names a necessary stage in the formation of the ego; only secondarily does it name a pathology, that extreme "libidinal cathexis of the ego" which entails the withdrawal of libido from objects (that is, love objects). The tension between the universal function of narcissism in the formation of the ego, and its more particular function in the etiology of neurosis, is less a defect of psychoanalytic theory than it is the mark of its "universalist" understanding of pathology as the always possible and perhaps inevitable consequence of the formation of the human subject. The link in theory between the universal and particular functions of narcissism (roughly corresponding in Freudian metapsychological terms to the distinction be-tween a "primary" and a "secondary" narcissism) thus disallows any simple reduction of narcissism to a pathology from which only certain individuals suffer, what medicalized psychology now calls "narcissistic personality disor-der." Similarly, psychoanalysis refuses to reduce narcissism to its ethical correlatives of self-love or selfishness, although it is obviously the case that such an equation circulates widely in "lay" discourse. I shall call the latter motif the "ethical" reduction of narcissism, and contend that it, like the pathological reduction, forgets that for psychoanalysis a narcissistic cathexis of the ego is essential to the formation of the human subject, and that it subsists in every subsequent act of self-identification.

In his essay of 1914, we further recall, Freud tells us that the question of narcissism is raised by the failure of what he originally called "auto-erotism" to account for the origin of the ego: "It is impossible to suppose that a unity comparable to the ego can exist in the individual from the very start; the ego has to develop. But the auto-erotic instincts are primordial; so there must be something added to auto-erotism—some new operation in the mind—in order that narcissism may come into being" (59). The simultaneous emergence of the ego and narcissism can be emphasized by plausibly revising the last phrase in the quotation to read: "in order that *the ego* may come into being." The ego would appear to take itself as an object—an object of love—before there is an "itself," and in this very process of objectification it supposedly becomes a self, a *subject*. This conundrum in Freud is not relieved by any further hypothesis about which comes first, the ego-as-subject or the ego-as-object, until the *The Ego and the Id* (1923), and then only in a footnote, where Freud suggests that "the ego is ultimately derived from bodily sensations, chiefly from those springing from the surface of the body . . . The ego is a bodily ego."[7] Clearly this conjecture authorizes Lacan's immensely influential extrapolation of the "mirror stage," where the unity or totality which is incapable of being experienced by the infant in the perception of its own body characterizes the ego in its primordial form by reference to the unity or totality of the body-*image*. What is at issue is not immediately the body but the body-image—or rather, the body-image as mediating the relation between the body and the ego. It is all the more obvious, then, as Jean Laplanche reminds us in his authoritative account of this episode in the metapsychology, that the ego has the status of a metaphor, or even a fiction. The ego "passes itself off" as a subject when it is in truth a particular kind of object.[8]

The primacy of ego-libido in the theory of narcissism, which has the effect of making object-libido only a *version* of that prior cathexis, draws Freud's theory into a complicated, if oddly unelaborated allusion to the myth of Narcissus. Yet this myth, in the form which Ovid gives it, seems to intimate the priority not of the ego but rather of the body-image, since Narcissus's first desire is not in any simple sense for himself, for his ego, but for his image in the water, which he loves initially as an *other* just because he does not recognize the image as his own. (We shall return to this point in connection with Milton's Eve.) While it is easy enough to read the subsequent recognition scene ("O I am he, I have felt it, I know now my own image. I burn with love of my own self." *Metamorphoses*, III, 463[9]) as a commentary on Narcissus's antecedent refusal of the love of another—the nymph called "Echo"—it would seem to be equally legitimate to read the very signifier "Echo" as a prolepsis of the image, an auditory self-reflection, and therefore as confirming what for both Freud and Lacan is the profoundest truth of narcissism: that the ego which becomes the object of love, is loved as an *other*, in a scenario of *unrequited* love.

The recognition that the ego is alienated as an other in narcissism generates the corollary proposition that object-love is always really narcissistic love. The hypothesis of an originally constitutive cathexis of the ego suggests for Freud that there is no reason for libido ever to leave the ego, except to seek out its likeness in another; hence his contention that the condition of being "in love" is at root narcissistic, that only narcissism can account for the typical overvaluation of the love object.[10] We shall encounter what seems to be a version of this overvaluation in Adam's love for Eve, with the same surprising intimation of narcissism; but this is not to credit either the legitimacy of Freud's theory, or Milton's apparent intimation of it. On the contrary, in both instances we are forced to recognize the extreme difficulty of producing a psychological account of how one can love oneself. What is this "love," such that it is both like and unlike the love one feels for others? The tendency of narcissism in Freud to be defined as a kind of object-love, and object-love to be defined as a kind of narcissism, is the symptom of a deep theoretical incoherence.

I should like to suggest that the problem is not just that both Freud and Lacan are attempting to construct narratives of ego-formation precedent, as Lacan says, to the subject's "social determination."[11] In his recent critique of this aspect of the theory of narcissism, Mikkel Borch-Jacobsen is quite right to insist that we "not dream, with Freud, of an ego whose existence would precede sociality."[12] But this dream, a *theoretical* fiction, is just by virtue of that fact much closer to a *poetic* fiction, or to that most eminently social form of fiction making, ideology. In this light, we might regard the taxonomy of object choices in Freud's essay on narcissism—in which he argues that the narcissistic type is especially characteristic of women—as much more than an *example* of how the theory of narcissism might illuminate a phenomenon such as sexual difference. There is a sense in which one might extrapolate the theory backwards from this difference:

> Further, the comparison of man and woman shows that there are fundamental differences between the two in respect of the type of object-choice, although these differences are of course not universal. Complete object-love of the anaclitic type is, properly speaking, characteristic of the man. It displays the marked sexual overvaluation which is doubtless derived from the original narcissism of the child, no doubt transferred to the sexual object. This sexual over-estimation is the origin of the peculiar state of being in love, a state suggestive of a neurotic compulsion, which is thus traceable to an impoverishment of the ego in respect of libido in favour of the love-object. A different course is followed in the type most frequently met with in women, which is probably the purest and truest feminine type. With the development of puberty the maturing of the female sexual organs, which up till then have been in a condition of latency, seems to bring about an intensification of the original narcissism, and this is unfavourable to the development of a true object-love with its accompanying sexual over-estimation; there arises in woman a certain

self-sufficiency (*especially when there is a ripening into beauty*) which compensates her for the social restrictions upon her object-choice. Strictly speaking, such women love only themselves with an intensity comparable to that of the man's love for them. Nor does their need lie in the direction of loving, but of being loved; and that man finds favour with them who fulfils this condition. (emphasis mine)[13]

The different trajectories of object-choice plotted by this theory may well be guaranteed by the phrase that looks at first like an aside: "especially when there is a ripening into beauty."[14] Here theoretical speculation leans on an unquestioned assumption about the distinctive social values attached to the body-images of men and women. Is it perhaps the case that the specificity of female narcissism is resting less on a psychogenetic account of object-choice, than it is on the casual association of narcissism with female beauty (*Schonheit*), and thus with female *vanity*? Let us bracket the question, then, of whether or not the theory of narcissism gives a convincing account of ego-formation, and raise the rather different question of whether the fiction of ego-formation is not constructed in order to make sense of certain social facts—such as, for example, the different relation of men and women to their body-images, and to their bodies. From this point of view the theory of the origin of the ego, which attempts to say something about the *universal* conditions of human existence, mistakes what is actually universal—the fact that every human being must establish a relation to his or her body-image, and that these relations can be very different for men and women—for an instrumentality of ego-formation. All human beings must negotiate their social identities (not just originally but continually) in relation to their body-images, a condition confirmed by the universality of the semiotic of dress and bodily adornment.

That this semiotic possesses a history is evident as soon as we reflect upon the fact that the male gender of Ovid's Narcissus is as integral to the story he wants to tell as the female Narcissus-figure is for Freud. For the same reason that the theory of narcissism can proceed for Freud only by occulting the figure of Narcissus himself—his ripening into beauty—behind the figure of the narcissistic woman, it can forget that its theoretical sex-change operation must integrate the body-image into that theory by insisting, both irrelevantly and extravagantly, that the narcissistic woman is in fact beautiful. The fiction of ego-formation is constructed, among other reasons, for the sake of repressing the exigent circumstance that the body-image is not merely the occasion of ego-formation, but that it is the inescapable horizon of the interminable process of self-identification. As such, it is the substratum of such historical transformations as that marked in the displacement of Ovid's Narcissus by the figure of the female narcissist.

Of this transformation we can say at present only that it has an *epochal* value, that it draws attention to classical civilization's very strikingly different relation to the body-image from our own. Further specification of the historicity of narcissism will require that we recognize that alongside the history of the body, which has become a major topos in recent historical criticism, there is a history of the body-image, of which the psychoanalytic theory of narcissism is itself an episode. This history has a certain relation to the discourses and practices out of which a history of the body is currently being constructed—medicine, anatomy, biology, sex codes, penal practices, hygiene, manners—but not a relation of identity. The body-image mediates relations to the body by transposing the body to the visual field. It is in the visual field that individual fantasy (how one sees one's body) and social fantasy (how others see it) can be said to intersect and interfere with one another, to produce those practices expressed in continually changing cultural standards of physical beauty, codes of dress, or bodily comportment—practices which can express both one's individual identity (that one looks like no one else), and one's belonging to a social category or group (class, gender etc.). For this reason the history of the body-image defines a history of the imaginary—not what the eye perceives but the "psyche." The body-image is thus the liminal field in which the relation of body to mind becomes (literally) visible.

STRIKING RESEMBLANCES

The marks of this history in the early modern period can be discerned in the regard of Adam and Eve for their own bodies, and for each other's; their acts of speculation reveal not only the fact of different bodies, but that they see bodies differently. The difference in psychoperceptual apparatus is for Milton *congenital*, a difference which is first underlined in Eve's account of her birth in Book 4:

> As I bent down to look, just opposite
> A Shape within the wat'ry gleam appear'd
> Bending to look on me, I started back,
> It started back, but pleas'd I soon return'd,
> Pleas'd it return'd as soon with answering looks
> Of sympathy and love; there I had fixt
> Mine eyes till now, and pin'd with vain desire,
> Had not a voice thus warn'd me, What thou seest
> What there thou seest fair Creature is thyself,
> With thee it came and goes: but follow me,
> And I will bring thee where no shadow stays
> Thy coming, and thy soft imbraces, hee
> Whose image thou art, him thou shalt enjoy
> Inseparably thine, to him shalt bear

Multitudes like thyself, and thence be call'd
Mother of human race: what could I do,
But follow straight, invisibly thus led
Till I espi'd thee, fair indeed and tall,
Under a Platan, yet methought less fair,
Less winning soft, less amiably mild,
Than that smooth wat'ry image; back I turn'd,
Thou following cri'd'st aloud, Return fair *Eve*,
Whom fli'st thou? whom thou fli'st, of him thou art,
His flesh, his bone; to give thee being I lent
Out of my side to thee, nearest my heart
Substantial Life, to have thee by my side
Henceforth an individual solace dear;
Part of my Soul I seek thee, and thee claim
My other half: with that thy gentle hand
Seiz'd mine, I yielded, and from that time see
How beauty is excell'd by manly grace
And wisdom, which alone is truly fair.

(4. 460–91)[15]

It will already be obvious that I intend to read Milton's scene of narcissism by taking at face value—that is, literally—Eve's cathexis of the body-image: "that smooth wat'ry image." By means of this literalism I hope to avoid the ethical reduction of narcissism. Reading Milton's allusion to Narcissus as something other or more than an ethical trope, as adumbrating a psychology, will depend initially upon recognizing in Milton's allusion a certain complexity in narrative sequence by which he reproduces in his text the same temporal gap we find in Ovid between Narcissus's cathexis of his body-image and his recognition of the image. (In the *Metamorphoses*, these moments are separated by 58 lines.) This sequencing *should* prevent the reader from taking Eve's original attraction to her body-image simply as the metaphoric vehicle for an expression of narcissism in the sense of "self-love," since Eve, like Narcissus, falls in love with her image before she knows it is an image of herself. Does the second moment—of self-recognition—simply give us the meaning of the first? This may indeed be Milton's own reading of Ovid, given that he has Eve "return" to her image even after being told that it *is* her image, and even after having been introduced to Adam. This return is, precisely, "secondary" narcissism, and it paves the way for the ethical / pathological reductions discussed above by permitting the universality of narcissistic identification with the body-image to be forgotten or suppressed, and thus for narcissism to be equated with a possible moral deficiency in Eve (as representative woman), or alternatively, with a less stigmatizing "narcissistic" phase through which she must pass on the way to a psychological normality.

I would insist, however, that in the scene of Eve's first encounter with her image, the body-image cannot be reduced to a metaphor of the ego, since Eve cannot be said yet to *have* an ego—this is just the sense in which the fiction of primary narcissism *is* the fiction of ego-formation. By allowing the moment of secondary narcissism—Eve's "return" to her image in the pool—to follow so hard upon her original cathexis of the image, Milton seems to encourage his readers to conflate the two scenes by way of an ethical reduction of narcissism. This is of course the basis for that reading which interprets Eve as by her very nature *tending* toward narcissism, a reading which disturbs the dogmatic premises of the poem by raising questions about Eve's innate fallenness that cannot be resolved in narrative terms, but only by vigorously reasserting the doctrinal distinction between unfallen and fallen states of being. This interpretive dilemma is only slightly improved by inserting Eve into a developmental psychology, by reading this scene as a revelation of her morally neutral but as yet immature personality;[16] or alternatively, by reading her instinctive refusal of Adam as a refusal not of object-choice but of domination by the patriarchal male.[17] In either case however, the cathexis of the body-image is read out of the scene; once the body-image is reduced to a metaphor, there is no longer any question of Eve's attraction to that image *as image*. In fact the body-image is not to be gotten rid of so easily as that.

It would be a tedious exercise indeed to demonstrate that readings of this passage typically interpret the body-image as a metaphor for the ego and thus fail to see that the body-image *remains* at the end of the passage, that it is always left over after narcissism is submitted to ethical or pathological reductions.[18] The problem is not simply that we tend casually to define narcissism as the excessive love of one's own *ego*; it is rather that positing the exemplary status of female narcissism seems to depend on reinstating the cathexis of the body-image as the *definitive instance* of narcissism. Furthermore, the correlation between femininity and narcissism underwrites the use of narcissism in psychoanalytic theories of neurosis and psychosis as a mechanism of regression, a retreat from the rigors of the Oedipus complex.[19] This agenda characterizes, for example, what is by far the most suggestive psychoanalytic reading of Milton, William Kerrigan's *The Sacred Complex: On the Psychogenesis of Paradise Lost*, which attempts to reinstate the primacy of the oedipal narrative against the tendency of post-Freudian theorists from Klein to Kohut to displace that narrative with heterodox or revisionary theories of narcissism. Kerrigan allows for an abundance of "narcissistic themes" in Milton, but insists that "these themes are located within and governed by an oedipal structure."[20] Without contesting the primacy of the oedipal in the *mythos* of *Paradise Lost*, we might shift the emphasis of Kerrigan's formula in order to say that narcissistic themes *subsist* within the oedipal structures of the poem, with effects which are by no means negligible, and certainly not governable. We might observe first of all, as Kerrigan does himself, that Eve's fall is only too capable of being read as a regression to the narcissistic phase, in other words a regression from that oedipal narrative in which she finds her place and her identity as wife and mother. The pressure exerted on the narrative of Eve's creation is all the greater, then, for raising this troubling issue of narcissism, and in this way marking the failure of the oedipal narrative to proceed toward its appropriate end without suffering a catastrophic detour in the Fall:

> [Eve's] entrancement with her form is transferred, as it were, to Adam, lifting the figure reflected in the mirror of narcissism into the higher dialectics of mutual love. In the end, to be sure, the self-love bound inevitably into their love will result in tragedy. The tempter reinflames Eve's adoration for her own image, and she offers the fatal meal to Adam in an inversion of the initial terms of her love, recreating the man as an image of herself, while Adam, too, remains under the spell of his own version of narcissistic idolatry, "fondly overcome with Female charm."
>
> (70)

Just as narcissism in this passage slides back and forth between "self-love" and love of the "image," so does it apparently have the capacity to characterize the fall of both Adam and Eve. But how does it do that? How is it that Adam's erotic attachment to *Eve's* image can constitute a "narcissistic idolatry"? This narcissism would on the face of it have to be very different from Eve's, since it does not seem to have been founded on any original cathexis of Adam's own body-image. And a quick check of Adam's account in Book 8 of his first awakening will confirm that he wastes scarcely a glance upon his body, nor does he pause beside the "murmuring Streams" to catch even a glimpse of those perfect features described earlier in Book 4. But the fact that the male body-image was not there to be cathected by Adam at his creation returns us to the scene of Eve by the pool to discover that this image is not here to be cathected by Eve either. What she is made to acknowledge in giving up her own narcissistic investment in her image is that "beauty is excell'd by manly grace / And wisdom, which alone is truly fair." It is not Adam's physical person that attracts her; it is manifestly "less fair, less winning soft." At this moment in the text, Milton seems disinclined to invoke that endlessly disseminated and circumambient Neoplatonism which recuperated physical beauty (potentially of either sex) as the signifier of ideal states of being—but this is to say that we cannot read the signifier "beauty" in this passage according to that code.

In a later essay, Kerrigan returns to this passage, in order to gloss the meaning of "beauty" more fully as follows: " 'Manly' modifies 'grace,' but not 'wisdom.' Wisdom is something separate from manly grace, though joined with it in their shared superiority to physical beauty; the true fairness of wisdom summarizes all the substitutions for the image in the pool. Beauty is excelled by manly grace. Eve is simply noting what her yielding meant, telling Adam that he is preferable as a love object to his rival, that she is, in other words, heterosexual."[21] The gloss exceeds Milton's own lines in the strenuousness of its effort to occult the male body-image behind the abstractions of manly grace and wisdom, accomplishing in the same gesture a complete feminization of beauty. I would argue, however, that if there is a feminization of beauty in Milton, this process is neither universal nor complete (to this point we shall return); its tenuous status can be measured here in the hyperbole of Kerrigan's gloss, according to which Eve's words are directed toward reassuring Adam of her heterosexual orientation. Not only the Edenic circumstance of there being no actual rival of either sex renders this conjecture excessive; there is a larger anachronism in the supposition that for Milton there is such a thing as heterosexuality—and a heterosexuality so marked by its other, by a homosexuality, that Eve's desire for her image raises the question of an *exclusively* same-sex desire.[22] It would be more accurate to say that Eve's desire for Adam cannot be expressed directly as an attraction to his physical person without acknowledging his specifically *male* beauty, because such an acknowledgment would upset the evaluative binarism of "beauty" and "manly grace." Given the capacity of the gender hierarchy to generate invidious distinctions in virtually every domain of comparison between the sexes, one may well wonder why male *beauty*, like the male *body*, is not superior to female beauty. Adam himself may wonder about just this point in Book 8, where, in puzzling over the intensity of his attraction to Eve's beauty, he reminds himself that her exterior "resembl[es] less / His image who made both." But in what sense could Adam's "outside" *more* resemble God than Eve's, if not in beauty? Exactly what aspect of his outside performs this imaging function? If we are tempted here to resort to the phallus to resolve this problem, we might as well admit that this is no resolution at all. The phallus is just what we *do not see*, for an obvious reason: its reference to the male genitalia cannot be foregrounded in the visual field. Thus neither Milton nor Adam can ground a hierarchical distinction between the sexes on genital difference.[23] The only sense in which Adam's body resembles God is the sense in which it can be occulted as an image, or as a body—this is the sense in which "manly grace / and wisdom" *reflects* the attribute of divinity.[24]

If the occultation of the male body-image is one possible condition for the much later distinction between homosexuality and heterosexuality—a distinction which polices desire by, among other strategies, voiding social discourse of a language for expressing the sexual attractiveness or beauty of the male body—we must nevertheless acknowledge that the immediate concern of this passage in Milton is with occulting the male body-image *as an image*, and not exclusively as the object of desire, or the object of an *exclusive* desire. Male beauty, as we shall see, is sacrificed in the process of this occultation, which paradoxically makes manifest (if not visible) the *ego* of Adam, the "manly grace / And wisdom" to which Eve yields her love. It is a question, then, of gender definition, although that question involves sexuality (Eve's sexual desire for Adam) as the casualty of its implacable trajectory. We can easily express in psychoanalytic terms what problem troubles this trajectory: The primary narcissism which sets a hypothetical ego-libido on its quest for an object finds in the image an object, to be sure, but no gender. *In the first place* narcissism has no relation to gender. And yet, if gender emerges *in the second place*, the place of a secondary narcissism, the latter seeks to backdate its discovery of sexual difference to that earlier scene by erasing the moment in which the male might have cathected his own body-image, at the same time that femininity is marked as the perpetual desire of the female to "return" to the body-image. This seems to be the case in both Milton and Freud—a striking resemblance! It now becomes possible to project the termini of these two trajectories from the way in which they revise their respective points of origin. At these termini we find what was there at the beginning, namely the body-image, but only *one* body-image: Eve's. This body-image is differently cathected in the man and the woman, a difference that is imputed to the very difference between how Adam and Eve see bodies, a difference that we must call both "imaginary" and "psychological." On Adam's side, then, the place of the occulted male body-image is supplied by the female body-image, which is cathected (with all the intensity of which sexual desire is capable) as a metaphor for the male *ego*. As such, the female body-image can be "overvalued," but the object of overvaluation is misrecognized as female beauty. In fact the overvaluation measures just the extent of the appropriately greater self-valuation of the male ego, given that this ego is alienated in the female body-image. This is precisely the sense of saying that Eve is the "image" of Adam: her beauty is what *in her* reflects his "manly grace / And wisdom," just as the latter is what *in him* reflects the Divine image.

The alienation of the male ego is certainly what is at issue when Adam comes later in Book 8 to describe the quality of his affect for Eve; in his attempt to rationalize this affect he simply transfers his own ego possessions—Wisdom, Authority, Reason—to Eve: "what she wills to do or say, / Seems wisest, virtuousest, discreetest, best . . ." (8. 549-550) The female body-image thus occupies the empty place (in theory) of the male body-image. Responding only to the symptom of male narcisissm—Adam's attachment to Eve's "outside"—not its structure or trajectory, Raphael urges Adam on to an act of "self-esteem": "weigh her with thyself; / Then value: Oft-times nothing profits more / Than self-esteem." Is the "self-esteem" which appears suddenly as an antidote to "the charm of beauty's powerful glance" (533) then a version of male narcissism? Apparently not, if Milton's critics are agreed that it is rather Adam's fondness for *Eve* that constitutes his "narcissistic idolatry." The fact that self-esteem appears as the *remedy* for male narcissism underlines the status of the former affect as a legitimate self-love, entirely distinct from the sin of pride. It is the greater value of the male "self" which is properly esteemed, implicitly by contrasting its status as psyche to the beauty of the female body.

At a later point we shall have to observe the effect here of a certain wound inflicted upon Milton's ontological monism whenever the dualism of gender cuts across that monistic continuum. We shall not be ready, however, to consider the larger philosophical concern until we have thoroughly "worked through" the issue of narcissism, and specifically its historical manifestation as a differential relation to the body-image. To return, then, to the question of a specifically female narcisissm, we are very aware now of the extent to which the perception of female beauty has entered into the genesis of male self-esteem.[25] Given this point, a theoretical objection must be raised to a reading of Eve's cathexis of her body-image as expressing a protofeminist repudiation of male domination.[26] For that cathexis operates, especially when Eve "returns" to her image in apparent recoil from a less physically attractive Adam, as the means to posit physical beauty as the constitutive link between femininity and an apparently "narcissistic" investment in the body-image. The critical strategy of heroicizing Eve, by reading her return to her body-image metaphorically as signifying a longing for a legitimate self-sufficiency, only reverses the sign of the ethical / pathological reduction occasioned by the scene of secondary narcissism. Such a reading fails to account for what is historically of greatest consequence in the scene, namely its insistence upon assigning a specific social value to female beauty in conjunction with an occultation of the male body-image, and of a specifically male beauty. If the transformation of Narcissus into a female figure has a certain epochal significance, we might suggest now that the occultation of the male body-image acquires its cultural import in that later phase of early modernity, when the prestige of an enormous array of Renaissance representational motifs, but mainly those which elevated the representation of the *nude* into a High Cultural value, is beginning to wane.[27] The narrative premise of Milton's epic, according to which the male and female protagonists must be presented as naked bodies, determines that on virtually every occasion of these bodies' representation as images, the question of the relative social values of male and female beauty will be raised. The fact that we seldom fail to be reminded of Eve's nudity in the poem, and only rarely of Adam's, is not simply the effect of Milton's presumed heterosexual desire, since such desire was not necessarily in the early modern period an impediment to the representation of male nudity. What remains insufficiently remarked in the poem's representational scheme is how the foregounding of Eve's nudity occults Adam's, and rather more effectively than any conveniently placed vegetation.

THE BEAUTY CONTEST

At this point we must take care to avoid an anachronistic reading of Milton's text that would identify the overvaluation of female beauty as the sole form of male narcissism. We have been examining several moments in Milton's poem, specifically those in which a masculine "self-esteem" is counterposed to female beauty, and to the identification of femininity with a cathexis of the female body-image; but these are not the only moments evoking the possibility of male narcissism. It will be essential to our understanding of Milton's transitional gender psychology to recognize that male narcissism appears in the poem in a more obvious form, namely as the cathexis of the male body-image. We shall see that this form of male narcissism is *equally* transitional. It is generally the case in early modern culture that the male's overvaluation of the female is universally considered to be "effeminizing," according to that system of gender distinction in which excessive erotic involvement with women tends to "soften" the natural "hardness" of the male.[28] But masculine concern with physical appearance is more culturally ambiguous. This ambiguity must be read against the background of the ascetic character of Christian morality, which would tend to condemn vanity in either sex while differentially seeking to discipline male desire against the provocations of female beauty.[29] The explicit condemnation of female vanity has a long history in Christian morality, but the question of male vanity is a more recent concern. It is primarily in the context of court society, in which male courtiers compete with each other on the terrain of fashion, that male beauty becomes a positive social value, and thus the potential object of social criticism (as in the discourse around the figure of the fop).[30] This competition on the field of velvet thus raises the issue of effeminacy among theorists of court society such as Castiglione, who remarks adversely in *The Book of the Courtier* on the imitation by courtiers of feminine modes of dress, including the use of jewelry and cosmetics.[31] The prevalence of masculine display in court society is also attested by the fact that the sixteenth and seventeenth centuries are conspicuous in the history of dress for developing sartorial fashions intended quite explicitly to reveal or draw attention to the male form.[32] The overdetermination of such display by a humanist culture in which classical norms of male beauty were revived throughout the representational arts insured that the cultural value of male beauty could not be simply negated by reasserting a norm of masculinity derived from ascetic or chivalric cultural precedents. For both humanist and court culture, the displacement of masculine self-assertion onto the terrain of refinement produced a somewhat paradoxical mode of masculine identification, as enduring as court society itself, in which male vanity could express at the same time both competition between males and the potential of effeminization.

The position of Milton with respect to this system of masculine identification is certainly complicated by his endorsement of the critique of court society that circulated within both Puritan and republican discourses; but this is not to say that male beauty ceases entirely to be a social value for him (any more than humanist culture ceased to be such a value). What psychoanalysis thus cannot explain (to invoke Greenblatt again) is the occasional presence in Milton's oeuvre of a version of male narcissism defined by an explicit cathexis of the male body-image, and mobilizing a recognizably High Renaissance ideal of male beauty. The copresence of this ideal in Milton with what we have otherwise identified as the occultation of the male body-image is not to be interpreted as a contradiction, then, but as something more like an "uneven development." How we understand this complex potentiality of the male body-image will determine how we read such a passage as the initial description of Adam in Book 4, in which Milton is scarcely averse to representing him as beautiful:

> His fair large front, and eye Sublime declared
> Absolute rule; and Hyacinthine Locks
> Round from his parted forelock manly hung
> Clustring, but not beneath his shoulders broad.
> (4. 300–3)

Only by invoking a fully pathologized conception of male narcissism, a pathology which for Freud grounds his theory of homosexuality, can we read Milton's allusion to Hyacinthus, the male lover of Apollo, as disturbing the scenario of masculine identification. (It may be useful to recall here that even the most effeminized of courtier figures, the fop, was not associated with predominantly homosexual desire until the eighteenth century.)[33] Milton's point is certainly not to undercut the masculinity of Adam's portrait, as every element of that portrait is taken to signify what is "manly." And of course it is precisely not masculinity that is called into question in Greek or Roman culture by the love between Apollo and Hyacinthus; that love is cited by Milton in conformity with a rhetorical practice of allusion in which a figure such as Hyacinthus stands as a type of male beauty.[34] Yet the difficulty of resisting an anachronistic reading of this passage is greatly increased when we recall that Milton uses the same epithet here to describe Adam's beauty ("*fair* large front") which he subjects to invidious distinction in the passage relating Eve's birth ("wisdom, which alone is truly fair"). It does not seem to me that these two passages can be made either to cohere with, or to contradict, one another. They must rather be seen as occupying the transitional cultural space of an uneven development, a space in which the male body-image is potentially *either* exhibited or occulted.

Book 4 alludes on another occasion, instructive for us, to Ovid's Narcissus, this time as the allusive pretext for the representation of male figures. In this scene (4. 810–50), Satan plays Narcissus and the mirror in which he sees his image, or fails to see it, is the angel Zephon, who, along with

Ithuriel, has surprised him in the shape of a toad at the ear of Eve, where he is inspiring her with the dream whose content is described as "Vain hopes, vain aims, inordinate desires." When Satan returns to "his own shape" at the touch of Ithuriel's spear, Zephon fails to recognize him, provoking in Satan a tirade of gigantic proto-Hegelian sputtering: "Know ye not then, said Satan, filled with scorn, / Know ye not mee . . . / Not to know me argues yourselves unknown" (4. 827–30). But the reason Zephon does not recognize such a celebrity as Satan is that his *looks* have suffered from residence in an inferior climate:

> Think not, revolted spirit, thy shape the same
> Or undiminisht brightness, to be known
> As when thou stoodst in Heaven upright and pure,
>   . . . thou resemblest now
> Thy sin and place of doom obscure and foul.
>
>   (4. 835–40)

In this instance Milton's monistic ontology is indistinguishable in its rhetorical effect from Neoplatonic commonplaces about the correspondence of virtue and beauty, vice and ugliness. While this ontology may provide Zephon with an effective put-down, however, it does not consistently govern the representational program of the poem. We have already seen Satan simulate persuasively the appearance of an unfallen angel before Uriel: "And now a stripling Cherub he appears, / Not of the prime, yet such as in his face / Youth smil'd Celestial" (3. 635–38). In the following lines Milton reinstitutes a representational system in which virtue and beauty are again correspondent:

> So spake the Cherub, and his grave rebuke
> Severe in youthful beauty, added grace
> Invincible. Abasht the devil stood,
> And felt how awful goodness is, and saw
> Virtue in her shape how lovely, saw, and pin'd
> His loss; but chiefly to find here observed
> His lustre visibly impaired.
>
>   (4. 844–50)

Zephon clearly presents Satan with the image of what he *once was*, an image evoking the youthful angels of High Renaissance visual art, certainly familiar to Milton from his Italian travels. This stock figure elicits through Satan an allusion to Narcissus; hence the spiral of libido depletion indicated by the recurrence of the Ovidian term "pin'd" (the usual translation in the Renaissance of Ovid's *tabuerit*).[35] The wavering of Zephon's body-image between genders ("Virtue in her shape how lovely") may also recapitulate another aspect of the visual representation of male beauty, that potential marking of extreme male beauty as female, which nevertheless does not signify the effeminization of the male as desiring subject.[36] The inflection of Zephon's beauty with the distinction of the female gender only reminds us that the society of the angels, like the society of Renaissance humanists, aspires to be exclusively male (the angels, we are told in Book 1, can assume either sex, but we never see them take female form—except, perhaps, here?). The status of gender in this passage is highly unstable, then, and for this reason the female gender is capable of signifying both the extremity of Zephon's male beauty and the figurative beauty of "virtue." The capacity to simulate such beauty is at this point withheld from Satan, and the effect of this constraint is to make his concern for his "lustre" seem merely trivial, merely narcissistic, as though he were a courtier out of fashion.[37]

The difficulty of sustaining a High Renaissance ideal of male beauty in the context of a hiatus in the history of court society is well exemplified by the anxiety that attends Milton's own descriptions of his personal appearance, but especially the extended self-portrait of his *Second Defense* (1654). That self-portrait responds to his anonymous antagonist's accusation that in physical appearance he resembles the Cyclops, "a monster, horrid, ugly, huge, and blind." That Milton's political monstrosity as a regicide should be reflected in his physical person is an assertion which can only be refuted according to the rules of this game by a counterportrait that exhibits Milton's beauty as the proper objectification of his "Virtue." We may guess that Milton will want to say of himself: "Virtue in his shape how lovely!" If the self-portrait he produces in the *Second Defense* can be understood as extending the rhetorical argument from "ethos" onto the terrain of personal appearance, we may nevertheless feel that Milton's response exceeds the exigency of polemic, as it produces in the margin of its excess a curious beauty contest:

> I certainly never thought I should have to contend with the cyclops for the point of beauty! But he immediately corrects himself. "He is not huge, it is true: for nothing can be more lean, bloodless, and shrivelled." Though it is to little purpose for a man to speak of his beauty [*Tametsi virum nihil attinet de forma dicere*]; yet at last, as I have reason, in this particular also. . . . I will say a few words.
>
> No one, who has only seen me, has ever to my knowledge, thought me ugly: whether handsome [*formosus*]or not, is a point I shall not determine. My stature, I own, is not tall: but may approach nearer to the middle than to the small size. And what if small, as many men have been, who were of the very first rank, both in peace and war.[38]

Milton goes on to boast of his skills with the broadsword, by way of attesting to his strength of person, and to comment on the "unclouded" appearance of his eyes, despite his blindness. He concludes his physical description as follows: "In my countenance, than which, as he has said, there is "nothing more bloodless," there still remains a colour so very opposite to the bloodless and pale, that, though turned of forty, there is scarcely any one who would not think me younger by nearly ten years. It is equally untrue, that either my body or my skin is shrivelled" (VII, 61). Milton is still, well into his forties it would seem, "severe in youthful beauty." If his protestations seem excessive, the possible anachronism in the imputation of excessive concern for appearance can be corrected by acknowledging that longstanding Renaissance conventions of male beauty are still operative in Milton's self-portrait, perhaps even those iconographic conventions governing the representation of angels as eternally youthful males. Nevertheless the question is not so simple as that. The perception of "narcissism" in this passage has the warrant of at least one of Milton's contemporaries, the respondent to the *Second Defense*, Alexander More, who argues in his *Public Faith of Alexander More* that Milton's belabored response to the Cyclops charge indeed proved that he was a "Narcissus." This charge was supported with an additional piece of evidence: Milton's vanity in having his portrait printed in the frontispiece to the 1645 edition of his poems. One may well understand, since this very portrait had been a sore point already with Milton, provoking him to point out in the Greek epigram subfixed to it how poor a likeness it conveyed, the exasperation which enters into his response to More in the *Defensio Pro Se* of 1655: "Now I am a Narcissus, because I did not choose by your limning to be made a cyclops, and because you have seen a picture of me totally without likeness 'prefixed to my poems'!" (IX, 125).

But what is a "Narcissus" in 1655? If it seems that Alexander More is attributing to Milton something like what we would call a *pathology*, the very pathology called "narcissism," it does not seem to be an irrelevant circumstance of the appearance of this pathology in Milton that he is in fact blind, that his narcissism must in some way be constructed by the literal occultation of his body-image to himself. Blindness is the pretext of the attack by Milton's polemical antagonists on his physical appearance, because it can so easily be made to signify divine reprobation; but blindness is also the basis for Milton's defense, since his report on his appearance relates not his own opinion of his beauty but the opinion of others, their "regard" for his appearance. This displacement of narcissistic regard produces a form of male narcissism which is not merely a version of female narcissism in the male; the difference inheres in a relation to the male body-image premised on a vehement protestation of *disregard* for that image: "it is not for a man to speak of his beauty." Thus Milton remembers the 1645 engraving not as an instance of injured vanity, but as the occasion on which he allowed his portrait to be engraved by a manifestly incompetent artist at the "importunity of the bookseller," a fact which "argues not that I was over-solicitous . . . but that I was indifferent about the matter." The disregard for his own image which is, as it were, accidentally literalized by blindness, thus functions not as an inhibition of narcissism but as the means to reconstruct it in a different form, the form of a complex relation between regard and disregard, a form in which the Zephon-like portrait of Milton's youthful beauty can continue to be produced alongside the assertion of disregard, of "indifference about the matter."

   If the norms of court society and humanist culture condition Milton's expression here of an apparently narcissistic regard, a version of that male narcissism long survives the decline of both court society and humanist culture. A complex relation between regard and disregard of the male body-image is nothing less than a condition of the modern fashion system, with its radical distinction between the degree of elaboration permitted in male and female dress. This distinction allows the strictest attention on the part of males to the signifying properties of dress at the same time that such attention can masquerade (a double mask!) as "disregard" by comparison to the much greater elaboration of female dress.[39] But I shall not pursue this question further into its modern occasions. I am only speaking here of a certain potentiality of cultural signification for the male body-image in the early modern period, a potentiality which does not yet exclude the possibility of male beauty as a publicly acknowledged cultural value. What does seem to be excluded more and more toward the end of the early modern period, however, is a certain sexual potential of that body-image, an exclusion coinciding with an increasingly perverse construction of the figure of the fop, and with the increasing vulnerability of court society to certain kinds of social criticism. When Milton describes Satan as "abasht" in response to the beauty of Zephon, the affect indicated by that word is entirely distinguishable from Satan's sexual arousal before the figure of Sin, even though the latter instance is equally governed by an oblique allusion to Narcissus. In the case of Zephon, the allusion seems to have the effect of *limiting* the desire expressed to the kind of male narcissism Milton exhibits in the *Defenses*, where it is likewise a question of "losing face" in a community of male contestants. If this loss of face is also quite literally a question of "lustre," of Milton's eyes remaining "as clear and bright, without the semblance of a cloud, as the eyes of those whose sight is most perfect," the vanity expressed in such a statement is legitimized only by denying its association with Narcissus. The allusion to Narcissus can circulate in more positive contexts in the Renaissance, as it did for Milton himself in his description of the two brothers in *Comus* as like "Narcissus." Exemplars of male beauty (especially youthful ones) might very well provoke sexual desire in the regard of males; but such desire was also capable, by way of just such allusions to Ganymede, Hyacinthus, or Narcissus himself, of troping male superiority. It was precisely the double potentiality of the male body-image—male beauty is the *literal* occasion of homosexual desire, and the desire aroused by male beauty is the *trope* for the social superiority of the male—which disappeared by the end of the early modern period. This supersession renders Milton's relation to his body-image difficult to interpret except by invoking anachronistic notions of narcissism, when in fact that narcissism defines what is most residual in his self-representations. On the other hand, the feminization of beauty and the occultation of the male body-image, which seem to have the warrant of the most traditional conceptions of gender, must be recognized as the site of an emergent psychologization of gender relations, with far-reaching transformative possibilities.

The question before us now is whether the development to which I have drawn attention can be said to inaugurate a "psychology of the sexes" more or less "dislocated" from the psychology implicit in the scholastic synthesis. We return, here, to Greenblatt's point that psychoanalysis follows upon the Renaissance, but does not explain it. We would like to be able to say that what precedes psychoanalysis in the Renaissance as its ultimate discursive condition is nothing other than a psychology—but a transitional, an "early modern" psychology. This is precisely what our analysis has fallen short of demonstrating in Milton, however, since a development in the history of imaginary relations to the body-image, even a development tending toward the psychologization of gender, does not yet amount to the institution of a distinct and autonomous *discourse* of psychology. We must settle at present with having isolated in Milton's text the expression of what will come to be a constitutive term of that psychology: a kind of self-love which at once solicits and refuses the name of narcissism. As we shall see, this "self-esteem," what in the early modern period would have been called a *passion*, is indeed "dislocated": it is no longer capable of being entirely integrated into received taxonomies of the virtues and vices, or into a Renaissance psychophysiology in which mental states are grounded deterministically in the infrastructure of the body, in its humors, its circulation of "spirits," or its sexually homologous organs. What declares itself in this passion is rather the possibility of a disjunct relation between body and psyche, the possibility of psychology. The concept of self-esteem brings us to the threshold of an autonomous psychological discourse, that discourse of the "passions" which set out from the fundamental principle of *amour-propre* or self-love, and which for at least a century after Milton functions as the dominant psychological discourse, supporting any number of other discourses and practices, from the novel to political economy, from moral philosophy to the fashion system of modernity.

A Psychology of the Passions

As I have already hinted, setting Milton's invocation of self-esteem in the context of a psychology of the passions will require inflicting a certain violence on the monistic ontology of *Paradise Lost*. For that ontology seems designed very much to resist the kind of distinction between body and psyche upon which psychology itself depends. Even today we are forced to assert such a dualism according to the following conventional test: where the somatic symptom has no "physical cause," there the psyche is manifest. If no materialism has yet overcome the incommensurability of body and mind, this fact testifies impressively to how thoroughly an alternative monistic materialism (such as Spinoza's) was defeated by the end of the early modern period. In this final section I would like to draw out some of the implications of what I take to be a premonition of that defeat in Milton's oeuvre. It will be necessary to begin the reconstruction of this wider context with some earlier elaborations in Milton's prose of the concept of self-esteem, composed almost certainly before he formulated his monistic ontology.

The first citation, from the *Apology for Smectymnuus* (1642), finds Milton responding to his polemical antagonist's charge that he frequented the bordellos of London in his youth, a charge that provokes one of the more famous self-characterizations in his prose: "he who would not be frustrate of his hope to write well hereafter in laudable things, ought himself to be a true poem, that is, a composition and pattern of the best and honorablest things." In the figure of the poet as poem, Milton reworks the familiar rhetorical argument from "ethos" by constructing the self as an effect of sheer moral resolution, an ethico-poetical project. But the following sentence discloses another ground of the ethical character, preceding and supporting the voluntarism of self-composition: "These reasonings, together with a certain niceness of nature, an honest haughtiness and self-esteem either of what I was, or what I might be (which let envy call pride), and last that modesty whereof, though not in the title-page, yet here I may be excused to make some beseeming profession; all these uniting the supply of their natural aid together, kept me still above those low descents of mind beneath which he must deject and plunge himself that can agree to saleable and unlawful prostitutions." Esteem of the self predisposes Milton to feats of moral voluntarism, of which "chastity" is not the least. If Milton asserts self-esteem for much the same motive here as later in *Paradise Lost*, he resists the temptations of the flesh neither in unreflective obedience to received moral precepts nor as an expression of an ascetic body-hatred, but on behalf of confirming his own high estimation of himself. Self-esteem is thus a kind of mental disposition of which chastity is only an outward manifestation; such a disposition makes "far less incontinences than this of the bordello" seem beneath Milton's dignity, scarcely temptations at all.[40] Struggling in this text with a lexicon that is manifestly inadequate to convey what he means by self-esteem, he is only able to give terms such as "niceness of nature" or "honest haughtiness" a positive valence by a kind of lexical violence. Most urgently, he is concerned to distinguish self-esteem from "pride," a manifest vice. To assert a distinction here is to trace a potential boundary between lexical fields, across which self-esteem and pride confront each other as *false* cognates.

Earlier in the same year, arguing in the *Reason of Church Government* for an abrogation of the church's power to enforce religious practice by resort to the punitive apparatus of the state, Milton posits the existence of a power in the "soul" already serving a punitive function. This propensity to self-punishment is related first to the social mechanism of "shame," but this is not what Milton is really thinking of:

> But there is yet a more ingenuous and noble degree of honest shame, or call it, if you will, an esteem, whereby men bear an inward reverence toward their own persons. And if the love of God, as a fire sent from heaven to be ever kept alive upon the altar of our hearts, be the first principle of all godly and virtuous actions in men, this pious and just honoring of ourselves is the second, and may be thought as the radical moisture and fountainhead whence every laudable and worthy enterprise issues forth. . . . Nor can he fear so much the offense and reproach of others, as he dreads and would blush at the reflection of his own severe and modest eye upon himself, if it should see him doing or imagining that which is sinful, though in the deepest secrecy. How shall a man know to do himself this right, how to perform this honorable duty of estimation and respect towards his own soul and body? Which way will lead him best to this hilltop of sanctity and goodness above which there is no higher ascent but to the love of God, which from this self-pious regard cannot be asunder?

The capacity of self-esteem to appear as a cognate of both pride and shame gives some indication of its complex relation to the field of morality. But the passage may seem more obviously striking to modern readers for employing motifs of internalization readily assimilable to the language of psychology. Hence Milton hypothesizes an origin for conscience even prior to internalized shame, in a "self-pious regard" which has the same relation to conscience as the Freudian "ideal ego" bears to the super-ego. Passages such as this solicit a reading in terms of narcissism (or psychoanalysis generally), but that reading tends to obscure the very negotiation between self-esteem and the field of morality that constitutes the occasion of the concept's formation. We might think of self-esteem here as extruded from the ethical field, in a discursive movement precisely the reverse of what occurs in psychoanalysis. The latter may be said to extrude ethical concepts, which have the uncomfortable status of false cognates in relation to the terms of psychoanalytic discourse. The appearance of such cognates is just what determines the "ethical reduction" of narcissism in lay discourse to a morally offensive self-love.

We must always take the question raised by narcissism quite seriously, then, especially when confronted, as in this text, with the gaze of an internal eye upon a soul figured as an internalized body, capable of no less a bodily function than "blushing." At the same time we must attempt to grasp what this question occludes, namely the status of self-esteem as a (false) cognate of pride. Does this circumstance imply that in being "dislocated," self-esteem has no discursive location? There is, to be sure, no way to reconstruct *superbia*, the sin by which the angels fell, as a virtue within the theological system of virtues and vices; but the culture of Christianity had never operated wholly within the norms of that system. From its beginnings, feudal culture imported as the central structural principle of its status hierarchy the classical virtue of "honor" or "glory," the virtue constitutive of the very identity of the feudal nobility. Yet as soon as we identify this principle as a socially legitimated pride and therefore as a precedent for "self-esteem," the difference between this cultural value and what Milton seems to be advocating is apparent. First of all, self-esteem is not associated in Milton with a particular stratum of the status hierarchy; in addition, the principle of "honor" or "glory," as the publicly acknowledged signifier of social status, is as emphatically exterior as Milton's self-esteem is interior—the difference therefore being, in our sense, "psychological." Nevertheless I should like to argue that these two principles are not unrelated.

At this point it will be possible to insert Milton's psychologizing rhetoric into a well-documented history, the history of "the passions and the interests" recounted by Albert O. Hirschman in his important study of that name.[41] Hirschman demonstrates that the emergence of an elaborate discourse of the passions in the later seventeenth century is premised on the delegitimation of the principle of glory, the very basis of the "chivalric, aristocratic ideal" (10). The "virtue" of honor had a career in Christian culture of nearly a millenium and a half, beginning with Augustine's partial endorsement of the motive of glory, despite the difficulty of reconciling this motivation to the deepest tendency of Christian morality. The ideology of honor (if we may call it that) does not recede in the Renaissance, but on the contrary is intensified and transformed in concert with the development of court society: it is virtue itself, the *virtu* of Machiavelli's prince. (This virtue, we might add, is one element in the overdetermination of masculine display, of which we have spoken above. *Virtu* seeks constant and extravagant modes of exteriorization and social validation.)[42] The same political crises of the early modern period which constitute the conditions for emphatic new conceptions of heroic virtue paradoxically enable a discourse of interiorized passions to emerge in the seventeenth century as the critique of heroic virtue itself; but this discourse surprisingly does not foreground the inherent contradictions between Christian and aristocratic virtue on behalf of reasserting an altruistic or otherworldly Christian morality. The critique, according to Hirschman, employs another strategy: "All the heroic virtues were shown to be forms of mere self-preservation by Hobbes, of self-love by La Rochefoucauld, of vanity and of frantic escape from real self-knowledge by Pascal" (11). How shall we describe this critique? It would not be inaccurate to say that a certain ethic—of heroic "virtue"—was subjected to critique by *psychological reduction*.

In Hirschman's account, the context of this psychology of the passions was the ongoing political crisis of early modernity, one in which the ends of government were seen by some theorists to be better served by an accurate knowledge of what motivated human action than by an unqualified endorsement of the quest for glory. This is not to say that the psychological reduction of glory was embraced by governments or the governing classes; it remained in the seventeenth century largely a counterdiscourse, as unassimilable in Hobbesian absolutist form as in its republican versions. At the same time the tendency of such a psychologizing critique was not merely negative, as the citations from Milton's polemical tracts demonstrate. If glory could be *reduced* to self-love in some contexts of governmental crisis (the Fronde), in other contexts (the Parliamentary debates on toleration of the sects in the 1640s), the cognate concept of self-esteem could be formulated as defining an ethically positive agency of self-government, obviating the necessity for intolerant state interventions into the religious practices of the citizenry. In this context, the *difference* between self-esteem and pride, the psychological difference, was crucial. It was just the psychological difference that permitted Milton to imagine a different governmental relation to religion, to explore a domain of "self-esteem" that could neither be denounced as the sin of pride, nor exalted as the virtue of aristocratic glory.

Hirschman has shown that advocates for a counterdiscourse of the passions argued that the passions ought to be governed less by repressive measures than by the exercise of a certain psychological canniness: one passion (or vice) might be pitted against another, in order to inhibit the indulgence of the less desirable passion (or vice). The interchangeability of vices and passions is entirely characteristic of this transitional psychology; it is just what allows an ethico-political arrangement to be orchestrated from underneath, as it were, by the manipulation of the passions. Hirschman further shows that the redefinition of self-love as a passion which can be pitted against other, more socially destructive passions was given a firmer basis in the early modern period as a result of the revival of interest in a Stoic morality emphasizing reason's control over the passions, as well as a revival of interest in classical republicanism, with its less violent, more socially responsible conception of political virtue.[43] The emphasis on reason in these classical revivals could be assimilated in some contexts to the development of new modes of behavioral self-control in accordance with radical Protestant doctrines of an indwelling "spirit"—an eclecticism Milton well exemplifies in his religio-political concept of "Christian liberty." These are the larger discursive contexts for the assertion of a concept of self-esteem in which government is internalized, projected inward as a mode of self-control. The particulars of this program in Milton follow very closely the strategy described by Hirschman: In the *Apology* the passion of self-esteem is pitted against the vice of sexual promiscuity, which it inhibits by a kind of psychological prior restraint. In *The Reason of Church Government*, "self-pious regard" is nothing less than the "fountainhead" of all virtuous action. The same self-esteem is asserted in *Paradise Lost* against the seductiveness of Eve's beauty ("here passion first I felt / Commotion strange")—only to fail, a failure that will concern us presently.

In *The Passions and the Interests*, Hirschman tells a longer story: the genealogy of the concept of "self-interest," which he discerns as a principle term in the eighteenth-century defense of capitalist enterprise. The relation of "passion" to "interest" is marked in Hirschman's narrative by a certain transposition: self-love becomes externalized as the rational calculation of one's long-term interests (31). By setting these interests against the immediate gratification of the passions, the latter are held in check; hence "self-interest" comes to signify nothing less than what in a seventeenth-century, neo-Stoic context would have been called reason's control over the passions. In a process too complex to be recounted here, self-interest tended in the eighteenth century increasingly to be defined in economic terms, and in this way the ethico-political defense of capitalism came to depend in part on a pre-existent psychology of the passions. Milton certainly belongs to this narrative, less as the explicit defender of capitalist enterprise than as the advocate of a legitimate self-love, the precursor of self-interest. Having glanced at this longer narrative, we can return to the genealogy of self-esteem, to the moment of psychologization, with a sense of what is at stake historically when psychological concepts begin to be extruded from the ethical field.

The province of self-esteem in Milton extends far beyond the particular uses of this term in his work. Everything that is evoked by the interpretive problem of "narcissism," by the biographical question of Milton's "egotism" (whether regarded as sublime or repellant), by the very choice in his epic poem of a *mythos* foregrounding the motive of pride, can be comprised under the problem of legitimizing self-love, of negotiating its discursive relations to "pride" and "glory." This problem is also that of the relation between a psychological and an ethical discourse, but it has deeper and disruptive connections with the epistemology and metaphysics of the period. The psychologized concept of self-love produces a kind of discursive momentum, a pressure to elaborate an interior domain, to enumerate the passions (we find these enumerations throughout the seventeenth century, in Hobbes, Descartes, La Rochefoucauld, Spinoza, and Locke). This pressure can be registered on the axis of the body-soul relation as the gradual transfer of psychological causality from the pole of the body to that of the psyche—in other words, as the recession of humoral psychology and its theories of somatic causation. This recession, it must be admitted, is very uneven, and marked by continuous recursions until well into the eighteenth century and perhaps beyond. More importantly, it is conditioned in complex and immensely consequential ways by the emergent "mechanical philosophy," for which the body itself could be assimilated to the domain of a purely mechanical causality. For this reason the trajectory of the recession of Aristotelian physics and metaphysics can be charted by the lexical instability of the concept of "spirit" in the seventeenth century, which oscillates in physiology (as in metaphysics) between material and immaterial significations, or both at once (the Cambridge Platonists). A definitive resolution of the body-soul problem could be attempted either by reducing psychological causation once again to the somatic, but a mechanical somatic (the solution of Hobbes), or by developing a psychology of the passions more or less independent of recourse to somatic causation (the solution of Locke).[44] But the latter is still only a dimly grasped possibility in midcentury. The more usual solutions tend to develop the discourse of the passions while continuing to rely for theories of causality either on traditional humoral physiologies or on newer mechanist ones. These more complex solutions describe respectively, Milton's animist materialism, which mingles physical and psychological causality on the ground of very traditional Aristotelian / Galenic notions,[45] and Descartes's dualism, which produces a mechanist account of the passions alongside a purely intrapsychic account, hypothesisizng only a single point of relation, the notorious pineal gland. Of all these solutions, however, we must insist that they are solutions to the *same problem*, the appearance in the Renaissance of the "mechanical" body. Milton extends the domain of matter to include spirit (and vice versa), while Descartes limits the domain of mechanical materiality to the human body, exclusive of the soul—but the effect of either solution is to necessitate a somewhat "dislocated" psychology to complement these complex solutions to the problem of the relation between bodies and souls.

If a psychology of the passions could be deployed in the form of a "psychological reduction" of cultural values such as "glory" (as in La Rochefoucauld's maxims on *amour-propre*), it could also take the obverse form in the notion of self-esteem—a kind of psychological *inflation*. In this context we can further generalize a certain conclusion already implicit in our reconsideration of narcissism in Milton: The question of narcissism is raised by Milton's oeuvre, to be sure, but not there only. By "working through" the question of narcissism, by thus inoculating our methodology against the anachronism of psychoanalysis, we have attempted to make visible the historical form of early modern psychology in the emergent problematic of self-love and the passions. To discern the emergence of this problematic into discourse is to recover the historical basis for a topos that otherwise circulates as the most impressionistic and anecdotal characterization of this period—its heroic self-confidence in disputing received orthodoxies in virtually every discursive realm, political, theological, or scientific. This confidence in the rightness of one's own opinion, the psychodynamic whose social correlative is sectarianism, is everywhere manifest as a character type of the period, as evident in Luther as in Galileo, in Hobbes as in Winstanley: it is what Hegel remarked as the "great obstinacy" of the moderns: "the kind of obstinacy which does honour to human beings, that they are unwilling to acknowledge in their attitudes anything which has not been justified by thought—and this obstinacy is the characteristic property of the modern age, as well as being the distinctive principle of Protestantism."[46] Such obstinacy is entirely socially determined, especially when it appears as the extraordinary arrogance, the "narcissism," of such exemplary figures of early modernity as Milton or Descartes. But this is a point that might be better appreciated by considering Descartes's elaboration of self-esteem into a full-scale passional psychology.[47]

The example of Descartes is very potent here, for the obvious reason that we need not look far to find invocations of narcissism in the interpretation of the Cartesian cogito.[48] The narrative of the *Meditations* conforms only too easily to a scenario of narcissistic withdrawal from every external object: "I will now shut my eyes, stop my ears, and withdraw all my senses. I will eliminate from my thoughts all images of bodily things."[49] The Cartesian meditation subtly revises the received theological doctrine according to which man is made in the image of God: for Descartes, the mind is such an image, but not the body. We need not belabor the point that reading this scene as narcissistic will produce the same anachronism as in the reading of *Paradise Lost*. Commenting on the narcissistic scenario in Descartes's *Meditations*, William Kerrigan and Gordon Braden remark on the consonance of that construction with the narrative of Adam's birth (not Eve's!) in *Paradise Lost*. What seems most compelling about this consonance is that both scenarios pivot around the moment of turning away from the body: Descartes turns from the merely mechanical body (an "automaton") to posit the existence of the ego as pure thought; Adam turns from a parcellated body ("Limb by Limb / Surveyed") scarely distinguished from any other natural object to query the source of his *ego's* existence: "But who I was, or where, or from what cause, / Knew not" (8. 270–71). He deduces the existence of God from the existence of his ego: "how came I thus, how here? / Not of myself, by some great Maker then." Kerrigan and Braden remind us that Dryden, in his rewriting of *Paradise Lost* into heroic couplets, was careful to insert the Cartesian cogito where Milton seems to have omitted it, between the turn from the body and the deduction of God's existence: "What am I? or from whence? For that I am, / I know, because I think."[50] The omission of the cogito in Milton's narrative is not without implication; it registers the Miltonic belief in the "ego" as an indivisible union of body and soul. If Adam's body-image is thereby less effectively occulted than Descartes's, this fact attests to the greater fragility of his self-esteem, expressed finally in the captivation of his male ego by the body of Eve. On the other hand, the apparent sexlessness of the Cartesian ego—sex must disappear with all the other "images of bodily things"—is only apparent since, as we have already seen, it is not the sexed body alone that implies a gendered psyche. We might legitimately ask whether it is the case for Descartes also that the very process of occulting the body-image introduces a certain gender difference at the level of the psyche.

The possibility of such an implication would depend first on whether we can argue that the cogito, in its transcendence of the body, is the basis in Descartes of a self-esteem. Recent revisionist readings by Michel Henry and Jean-Luc Marion have suggested that the cogito *should* be read as an affective concept, and that the usual reflexive interpretation that translates the cogito as self-representation—"I know that I think, therefore I am" (already Dryden's translation)—fails to capture the immediacy or "auto-affection" of the soul in the Cartesian meditation.[51] Without attempting to recapitulate the complex revisionary arguments of Henry and Marion, it must suffice to draw attention to their suggestion that the cogito might be reinterpreted from the point of view of Descartes's late treatise, *The Passions of the Soul* (1649), where the concept of self-esteem emerges as the key principle of Descartes's ethico-psychology. In the view of Marion, the cogito must be understood as "I esteem (myself), therefore I am."[52]

Descartes stresses in his preface to *The Passions of the Soul* that he intends to produce a mechanistic account of the passions: "my purpose has not been to explain the Passions as an Orator, or even as a moral Philosopher, but only as a Physicist."[53] This intention must be taken entirely seriously if one is to appreciate the speculative effort that goes into displacing the Aristotelian / Galenic somatic psychology with a purely mechanist one. And yet it is this aspect of the treatise—its recondite description of the machinery of the passions—which is most irremediably alien to modern readers, and which has permitted the treatise to be received primarily as an *ethics*. Our analysis will have to keep in mind the question of discursive affiliation, as it is crucial for understanding the fate of early modern psychology. We must begin, then, with a certain problem that arises as a consequence of Descartes' determination to write as a physicist: the fact that not all of the passions seem capable of reduction to mechanical causality. Within the terms of Descartes's mechanist system, a "passion" is supposed to be caused when the senses are excited either by external objects or by some "temperament of the body alone." In both cases a sensation is communicated by the "spirits" (in Cartesian physiology, very tiny fast-moving bodies) through the nerves to the pineal gland, which represents the sensation to the soul, and which then experiences a "passion." But Descartes also allows that certain passions are excited by the "action of the soul" alone, and though these passions may be expressed in the body, the body is not their origin. These intrapsychic passions derive from the "first of all the passions," which Descartes designates as "Wonder," and which is elicited in the soul when "the first encounter with some object surprises us, and we judge it to be new, or very different from what we knew in the past or what we supposed it was going to be" (52). While one would think that many different external objects might occasion this passion, Descartes regards the primary object of wonder to be the soul itself: "Esteem or Scorn is joined to Wonder according as it is the greatness of an object or its smallness we are wondering at. And we can thus esteem or scorn our own selves, whence come the passions and then the dispositions of Magnanimity or Pride, and Humility or Servility" (52). The major terms of Descartes's psychology are in this way generated out of a purely intrapsychic occurrence, the soul's wonder at itself.

That the "first of all the passions" is not given a mechanical causation is perhaps already an exception too great for a physics of the passions to overcome. How is it, moreover, that the self or the psyche can appear so continually "new" as to be an occasion for wonder again and again? For the very reason, Descartes argues, that distinguishes the soul substantially from the body, that it has free will: "I observe but a single thing in us which could give us just cause to esteem ourselves, namely the use of our free will and the dominion we have over our volitions." The intricate oscillations of esteem and scorn will thus follow the motions of the will, which are essentially moral decisions: "For it is only the actions that depend on that free will for which we could rightly be praised or blamed" (103). Descartes goes on to name this legitimate self-esteem "Generosity," which "makes a man esteem himself as highly as he can legitimately esteem himself" (104). The famous concept of *generosité*, resonant with neo-Stoic implication—the generous are "masters of their Passions"—is then installed as the cardinal principle of what the history of philosophy regards as Descartes's ethics; but if the concept is thus narrowly defined as ethical, the genealogy of self-esteem in an *exception* to the mechanist account of the passions disappears from view.

Descartes plays additionally on the association of *generosité* with traditional aristocratic virtue (already invoked in his earlier use of the Aristotelian "magnanimity"); but as with Milton's concept of self-esteem, the exercise of generosity is not limited to a stratum of the status hierarchy.[54] The ethics projected by his treatise thus cannot be reduced to a repetition of its historical precedents, classical or Christian, precisely because his taxonomy of virtues and vices is at the same time a psychology. The very possibility of a distinction between self-esteem and pride is contingent upon the dual citizenship of these concepts within both psychology and ethics. Thus it is as important for Descartes to establish the passional genealogy of pride as it is to condemn pride as a vice: "Furthermore, it is easy to understand that Pride and Servility are not only vices but also Passions, because their excitation is very noticeable externally in those who are suddenly puffed up or cast down by some new occasion" (107). The recognition of a passion in another is obviously contingent upon our ability to see across the ontological gap separating the body from the soul, or what amounts to the same thing, to read in the body-image the trace, the footprint, of the invisible passion. The very immateriality of the soul, which guarantees freedom of the will and thus the possibility of an ethics, challenges the premise of the Cartesian psychology by making intrapsychic passions inaccessible except as they are expressed in the body, at the same time that this psychology is *founded* on the purely intrapsychic experience of self-esteem or self-scorn, that is, on the soul's transcendence of the body. The exception at the founding moment of the system forces Descartes to conclude that while Pride and Generosity are distinguished within ethics, as vice and virtue respectively, from the point of view of psychology they are the same thing: "And because Pride and Generosity consist only in the good opinion we have of ourselves, and differ only in that this opinion is unjust in one and just in the other, it seems to me that they can be referred to a single Passion" (107). This is perhaps as far as early modern psychology may go in establishing its discursive autonomy, occupying as it does a liminal discursive terrain between the voluntarism of ethical discourse and the determinism of physiology.[55] A passion such as self-esteem can never again be made to coincide exactly with its precursor concepts of pride or glory in ethical discourse, even though the concept of self-esteem will be returned to circulation within ethical discourse by way of discrimination into a virtue ("generosity") and a vice ("pride"). The filtering of the virtues and vices through a psychology of the passions transmutes them irrevocably. Psychology thereafter is forced to function as an ethics at the same time that it seeks always to give a causal account of the passions. The truth of this history is already apparent in the reception of *Paradise Lost*, in the fact that the poem refuses an exclusively ethical (voluntarist) reading just as it refuses an exclusively psychological (determinist) one.

On what basis could psychology in the early modern period have been regrounded in physiology rather than returned to ethics? Only on the basis, one would have to say, of a *determinist* materialism such as that of Hobbes or Spinoza, the losers in the great discursive battle of the seventeenth century. The preceding analysis might be summed up as the proposition that the reversion of the passions to virtues and vices, to an ethical system, is a consequence of the failure of materialism to ground a psychology of the passions. Early modern psychology thus becomes an ethico-psychology constituted on a dualism of body and soul. This does not necessarily imply, however, that the emergence of an early modern psychology is entirely dependent on a strict ontological dualism such as Descartes advocates. Less strict versions of dualism will produce the same effect of at once instituting a psychological discourse and resubordinating that discourse to an ethics. It is only a question of where and how this dualism is asserted. With this very large point in mind, we can return to Milton, in the recognition that what he shares "epistemically" with Descartes—his ethical voluntarism—is in the long term more consequential than the conspicuous difference of his monistic materialism. The burden of the difference is that Milton's deployment of the concepts of "body" and "soul" will have to have some other ground than the substantial dualism favored by Descartes.

That this ground in Milton is gender will be clear enough if we reproduce the taxonomy of the passions in Descartes for the purpose of comparison
with the genealogy of self-esteem in Milton:[56]

```
                    wonder
                   /      \
             esteem        scorn
            /    \         /    \
   generosity  pride  humility  servility
```

If Adam and Eve both awaken in wonder at their own bodies, the different
trajectories of their self-identifications depend as we have already seen upon
whether and to what extent the "self" as object of wonder is reidentified as
something other than a body—not substantially other, as in Descartes, but
other nonetheless. It is important to remember here that a distinction between body and soul persists within Milton's monism, and allows him to
speak, coherently enough within the terms of his system, of all creation as
deriving from "one first matter" at the same time that the prelapsarian bodies
of Adam and Eve are supposed to "turn all to spirit" (5.472, 498). While
the distinction between body and soul is not ontological, then, it continues
to operate as an *evaluative* or ethical distinction; the moral state of any being
in Milton's cosmos can be signified by its ratio of "spirit" to "matter." That
such an ethical dualism provides a kind of back-door for the reentry of
metaphysical dualism is confirmed by the fact that masculine self-esteem is
founded in Milton's poem on the occultation of the male body-image. Conversely, Adam's appropriately lesser esteem for Eve ("scorn" in the strict
sense of a relative disesteem) is commensurate with her greater presence in
the visual field as a body (in Raphael's words, as an "outside"). The relation
of body to psyche is thus negotiated through the body-image, in the manner
already indicated: as the difference between the relative presence of male and
female bodies in the visual field. Only in this way can the distinction between
the determinism of the body and the voluntarism of the spirit be aligned
with the distinction of gender. Adam's self-esteem is nothing less than the
soul's esteem of itself as non-determined by the materiality of the body, as
ethically free. Eve's self-esteem (or more accurately, self-disesteem) is on the
other hand from the beginning defined by a cathexis of the body-image,
which introduces into her "psychology" an unfreedom, a determinism, it
never overcomes. The irresolvable alternatives in Milton criticism between
ethical voluntarist and psychological determinist accounts of the Fall thus
reproduce a distinction already given narrative form in the difference between
Adam's fall and Eve's; it is just the voluntarism of the former and the
irremovable taint of determinism in the latter that has never ceased to trouble
criticism of the poem.[57]

The Cartesian taxonomy gives us a precise ethico-psychological formula for the poem's two trajectories of gender identification: in Adam's case, wonder—self-esteem—generosity; in Eve's wonder—self-scorn—humility. The distinction between self-esteem and self-scorn translates the distinction between soul and body into the register of the psychological, as a distinction between male and female psyches. In a similar fashion, Descartes's taxonomy suggests an ethico-psychological formula for the Fall itself: in Adam's case, wonder—self-scorn—servility; in Eve's, wonder—self-esteem—pride. The scenario of Eve's fall begins in fact with "the first of all the passions," wonder: "Wonder not, sovran Mistress"—wonder at a startling object, to be sure, a talking snake; but the poem proceeds immediately to record Satan's inducement in Eve of wonder at herself:" . . . who are sole Wonder . . . Fairest resemblance of thy Maker fair, / Thee all things gaze on" (9. 532–539). While Descartes's taxonomy makes no distinction of gender in its celebration of self-esteem, Milton's scenario of the Fall makes it easy to see how gender can be reimposed on the template of the body-soul dualism. The female self esteemed in the opening moments of Eve's fall is manifestly a self put forward as body: "Thee all things gaze on"; for this very reason the pride to which she yields, the sin of pride, can be misrecognized as female vanity, misrecognized as "narcissism." It is important to understand, however, that this female vanity is the *occasion* and not the equivalent of the sin of "pride."[58] Eve's sin is not love of her image, but the desire to see herself in the place of Adam:"to add what wants / In female sex." What could this mean, if not to be a man? Pride must be understood exactly as it is in Descartes's ethico-psychology, as an "unjust" opinion of oneself. What is "unjust" in Eve's estimation of herself is not the fact of her beauty, which is granted all around by the male spectators in the poem; it is rather her claim to the very freedom of male self-esteem: "for inferior who is free?" (9. 825).

In an essay commenting on the long history of the vexed relation between women and philosophy, Michelle Le Doeuff remarks on what appears to be an intensification of antifeminist polemic among philosophers after the seventeenth century, in a social milieu transformed by the revolutions of the early modern period: "It would still remain to be explained why it was the bourgeoisie who were anxious to confine woman to the sphere of *feelings* ("love is an episode in men's lives and the whole story of women's") when the psychology of the royal age (Racine) had not laid down any fundamental inequality between man and woman with respect to *passion* (in the *Traité des passions* Descartes does not refer to sexual differences)."[59] The narrative of *Paradise Lost* may tell us why Descartes did not have to make such a distinction in constructing a psychology of the passions, and also why that psychology could become the condition for the very antifeminist polemic to which Le Doeuff is pointing. The same self-love that was denounced as the basis of all the passions, the greatest of the vices, was also extolled in another guise as self-esteem, the reward of those who "are entirely masters of their passions." It is hardly surprising that such a discourse of mastery, as so many others before it, became the possession of those who practiced as well as preached the virtue of self-esteem.

Notes

1. Jacques Lacan, "The Mirror Stage as Formative of the I" in *Ecrits*, trans. Alan Sheridan (New York: W. W. Norton, 1977), 2.

2. Stephen Greenblatt, "Psychoanalysis and Renaissance Culture," in *Literary Theory / Renaissance Texts*, ed. Patricia Parker and David Quint (Baltimore: The Johns Hopkins University Press, 1986), 215.

3. A. J. Krailsheimer, *Studies in Self-Interest: From Descartes to La Bruyere* (Oxford: Clarendon Press, 1962), 2.

4. Ian Maclean, *The Renaissance Notion of Woman* (Cambridge: Cambridge University Press, 1980), 89.

5. This indeterminacy is writ large in the text of Robert Burton's *Anatomy of Melancholy* (New York: Random House, 1977) and authorizes the double-duty of the book: "It is a disease of the soul on which I am to treat, and as much appertaining to a divine as to a physician, and who knows not what an agreement there is betwixt these two professions?" (37).

6. Sigmund Freud, "On Narcissism: An Introduction," in *General Psychological Theory*, ed. Philip Rieff (New York: Collier Books, 1963).

7. Sigmund Freud, *The Ego and the Id*, ed. James Strachey (New York: Norton, 1962).

8. Jean Laplanche, *Life and Death in Psychoanalysis*, trans. Jeffrey Mehlman (Baltimore: Johns Hopkins University Press, 1976), 74.

9. Ovid, *Metamorphoses*, Loeb Classical Library, trans. Frank Justus Miller (Cambridge: Harvard University Press, 1916), 157.

10. Freud, "On Narcissism," 68.

11. Lacan, *Ecrits*, 19.

12. Mikkel Borch-Jacobsen, *The Freudian Subject*, trans. Catherine Porter (Stanford: Stanford University Press, 1988), 93.

13. Freud, "On Narcissism," 69.

14. Freud's text in German does not enclose this clause in parentheses; it clearly struck the translator as parenthetical.

15. Quotations from Milton's poetry are cited from Merrit Hughes, *John Milton: Complete Poetry and Major Prose* (Indianapolis: The Odyssey Press, 1957).

16. See, for example, the reading of Marshall Grossman, in *"Authors to Themselves": Milton and the Revelation of History* (New York: Cambridge University Press, 1987), 216.

17. Christine Froula, "When Eve Reads Milton: Undoing the Canonical Economy," *Critical Inquiry* 10 (1983).

18. Invocations of "narcissism" are too common in critical discussions of Eve to be listed here. The point of the present analysis is rather to question the extrapolation of "narcissism" from the allusion to Narcissus. For representative examples of the reading of Milton's allusion, see Richard J. DuRocher, *Milton and Ovid* (Ithaca: Cornell University Press, 1985); Kenneth J. Knoespel, "The Limits of Allegory: Textual Expansion of Narcissus in *Paradise Lost*," *Milton Studies* 22 (1986), 79–99; James Earl, "Eve's Narcissism," *Milton Quarterly* 19 (1985), 13–16.

19. As, for example, in Freud's theory of the genesis of homosexuality.

20. William Kerrigan, *The Sacred Complex: On the Psychogenesis of Paradise Lost* (Cambridge: Harvard University Press, 1983), 74.

21.   William Kerrigan and Gordon Braden, *The Idea of the Renaissance* (Baltimore: Johns Hopkins University Press, 1989), 203. The following critique is not intended to diminish the persuasiveness of Kerrigan's larger argument, to the effect that Milton's poem is as oedipal as he can possibly make it. Unfortunately for both Milton and Freud, the oedipal outcome is contingent first and last upon the mechanism of narcissistic identification, which represents at the same time the greatest threat to that outcome. That is why homosexuality should seem to be the most catastrophic failure of oedipalization, and therefore the triumph of narcissism.

22.   The history of sexuality has now firmly established the belatedness of conceptions of homosexuality as exclusively same-sex desire. For a persuasive revisionary account of expressions of homosexual desire in the Renaissance, see Alan Bray, *Homosexuality in Renaissance England* (Boston: Gay Men's Press, 1982). I have benefitted also from Jonathan Goldberg's thorough reconsideration of this question in the context of Renaissance literature, *Sodometries: Renaissance Texts, Modern Sexualities* (Stanford: Stanford University Press, 1992).

23.   The hierarchical distinction of the sexes is founded in traditional physiology on such notions as the heat-differential between male and female bodies. Visual appearance would seem to be secondary in relation to such intrinsic physical qualities as hot and cold, dry and moist, hard and soft, which correspond to a metaphysical hierarchy of activity and passivity, domination and subordination. On the tendency of traditional sex distinction to be expressed in a system in which what one *sees* (anatomy) is determined by what one *knows* (metaphysics), see Thomas Lacqueur, *Making Sex: Body and Gender from the Greeks to Freud* (Cambridge: Harvard University Press, 1990).

24.   See Ian Maclean, in *The Renaissance Idea of Woman*, 13 ff., on the debate in the theological tradition over whether woman was made in the image of God. The very fact that this point was debated indicates its complexity, and also its apparent irresolution for Renaissance writers.

25.   The insistence of this connection in Freud has been pointed out by Sarah Kofman in her important study, *The Enigma of Woman*. Kofman discovers in Freud's concept of female narcissism a kind of perforation along which it can be separated into two types. In the first type of narcissism, Freud seems to suggest the possibility of a complete erotic self-sufficiency: "such women love only themselves." And presumably the self they love is not reducible to the body-image; they do not, like Narcissus, pine with vain desire for that image. One may reasonably doubt, however, whether these erotically self-sufficient women exist anywhere except in the imaginary regard of the male. The latter hypothesis seems more likely, given the fact that Freud compares the "charm" of the female narcissist to that of "certain animals which seem not to concern themselves about us, such as cats and the large beasts of prey. In literature, indeed, even the great criminal and the humorist compel our interest by the narcissistic self-importance with which they manage to keep at arm's length everything which would diminish the importance of their ego. It is as if we envied them their power of retaining a blissful state of mind—an unassailable libido-position which we ourselves have since abandoned" (70). Such figures express a kind of contempt for the demands of civility (the oedipal narrative), at once frightening and fascinating to the male ("we ourselves"). Coexisting with this autonomous narcissist in Freud's text, according to Kofman, is a less fascinating, as well as less frightening, type defined by the woman's investment in her body-image as the *lure* of male desire. Such a cathexis would account for the techniques of female vanity by giving its various social forms a relatively simple motive. The reduction of female narcissism to the techniques of vanity (the entire realm of dress, cosmetics etc.) may be reassuring to the male, in that it posits a female body-image cathected by the woman *only* as the object of male desire. But the fact that Freud himself wavers uneasily between the two types of narcissism identified by Kofman suggests rather that this distinction is impossible to maintain empirically, and that female vanity always raises the possibility of female erotic self-sufficiency. [The story of the film *All About Eve* concerns aging and identification. Consider that other

Eve, to whom Margot Channing remarks that she should put her award "where her heart should be."] Freud would not otherwise have suggested that the dangerously autonomous female was the most attractive to men, because often the most beautiful: "Such women have the greatest fascination for men, not only for aesthetic reasons, since as a rule they are the most beautiful, but also because of certain interesting psychological constellations. . . ." The insistence on the beauty of the female narcissist continues to guarantee the exemplary status of female narcissism in the theory of narcissism, at the same time that it betrays that theory's failure to define narcissism as an originary cathexis of the ego, prior to the perception of gender. The speculative etiologies of narcissism thus continue to rely on the empirical fact of the body-image, and thus on the relative social values of male and female beauty.

26. See, for example, the argument of Christine Froula, "When Eve Reads Milton: Undoing the Canonical Economy," *Critical Inquiry* 10 (1983). While the main point of Froula's argument seems to me wrong, for reasons made clear in the text, I would second her insistence on the significance of the invisibility of male authority in this scene. I have attempted to provide a historical context for understanding this invisibility in Milton, without assimilating it to the invisibility of the Hebraic / Christian God (this God, it should be remembered, is capable of visual manifestation in various forms, including that of the Messiah).

27. The basic study of this question remains Kenneth Clark's *The Nude: A Study in Ideal Form* (New York: Pantheon Books, 1953). Without endorsing some of the cultural prejudices expressed in this work, we must respect its confrontation with the puzzling circumstance of the rise and decline of the nude as a major cultural form of visual representation in the Renaissance. The compatibility of Milton's prelapsarian mise-en-scène with the revival of classical canons of bodily representation makes a certain rhetorical agenda possible for Milton, a merging of his sexual ideology with these canons. At the same time Milton is writing both as a Northern European Protestant, and in the larger culture of post-Tridentine Europe, when (for example), the male genitals in Michelangelo's Sistine Chapel frescos have been modestly covered with painted wisps of drapery.

28. On this topos in Western thought, descending from the concept of *mollities* in Aristotle's *Nicomachean Ethics*, see Maclean, *The Renaissance Notion of Woman*, 51.

29. See Ian Maclean, *Feminism in French Literature*, 41 ff.; also Peter Brown, *The Body and Society*, (New York: Columbia University Press, 1988).

30. For a discussion of the fop in the context of the history of sexuality, see Rudolph Trumbach, "The Birth of the Queen: Sodomy and the Emergence of Gender Equality in Modern Culture, 1660–1750," in *Hidden from History: Reclaiming the Gay and Lesbian Past*, ed. Martin Duberman et al. (Harmondsworth: Penguin Books, 1989), 129–40. The following discussion is indebted throughout to Norbert Elias's study of court society, *The Civilizing Process*. For a comment on the place of fashion in that society, see also *The Court Society*, trans. Edmund Jephcott (New York: Pantheon Books, 1983), 231 ff.

31. Baldesar Castiglione, *The Book of the Courtier*, trans. George Bull (Harmondsworth: Penguin Books, 1967), 61: "I don't want him [the courtier] to appear soft and feminine as so many try to do, when they not only curl their hair and pluck their eyebrows but also preen themselves like the most wanton and dissolute creatures imaginable."

32. On the tendency of Renaissance male fashion to emphasize the shape of the male body, and even to gesture (as with the codpiece) to the male genitalia, see Anne Hollander, *Seeing Through Clothes* (Berkeley: University of California Press, 1975), 208 ff.; 234 ff.

33. See Rudolph Trumbach, "The Birth of the Queen," 134.

34. For this subject see James Saslow, *Ganymede in the Renaissance: Homosexuality in Art and Society* (New Haven: Yale University Press, 1986).

35. As in Sandys's translation of *Metamorphoses* III, 445: "Have you ever known any thus to pine away."

36. This double-genderedness defines an always possible relation, of course, to the

beardless boys of the Renaissance theater. See also Bruce Smith's comment on the original *Arcadia*, the passage in which Musidorus's desire is clearly incited by Pyrocles' feminine disguise, provoking also an allusion to Narcissus: "I pray you take heed of looking yourself in a glass lest Narcissus's fortune fall to you." Bruce Smith, *Homosexual Desire in Shakespeare's England* (Chicago: The University of Chicago Press, 1991), 141–42.

37.   Satan has already been implicitly represented as a courtier earlier in this scene by Gabriel, 4. 958: "who more than thou / Once fawned, and cring'd, and servilely adored / Heaven's awful Monarch."

38.   *The Works of John Milton*, ed. Frank Allen Patterson et al. (New York: Columbia Press, 1933), VII, 59–61.

39.   On this subject, see Elizabeth Wilson, *Adorned in Dreams: Fashion and Modernity* (Berkeley: University of California Press, 1985), 16–47.

40.   Milton's notion of a "certain reservedness of natural disposition" has a precedent in the Aristotelian / Scholastic notion of "habit", for which see Aristotle's *Nicomachaen Ethics* II, 1, and Aquinas's *Summa Theologica* Q. 51. Art. 1. Aquinas says interestingly that "no habit is natural in its beginning, on the part of the soul itself, as to the substance of the habit; but only as to certain of its principles. . . . But on the part of the body, in respect of the individual nature, there are some appetitive habits by way of natural beginnings. For some are disposed from their own bodily temperament to chastity or meekness or the like." It does not seem to me that Milton would wish to ground his "self-esteem" in a "bodily temperament," as this would remove the basis for its expression in feats of moral voluntarism. The problem has to do with the complex balance in Milton's *ethos* between his "natural disposition" and his acts of projective self-fashioning. "Self-esteem" is situated at the border between these two constructions of *ethos*.

41.   Albert O. Hirschman, *The Passions and the Interests: Political Arguments for Capitalism before its Triumph* (Princeton: Princeton University Press, 1977).

42.   For a comment on the "complete externalization of the rules of behavior" in court society, see Jacques Revel, "The Uses of Civility," in *A History of Private Life: Passions of the Renaissance*, ed. Philippe Aries et al. (Cambridge: Harvard University Press, 1989), 195.

43.   For the seminal treatment of this topos, see J. G. A. Pocock, *The Machiavellian Moment: Florentine Political Thought and the Atlantic Republican Tradition* (Princeton: Princeton University Press, 1975), especially the discussion of glory, 133 ff.

44.   So Locke announces on the first page of the *Essay Concerning Human Understanding*: "I shall not at present meddle with the Physical consideration of the Mind; or trouble my self to examine, wherein its Essence consists, or by what Motions of our Spirits, or Alterations of our Bodies, we come to have any Sensation by our Organs, or any *Ideas* in our Understandings; and whether those *Ideas* do in their Formation, any, or all of them, depend on Matter, or no. These are Speculations, which, however curious and entertaining, I shall decline as lying out of my Way, in the Design I am now upon."

45.   Milton's animist materialism is thus superimposed upon an obviously conventional terminology. Even the famous passage from Book 5, 470 ff, in which he asserts his materialism most explicitly, redeploys an only slightly idiosyncratic tripartite division of the soul into "vital, animal, and intellectual spirits." Elsewhere, the terms of faculty psychology and humors are redeployed as well. For a good analysis of Milton's unorthodox use of orthodox Aristotelian science, see Harinder Singh Marjara, *Contemplation of Created Things: Science in Paradise Lost* (Toronto: University of Toronto Press, 1992), 234 ff. The best study of Milton's relation to seventeenth century philosophy is Stephen Fallon, *Milton among the Philosophers: Poetry and Materialism in Seventeenth-Century England* (Ithaca: Cornell University Press, 1991).

46.   G. W. F. Hegel, *Elements of the Philosophy of Right*, ed. Allen W. Wood (Cambridge: Cambridge University Press, 1991), 22.

47.   The concept of self-love is, as I have remarked, crucial for the development of passional psychology in the seventeenth century. We might briefly note here, before giving

an account of Descartes's treatise, the analogous moments in Hobbes and Spinoza. As we might expect, Hobbes in the *Leviathan* is rigorously reductionist on mechanical materialist grounds, and hence he makes no distinction between a legitimate self-esteem and the cognate concepts of "power, worth, dignity, honour;" but neither does he reduce the latter to the sin of pride. In this strategy he anticipates the concept of self-interest in the eighteenth century. Spinoza makes a distinction closer to Milton's and Descartes's in the *Ethics* IV between pride or glory and "self-contentment *(acquiescentia in se ipso),*" which "arises from reason," and "is the highest good we can hope for."

48.   For a reading of Descartes's *Meditations* through the lens of narcissism, see David Michael Levin, "Visions of Narcissism: Intersubjectivity and the Reversals of Reflection" in *Merleau-Ponty Vivant,* ed . M. C. Dillon (Albany: State University of New York Press, 1991), 47–90.

49.   *The Philosophical Writings of Descartes,* 3 vols. trans. John Cottingham et al. (Cambridge: Cambridge University Press, 1984), 11, 24.

50.   *The Idea of the Renaissance,* 147 ff.

51.   Michel Henry, *The Genealogy of Psychoanalysis,* trans. Douglas Brick (Stanford: Stanford University Press, 1993); and Jean-Luc Marion, "Generosity and Phenomenology: Remarks on Michel Henry's Interpretation of the Cartesian *Cogito,*" in *Essays on the Philosophy and Science of Rene Descartes,* ed. Stephen Voss (New York: Oxford University Press, 1993), 52–74.

52.   Marion, "Generosity and Phenomenology": "Existence immediately apparent to itself by thought (in auto-affection) would culminate in esteem of self, with *res cogitans* repeating and reaffirming itself through the modality of its will. In this way it would gain the existence of the *ego,* by carrying out auto-affection in the mode of a volition, volition esteeming itself; by consequently interpreting representation (of self) as an esteem (of self)."

53.   Rene Descartes, *The Passions of the Soul,* trans. Stephen Voss (Indiannapolis: Hackett Publishing Company, 1989), 17.

54.   Marion points out, "Generosity and Phenomenology," 73, that the distinction between generosity and Aristotle's magnanimity is also evident in the fact that for Aristotle magnanimity does not derive from wonder (*Nicomachaean Ethics,* IV, 8: "He is not given to admiration, for nothing is great to him.").

55.   This liminality persists into the modern psychological discourses. The function of a scientific psychology in positing affects, mental states, illness etc. as *determined* can never be reconciled to its de facto status as an ethics of modern culture. The tendency of narcissism to circulate in the form of its "ethical reduction" has taught us that. For this reason, psychology has been given the police function of patrolling the border between ethical responsibility and mental illness. as an ironic burden of the formation of a psychological discourse in the wake of the "mind-body" problem.

56.   On the link between dualism and gender, see the shrewd essay of Stephen Fallon, "The Metaphysics of Milton's Divorce Tracts," in *Politics, Poetics, and Hermeneutics in Milton's Prose,* ed. David Loewenstein and James Grantham Turner (Cambridge: Cambridge University Press, 1990), 69–84. Fallon argues that the divorce tracts are marked by a contradictory tendency to ground an idealization of marriage on an incipient monism at the same time that the grounds for divorce from the incompatible wife evoke a dualism condemning the woman to the status of spiritless matter. This seems to me essentially right, and I regard this contradiction (Fallon does not) as persisting in *Paradise Lost.* It does not seem to me necessary, in order to make the argument Fallon wishes to make on behalf of the sophistication and interest of Milton's materialism, to portray that materialism as the happy solution to all of the representational problems Milton sets himself in his poem (see *Milton Among the Philosophers,* 254–55). Interpreting Milton's materialism as internally coherent imposes an unnecessary constraint upon interpretation (the poem is not better or worse for being philosophically coherent or incoherent) at the same time that it forces Fallon into the peculiar

position of having to argue for an early dating of *Samson Agonistes*, because this poem does not seem to reflect Milton's mature metaphysics (248–251). An application of Ockham's razor here would allow us to discard this unprovable hypothesis in favor of the recognition that Milton simply never reconciled his monistic materialism to the dualist metaphysics of gender, and that his metaphysics falls short of consistency precisely on this score. I believe this point distantly supports Fredric Jameson's very suggestive remarks concerning the implications of Milton's sexual politics in his "Religion and Ideology: *Paradise Lost*," in *Literature, and Theory*, ed. Francis Barker et al. (London: Methuen, 1986), 35–56. If radical politics of one sort or another become associated in midcentury with the materialist position in metaphysics, then dualism must be recognized as what *limits* and finally defeats that politics. The reintroduction of dualism via the question of gender is not just a by-product of that defeat. This is to say that the reconstruction of gender hierarchy in the early modern period is an essential element of the transition itself.

57. Not the least of these "troubling" cruxes of interpretation is provided by Milton's insistence that Eve's temptation begins *in her body*, in the "organs of her Fancy," and in Satan's tainting of her "animal spirits" (4. 802, 805). In order to remove the implication of determinism here, Adam is forced to assert a dualism of mind and body more than a little compatible with Descartes's. "Evil into the mind of God or Man / May come and go, so unapprov'd, and leave / No spot or blame behind" (5. 117–19).

58. Raphael's 1510 painting of the temptation scene, in which the head of the serpent is depicted with Eve's features, makes an interesting analogical test case. We are of course invited, as with Milton, to conflate female vanity on the basis of this iconography with the sin of pride. In order to preempt the anachronism of such a reading, we must consider the possibility that in Raphael's painting the mirroring of Satan and Eve is a kind of metaphor for the sin of pride, of inordinate self-love. In Milton we are asked to take Eve's vanity quite literally as vanity, as a cathexis of the body-image; this is emphasized at a number of points in the temptation scene. This vanity then becomes the occasion of pride, in the sense that Eve aspires in the following lines to what she calls "inward freedom" (762), transcending the determinism of her bodily being. The two moments, of vanity and pride, are thus separated in the scenario of the Fall.

59. Michele Le Doeuff, *The Philosophical Imaginary*, trans. Colin Gordon (Stanford: Stanford University Press, 1989), 110. The relation of *The Passions of the Soul* to the question of gender can be recovered in the immediate circumstances of the text's production, in the request by the Princess Elizabeth, with whom Descartes maintained a well-known and impressive philosophical correspondence, for a more thorough elucidation of the body-soul interaction. Marjorie Grene, in her *Descartes* (Minneapolis: University of Minnesota Press, 1985), 41 ff. emphasizes the crucial importance of this correspondence, as well as the incoherence of Descartes's position. For an argument about the implications of Cartesian dualism for women, see Genevieve LLoyd, *The Man of Reason: "Male" and "Female" in Western Philosophy* (Minneapolis: University of Minnesota Press, 1984), 38–50.

Index

♦

Accademia Fiorentina, 152
Accademia degli Incogniti, 153, 162n11
Addison, Joseph, 9
Albizzi, Giovanna degli, 64
Allegory. *See Comus*
Androgyny, 167
Annotations Upon All the Books of the Old and New Testaments, 175–77
Aristotle, 138, 139, 145nn. 13, 14, 16; *Poetics*, 132, 135, 136
Arminianism, 133, 144n3
Arnold, Matthew, 10, 14n21
Astell, Mary: *Reflections upon Marriage*, 188–89
Austin, J. L., 20

Bacon, Francis, 159
Baker, Arthur, 137
Bal, Mieke, 167, 168, 189
Balaam, 83
Baron, Hans, 154
Barthes, Roland, 119
Beauty, 60–63, 207, 208; and female self-sufficiency, 201, 229–30n25; feminization of, 194, 206, 214–15; male, 208–10, 211–12, 214. *See also* Body image, Narcissism
Bentley, Richard, 2–3, 9, 13n4–5, 37
Blake, William, 8, 23, 35, 36, 38
Bodin, Jean, 154
Body image, 199, 202–4, 224; and fashion, 209, 214, 218; and gender, 201, 204, 205–9, 211, 215, 226, 229–30n25. *See also* Vanity
Book market, expansion of, 3

Borch-Jacobsen, Mikkel, 200
Boswell, James, 149
Botero, Giovanni, 163n15
Botticelli, Sandro: *Primavera*, 64, 68
Braden, Gordon, 222
Bridgewater, Earl of, 150, 157
Brooke, Lord: *A Discourse Opening the Nature of Episcopacy*, 80
Brooks, Cleanth, 188
Bunyan, John, 28, 31, 49
Burton, Robert: *Anatomy of Melancholy*, 228n5

Calvin John, 168, 169, 172, 179
Capitalism, emergence of, 176–77, 185, 220
Castiglione, Baldesar: *The Book of the Courtier*, 209
Causation, 136, 143
Cavell, Stanley, 55
Charles I, 24, 29, 43n5, 95–114, 143; as icon, 115–16, 118, 120; as martyr, 98–103, 115, 117–18; Milton's depiction of, 119–20; and *Paradise Regained*, 107, 108–9, 110, 111
Charles II, 102–3
Chastity, 6, 7, 58, 66, 68; in the *Aeneid*, 57, 64; and beauty, 60–63, 68; as expression of love, 66, 68, 69; interpretive, 49, 50; of Lady in *Comus*, 47, 48, 51, 54, 57, 66; and self-esteem, 66, 216
Christian liberty vs. responsibility, 80, 219
Civic humanism, 154–55, 156, 158, 160
Commonwealth, 39. *See also* English Civil War

Condee, Ralph, 93n13
Conscience, 50
Contarini, Gasparo: *De Magistratibus et Republica Venetorum*, 155, 163n15
Cook, John, 96
Cosimo I, 152
Counter-Reformation, 155
Creaser, John, 157
Creation accounts, 166, 167–89; and capitalism, 176–77, 185; and feminism, 185, 189; in *Paradise Lost*, 181–89; Protestant exegesis of 168–69, 171–72, 173–77, 179–80, 187
Cromwell, Oliver, 8, 124

De Man, Paul, 136
Democracy, 14n21
Derrida, Jacques, 41, 184
Descartes, René, 220, 221, 222–27; *Meditations*, 222; *The Passions of the Soul*, 223
Diodati, John, 188
Divorce tracts, 5, 6, 40, 55, 56, 125, 232–33n56; and chastity, 66, 67–68; creation account in, 167–80; doctrine of marriage in, 169, 178–80, 183
Doctrine of things indifferent, 79–85, 88, 90
Dryden, John, 9, 222
Dualism, 197, 225, 226, 227, 233n57; and gender, 208, 232–33n56

Eagleton, Terry: "English Literature Song," 23
Ego, 198–99, 201, 204, 222; male (*see* Self-esteem)
Eikon Basilike, 95, 98–100, 105, 115, 117, 123; frontispiece of, 108, 117–18, 123; Milton's refutation of, 103–4, 115, 118, 119; publication of, 98, 102
Eliot, T. S., 8, 21, 22, 23–27, 29–30, 34, 42; and F. R. Leavis, 13n1, 28, 31; and formalism, 40; *Little Gidding*, 43n5; and Milton's political philosophy, 23–25, 41; and religion, 27, 33, 38; *The Waste Land*, 30
Emblem, 49, 55
Empson, William, 2, 22, 33, 36–42; and Christianity, 11, 37–39, 41, 44n12; *Milton's God*, 11, 12, 21, 36, 38; political philosophy, 39, 41

English Civil War, 24, 39, 43n5, 99, 189
Eve (*Paradise Lost*), 166, 180, 184–88, 202–3; beauty of, 61, 62; in creation accounts, 172, 182; and narcissism, 194, 203–8; as protofeminist, 208; and self-esteem, 226–27

Fallon, Stephen, 232–33n56
Fascism, 24, 42
Feminism, 6, 14n12, 165, 185, 188–89
Fish, Stanley, 48, 50, 51, 53, 54, 59, 62
Fletcher, Angus, 49
Forgery, literary, 3
Fomalism, 40, 41
Foucault, Michel, 41, 96, 97, 104
Foxe, John: "Book of Martyrs," 98, 99, 100, 101, 102, 105
Freud, Sigmund, 194–95, 198–200, 201, 210, 229–30n25
Friedman, Donald, 48, 50, 51
Froula, Christine, 185
Frye, Northrop, 93n13

Gauden, John, 98, 99, 100, 105, 117
Gender equality, 165, 192n29, 227; and reproduction, 176–77. *See also* Feminism, Mutuality
Genette, Gérard, 168
Gilman, Ernest, 116
Glory, psychological reduction of, 218–19, 221
Good works vs. faith, 84–85
Graces, 64, 66
Grand Style, 8, 15n21, 29, 31, 35, 40
Greenblatt, Stephen, 195–97, 198, 210, 215
Greg, Sir Walter, 50–51, 63, 68, 69
Guerre, Martin, 196
Guillory, John, 133–34, 146n23

Hakewell, George, 124
Hegel, G. W. F., 221–22
Henry, Michel, 223
Henry, Philip, 97
Herbert, George, 92
Hill, Christopher, 11–12, 41, 113n25, 137
Hirschman, Albert O., 218–20
Hobbes, Thomas, 218, 219, 220, 221, 225; *Leviathan*, 231–32n47
Hog, William, 2
Homeric/Virgilian epic, 32, 34, 35
Hume, David, 136

Hypocrisy, 69

Iconoclasm, 115–30, 142; and the
    Apocalypse, 124, 126; literary nature
    of, 126; and theatricality, 121–22,
    127
Identity, determination of, 196, 197, 198;
    and body image, 201, 202
Idolatry: of Charles I, 103; temptation of,
    81, 85, 89
Imagery, 25, 28, 116, 118, 119–120
Individualism, 180, 189
Intentionalism, 1, 39
Interpretation, 59, 62

Jaeger, Werner, 65
Jayne, Sears, 48, 49, 51, 70
Jewel, John, 118
Johnson, Samuel, 8, 13nn. 3, 5, 24,
    134–37, 143; and patronage system,
    149; and republicanism, 161
Jonson, Ben, 145
Judgment, temptation of, 81

Kahn, Victoria, 52, 54
Kant, Immanuel, 136; *Critique of Judgment*,
    20
Keats, John: *To Autumn*, 28
Kerrigan, William, 204, 205, 222
Knight, Wilson, 29
Kofman, Sara: *The Enigma of Woman*,
    229–30n25
Krailsheimer, A. J., 197

La Rochefoucauld, François de, 218, 220,
    221
Lacan, Jacques, 195, 198, 199, 200
Language, 26, 29, 30, 35; and
    contradiction, 40; sexual, 60, 61; and
    speech, 43n6
Laplanche, Jean, 199
Lauder, William, 2, 3, 9, 13n3–5
Lawes, Henry, 150, 157
Lawrence, D. H., 22, 23, 27, 31
Le Doeuff, Michelle, 227
Leavis, F. R., 21–22, 25, 27–29, 30, 33,
    42; and formalism, 40; sociopolitical
    philosophy, 27, 30, 39, 41; and T. S.
    Eliot, 13n1, 28, 31, 35; and William
    Empson, 36, 39
Leo the Iconoclast, 116
Leonard, John, 63, 68
Lewalski, Barbara, 89, 159

Lewis, C. S., 8–9, 22, 31–36, 37,
    38–39, 42; and Christian orthodoxy,
    32, 33, 35–36; *Perelandra*, 33; *A
    Preface to "Paradise Lost,"* 21, 31–32;
    and style, 40
Literary criticism, 19–21, 38;
    performative, 20; single-author,
    20–21. *See also* individual critics
Lloyd George, David, 43n6
Locke, John, 220, 221
Loewenstein, David, 145n23
Luther, Martin, 68, 69, 71, 132, 221

Macherey, Pierre, 38, 39, 41
Mack, Maynard, 149
Maclean, Ian: *The Renaissance Notion of
    Woman*, 197
Manso, Giovanni Battista, 151–52, 153
Marion, Jean-Luc, 223, 232n54
Marriage, 7, 55, 56, 65, 66, 173, 174,
    183; companionate, 165, 177;
    feminist critique of, 188–89; as first
    institution, 178–80, 183
Marshall, Stephen, 129n32
Martyrdom, 104, 107
Martyrology, 101–3, 105, 106, 108. *See
    also* Charles I
Marvell, Andrew, 119, 124, 126
Marx, Karl, 23
Mary I, 99
Masculine identification, 209–10
Masque, 48, 49, 57. *See also* Milton, John:
    Comus
Mason, Francis, 79–80
Metaphor, 29, 78, 204, 207
Middle class, 3, 41
Milton, John: attacks on, 2–3 (*see also*
    Eliot, Leavis); biographies of, 10, 11;
    blindness, 2, 5, 26, 213; critical
    studies of, 1; identification with,
    1–11; in Italy, 151–56, 211;
    marriage, 5, 7; as national poet, 9;
    and patronage system, 150; as
    political philosopher, 23–24; as prose
    writer, 150, 156; and religion, 4–5,
    8; as revolutionary, 4, 8–9, 23, 24,
    29, 34, 40, 115, 125, 127; rhetorical
    style, 25, 30 (*see also* Versification);
    and self-esteem, 4, 216; self-portrait,
    212–13, 214

POETRY
L'Allegro, 25

Comus, 5, 47–73, 150, 151, 160, 214; as allegory, 47; and appearances, 58; dialogue in, 49; nature in, 67; obstacles of plot in, 50–51, 53–55, 57; Platonism in, 50, 51, 54–55, 57, 59; publication of, 150, 157. *See also* Chastity

"Lycidas," 5, 150, 157

Ode on the Morning of Christ's Nativity, 5, 76

"On Shakespeare," 137, 139

Paradise Lost, 67, 126, 145–46n20, 180–89; attacks on, 2–3, 22 (*see also* Eliot, Leavis); and Christianity, 11, 32–33; and classicism, 32–33; contradictions in, 38–39, 40–41; and critical identification, 1–11; debate on active vs. contemplative life in, 158–60; depiction of Eden in, 158–60; editions of, 2, 8; Eve in (*see* Eve); and Genesis, 167, 181, 182, 183–84; and historical-political criticism, 10–11; and Milton's biography, 5, 39; as national poem, 9–10; psychoanalytic interpretation of, 194–95; publication of, 149, 150–51, 160; and revolutionary politics, 8–9; Satan's speeches in, 26, 34, 211; self-esteem in, 219, 222, 226–27

Paradise Regained, 5, 14n10, 74–94, 105–111; criticism of, 88–87, 93, 94n13, 113n25; evasive language in, 82–85, 89; iconoclasm in, 123; and meaning of martyrdom, 105, 108; and rejection of Passion, 107; and revolutionay politics, 8; and sexual politics, 6; temptation in, 77–78, 81–85, 87–90, 92, 106, 108, 110; war for the soul in, 74–76

Il Penseroso, 56

Poems (collection), 150, 151, 156, 157, 160

Poems, &, on Several Occasions (collection), 157

Poems of Mr John Milton (collection), 157

Samson Agonistes, 5, 14n9, 118, 120–30, 131–46, 232–33n56; agency in, 131–34, 143; Dalila in, 81, 120, 142, 143; and iconoclasm, 116, 117, 120–30; irony in, 121, 123, 133; lack of event in, 134, 137, 143; language of, 135, 141–42; prefatory epistle to, 132, 138, 140; restraint in, 133–34; and revolutionary politics, 8, 115; and sexual politics, 6; as tragedy, 139

PROSE

Animadversions, 68, 122, 123

Apology for Smectymnuus, An, 58, 68, 70, 122, 216, 219; on chastity, 65, 67, 69

Areopagitica, 40, 58, 80, 156, 157; and iconoclasm, 122; and truth seeking, 57, 69, 70, 159–60

Colasterion, 177

Defensio Pro Se, 213

Doctrine and Discipline of Divorce, The, 62, 65, 125, 126, 127, 156, 163n18. *See also* Divorce tracts

Eikonoklastes, 103–5, 109, 110, 111, 115–20, 122, 156; as revolutionary polemic, 115–16, 117–19, 123, 127; theatricality of, 118, 127

Likeliest Means to Remove Hirelings, 156

Of Christian Doctrine, 56, 84, 122, 124, 125

Of Education, 157

Of Reformations, 122, 156

Readie and Easie Way, The, 156, 160

Reason of Church-Government, The, 125, 157, 216, 219

Second Defence of the English People, 151, 153, 161n5, 212

Tetrachordon, 125, 156, 169–70, 172–73, 175, 178; and creation accounts, 177; and iconoclasm, 125

Mind-body relationship, 196, 197, 216, 220–21, 222, 226, 233n57

Minsheu, John, 164n30

Moral action, nature of, 75–76, 77–78, 81

Misogyny, 6–7, 167

Monism, 7, 208, 211, 216, 222, 226, 232–33n56

More, Alexander, 213

Moseley, Humphrey, 150, 157, 160

Mutuality, in gender relations, 165, 167, 171, 173, 175

Narcissism, 197, 198–215, 227, 229–30n25; and body image, 201, 203–4; and ego formation, 198–99, 201; and female subjectivity, 186, 187, 194; love as, 200; male, 207–210, 214; in Milton, 212–14

Narcissus myth, 186, 195, 198, 199, 201, 203, 210–11, 214

Nationalism, 4, 9–10

Neoplatonism, 50, 55, 205; and incongruity, 58–59, 64, 65–66, 211

New Criticism, 19
New Historicism, 10, 117
Niccholes, Alexander, 174–75
Novel, rise of, 188

Obedience, 76–77, 78, 84, 90, 108
Obstinacy, 221–22
Oedipus complex, 204–5
O'Connell, Michael, 116
Ovid: *Metamorphoses*, 198, 200, 203, 210, 211. *See also* Narcissus
Owens, John, 119

Paradise of Fools, 158
Pareus, 168
Parker, William Riley, 150
Paruta, Paolo, 155, 158, 159
Patriarchy, 6, 167, 185, 187
Patronage system, 149, 160, 161; in Italy, 151–53
Plato, 65, 154
Polybius, 154
Pope, Alexander, 3, 149
Positivism, 19–20, 33
Property, concept of, 196
Protestant Reformation, 116, 118, 222
Prynne, William, 118
Psychoanalysis, 195; and narcissism, 198, 217; and Renaissance culture, 195–96, 197, 210, 215
Psychology, 196–97, 215, 217, 218–20, 223–27; Cartesian, 222–25; of gender, 215
Public trial/execution as drama, 96–100

"Querelle des Femmes," 173, 189

Radzinowicz, Mary Ann, 159
Rajan, Balanchandra, 49
Ransom, John Crowe, 47
Reading, act of, 135, 136, 137, 139–40, 141, 143; and seeing, 146n21
Regicide. *See* Charles I
Relaxation, temptation to, 81
Renaissance: honor in, 218; Neoplatonism, 58–59, 66; psychology, 196–97, 215, 221; representational motifs, 208, 210, 211, 213; self-fashioning, 117, 118; women's status in, 197
Republicanism, 4, 151, 161, 219; Milton's arguments for, 156, 159–60; in Venice, 154, 155. *See also* Milton, John, as revolutionary

Restoration, 29, 39, 40, 102–3, 105, 108

Sadler, Anthonie, 102
St. John Damascene, 159
St. Thomas Aquinas, 231n40
Samuel, Irene, 93–94n13
Sarpi, Paolo, 155–56, 158
Scholasticism, 197
Scrutiny, 22
Self-esteem, 194, 207–8, 209, 215–28, 231n40; Descartes's psychology of, 223, 224–25, 227; vs. pride, 216, 217, 219, 224
Sexism, idiosyncratic, 4, 6–8
Sexuality, 6, 67, 207, 229nn. 24–26
Shakespeare, William, 136, 137, 140, 143, 145n15; *Antony and Cleopatra*, 139, 143, 145nn. 15, 19
Shame, internalization of, 217
Sharpe, Joan, 173
Shelley, Percy Bysshe, 23, 35, 36, 37, 38, 39
Social dislocation, 29–30, 31
Socialism, 24, 42
Speght, Rachel, 173–74, 179–80
Spenser, Edmund, 71–72
Steiner, George, 19
Stevens, Paul, 48, 50, 51
Stoics, 79, 80
Stratford, Earl of, 118, 122
Subscription publishing, 160–61
Supplementarity, logic of, 184
Swetnam, Joseph, 173, 174
Swift, Jonathan, 3

Tableau, 49, 50
Tasso, Torquato, 151–52
Tayler, Edward, 86
Temptations. *See Paradise Regained*, temptation in
Theater, 137–38, 141, 142, 145n15. *See also* Masque
Theatricality, 103, 106, 117, 118, 121, 122, 127; and Puritanism, 118–19
Tillyard, E. M. W., 33
Tonson, Jacob, 13n4, 160
Tragedy, 138–39, 142, 145n17
Trible, Phyllis, 166–67, 168, 189
Truthfulness, 109

Value, location of, 89, 90
Vanity, 201, 209, 214, 229–30n25, 233n58

Venice, 151, 153–56; government of,
154, 163n15
Versification, 26, 27, 28, 30
Virtue, heroic, 218
Vocationalism, 4–6, 133
Voltaire, 37, 39
Vondel, Joost Van Den, 121

Waldcock, A. J. A., 28, 39
Webber, Joan, 91
Weber, Max, 133
Williams, Charles, 35

Wind, Edgar, 58, 64, 68
Wither, George, 160
Witnessing vs. bearing witness, 132, 133,
135
Wittgenstein, Ludwig, 56
Wittreich, Joseph, 130n35
Woodbridge, Linda, 6
Woodhouse, A. S. P., 93n13
Wotton, Sir Henry, 150, 151, 155, 157, 160
Writing, 29

Zagorini, Peter, 119